COMMON CORE MATHEMATICS

A Story of Units

Grade 2, Module 7: Problem Solving with Length, Money, and Data

JB JOSSEY-BASS™
A Wiley Brand

Cover design by Chris Clary

Published by Jossey-Bass
A Wiley Brand
One Montgomery Street, Suite 1200, San Francisco, CA 94104-4594—www.josseybass.com

ISBN: 978-1-118-81158-0

Printed in the United States of America
FIRST EDITION
PB Printing 10 9 8 7 6 5 4 3 2 1

WELCOME

Dear Teacher,

Thank you for your interest in Common Core's curriculum in mathematics. Common Core is a non-profit organization based in Washington, DC dedicated to helping K-12 public schoolteachers use the power of high-quality content to improve instruction.[1] We are led by a board of master teachers, scholars, and current and former school, district, and state education leaders. Common Core has responded to the Common Core State Standards' (CCSS) call for "content-rich curriculum"[2] by creating new, CCSS-based curriculum materials in mathematics, English Language Arts, history, and (soon) the arts. All of our materials are written by teachers who are among the nation's foremost experts on the new standards.

In 2012 Common Core won three contracts from the New York State Education Department to create a PreKindergarten–12th grade mathematics curriculum for the teachers of that state, and to conduct associated professional development. The book you hold contains a portion of that work. In order to respond to demand in New York and elsewhere, modules of the curriculum will continue to be published, on a rolling basis, as they are completed. This curriculum is based on New York's version of the CCSS (the CCLS, or Common Core Learning Standards). Common Core will be releasing an enhanced version of the curriculum this summer on our website, commoncore.org. That version also will be published by Jossey-Bass, a Wiley brand.

Common Core's curriculum materials are not merely aligned to the new standards, they take the CCSS as their very foundation. Our work in math takes its shape from the expectations embedded in the new standards—including the instructional shifts and mathematical progressions, and the new expectations for student fluency, deep conceptual understanding, and application to real-life context. Similarly, our ELA and history curricula are deeply informed by the CCSS's new emphasis on close reading, increased use of informational text, and evidence-based writing.

Our curriculum is distinguished not only by its adherence to the CCSS. The math curriculum is based on a theory of teaching math that is proven to work. That theory posits that mathematical knowledge is most coherently and

---

1. Despite the coincidence of name, Common Core and the Common Core State Standards are not affiliated. Common Core was established in 2007, prior to the start of the Common Core State Standards Initiative, which was led by the National Governors Association and the Council for Chief State School Officers.

2. *Common Core State Standards for English Language Arts & Literacy in History/Social Studies, Science, and Technical Subjects* (Washington, DC: Common Core State Standards Initiative), 6.

effectively conveyed when it is taught in a sequence that follows the "story" of mathematics itself. This is why we call the elementary portion of this curriculum "A Story of Units," to be followed by "A Story of Ratios" in middle school, and "A Story of Functions" in high school. Mathematical concepts flow logically, from one to the next, in this curriculum. The sequencing has been joined with methods of instruction that have been proven to work, in this nation and abroad. These methods drive student understanding beyond process, to deep mastery of mathematical concepts. The goal of the curriculum is to produce students who are not merely literate, but fluent, in mathematics.

It is important to note that, as extensive as these curriculum materials are, they are not meant to be prescriptive. Rather, they are intended to provide a basis for teachers to hone their own craft through study, collaboration, training, and the application of their own expertise as professionals. At Common Core we believe deeply in the ability of teachers and in their central and irreplaceable role in shaping the classroom experience. We strive only to support and facilitate their important work.

The teachers and scholars who wrote these materials are listed beginning on the next page. Their deep knowledge of mathematics, of the CCSS, and of what works in classrooms defined this work in every respect. I would like to thank Louisiana State University professor of mathematics Scott Baldridge for the intellectual leadership he provides to this project. Teacher, trainer, and writer Robin Ramos is the most inspired math educator I've ever encountered. It is Robin and Scott's aspirations for what mathematics education in America *should* look like that is spelled out in these pages.

Finally, this work owes a debt to project director Nell McAnelly that is so deep I'm confident it never can be repaid. Nell, who leads LSU's Gordon A. Cain Center for STEM Literacy, oversees all aspects of our work for NYSED. She has spent days, nights, weekends, and many cancelled vacations toiling in her efforts to make it possible for this talented group of teacher-writers to produce their best work against impossible deadlines. I'm confident that in the years to come Scott, Robin, and Nell will be among those who will deserve to be credited with putting math instruction in our nation back on track.

Thank you for taking an interest in our work. Please join us at www.commoncore.org.

Lynne Munson
President and Executive Director
Common Core
Washington, DC
October 25, 2013

Common Core's K-5 Math Staff

Scott Baldridge, Lead Mathematician and Writer
Robin Ramos, Lead Writer, PreKindergarten-5
Jill Diniz, Lead Writer, 6-12
Ben McCarty, Mathematician

Nell McAnelly, Project Director
Tiah Alphonso, Associate Director
Jennifer Loftin, Associate Director
Catriona Anderson, Curriculum Manager, PreKindergarten-5

Sherri Adler, PreKindergarten
Debbie Andorka-Aceves, PreKindergarten

Kate McGill Austin, Kindergarten
Nancy Diorio, Kindergarten
Lacy Endo-Peery, Kindergarten
Melanie Gutierrez, Kindergarten
Nuhad Jamal, Kindergarten
Cecilia Rudzitis, Kindergarten
Shelly Snow, Kindergarten

Beth Barnes, First Grade
Lily Cavanaugh, First Grade
Ana Estela, First Grade
Kelley Isinger, First Grade
Kelly Spinks, First Grade
Marianne Strayton, First Grade
Hae Jung Yang, First Grade

Wendy Keehfus-Jones, Second Grade
Susan Midlarsky, Second Grade
Jenny Petrosino, Second Grade
Colleen Sheeron, Second Grade
Nancy Sommer, Second Grade
Lisa Watts-Lawton, Second Grade
MaryJo Wieland, Second Grade
Jessa Woods, Second Grade

Eric Angel, Third Grade
Greg Gorman, Third Grade
Susan Lee, Third Grade
Cristina Metcalf, Third Grade
Ann Rose Santoro, Third Grade
Kevin Tougher, Third Grade
Victoria Peacock, Third Grade
Saffron VanGalder, Third Grade

Katrina Abdussalaam, Fourth Grade
Kelly Alsup, Fourth Grade
Patti Dieck, Fourth Grade
Mary Jones, Fourth Grade
Soojin Lu, Fourth Grade
Tricia Salerno, Fourth Grade
Gail Smith, Fourth Grade
Eric Welch, Fourth Grade
Sam Wertheim, Fourth Grade
Erin Wheeler, Fourth Grade

Leslie Arceneaux, Fifth Grade
Adam Baker, Fifth Grade
Janice Fan, Fifth Grade
Peggy Golden, Fifth Grade
Halle Kananak, Fifth Grade
Shauntina Kerrison, Fifth Grade
Pat Mohr, Fifth Grade
Chris Sarlo, Fifth Grade

Additional Writers

Bill Davidson, Fluency Specialist
Robin Hecht, UDL Specialist
Simon Pfeil, Mathematician

Document Management Team

Tam Le, Document Manager
Jennifer Merchan, Copy Editor

Table of Contents

GRADE 2 • MODULE 7

Problem Solving with Length, Money, and Data

Grade 2 • Module 7

Problem Solving with Length, Money, and Data

OVERVIEW

Module 7 presents an opportunity for students to practice addition and subtraction strategies within 100 and problem-solving skills as they learn to work with various types of units within the contexts of length, money, and data. Students represent categorical and measurement data using picture graphs, bar graphs, and line plots. They revisit measuring and estimating length from Module 2, though now using both metric and customary units.

Module 7 opens with students representing and interpreting categorical data. In Grade 1, students learned to organize and represent data with up to three categories. Now, in Grade 2, students build upon this understanding by drawing both picture and bar graphs (**2.MD.10**). First, they record category counts in a table, solving problems based on the information in the table. Next, they draw picture graphs in which each picture represents one object. Finally, they represent the same data set in the form of a bar graph where one axis names the categories and the other shows a single-unit count scale. Students use the information to solve *put-together, take-apart,* and *compare* problems (**2.MD.10**), making connections to finding sums and differences on a number line diagram (**2.MD.6**). In the final lesson of Topic A, students display money data in the form of a bar graph, thus establishing a connection to word problems with coins in Topic B.

In Topic B, students work with the most popular units of all, bills and coins. Students apply their knowledge of coin values, place value strategies, and the properties of operations to solve addition and subtraction word problems (**2.NBT.5**, **2.MD.8**) to find the total value of a group of coins or bills. Next, they use coins to find multiple ways to represent the same quantity, sometimes using the fewest number of coins. Students then focus on the decomposition of a dollar, where they see that this unit behaves like all others they have seen before (e.g., 100 ones = 1 hundred, 100 cm = 1 m, etc.). Students learn how to make change from one dollar using counting on, simplifying strategies (e.g., number bonds), and the relationship between addition and subtraction. As students use coins or bills to solve addition and subtraction word problems within 100,[1] they use drawings and equations to represent the unknown in various situations. The Application Problems throughout this module include solving two-step word problems involving two-digit money amounts (e.g., $28 + $47 or 28¢ + 47¢), as students use this new context to increase fluency with addition and subtraction within 100 (**2.NBT.5**).

After the Mid-Module Assessment, Topic C reviews the measurement concepts and skills presented in Module 2, now with a focus on customary units. Students deepen their understanding of a *length unit* as they lay one-inch square tiles end-to-end to create simple inch rulers, just as they created centimeter rulers in Module 2. They see again that the smaller the unit, the more iterations are necessary to cover a given distance. Students measure the length of various objects with their new unit rulers (**2.MD.1**), applying important concepts such as the understanding that the zero point on a ruler is the beginning of the total

[1] Totals are limited to within 100 cents, or 1 dollar, when working with coins, and 100 dollars when working with bills.

length and that *7* on a ruler means the distance covered by 7 length units.

In Topic D, students apply their measurement skills and knowledge of the ruler to measure a variety of objects using the appropriate measurement tools, such as inch rulers and yardsticks, just as they measured with centimeter rulers, meter sticks, and meter tape in Module 2 (**2.MD.1**). Students thereby add to their bank of benchmark lengths, such as an inch being the distance across a quarter. In doing so, students develop mental images of an inch, a foot, or a yard, which empowers them to estimate a given length (**2.MD.3**).

In addition, in Topic D students measure objects twice using metric and customary length units, thereby developing an understanding of how the number of units needed depends upon the size of the unit chosen (**2.MD.2**). As in Topic C, students recognize, for example, that the smaller the length unit, the more iterations are necessary to cover a given distance. Topic D concludes with students measuring to determine how much longer one object is than another (**2.MD.4**). Students use addition and subtraction to compare two lengths, subtracting the length of the shorter object from the length of the longer object to determine the difference (e.g., 40 in – 35 in = 5 in, or 35 in + _____ = 40 in).

Whereas in Topic D students used rulers to compare lengths, in Topic E students use drawings (e.g., tape diagrams and number bonds) and equations with an unknown to represent addition and subtraction word problems (**2.MD.5**). Once they have a solid conceptual understanding of length, students are ready to represent whole numbers as lengths on a number line (**2.MD.6**) and to apply their knowledge of the ruler to a number line diagram. In Topic E, they are asked to identify unknown numbers on a number line by using place value, reference points (e.g., 5, 10, 25, and 50), and the distance between points. Students are also asked to represent two-digit sums and differences using the number line as a measurement model for combining and comparing lengths.

Topic F follows naturally, with students generating measurement data and representing it with a line plot (**2.MD.9**). Students position data along a horizontal scale with whole number markings, drawn as a number line diagram (**2.MD.6**). Since students are working with length, the scale on their line plots corresponds to the scale on their rulers. After generating measurement data, students create line plots from different data sets, and then they discuss and interpret the results.

The Mid-Module Assessment follows Topic B, and the End-of-Module Assessment follows Topic F.

Distribution of Instructional Minutes

This diagram represents a suggested distribution of instructional minutes based on the emphasis of particular lesson components in different lessons throughout the module.

- Fluency Practice
- Concept Development
- Application Problems
- Student Debrief

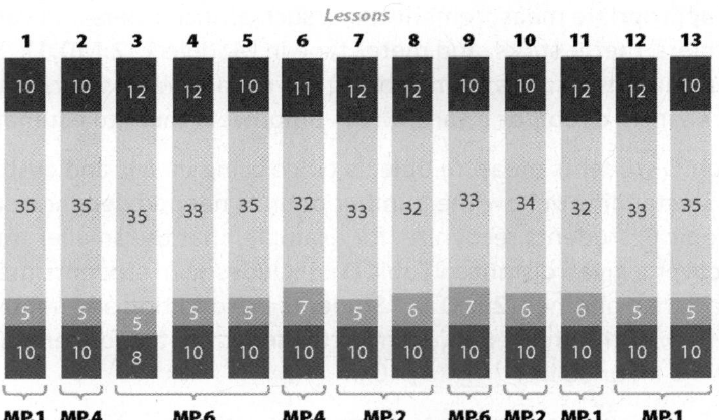

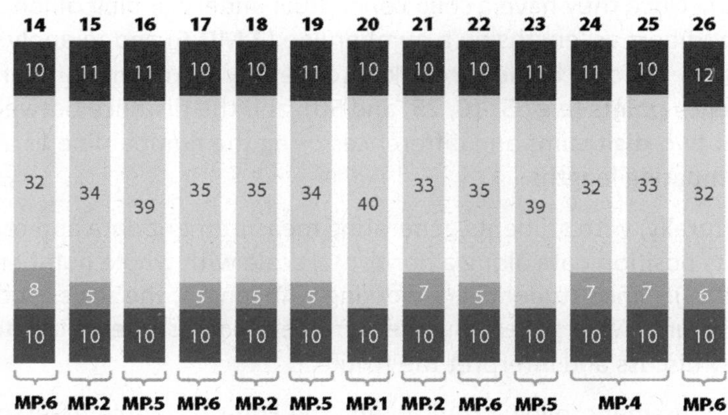

MP = Mathematical Practice

Focus Grade Level Standards

Use place value understanding and properties of operations to add and subtract.

2.NBT.5 Fluently add and subtract within 100 using strategies based on place value, properties of operations, and/or the relationship between addition and subtraction.

Measure and estimate lengths in standard units.

2.MD.1 Measure the length of an object by selecting and using appropriate tools such as rulers, yardsticks, meter sticks, and measuring tapes.

2.MD.2 Measure the length of an object twice, using length units of different lengths for the two measurements; describe how the two measurements relate to the size of the unit chosen.

2.MD.3 Estimate lengths using inches, feet, centimeters, and meters.

2.MD.4 Measure to determine how much longer one object is than another, expressing the length difference in terms of a standard length unit.

Relate addition and subtraction to length.

2.MD.5 Use addition and subtraction within 100 to solve word problems involving lengths that are given in the same units, e.g., by using drawings (such as drawings of rulers) and equations with a symbol for the unknown number to represent the problem.

2.MD.6 Represent whole numbers as lengths from 0 on a number line diagram with equally spaced points corresponding to the numbers 0, 1, 2, ..., and represent whole-number sums and differences within 100 on a number line diagram.

Work with time and money.[2]

2.MD.8 Solve word problems involving dollar bills, quarters, dimes, nickels, and pennies, using $ and ¢ symbols appropriately. *Example: If you have 2 dimes and 3 pennies, how many cents do you have?*

Represent and interpret data.

2.MD.9 Generate measurement data by measuring lengths of several objects to the nearest whole unit, or by making repeated measurements of the same object. Show the measurements by making a line plot, where the horizontal scale is marked off in whole-number units.

2.MD.10 Draw a picture graph and a bar graph (with single-unit scale) to represent a data set with up to four categories. Solve simple put-together, take-apart, and compare problems using information presented in a bar graph.

Foundational Standards

1.MD.2 Express the length of an object as a whole number of length units, by laying multiple copies of a shorter object (the length unit) end to end; understand that the length measurement of an object is the number of same-size length units that span it with no gaps or overlaps. *Limit to contexts where the object being measured is spanned by a whole number of length units with no gaps or overlaps.*

1.MD.4 Organize, represent, and interpret data with up to three categories; ask and answer questions about the total number of data points, how many in each category, and how many more or less are in one category than in another.

2.OA.1 Use addition and subtraction within 100 to solve one- and two-step word problems involving situations of adding to, taking from, putting together, taking apart, and comparing, with unknowns in all positions, e.g., by using drawings and equations with a symbol for the unknown number to represent the problem. (See CCLS Glossary, Table 1.)

[2] Focus on money. Time is taught in Module 8.

2.NBT.2 Count within 1000; skip-count by 5s,[3] 10s, and 100s.

2.NBT.4 Compare two three-digit numbers based on meanings of the hundreds, tens, and ones digits, using >, =, and < symbols to record the results of comparisons.

2.NBT.6 Add up to four two-digit numbers using strategies based on place value and properties of operations.

Focus Standards for Mathematical Practice

MP.1 **Make sense of problems and persevere in solving them.** Students draw to determine the part–whole relationships embedded within various word problem types, and based on their analysis, they persevere to use various addition and subtraction strategies to solve problems. They then persist in making a statement of the solution to answer the question in the original context. In this module, the problem solving contexts involve length, money, and data.

MP.2 **Reason abstractly and quantitatively.** Students compare measurements using rulers, tape diagrams, and graphs. After they abstract the number of units or length measurements to calculate differences, they reinterpret the difference using the given units within a problem. Students also abstract the value from a set of coins to find the total value and then express that value once again in terms of dollars or cents.

MP.4 **Model with mathematics.** Students create drawings (e.g., tape diagrams) and write equations to model and solve word problems involving units of length, money, and data. Students use appropriate representations (e.g., line plot, bar graph, and picture graph) to visually display data. Students also use the number line to understand numbers and their relationships and to represent sums and differences within 100. Students organize their thinking about money by modeling with dollars and coins to solve addition and subtraction word problems.

MP.5 **Use appropriate tools strategically.** Students apply their measurement skills and knowledge of the ruler to measure a variety of objects using the appropriate measurement tools, such as inch rulers and yardsticks. When conventional measurement tools are not available, students make decisions about which resources might be helpful, such as using iteration with a shoe, a book, or a lima bean, while recognizing the limitations of such tools.

MP.6 **Attend to precision.** Students attend to precision when they iterate a physical unit to create inch rulers. They align the zero point on a ruler as the beginning of the total length, and they use various measurement tools and precise language to describe their experience: "I used an inch as the length unit." Students learn estimation strategies for measurement and make closer and closer approximations to the actual length. They assign specific values to different coins and count up starting with the largest value. Students generate and represent data in a bar graph, picture graph, or line plot, labelling axes appropriately and specifying the unit of measure.

---

[3] Use analog clock to provide a context for skip-counting by fives.

Overview of Module Topics and Lesson Objectives

Standards		Topics and Objectives	Days
2.MD.10 2.MD.6	A	**Problem Solving with Categorical Data** Lesson 1: Sort and record data into a table using up to four categories; use category counts to solve word problems. Lesson 2: Draw and label a picture graph to represent data with up to four categories. Lesson 3: Draw and label a bar graph to represent data; relate the count scale to the number line. Lesson 4: Draw a bar graph to represent a given data set. Lesson 5: Solve word problems using data presented in a bar graph.	5
2.NBT.5 **2.MD.8** 2.NBT.2 2.NBT.6	B	**Problem Solving with Coins and Bills** Lesson 6: Recognize the value of coins and count up to find their total value. Lesson 7: Solve word problems involving the total value of a group of coins. Lesson 8: Solve word problems involving the total value of a group of bills. Lesson 9: Solve word problems involving different combinations of coins with the same total value. Lesson 10: Use the fewest number of coins to make a given value. Lesson 11: Use different strategies to make \$1 or make change from \$1. Lesson 12: Solve word problems involving different ways to make change from \$1. Lesson 13: Solve two-step word problems involving dollars or cents with totals within \$100 or \$1.	8
		Mid-Module Assessment: Topics A–B (assessment ½ day, return ½ day, remediation or further applications 1 day)	2
2.MD.1	C	**Creating an Inch Ruler** Lesson 14: Connect measurement with physical units by using iteration with an inch tile to measure. Lesson 15: Apply concepts to create inch rulers; measure lengths using inch rulers.	2

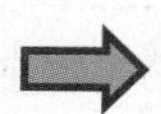

Standards		Topics and Objectives	Days
2.MD.1 **2.MD.2** **2.MD.3** **2.MD.4**	D	**Measuring and Estimating Length Using Customary and Metric Units** Lesson 16: Measure various objects using inch rulers and yardsticks. Lesson 17: Develop estimation strategies by applying prior knowledge of length and using mental benchmarks. Lesson 18: Measure an object twice using different length units and compare; relate measurement to unit size. Lesson 19: Measure to compare the differences in lengths using inches, feet, and yards.	4
2.MD.5 **2.MD.6** 2.NBT.2 2.NBT.4 2.NBT.5	E	**Problem Solving with Customary and Metric Units** Lesson 20: Solve two-digit addition and subtraction word problems involving length by using tape diagrams and writing equations to represent the problem. Lesson 21: Identify unknown numbers on a number line diagram by using the distance between numbers and reference points. Lesson 22: Represent two-digit sums and differences involving length by using the ruler as a number line.	3
2.MD.6 **2.MD.9** 2.MD.1 2.MD.5	F	**Displaying Measurement Data** Lesson 23: Collect and record measurement data in a table; answer questions and summarize the data set. Lesson 24: Draw a line plot to represent the measurement data; relate the measurement scale to the number line. Lessons 25–26: Draw a line plot to represent a given data set; answer questions and draw conclusions based on measurement data.	4
		End-of-Module Assessment: Topics A–F (assessment ½ day, return ½ day, remediation or further applications 1 day)	2
Total Number of Instructional Days			**30**

Terminology

New or Recently Introduced Terms

- Bar graph (diagram showing data using lines or rectangles of equal width)
- Category (group of people or things sharing a common characteristic, e.g., bananas are in the fruit category)
- Data (facts assembled for analysis or information)
- Degree (unit of temperature measure)
- Foot (ft, unit of length measure equal to 12 inches)
- Inch (in, unit of length measure)
- Legend (notation on a graph explaining what symbols represent)
- Line plot (graph representing data with an X above each instance of value on a number line)
- Picture graph (representation of data like a bar graph, using pictures instead of bars)
- Scale (system of ordered marks at fixed intervals used as a reference standard in measurement)
- Survey (collecting data by asking a question and recording responses)
- Symbol (picture that represents something real)
- Table (representation of data using rows and columns)
- Thermometer (temperature measuring tool)
- Yard (yd, unit of length measure equal to 36 inches or 3 feet)

Bar Graph

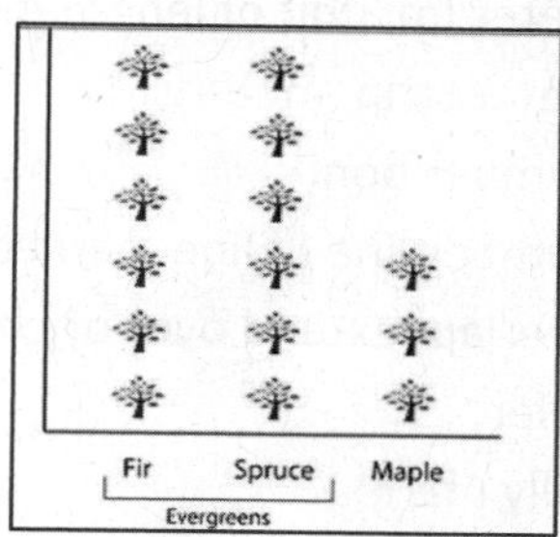

Picture Graph

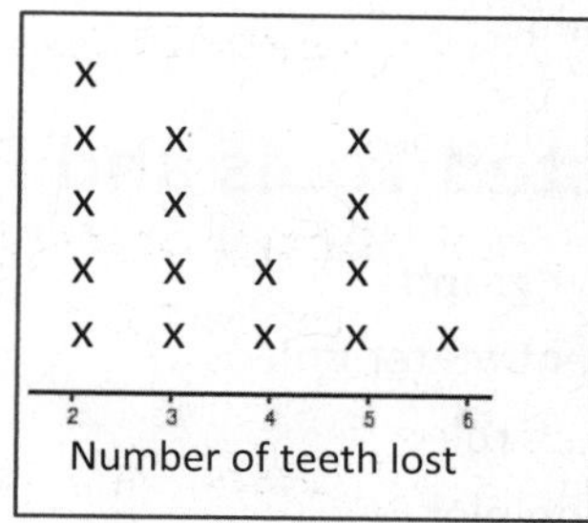

Line Plot

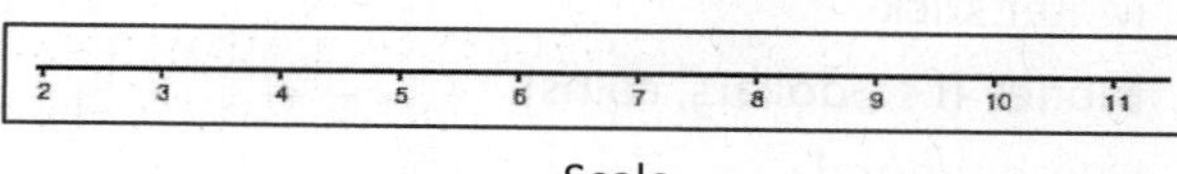

Scale

Familiar Terms and Symbols[4]

- Benchmark (e.g., round numbers like multiples of 10)
- Centimeter (cm, unit of length measure)
- Cents (e.g., 5¢)
- Coins (e.g., penny, nickel, dime, and quarter)
- Compare
- Compose
- Decompose
- Difference
- Dollars (e.g., $2)

[4] These are terms and symbols students have seen previously.

- Endpoint
- Equation
- Estimation (an approximation of the value of a quantity or number)
- Hash mark (the marks on a ruler or other measurement tool)
- Height
- Length
- Length unit
- Meter (m, unit of length measure)
- Meter strip, meter stick
- Number bond
- Number line (a line marked at evenly spaced intervals)
- Overlap (extend over or cover partly)
- Ruler
- Tally mark
- Tape diagram
- Unit
- Value

Suggested Tools and Representations

- Bar graph
- Centimeter Ruler
- Inch ruler
- Line plot
- Meter stick
- Money (i.e., dollars, coins)
- Number bond
- Number line
- Picture graph
- Table
- Tape diagram
- Yardstick

Scaffolds[5]

The scaffolds integrated into *A Story of Units* give alternatives for how students access information as well as express and demonstrate their learning. Strategically placed margin notes are provided within each lesson elaborating on the use of specific scaffolds at applicable times. They address many needs presented by English language learners, students with disabilities, students performing above grade level, and students performing below grade level. Many of the suggestions are organized by Universal Design for Learning (UDL) principles and are applicable to more than one population. To read more about the approach to differentiated instruction in *A Story of Units,* please refer to "How to Implement *A Story of Units*."

Assessment Summary

Type	Administered	Format	Standards Addressed
Mid-Module Assessment Task	After Topic B	Constructed response with rubric	2.NBT.5 2.MD.8 2.MD.10
End-of-Module Assessment Task	After Topic F	Constructed response with rubric	2.NBT.5 2.MD.1 2.MD.2 2.MD.3 2.MD.4 2.MD.5 2.MD.6 2.MD.8 2.MD.9 2.MD.10

[5] Students with disabilities may require Braille, large print, audio, or special digital files. Please visit the website, www.p12.nysed.gov/specialed/aim, for specific information on how to obtain student materials that satisfy the National Instructional Materials Accessibility Standard (NIMAS) format.

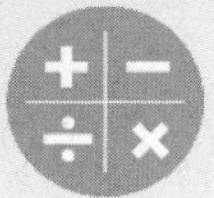

Topic A

Problem Solving with Categorical Data

2.MD.10, 2.MD.6

Focus Standard:	2.MD.10	Draw a picture graph and a bar graph (with single-unit scale) to represent a data set with up to four categories. Solve simple put-together, take-apart, and compare problems using information presented in a bar graph.
Instructional Days:	5	
Coherence -Links from:	G1–M3	Ordering and Comparing Length Measurements as Numbers
-Links to:	G3–M6	Collecting and Displaying Data

In Topic A, student work revolves around categorical data, which is produced by sorting objects or information into categories. For example, students learn about categories of animal classes and habitats and then record those data in a table. Students also learn to use picture graphs and bar graphs to organize and represent the data in as many as four categories (**2.MD.10**). They learn that this organizing of information makes it easier to compare data and can help them solve problems.

In Lesson 1, working within a science context, students categorize animals into classes (mammals, birds, fish, and reptiles), organize them in the form of a table, and then use the category counts to solve simple *put-together, take-apart,* and *compare* word problems (**2.MD.10**). Students then repeat the process, sorting animals by habitat to create a second data set. They record category counts in the tables with both numerals and tally marks (see image below).

Animal Habitats		
Arctic	**Ocean**	**Woodland**
卌 I	卌	卌 卌 IIII

Animal Classification			
Birds	**Fish**	**Mammals**	**Reptiles**
6	5	11	3

In Lesson 2, students learn to draw and label a picture graph using the data from Lesson 1. Grid paper provides support as students construct these graphs. They learn that a graph can be oriented horizontally or vertically, and that each picture represents one object.[1] Students ask and answer questions based on the information displayed in the graphs.

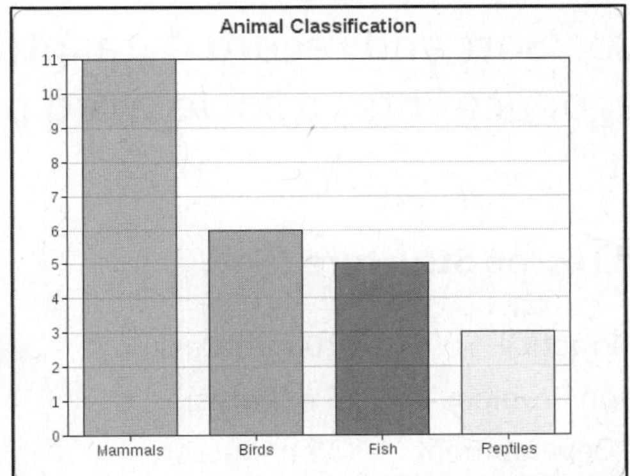

Following the same procedure and using the same data as in Lesson 2, students learn to draw and label a bar graph in Lesson 3. They learn that one axis names the category while the other shows a single-unit count scale. As students ask and answer questions based on the data in the graphs, they relate the count scale to finding sums and differences on a number line diagram (**2.MD.6**). In Lesson 4, students continue working with bar graphs to represent new data sets and solve simple word problems.

Topic A culminates in Lesson 5, as students display money data in a bar graph and use this data to solve word problems. This leads into problem solving with coins in Topic B.

A Teaching Sequence Towards Mastery of Problem Solving with Categorical Data

Objective 1: **Sort and record data into a table using up to four categories; use category counts to solve word problems.**
(Lesson 1)

Objective 2: **Draw and label a picture graph to represent data with up to four categories.**
(Lesson 2)

Objective 3: **Draw and label a bar graph to represent data; relate the count scale to the number line.**
(Lesson 3)

Objective 4: **Draw a bar graph to represent a given data set.**
(Lesson 4)

Objective 5: **Solve word problems using data presented in a bar graph.**
(Lesson 5)

[1] Note that pictures can represent more than one object beginning in Grade 3.

Lesson 1

Objective: Sort and record data into a table using up to four categories; use category counts to solve word problems.

Suggested Lesson Structure

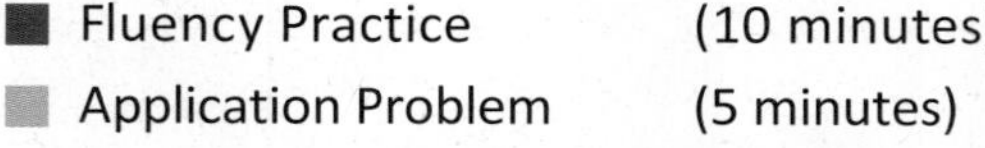

Fluency Practice	(10 minutes)
Application Problem	(5 minutes)
Concept Development	(35 minutes)
Student Debrief	(10 minutes)
Total Time	**(60 minutes)**

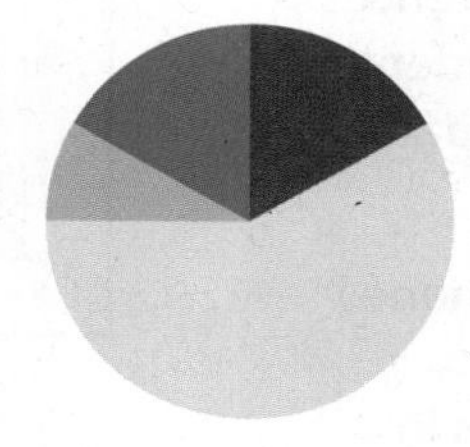

Fluency Practice (10 minutes)

- Count by 10 or 5 with Dimes and Nickels **2.NBT.2** (5 minutes)
- Grade 2 Core Fluency Differentiated Practice Sets **2.OA.2** (5 minutes)

Count by 10 or 5 with Dimes and Nickels (5 minutes)

Materials: (T) 20 dimes, 20 nickels

Note: This activity uses dimes and nickels as representations of tens and fives to help students become familiar with coins, while providing practice with counting forward and back by 10 or 5

- Arrange 10 nickels in a ten-frame formation and count up by 5 from 50 to 100. Ask how many nickels make 100 cents, how many fives are in 100 cents, and how many ones are in 100 cents. Add and subtract by 5 as you place and take away nickels.
- Arrange 9 dimes in a ten-frame formation and count up by 10 to 150. Ask how many dimes make 150 cents, how many tens are in 150 cents, how many fives are in 150 cents, and how many ones are in 150 cents. Continue counting to 200. Ask how many dimes make 200 cents, how many tens are in 200 cents, and how many ones are in 200 cents. Add and subtract by 10 as you place and take away dimes.

Grade 2 Core Fluency Differentiated Practice Sets (5 minutes)

Materials: (S) Core Fluency Practice Sets

Note: During G2–M7–Topic A and for the remainder of the year, each day's fluency includes an opportunity for review and mastery of the sums and differences with totals through 20 by means of the Core Fluency Practice Sets or Sprints. Five options are provided in this lesson for the Core Fluency Practice Set, with Sheet

A being the most simple to Sheet E being the most complex. Start all students on Sheet A.

Students complete as many problems as they can in 120 seconds. The recommended goal is 100% accuracy and completion before moving to the next level. Collect any Practice Sets that have been completed within the 120 seconds and check the answers. The next time Core Fluency Practice Sets are used, students who have successfully completed their set can be provided with the next level. Keep a record of student progress.

Consider assigning early finishers a counting pattern and start number (e.g., count by fives from 195). Celebrate improvement as well as advancement. Students should be encouraged to compete with themselves rather than their peers. Discuss with students possible strategies to solve. Notify caring adults of each student's progress.

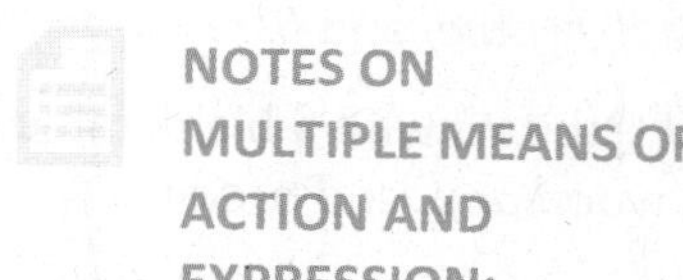
NOTES ON MULTIPLE MEANS OF ACTION AND EXPRESSION:

Scaffold the Application Problem for your students with disabilities by talking through it step by step and by asking questions such as, "How many penguins? How many whales? Are there more penguins or whales?" Watch students as they draw their tape diagrams to solve the problem and insist that they represent the problem accurately.

Application Problem (5 minutes)

There are 24 penguins sliding on the ice. There are 18 whales splashing in the ocean. How many more penguins than whales are there?

Note: This problem's context leads into today's Concept Development, as students will be sorting animals by habitat. Also, it is a comparative problem type that lends itself to a tape diagram drawing. This sets the stage for students to notice the similarity between the bars of a tape diagram and the bars of a bar graph in G2–M7–Lesson 3.

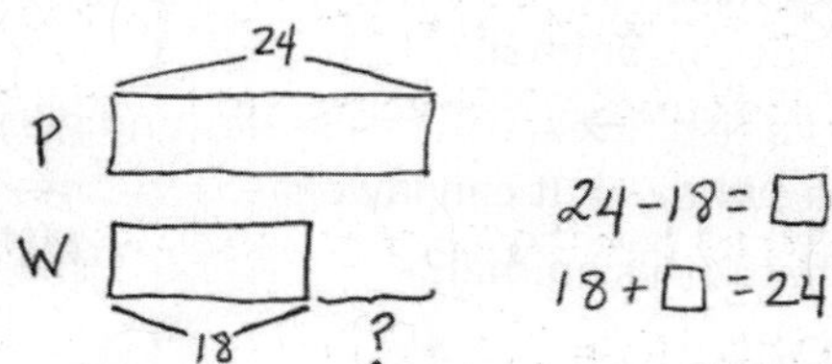

Concept Development (35 minutes)

Materials: (T) 4 pieces of chart paper (see chart list below)
(S) Personal white boards, one animal picture from the picture sheet per pair of students

Note: Prior to this lesson, consider laminating the picture sheet to make reusable cards. Cut the sheet into individual pictures. Also, prepare the four charts listed below. Save these charts for work in G2–M7–Lessons 1, 2, and 3.

Chart 1: Animal Characteristics with a blank tree map labeled *bird, mammal, reptile,* and *fish.*

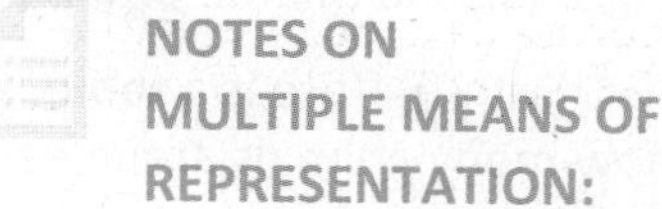
NOTES ON MULTIPLE MEANS OF REPRESENTATION:

Support English language learners by introducing essential terms like *characteristics, categories, data,* and *table* to them using visuals and multiple examples. Ask them to practice using the terms, pick out examples, and label pictures as examples of the different terms.

Chart 2: Sentence frames to support language production.

Chart 3: Animal Classification with a blank table labeled *bird, mammal, reptile,* and *fish.*

Chart 4: Animal Habitats with a blank table labeled *arctic, woodland,* and *ocean.*

Have students sit on the carpet in a circle.

T: Let's play a guessing game!

T: I have two legs, wings, feathers, and I can fly. What am I? Whisper to your partner.

S: A bird!

T: Of course! I just described the characteristics of a bird. (Post Chart 1.) Where do you see the characteristics of a bird listed on this chart?

S: On the left! → Under the word *bird*.

T: (Show a picture of a fish. Point to Chart 2.) Use these sentence frames to tell your partner about this animal.

S: It is a fish. → A fish has scales and gills. → It can swim. → It can lay eggs.

T: What is this animal?

S: A fish!

T: So what are the characteristics of a fish?

S: It has scales. → It has fins and gills. → It swims.

T: Yes! Let's sort animals into **categories**, or groups, based on their characteristics.

Chart 1

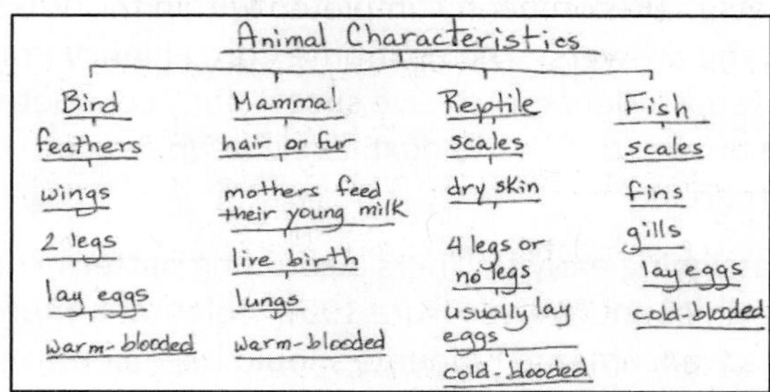

Chart 2

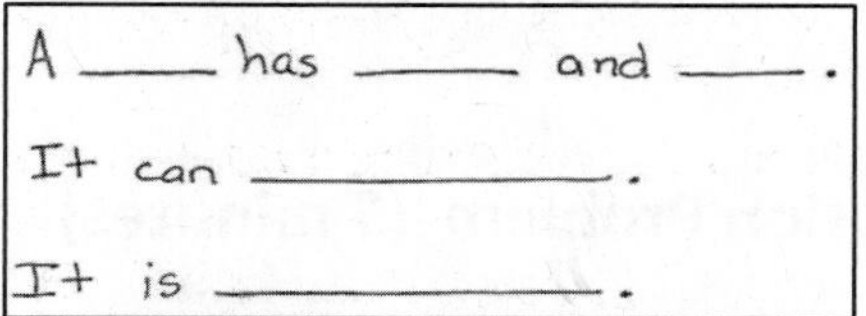

Chart 3

Animal Classification

Bird	||||
Mammal	卌 |||
Reptile	卌
Fish	|||

Pass out one picture card to each pair of students. Have partners take turns using the sentence frames and the animal characteristics chart to describe their animal to each other. Then have students sort the pictures into piles by category in the middle of the circle.

T: (Display Chart 3.) Here is a **table**. How can we organize our information, or **data**, so it's easier to know how many animals are in each category?

S: We could tape the pictures down in the row where they belong. → We could count how many are in each group and write the number in that row. → We could use tally marks.

T: Those are all excellent ideas! Let's record our category counts on this table using tally marks.

T: Count with me and make tally marks in the air as I record each amount.

T: How many birds do we have?

Call on volunteers to count each pile of pictures one by one. Make tally marks for each amount in the appropriate category, as students make tally marks in the air as they count aloud with you.

T: Now that the data is organized in this table, is it easy to see and count how many animals belong to each category?

S: Yes!

T: Let's count the tally marks in each category, while I record the totals as numbers directly on the table. (Record the numbers to the right of the tally marks.)

T: Now we can use the data to answer some questions.

Pose questions such as those below, and have students write their answers on their personal boards. Then invite students to pose questions to the class based on the data.

- How many categories does this table have?
- How many animals did we sort all together?
- How many more birds and mammals are there than reptiles and fish?
- How many fewer birds and fish are there than mammals and reptiles?
- How would the table change if we counted four more birds?

T: What are some other ways we could organize these animals?

S: We could sort them by what they eat. → Or, by where they live. → We could sort them by whether they are predators or prey!

T: I like your thinking! Let's sort them by their habitat, or where they live. (Display Chart 4.)

Chart 4

Animal Habitats		
Arctic	Woodland	Ocean
4	10	6

Repeat the process with animal habitats, but this time record numbers instead of tally marks.

Prompt students to discuss which recording is easier to read, tally marks or numbers. Some students may say numbers, because the total is given so they don't have to count the tally marks. However, some students may reference the visual length of the tally marks as helpful, particularly with questions of most and least. This touches on the tally's resemblance to bars in a tape diagram, a relationship that will be more pronounced when students create and use bar graphs in G2–M7–Lesson 3.

Make a quick drawing to show Chart 4 drawn vertically. Ask students whether the orientation of the table affects the data in any way.

After creating the table on Chart 4, have students write their answers as you ask questions such as those below. Then invite partners to ask and answer questions that they create.

- How many categories does this table have?
- Which category has the fewest animals? Which has the most?
- How many animals altogether live in the woodland and the ocean?

MP.1

- How many fewer animals live in the arctic than in the ocean?
- How many more animals would need to be in the arctic category to have the same number as animals in the woodland category?
- How many more arctic and ocean animals are there than woodland animals? (Note that some students will believe the wording *how many more* means there must be a difference. Have students who answer correctly explain their answer.)

Problem Set (10 minutes)

Students should do their personal best to complete the Problem Set within the allotted 10 minutes. Some problems do not specify a method for solving. This is an intentional reduction of scaffolding that invokes MP.5, Use Appropriate Tools Strategically. Students should solve these problems using the RDW approach used for Application Problems.

For some classes, it may be appropriate to modify the assignment by specifying which problems students should work on first. With this option, let the careful sequencing of the Problem Set guide your selections so that problems continue to be scaffolded. Balance word problems with other problem types to ensure a range of practice. Assign incomplete problems for homework or at another time during the day.

Name Jessie Date

1. Count and categorize each picture to complete the table with tally marks.

No Legs	2 Legs	4 Legs
II	III	IIII

2. Count and categorize each picture to complete the table with numbers.

Fur	Feathers
IIII	III

3. Use the Animal Habitats table to answer the following questions.

Animal Habitats		
Forest	Wetlands	Grasslands
~~IIII~~ I	~~IIII~~	~~IIII~~ ~~IIII~~ IIII

a. How many animals have habitats on grasslands and wetlands? 19

b. How many fewer animals have forest habitats than grasslands habitats? 8 (14 − 6 = 8)

c. How many more animals would need to be in the forest category to have the same number as animals in the grasslands category? 8

d. How many total animal habitats were used to create this table? 25

4. Use the Animal Classification table to answer the following questions about the types of animals Ms. Lee's second-grade class found in the local zoo.

Animal Classification			
Birds	Fish	Mammals	Reptiles
6	5	11	3

a. How many animals are birds, fish, or reptiles? 14

b. How many more birds and mammals are there than fish and reptiles? 9 (17 − 8 = 9)

c. How many animals were classified? 25 (6 + 5 = 11, 11 + 3 = 14, 11 + 14 = 25)

d. How many more animals would need to be added to the chart to have 35 animals classified? 10

e. If 5 more birds and 2 more reptiles were added to the table, how many fewer reptiles would there be than birds? 6 (6 + 5 = 11, 3 + 2 = 5, 11 − 5 = 6)

Student Debrief (10 minutes)

Lesson Objective: Sort and record data into a table using up to four categories; use category counts to solve word problems.

The Student Debrief is intended to invite reflection and active processing of the total lesson experience.

Invite students to review their solutions for the Problem Set. They should check work by comparing answers with a partner before going over answers as a class. Look for misconceptions or misunderstandings that can be addressed in the Debrief. Guide students in a conversation to debrief the Problem Set and process the lesson.

You may choose to use any combination of the questions below to lead the discussion.

- Look at your Problem Set with a partner. Do you both have the same number of tallies in the table about animal legs? If you have a different number of tallies, talk to your partner about why that is. (A possible misstep is making a tally mark for each leg as opposed to one tally for the animal with four legs).
- Look at the next table on your Problem Set. Could I have drawn the table like this? (Draw the

table vertically and write the categories in the left column.) If I make the table like this does it change the data inside the table? Why or why not?

- Look at Problem 3(b) about animal habitats. Tell your neighbor what counting strategy you used to figure out how many fewer animals have forest habitats than grasslands habitats. (Subtraction, matched marks and counted the extra, drew a picture, or crossed out objects.)
- Think about the two ways we recorded the value of our groups of animals in the tables we made today. Tell your neighbor which way you like to record information in a table. Can the same group of things be recorded in different ways? If yes, will the tallies or numbers be different in each table?

Exit Ticket (3 minutes)

After the Student Debrief, instruct students to complete the Exit Ticket. A review of their work will help you assess the students' understanding of the concepts that were presented in the lesson today and plan more effectively for future lessons. You may read the questions aloud to the students.

Name ______________________________ Date ______________

1.	10 + 2 =	21.	7 + 9 =
2.	10 + 7 =	22.	5 + 8 =
3.	10 + 5 =	23.	3 + 9 =
4.	4 + 10 =	24.	8 + 6 =
5.	6 + 11 =	25.	7 + 4 =
6.	12 + 2 =	26.	9 + 5 =
7.	14 + 3 =	27.	6 + 6 =
8.	13 + 5 =	28.	8 + 3 =
9.	17 + 2 =	29.	7 + 6 =
10.	12 + 6 =	30.	6 + 9 =
11.	11 + 9 =	31.	8 + 7 =
12.	2 + 16 =	32.	9 + 9 =
13.	15 + 4 =	33.	5 + 7 =
14.	5 + 9 =	34.	8 + 4 =
15.	9 + 2 =	35.	6 + 5 =
16.	4 + 9 =	36.	9 + 7 =
17.	9 + 6 =	37.	6 + 8 =
18.	8 + 9 =	38.	2 + 9 =
19	7 + 8 =	39.	9 + 8 =
20.	8 + 8 =	40.	7 + 7 =

Name ______________________ Date ____________

1.	10 + 6 =	21.	3 + 8 =
2.	10 + 9 =	22.	9 + 4 =
3.	7 + 10 =	23.	_____ + 6 = 11
4.	3 + 10 =	24.	_____ + 9 = 13
5.	5 + 11 =	25.	8 + _____ = 14
6.	12 + 8 =	26.	7 + _____ = 15
7.	14 + 3 =	27.	_____ = 4 + 8
8.	13 + _____ = 19	28.	_____ = 8 + 9
9.	15 + _____ = 18	29.	_____ = 6 + 4
10.	12 + 5 =	30.	3 + 9 =
11.	_____ = 2 + 17	31.	5 + 7 =
12.	_____ = 3 + 13	32.	8 + _____ =14
13.	_____ = 16 + 2	33.	_____ = 5 + 9
14.	9 + 3 =	34.	8 + 8 =
15.	6 + 9 =	35.	_____ = 7 + 9
16.	_____ + 5 = 14	36.	_____ = 8 + 4
17.	_____ + 7 = 13	37.	17 = 8 + _____
18.	_____ + 8 = 12	38.	19 = _____ + 9
19	8 + 7 =	39.	12 = _____ + 7
20.	7 + 6 =	40.	15 = 8 + _____

Name ______________________ Date ____________

1.	13 - 3 =	21.	16 - 8 =
2.	19 - 9 =	22.	14 - 5 =
3.	15 - 10 =	23.	16 - 7 =
4.	18 - 10 =	24.	15 - 7 =
5.	12 - 2 =	25.	17 - 8 =
6.	11 - 10 =	26.	18 - 9 =
7.	17 - 13 =	27.	15 - 6 =
8.	20 - 10 =	28.	13 - 8 =
9.	14 - 11 =	29.	14 - 6 =
10.	16 - 12 =	30.	12 - 5 =
11.	11 - 3 =	31.	11 - 7 =
12.	13 - 2 =	32.	13 - 8 =
13.	14 - 2 =	33.	16 - 9 =
14.	13 - 4 =	34.	12 - 8 =
15.	12 - 3 =	35.	16 - 12 =
16.	11 - 4 =	36.	18 - 15 =
17.	12 - 5 =	37.	15 - 14 =
18.	14 - 5 =	38.	17 - 11 =
19	11 - 2 =	39.	19 - 13 =
20.	12 - 4 =	40.	20 - 12 =

Name ______________________ Date ______________

1.	17 - 7 =	21.	16 - 7 =
2.	14 - 10 =	22.	17 - 8 =
3.	19 - 11 =	23.	18 - 7 =
4.	16 - 10 =	24.	14 - 6 =
5.	17 - 12 =	25.	17 - 8 =
6.	15 - 13 =	26.	12 - 8 =
7.	12 - 3 =	27.	14 - 7 =
8.	20 - 11 =	28.	15 - 8 =
9.	18 - 11 =	29.	13 - 5 =
10.	13 - 5 =	30.	16 - 8 =
11.	_____ = 11 - 2	31.	14 - 9 =
12.	_____ = 12 - 4	32.	15 - 6 =
13.	_____ = 13 - 5	33.	13 - 6 =
14.	_____ = 12 - 3	34.	_____ = 13 - 8
15.	_____ = 11 - 4	35.	_____ = 15 - 7
16.	_____ = 13 - 2	36.	_____ = 18 - 9
17.	_____ = 11 - 3	37.	_____ = 20 - 14
18.	17 - 8 =	38.	_____ = 20 - 7
19	14 - 6 =	39.	_____ = 20 - 11
20.	16 - 9 =	40.	_____ = 20 - 8

Name ____________________ Date ____________

1.	11 + 9 =	21.	13 - 7 =
2.	13 + 5 =	22.	11 - 8 =
3.	14 + 3 =	23.	15 - 6 =
4.	12 + 7 =	24.	12 + 7 =
5.	5 + 9 =	25.	14 + 3 =
6.	8 + 8 =	26.	8 + 12 =
7.	14 - 7 =	27.	5 + 7 =
8.	13 - 5 =	28.	8 + 9 =
9.	16 - 7 =	29.	7 + 5 =
10.	17 - 9 =	30.	13 - 6 =
11.	14 - 6 =	31.	14 - 8 =
12.	18 - 5 =	32.	12 - 9 =
13.	9 + 9 =	33.	11 - 3 =
14.	7 + 6 =	34.	14 - 5 =
15.	3 + 9 =	35.	13 - 8 =
16.	6 + 7 =	36.	8 + 5 =
17.	8 + 5 =	37.	4 + 7 =
18.	13 - 8 =	38.	7 + 8 =
19	16 - 9 =	39.	4 + 9 =
20.	14 - 8 =	40.	20 - 8 =

Name ______________________________ Date ________________

1. Count and categorize each picture to complete the table with tally marks.

No Legs	2 Legs	4 Legs

2. Count and categorize each picture to complete the table with numbers.

Fur	Feathers

3. Use the Animal Habitats table to answer the following questions.

Animal Habitats		
Forest	**Wetlands**	**Grasslands**
卌 |	卌	卌 卌 ||||

a. How many animals have habitats on grasslands and wetlands? ________

b. How many fewer animals have forest habitats than grasslands habitats? _______

c. How many more animals would need to be in the forest category to have the same number as animals in the grasslands category? ________

d. How many total animal habitats were used to create this table? __________

4. Use the Animal Classification table to answer the following questions about the types of animals Ms. Lee's second-grade class found in the local zoo.

Animal Classification			
Birds	**Fish**	**Mammals**	**Reptiles**
6	5	11	3

a. How many animals are birds, fish, or reptiles? _______

b. How many more birds and mammals are there than fish and reptiles? _______

c. How many animals were classified? _______

d. How many more animals would need to be added to the chart to have 35 animals classified? _______

e. If 5 more birds and 2 more reptiles were added to the table, how many fewer reptiles would there be than birds? _______

Name ______________________________ Date ______________

Use the Animal Classification table to answer the following questions about the types of animals at the local zoo.

Animal Classification			
Birds	**Fish**	**Mammals**	**Reptiles**
9	4	17	8

1. How many animals are birds, fish, or reptiles? ______

2. How many more mammals are there than fish? ______

3. How many animals were classified? ______

4. How many more animals would need to be added to the chart to have 45 animals classified? ______

Name ______________________________ Date ________________

1. Count and categorize each picture to complete the table with tally marks.

No Legs	2 Legs	4 Legs

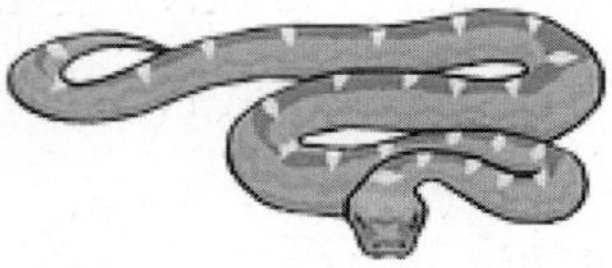

2. Count and categorize each picture to complete the table with numbers.

Fur	Feathers

3. Use the *Animal Habitat* table to answer the following questions.

Animal Habitats		
Arctic	**Forest**	**Grasslands**
6	11	9

a. How many animals live in the arctic? ________

b. How many animals have habitats in the forest and grasslands? ________

c. How many fewer animals have arctic habitats than forest habitats? _______

d. How many more animals would need to be in the grassland category to have the same number as the arctic and forest categories combined? _______

e. How many total animal habitats were used to create this table? __________

4. Use the *Animal Classification* table to answer the following questions about the class pets in West Chester Elementary School.

Animal Classification			
Birds	**Fish**	**Mammals**	**Reptiles**
7	15	18	9

a. How many animals are birds, fish, or reptiles? _______

b. How many more birds and mammals are there than fish and reptiles? _______

c. How many animals were classified? _______

d. If 3 more birds and 4 more reptiles were added to the table, how many fewer birds would there be than reptiles? _____

1 2 3

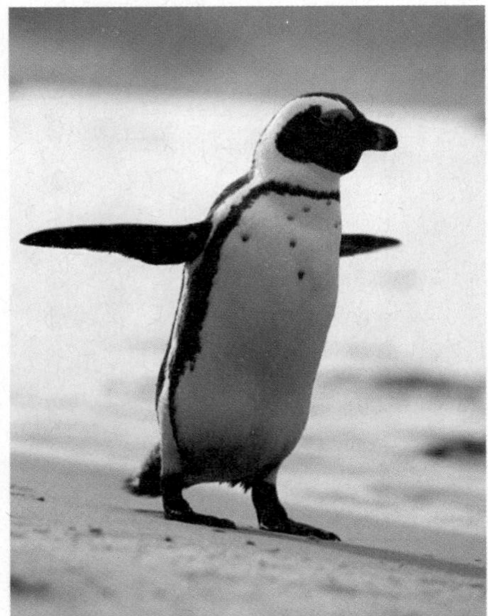

African Penguin

The African penguin lays 2 eggs at a time.

Clown Anemonefish

The clown anemonefish has scales, fins, and gills.

Polar Bear

The polar bear's thick coat of insulated fur protects against the arctic cold.

4 5

Barn Owl

The barn owl usually lays 4-7 eggs at a time.

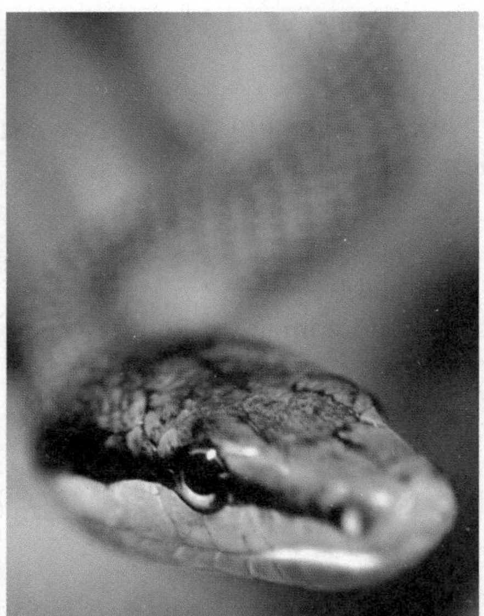

Rough Green Snake

Rough green snakes lay 4–12 sticky eggs under a flat stone or log.

Seahorse

Male seahorses carry eggs in brood pouches. They swim using a small fin on their back.

6

Arctic Fox

The female arctic fox can give birth to a litter of up to 14 pups.

7

Bottlenose Dolphin

Dolphins have lungs. They breathe air through a blowhole at the top of the head.

8

Brown Bear

Brown bear mothers give birth to cubs during hibernation. They don't even have to wake up!

9

Rabbit

Mother rabbits feed their babies milk once or twice a day.

10

Leopard Gecko

Leopard geckos are cold-blooded and absorb sunlight for warmth.

11

Green Iguana

Green iguanas often live in trees, but come to the ground to lay eggs.

12

California Mountain Kingsnake

This snake is a cold-blooded animal with scales.

13

Bull Shark

The bull shark's gills allow them to live in the shallow, warm waters of the ocean.

Brown Field Mouse

Female field mice give birth to 4-7 babies at a time.

British Robin

Females lay 4-6 pale blue speckled eggs in a nest in the spring.

Rooster

These warm-blooded creatures are known for crowing at dawn.

Orca Whale

A baby orca, or calf, is born tail-first and may weigh about 400 pounds.

Sea Turtle

Females lay eggs in a nesting hole in the sand.

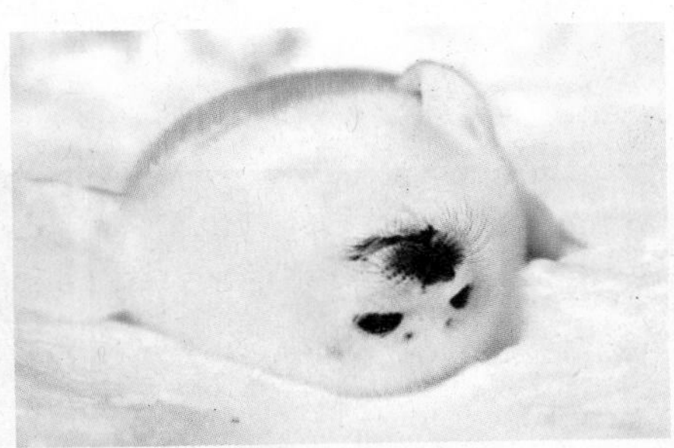

Baby Harp Seal

Seal mothers give birth in the spring and can identify their babies by their smell.

Lesson 2

Objective: Draw and label a picture graph to represent data with up to four categories.

Suggested Lesson Structure

■ Fluency Practice	(10 minutes)
■ Application Problem	(5 minutes)
■ Concept Development	(35 minutes)
■ Student Debrief	(10 minutes)
Total Time	**(60 minutes)**

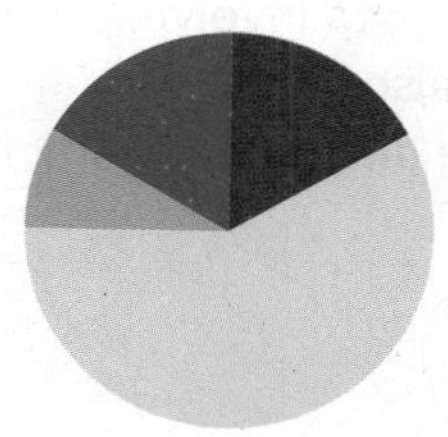

Fluency Practice (10 minutes)

- Grade 2 Core Fluency Differentiated Practice Sets **2.OA.2** (5 minutes)
- Coin Drop **2.OA.2, 2.NBT.2** (5 minutes)

Grade 2 Core Fluency Differentiated Practice Sets (5 minutes)

Materials: (S) Core Fluency Practice Sets from G2–M7–Lesson 1

Note: During G2–M7–Topic A and for the remainder of the year, each day's fluency includes an opportunity for review and mastery of the sums and differences with totals through 20 by means of the Core Fluency Practice Sets or Sprints. The process is detailed and Practice Sets are provided in G2–M7–Lesson 1.

Coin Drop (5 minutes)

Materials: (T) 10 dimes, 10 nickels, 10 pennies, can

Note: In this activity, students practice adding and subtracting ones, fives, and tens with coins.

T: (Hold up a nickel.) Name my coin.

S: A nickel.

T: How much is it worth?

S: 5 cents.

T: Listen carefully as I drop coins in my can. Count along in your minds.

Drop in some nickels and ask the value of the money in the can. Take out some of the nickels and show them. Continue adding and subtracting nickels for a minute or so. Then repeat the activity with dimes, then with nickels and pennies, and then dimes and pennies.

Application Problem (5 minutes)

Gemma is counting animals in the park. She counts 16 robins, 19 ducks, and 17 squirrels. How many more robins and ducks did Gemma count than squirrels?

Note: This comparative problem type invites the use of a tape diagram. It leads into today's lesson in which students will use data involving animals to solve simple *compare* word problems. It also prepares students to notice the relationship between the tape diagram and the bars on a bar graph in G2–M7–Lesson 3.

$16 + 19 = 15 + 20 = 35$

R and D [35]

S [17] ?

$35 - 17 = \square$

$17 + \square = 35$

Gemma saw 18 more robins and ducks than squirrels.

Concept Development (35 minutes)

Materials: (T) Animal Classification and Animal Habitats tables (Charts 3 and 4 from G2–M7–Lesson 1), 1 piece of chart paper (see below) (S) Template 1 graph, Template 2 graph, crayons or colored pencils, personal white board, paper or math journal

Note: Prior to this lesson, prepare a chart for a new table: Favorite Class of Animal. At the end of the lesson, save this new table and Template 1 and Template 2 graphs for work in G2–M7–Lesson 3.

Part 1: Use the picture graph template.

T: (Display Animal Classification table.) Yesterday, we organized information, or data, about animals into tables using tally marks and numbers.

T: A **picture graph** is another way we can show data. What do you think we use to show data on a picture graph?

S: Pictures!

T: Yes! Let's create a picture graph of the data in the Animal Classification table.

Pass out the picture graph template and have students slide the sheet into their personal boards. This way, the template can be used until students demonstrate proficiency in recording data.

Project or draw the first graph (vertical orientation on Template 1) on the board next to the Animal Classification table.

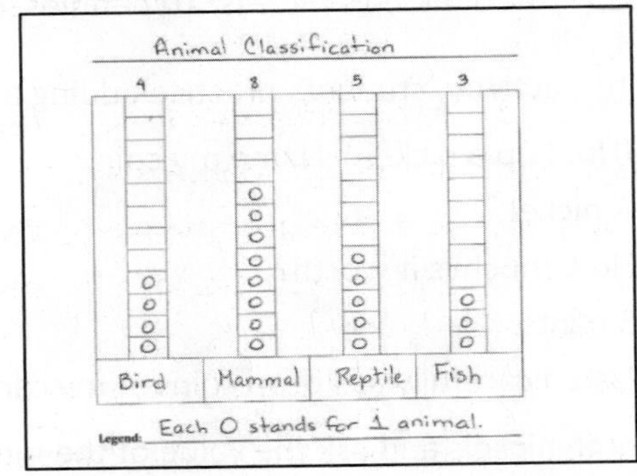

Template 1

T: Since graphs help us understand information, we need to know what the graph is about. What is the title of our table?

S: Animal Classification.

T: Yes. Our picture graph is going to show the same information, so write this same title on the line above the first graph. (Model as students do the same.)

T: What are the four categories of animals we classified?

S: Bird. → Mammal. → Reptile. → Fish.

T: Let's write these labels in the same order as they appear on the table. (Model as students do the same.)

T: Why do you think it matters that we write the categories in the same order as they appear on the table?

S: So we don't get confused. → So the information looks the same.

T: Yes, we want to be sure our data matches up.

T: Now, we're going to draw a picture in each box to represent each animal recorded by a tally mark on our table.

T: As always, it's math not art, so we want to be quick and efficient. We don't have the time or enough space to draw a whale or a polar bear over and over in these little boxes, do we?

S: No!

T: What do we use in our math drawings that's quick and efficient?

S: Circles!

T: Absolutely! A circle is a fast way to draw something, and it can stand for whatever we want it to stand for!

T: Today, our circles will be our picture, or **symbol**, for animals. Each circle will represent one animal, and we'll draw one circle in each box.

T: How many circles should we draw in the *bird* column?

S: Four circles!

T: Draw with me. (Model as students do the same. Continue this way to complete the picture graph.)

T: We need to add one more piece of information to our graph. We have to tell people what those circles stand for, so we need a **legend**, or key.

T: Does a circle stand for a box of crayons?

S: No!

T: What does each circle represent?

S: Each circle stands for one animal.

T: Excellent! Add the legend on your graph. (Model as students do the same.)

T: It's also helpful to write the total for each category count right on the graph. Let's do that. (Model as students do the same.)

T: Now we're ready to use our graph to ask and answer questions about the data.

Pose questions such as those below, and have students write their answers on their personal boards.

- How many birds, mammals, and reptiles did we count?

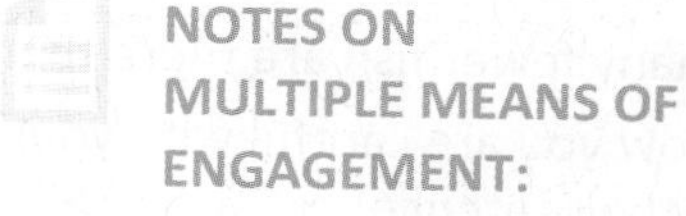

NOTES ON MULTIPLE MEANS OF ENGAGEMENT:

Use Google Images to show visuals of unusual animals such as the Komodo dragon or the chameleon, and share interesting facts. Invite students from other countries to share any animals that may be specific to that geographic area.

NOTES ON MULTIPLE MEANS OF ACTION AND EXPRESSION:

Support English language learners with sentence frames to guide them in posing and answering questions based on the data. For example, "We counted _____ birds, mammals, and reptiles," and, "The category with the fewest animals is _____."

- Which category has the fewest animals? The most?
- How many fewer reptiles are there than mammals?

T: Now it is your turn to ask a comparison question. Use the sentence frame "How many fewer _____ are there than _______?" to ask your partner a question about the graph.

S: How many fewer fish are there than reptiles? → How many fewer birds are there than mammals?

T: I like how you are careful with your questions. You made sure to put the class with fewer animals first in the sentence.

T: Let's ask another type of comparison question. This time use the sentence frame, "How many more _____ are there than _____?"

S: How many more mammals are there than reptiles? → How many more birds are there than fish?

T: Which class of animals did you say first in this question?

S: The one with more. → The one with a greater number of animals.

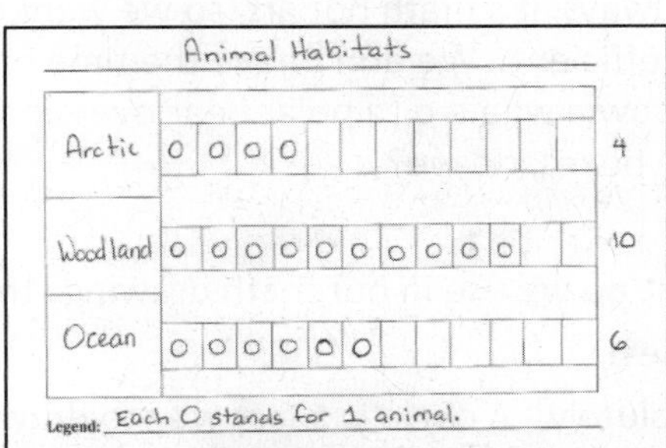

Template 1

Repeat the process to create a picture graph of the data from the Animal Habitats table, using the second graph (horizontal orientation) on Template 1. As students demonstrate understanding, allow them to work with a partner or independently.

After creating the graph, invite partners to ask and answer questions based on the data.

Part 2: Create picture graphs on graph paper.

Note: This next activity is designed to scaffold from the isolated columns and rows on Template 1 to the use of grid paper to create a picture graph (Template 2).

T: Now that we've learned how to classify certain animals, let's gather some more data. I will **survey** the class to find out what your favorite class of animal is. (Display Favorite Class of Animal table.)

T: You each get one vote, and I will record your votes on this table. (Survey students and record votes, then distribute Template 2.)

T: We're going to create a picture graph of this data, this time using grid paper.

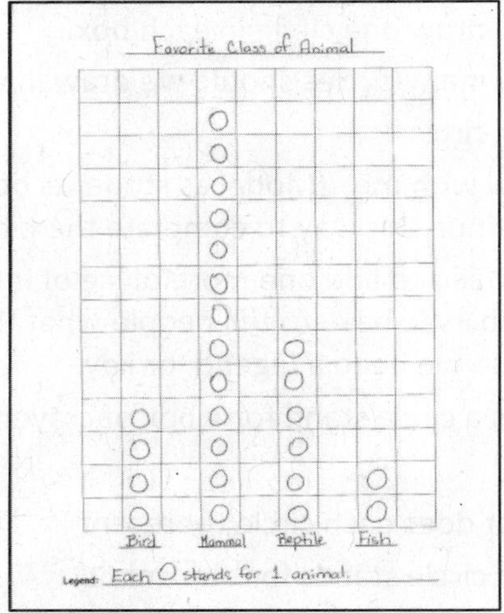

Template 2

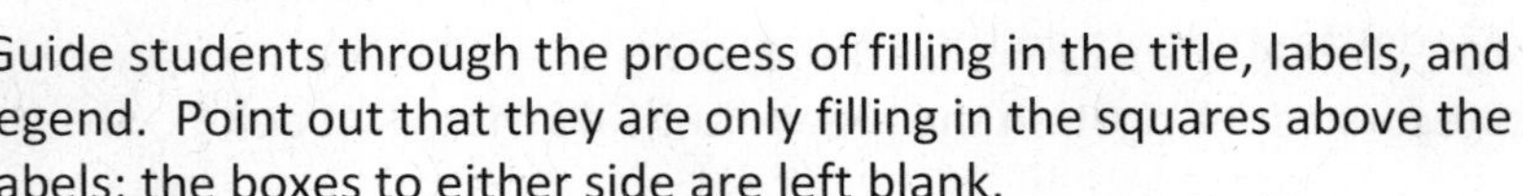

MP.4

Guide students through the process of filling in the title, labels, and legend. Point out that they are only filling in the squares above the labels; the boxes to either side are left blank.

After completing the graph, ask partners to ask and answer comparison questions based on the data.

Favorite Class of Animal

Bird	Mammal	Reptile	Fish
4	13	6	2

As students demonstrate proficiency creating and interpreting the graph, allow them to move on to the Problem Set. Continue working with any students who need support.

Problem Set (10 minutes)

Students should do their personal best to complete the Problem Set within the allotted 10 minutes. For some classes, it may be appropriate to modify the assignment by specifying which problems they work on first. Some problems do not specify a method for solving. Students solve these problems using the RDW approach used for Application Problems.

Name Amber Date

1. Use grid paper to create a picture graph below using data provided in the table. Then answer the questions.

Central Park Zoo Animal Classification			
Birds	Fish	Mammals	Reptiles
6	5	11	3

Central Park Zoo Animal Classification

Birds Fish Mammals Reptiles

Legend: Each ○ is 1 animal.

a. How many more animals are mammals than fish? 6

b. How many more animals are mammals and fish than birds and reptiles? 7
16 - 9 = 7

c. How many fewer animals are reptiles than mammals? 8

d. 4. Write one question comparing the number of two different animals.

Question: How many more birds are there than reptiles?

Answer: 3

2. Use the table below to create a picture graph in the space provided.

Animal Habitats		
Desert	Tundra	Grassland
卌 I	卌	卌 卌 IIII

Title: Animal Habitats

Desert ○○○○○○

Tundra ○○○○○

Grassland ○○○○○○○○○○○○○○

Legend: Each ○ is 1 habitat.

a. How many more animal habitats are in the grassland than in the desert? 8

b. How many fewer animal habitats are in the tundra than in the grassland and desert combined? 15

c. Write a comparison question that you can answer using the data from your picture graph.

Question: How many more habitats are grasslands than tundra?

Answer: 9

Student Debrief (10 minutes)

Lesson Objective: Draw and label a picture graph to represent data with up to four categories.

The Student Debrief is intended to invite reflection and active processing of the total lesson experience.

Invite students to review their solutions for the Problem Set. They should check work by comparing answers with a partner before going over answers as a class. Look for misconceptions or misunderstandings that can be addressed in the Debrief. Guide students in a conversation to debrief the Problem Set and process the lesson.

You may choose to use any combination of the questions below to lead the discussion.

- Talk to your neighbor about why we call these graphs picture graphs. Are there pictures in the graph?
- Look at the first page of the Problem Set. Question 1(a) asks how many more mammals than fish are in the table. Point to the pictures on your graph that tells the answer. Show your neighbor. (Guide students to see that in comparison problems, *more than* and *fewer than* refer to the extra circles of the two groups being compared.)
- Look at your Problem Set. Why does the grid paper make it easier to make a picture graph?
- Share the graph you created on the second page of the Problem Set with your neighbor. Do your graphs look the same? Can you understand your

neighbor's graph? Is the information in the graph correct? Are there labels?

- Does it matter if we record our pictures or circles in rows or columns? Does it change the information in the graph?
- What is a picture graph good for? What does it help us do?

Exit Ticket (3 minutes)

After the Student Debrief, instruct students to complete the Exit Ticket. A review of their work will help you assess the students' understanding of the concepts that were presented in the lesson today and plan more effectively for future lessons. You may read the questions aloud to the students.

Name ______________________________ Date ______________

1. Use grid paper to create a picture graph below using data provided in the table. Then answer the questions.

Central Park Zoo Animal Classification			
Birds	Fish	Mammals	Reptiles
6	5	11	3

a. How many more animals are mammals than fish? _______

b. How many more animals are mammals and fish than birds and reptiles? _______

c. How many fewer animals are reptiles than mammals? _______

Legend: ______________________

d. Write one question comparing the number of two different animals.

Question: ____

Answer: ____

2. Use the table below to create a picture graph in the space provided.

Animal Habitats		
Desert	**Tundra**	**Grassland**
𝍸 |	𝍸	𝍸 𝍸 ||||

Title: ______________________

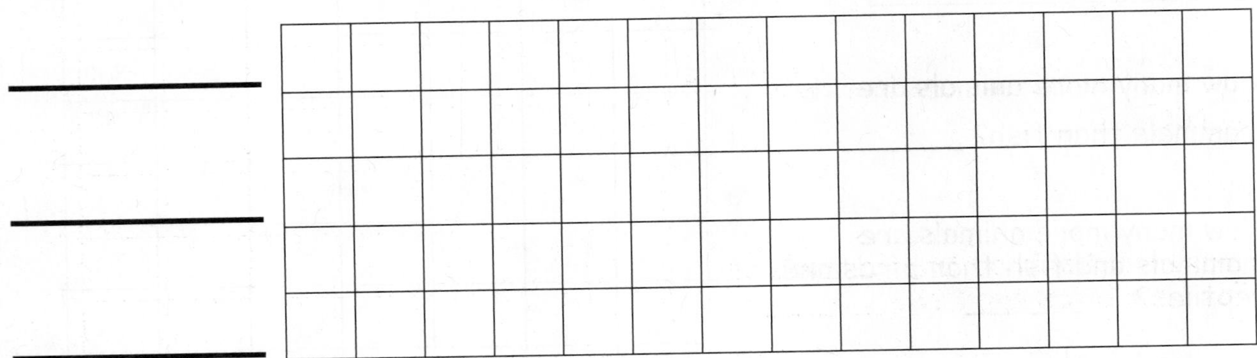

Legend: ______________________

a. How many more animal habitats are in the grassland than in the desert? ______

b. How many fewer animal habitats are in the tundra than in the grassland and desert combined? ______

c. Write a comparison question that you can answer using the data from your picture graph.

Question: ______________________

Answer: ______________________

Name ______________________________ Date ______________

Use grid paper to create a picture graph below using data provided in the table. Then answer the questions.

Central Park Zoo Animal Classification			
Birds	**Fish**	**Mammals**	**Reptiles**
8	4	12	5

a. How many more animals are mammals than birds? ______

b. How many more animals are mammals and reptiles than birds and fish? ______

c. How many fewer animals are fish than birds? ________

______ ______ ______ ______

Legend: ______________________________

Name ______________________________ Date ______________

1. Use grid paper to create a picture graph below using data provided in the table. Then answer the questions.

Favorite Mammals			
Tiger	Panda	Snow Leopard	Gorilla
8	11	7	12

a. How many more animals are gorillas than tigers? ______

b. How many more animals are tigers and gorillas than pandas and snow leopards? ______

c. How many fewer animals are tigers than pandas? ______

Legend: ______________________

d. Write one question comparing the number of two different animals.

Question: ____

Answer: ____

2. Use the data of Mr. Clark's class vote to create a picture graph in the space provided.

Favorite Birds		
Penguin	Flamingo	Peacock
卌 I	卌	卌 卌 IIII

Title: ______________________

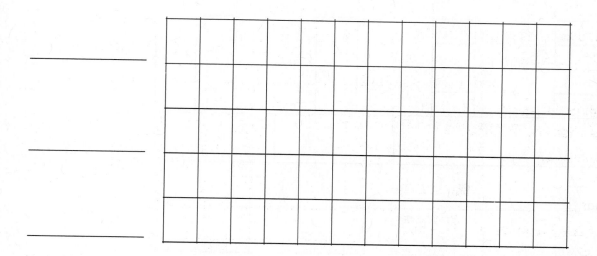

Legend: ______________________

a. How many more students voted for peacocks than penguins? ______

b. How many fewer flamingos than penguins or peacocks? ______

c. Write a comparison question that you can answer using the data from your picture graph.

Question: ____

Answer: ____

____

Legend: ____

____

Legend: ____

____

______ ______ ______ ______

Legend: ______________________________

Lesson 3

Objective: Draw and label a bar graph to represent data; relate the count scale to the number line.

Suggested Lesson Structure

■ Fluency Practice	(12 minutes)
■ Application Problem	(5 minutes)
■ Concept Development	(35 minutes)
■ Student Debrief	(8 minutes)
Total Time	**(60 minutes)**

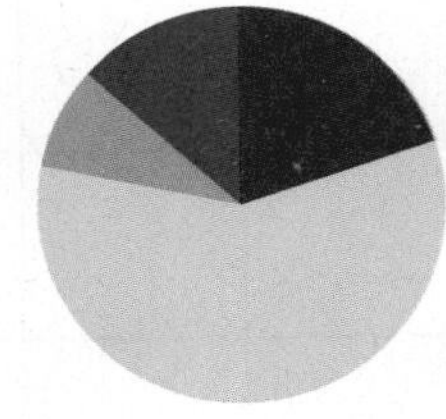

Fluency Practice (12 minutes)

- Sprint: Addition and Subtraction by 5 **2.NBT.2** (9 minutes)
- Coin Drop **2.NBT.2, 2.OA.2** (3 minutes)

Sprint: Addition and Subtraction by 5 (9 minutes)

Materials: (S) Addition and Subtraction by 5 Sprint

Note: This Sprint gives practice adding and subtracting by 5 in preparation for counting nickels in G2–M7–Topic B.

Coin Drop (3 minutes)

Materials: (T) 10 dimes, 5 nickels, can

Note: In this activity, students practice adding and subtracting fives, and tens.

T: (Hold up a nickel.) Name my coin.
S: A nickel.
T: How much is it worth?
S: 5 cents.
T: Listen carefully as I drop coins in my can. Count along in your minds.

Drop in some nickels and ask how much money is in the can. Take out some of the nickels and show them. Ask how much money is still in the can. Continue adding and subtracting nickels for a minute or so. Then repeat the activity with dimes and nickels.

Application Problem (5 minutes)

Materials: (T) Tally chart (S) Picture graph template

a. Use the tally chart to fill in the picture graph.

Number of Books Read

Jose	Laura	Linda
𝍸 III	𝍸	

Number of Books Read

Jose Laura Linda

Each ● stands for 1 book.

b. Draw a tape diagram to show how many more books Jose read than Laura.

c. If Jose, Laura, and Linda read 21 books altogether, how many books did Linda read? Complete the tally chart and the graph to show the answer.

Note: This problem reviews creating and interpreting picture graphs. It also anticipates one element of the Concept Development, in which students relate the bars of a graph to the bars of a tape diagram.

Number of Books Read

Jose	Laura	Linda
𝍸 III	𝍸	𝍸 III

Number of Books Read

Jose Laura Linda

Each ● stands for 1 book.

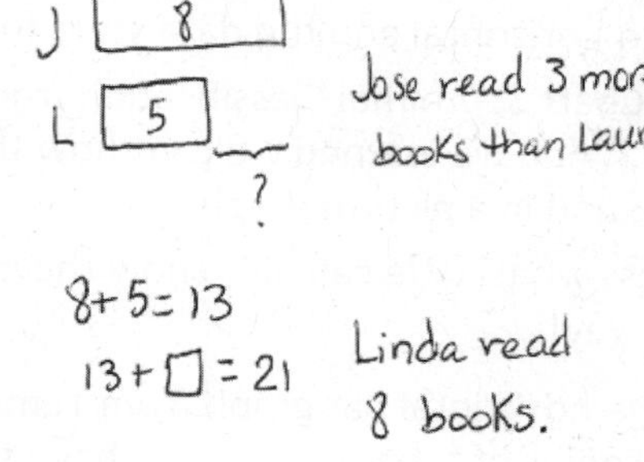

J 8
L 5
?
Jose read 3 more books than Laura.
8+5=13
13+□=21
Linda read 8 books.

Concept Development (35 minutes)

Materials: (T) Template 3 (blank bar graphs), Chart 3: Animal Classification and Chart 4: Animal Habitats (from G2–M7–Lesson 1), completed Template 1 (from G2–M7–Lesson 2) (S) Tape diagrams from Application Problem, Template 3, personal white board, paper or math journal

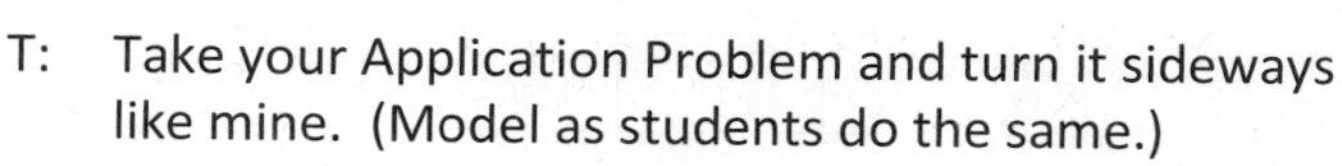

T: Take your Application Problem and turn it sideways like mine. (Model as students do the same.)

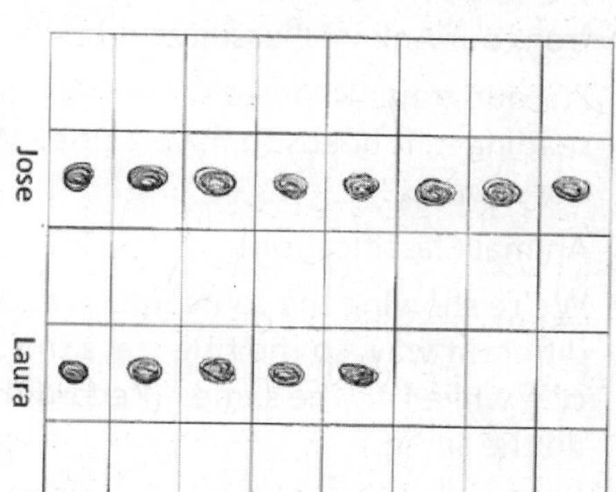

T: Talk with your partner: What do you notice about the picture graph when it's turned this way?

S: Hey! It looks just like a tape diagram! → The bars on the tape diagram show the same amount as the circles on the graph. → They both show that 8 is longer than 5. → They both show the difference between 8 and 5, but you can count the three empty spaces on the graph.

T: (Display Template 1 graph from G2–M7–Lesson 1, pictured below at right.)

T: Talk with your partner: How can you tell by looking at the graph which category has more and which has less?

S: The category with the most is the tallest, and the category with the least is the shortest.

T: Does the data change if I turn the graph sideways? (Rotate graph to horizontal position.)

S: No!

T: True! So, we're learning some interesting things about graphs. We can change the position of the graph from vertical to horizontal and the data stays the same.

T: (Display Chart 3: Animal Classification from G2–M7–Lesson 1.) And we learned we can show the same data in a table and in a picture graph.

T: Well guess what? We can also show the information another way!

Project or draw the horizontal bar graph from Template 3. Then pass out student copies of the template and have students slide the sheet into their personal boards.

T: We're going to create a **bar graph** to show the data from our Animal Classification table.

T: For our graph to make sense to someone who's reading it, it needs to have a title. What is the title of our chart?

S: Animal Classification!

T: We're showing the same information, just in a different way, so the title stays the same. Fill in the title while I do the same. (Record the title as students do the same.)

T: How many categories of animals did we classify?

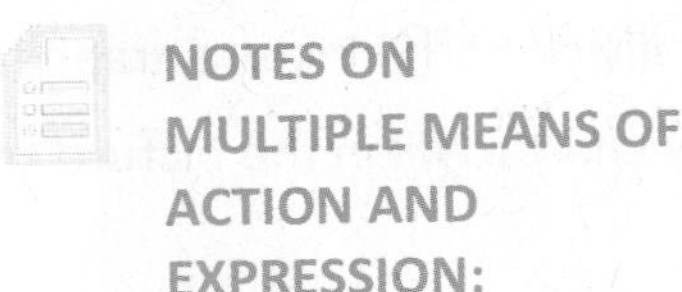

NOTES ON MULTIPLE MEANS OF ACTION AND EXPRESSION:

The language of comparison can be challenging for English language learners. Allow them to choose the language they prefer for discourse. Also, accompany comparative language such as *more, less, taller,* and *shorter,* with illustrative gestures.

Template 1 from G2–M7–Lesson 1

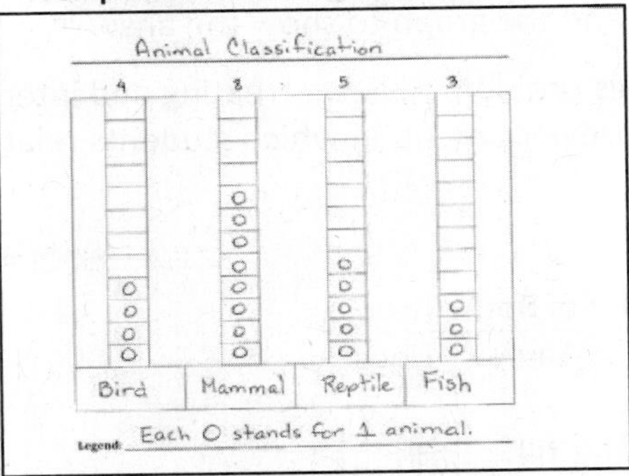

Chart 3 from G2–M7–Lesson 1

Animal Classification

Bird	IIII
Mammal	卌 III
Reptile	卌
Fish	III

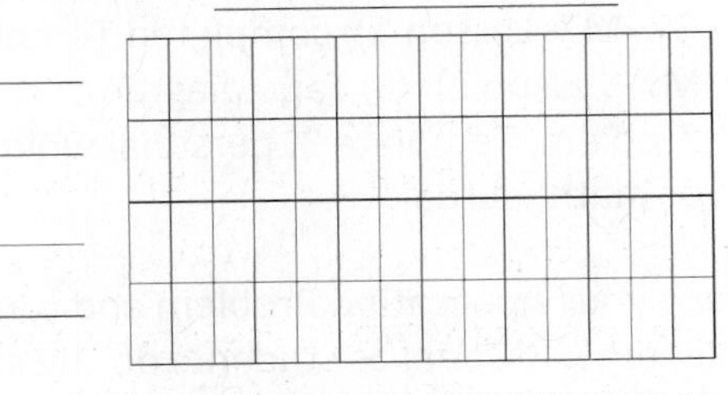

Template 3

S: Four!

T: Let's label those same categories in the same order on the bar graph. (Record as students do the same.)

T: How did we record the number of animals on the table?

S: We used tally marks.

T: And how did we represent the number of each animal on the picture graph?

S: We drew a picture to represent each animal.

T: Watch how we represent data on a bar graph. (Fill in the scale.)

T: (Point to the numbers.) First, I fill in the **scale**. What are we counting by?

S: Ones!

T: Yes. Whisper to your partner what the scale reminds you of.

MP.6

S: It's like a meter strip. → It's like the numbers on a ruler. → It's a number line!

T: The scale tells us that each box equals one, so how many boxes should we color in for the *bird* category?

S: Four boxes!

T: Color four boxes in the bird row. (Model as students do the same. Continue in this way to complete the graph.)

T: Now, just as with the picture graph, we can use the bar graph to ask and answer questions.

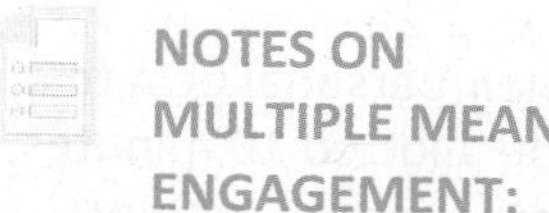

NOTES ON MULTIPLE MEANS OF ENGAGEMENT:

When comparing categories, have students make the "hop" with their fingers to show how they add and subtract on the number line. Alternately, call students up to make live bars to compare categories. For example, to compare bird and fish, have a row of four students face a row of three students. Three students from each "bar" can hold hands, making it easy to see the difference.

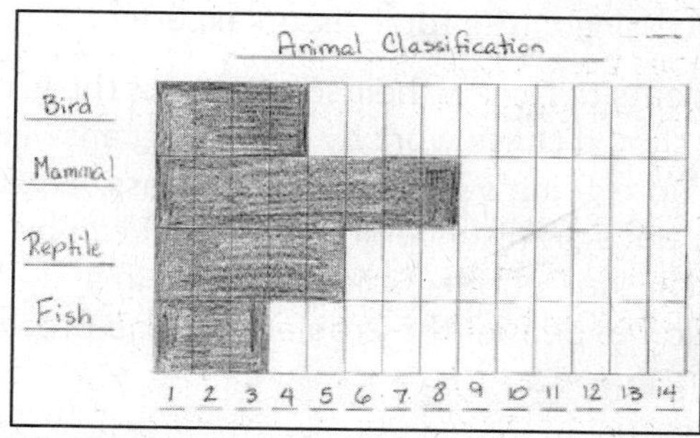

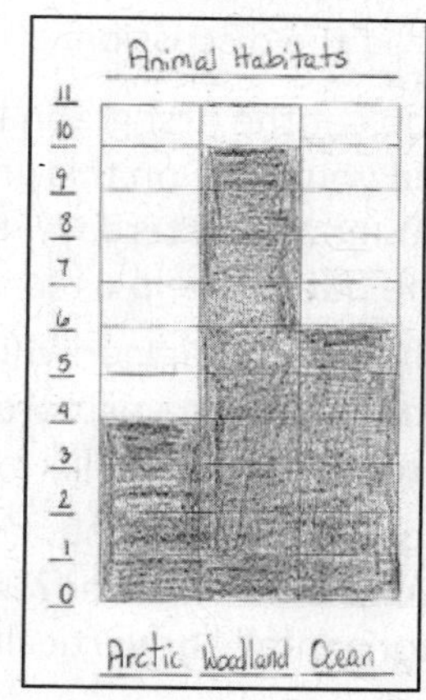

Template 3

Pose questions such as those below, and have students write their answers on paper or in a math journal. Then, invite students to pose questions to the class based on the picture graph. Invite students to utilize the *compare* question sentence frames from G2–M7–Lesson 2 as needed.

- How many more mammals than reptiles are there?
- How many fewer birds than reptiles are there?
- How would the graph change if we added four more birds to the *bird* category?

Repeat the process to create a bar graph of the data from the Animal Habitats table, using the second graph (vertical orientation) on Template 3.

After creating the graph, invite partners to ask and answer questions based on the data.

As students demonstrate proficiency creating and interpreting the graph, allow them to move on to the Problem Set. Continue working with any students who need support.

Problem Set (8 minutes)

Students should do their personal best to complete the Problem Set within the allotted 10 minutes. For some classes, it may be appropriate to modify the assignment by specifying which problems they work on first. Some problems do not specify a method for solving. Students solve these problems using the RDW approach used for Application Problems.

NYS COMMON CORE MATHEMATICS CURRICULUM — Lesson 3 Problem Set 2•7

Name Avery Date

1. Complete the bar graph below using data provided in the table. Then answer the questions about the data.

Animal Classification			
Birds	Fish	Mammals	Reptiles
6	5	11	3

Birds, Fish, Mammals, Reptiles

1 2 3 4 5 6 7 8 9 10 11 12

a. How many more animals are birds than reptiles? 3

b. How many more birds and mammals are there than fish and reptiles? 9 (6 + 11 = 17, 5 + 3 = 8, 17 - 8 = 9)

c. How many fewer animals are reptiles or fish than mammals? 3

d. Write and answer your own comparison question based on the data.
Question: How many more fish than reptiles?
Answer: 2

Student Debrief (8 minutes)

Lesson Objective: Draw and label a bar graph to represent data; relate the count scale to the number line.

The Student Debrief is intended to invite reflection and active processing of the total lesson experience.

Invite students to review their solutions for the Problem Set. They should check work by comparing answers with a partner before going over answers as a class. Look for misconceptions or misunderstandings that can be addressed in the Debrief. Guide students in a conversation to debrief the Problem Set and process the lesson.

You may choose to use any combination of the questions below to lead the discussion.

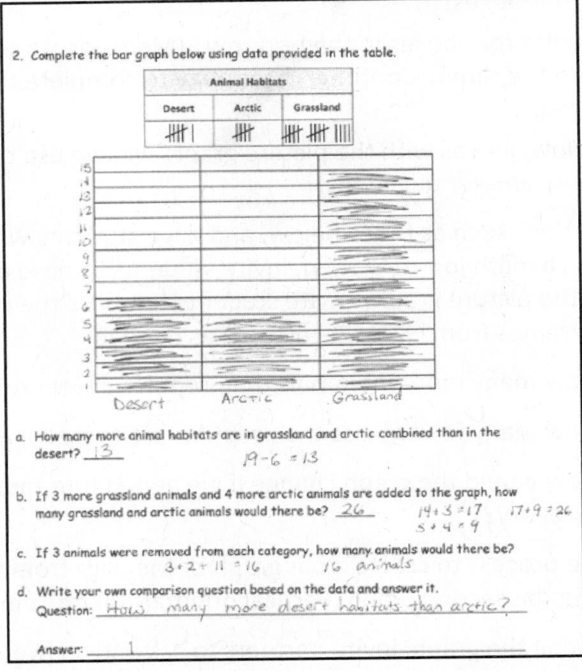

2. Complete the bar graph below using data provided in the table.

Animal Habitats		
Desert	Arctic	Grassland
𝍸 I	𝍸	𝍸 𝍸 IIII

Desert, Arctic, Grassland

a. How many more animal habitats are in grassland and arctic combined than in the desert? 13 (19 - 6 = 13)

b. If 3 more grassland animals and 4 more arctic animals are added to the graph, how many grassland and arctic animals would there be? 26 (14 + 3 = 17, 5 + 4 = 9, 17 + 9 = 26)

c. If 3 animals were removed from each category, how many animals would there be? 16 animals (3 + 2 + 11 = 16)

d. Write your own comparison question based on the data and answer it.
Question: How many more desert habitats than arctic?
Answer: 1

- Look at the first graph in your Problem Set. What did you write on this graph that we didn't put on our graph yesterday? How do the numbers on the bottom help us to record data in a bar graph?
- Show your partner which part of your graph shows how many more birds than reptiles there are.
- Look at your neighbor's habitat graph. Did they make a number line? Are the numbers written horizontally or vertically?
- When you were coloring the boxes to record how many animals live in the grasslands, did you count each box or did you look at the numbers you wrote? Which strategy would be faster?
- Why are bar graphs good for making comparisons? Can you tell which category has more or less without using the scale? How does the scale help you make more precise comparisons?

- How does writing numbers on our graphs help us to use tape diagrams? How do bar and picture graphs help us to draw tape diagrams so that we can see the difference (more than or fewer than) between groups?
- Tell your partner the different types of graphs you know how to use. What are the differences and similarities between them? Do they all use numbers?

Exit Ticket (3 minutes)

After the Student Debrief, instruct students to complete the Exit Ticket. A review of their work will help you assess the students' understanding of the concepts that were presented in the lesson today and plan more effectively for future lessons. You may read the questions aloud to the students.

A

Correct ______

Add or subtract.

1	0 + 5 =		23	10 + 5 =	
2	5 + 5 =		24	15 + 5 =	
3	10 + 5 =		25	20 + 5 =	
4	15 + 5 =		26	25 + 5 =	
5	20 + 5 =		27	30 + 5 =	
6	25 + 5 =		28	35 + 5 =	
7	30 + 5 =		29	40 + 5 =	
8	35 + 5 =		30	45 + 5 =	
9	40 + 5 =		31	0 + 50 =	
10	45 + 5 =		32	50 + 50 =	
11	50 - 5 =		33	50 + 5 =	
12	45 - 5 =		34	55 + 5 =	
13	40 - 5 =		35	60 - 5 =	
14	35 - 5 =		36	55 - 5 =	
15	30 - 5 =		37	60 + 5 =	
16	25 - 5 =		38	65 + 5 =	
17	20 - 5 =		39	70 - 5 =	
18	15 - 5 =		40	65 - 5 =	
19	10 - 5 =		41	100 + 50 =	
20	5 - 5 =		42	150 + 50 =	
21	5 + 0 =		43	200 - 50 =	
22	5 + 5 =		44	150 - 50 =	

B Improvement _____ # Correct _____

Add or subtract.

1	5 + 0 =		23	10 + 5 =	
2	5 + 5 =		24	15 + 5 =	
3	5 + 10 =		25	20 + 5 =	
4	5 + 15 =		26	25 + 5 =	
5	5 + 20 =		27	30 + 5 =	
6	5 + 25 =		28	35 + 5 =	
7	5 + 30 =		29	40 + 5 =	
8	5 + 35 =		30	45 + 5 =	
9	5 + 40 =		31	50 + 0	
10	5 + 45 =		32	50 + 50 =	
11	50 - 5 =		33	5 + 50 =	
12	45 - 5 =		34	5 + 55 =	
13	40 - 5 =		35	60 - 5 =	
14	35 - 5 =		36	55 - 5 =	
15	30 - 5 =		37	5 + 60 =	
16	25 - 5 =		38	5 + 65 =	
17	20 - 5 =		39	70 - 5 =	
18	15 - 5 =		40	65 - 5 =	
19	10 - 5 =		41	50 + 100 =	
20	5 - 5 =		42	50 + 150 =	
21	0 + 5 =		43	200 - 50 =	
22	5 + 5 =		44	150 - 50 =	

Name ______________________________ Date ______________

1. Complete the bar graph below using data provided in the table. Then answer the questions about the data.

Animal Classification			
Birds	Fish	Mammals	Reptiles
6	5	11	3

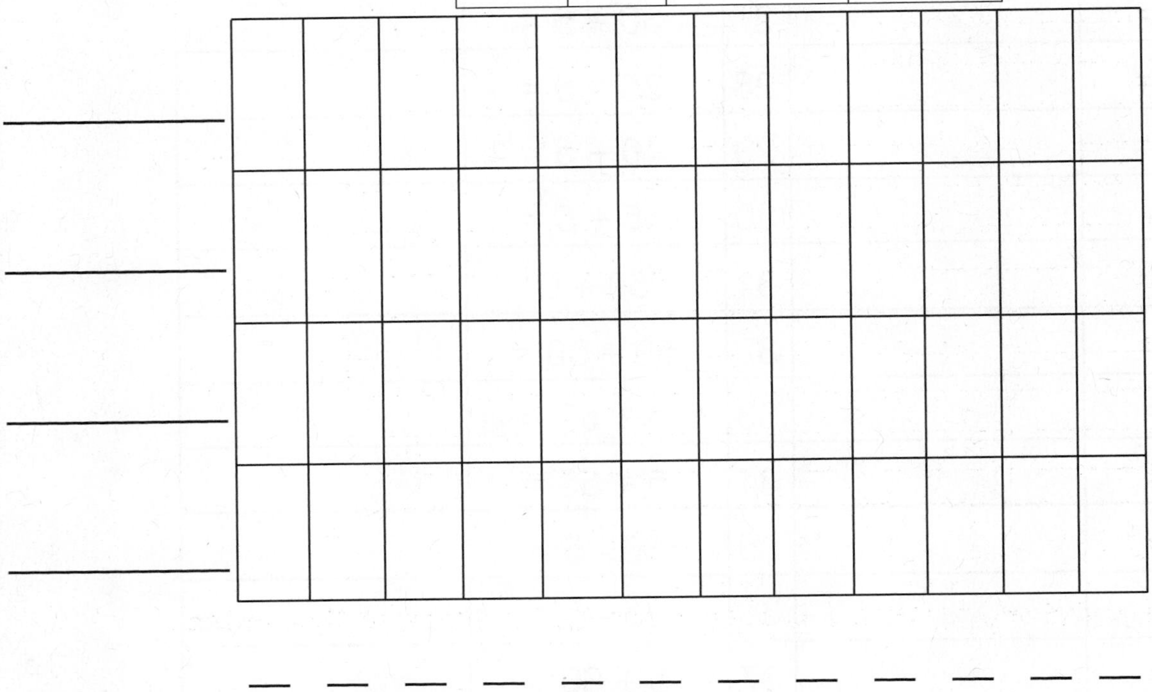

a. How many more animals are birds than reptiles? ______

b. How many more birds and mammals are there than fish and reptiles? ______

c. How many fewer animals are reptiles or fish than mammals? ______

d. Write and answer your own comparison question based on the data.
Question: ______________________________

Answer: ______________________________

2. Complete the bar graph below using data provided in the table.

Animal Habitats		
Desert	Arctic	Grassland
𝍸 |	𝍸	𝍸 𝍸 ||||

a. How many more animal habitats are in grassland and arctic combined than in the desert? ______

b. If 3 more grassland animals and 4 more arctic animals are added to the graph, how many grassland and arctic animals would there be? ______

c. If 3 animals were removed from each category, how many animals would there be?

d. Write your own comparison question based on the data and answer it.

Question: ____

Answer: ____

Name ______________________________ Date ______________

Complete the bar graph below using data provided in the table. Then answer the questions about the data.

Animal Classification			
Birds	**Fish**	**Mammals**	**Reptiles**
7	12	8	6

a. How many more animals are fish than reptiles? ______

b. How many more fish and mammals are there than birds and reptiles? ______

Name ______________________________ Date ________________

1. Complete the bar graph below using data provided in the table. Then answer the questions about the data.

Various Animal Coverings at Jake's Pet Shop			
Fur	**Feathers**	**Shells**	**Scales**
12	9	8	11

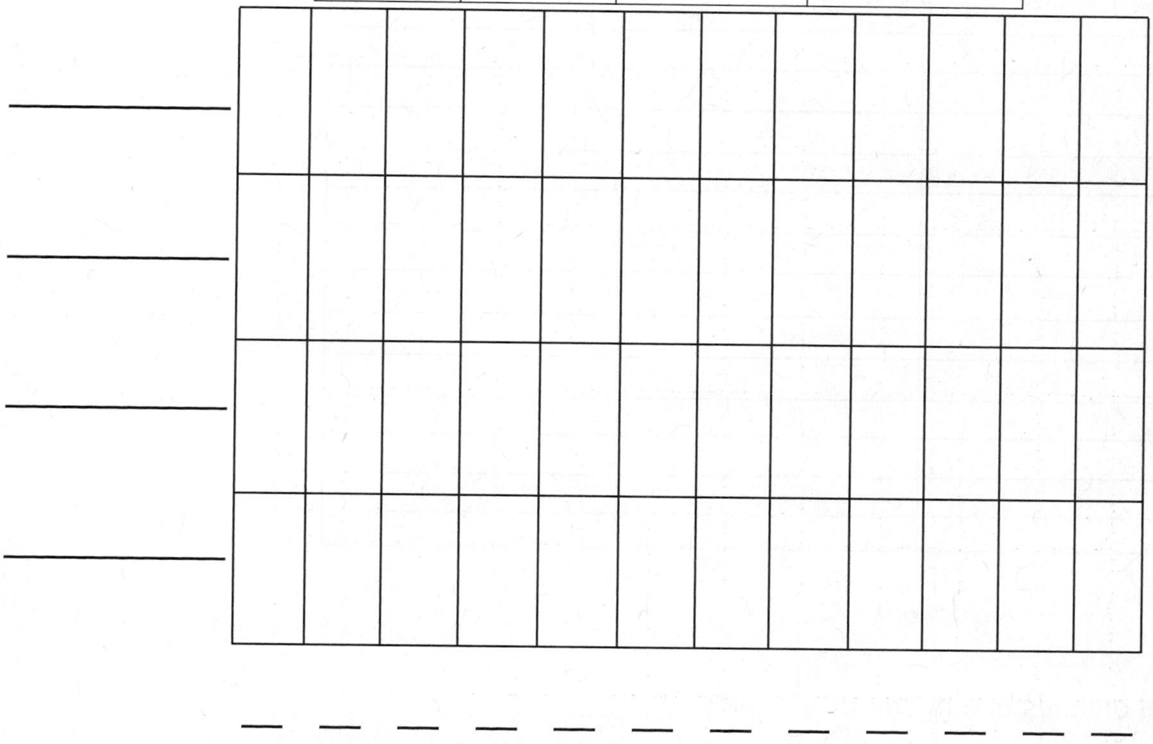

a. How many more animals have fur than shells? ______

b. Which pair of categories has more? Fur and feathers or shells and scales? How much more? ____

c. Write and answer your own comparison question based on the data.

Question: ____

Answer: ____

2. Complete the bar graph below using data provided in the table.

City Shelter Animal Diets		
Meat Only	**Plants Only**	**Meat and Plants**
𝍸 |||	𝍸 ||||	𝍸 𝍸 ||||

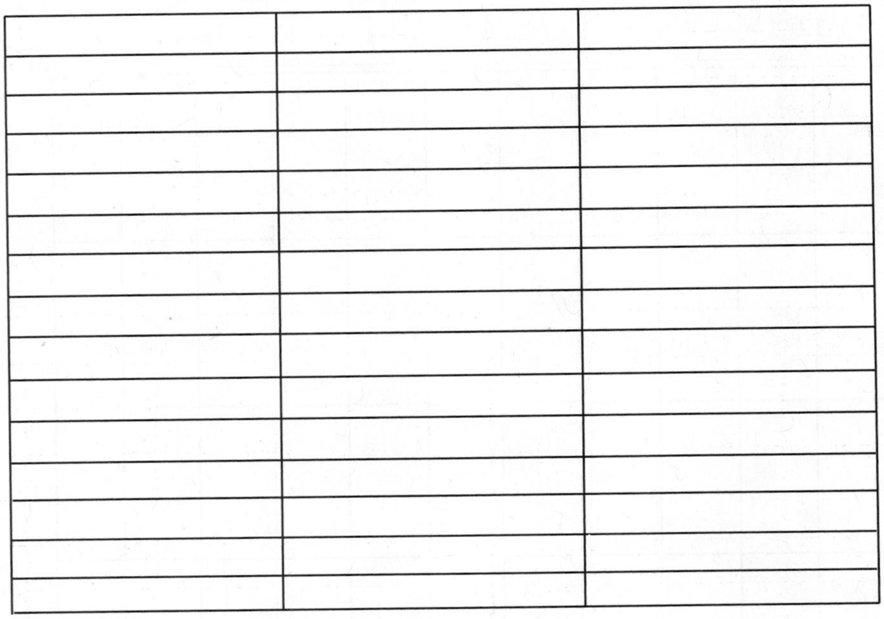

a. How many total animals are in the city shelter? ______

b. How many more meat and plant eating animals are there than meat only? ______

c. If 3 animals were removed from each category, how many animals would there be?

d. Write your own comparison question based on the data and answer it.

Question: ____

Answer: ____

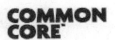

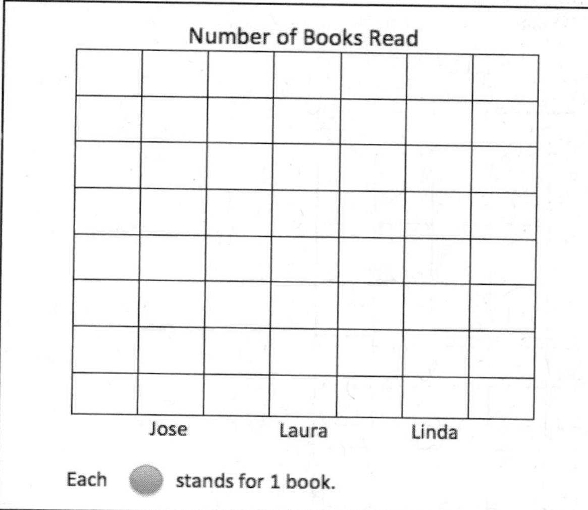
Number of Books Read
Jose
Laura
Linda
Each
stands for 1 book.

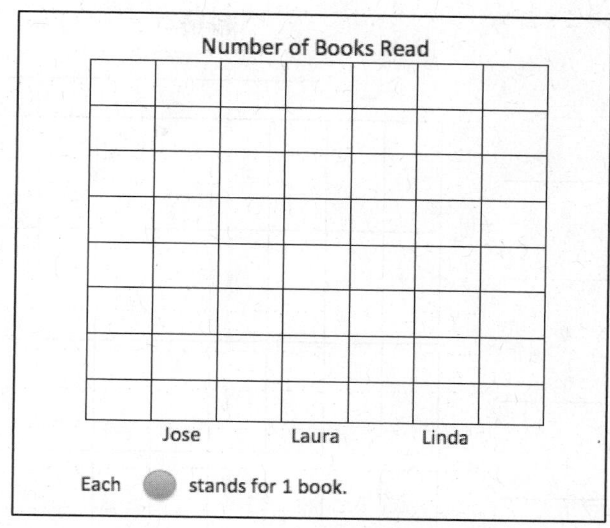
Number of Books Read
Jose
Laura
Linda
Each
stands for 1 book.

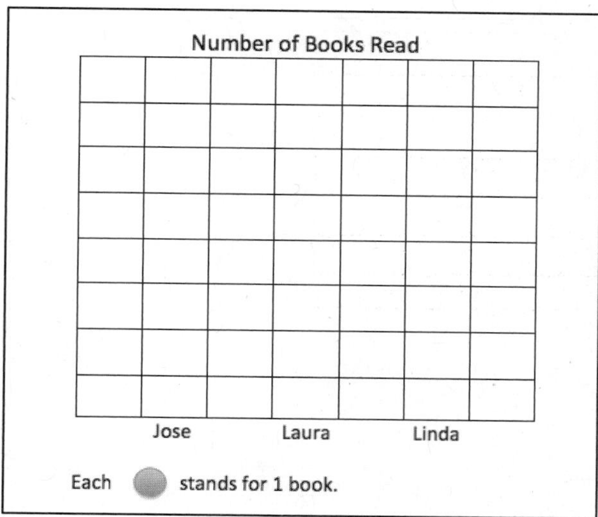
Number of Books Read
Jose
Laura
Linda
Each
stands for 1 book.

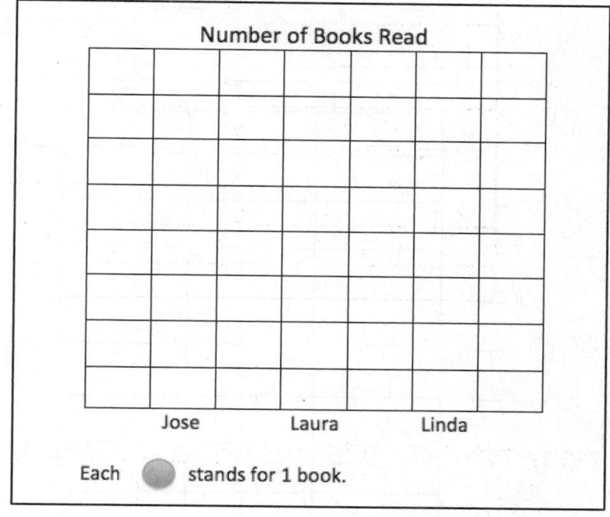
Number of Books Read
Jose
Laura
Linda
Each
stands for 1 book.

Lesson 4

Objective: Draw a bar graph to represent a given data set.

Suggested Lesson Structure

■ Fluency Practice	(12 minutes)
■ Application Problem	(5 minutes)
■ Concept Development	(35 minutes)
■ Student Debrief	(8 minutes)
Total Time	**(60 minutes)**

Fluency Practice (12 minutes)

- Coin Drop **2.NBT.2, 2.OA.2** (3 minutes)
- Sprint: Skip-Counting by 5 **2.NBT.2** (9 minutes)

Coin Drop (3 minutes)

Materials: (T) 2 quarters, 10 pennies, can

Note: In this activity, students practice adding and subtracting ones.

T: (Hold up a quarter.) Name my coin.
S: A quarter.
T: How much is it worth?
S: 25 cents.
T: Watch carefully as I drop the quarter and some pennies in my can. Count along in your minds.

Drop in a quarter and some pennies and ask how much money is in the can. Take out some pennies and show them. Ask how much money is still in the can. Continue adding and subtracting pennies for a minute or so. Then repeat the activity with two quarters and pennies.

Sprint: Skip-Counting by 5 (9 minutes)

Materials: (S) Skip-Counting by 5 Sprint

Note: This Sprint gives practice skip-counting by 5 in preparation for counting with coins in G2–M7–Topic B.

Application Problem (5 minutes)

After a trip to the zoo, Ms. Anderson's students voted on their favorite animals. Use the bar graph to answer the following questions.

a. Which animal got the fewest votes?

b. Which animal got the most votes?

c. How many more students liked komodo dragons than koala bears?

Favorite Animals

Flamingo

Snow Leopard

Komodo Dragon

Koala Bear

1 2 3 4 5 6 7 8 9 10 11 12 13 14

d. Later, two students changed their votes from koala bear to snow leopard. What was the difference between koala bears and snow leopards then?

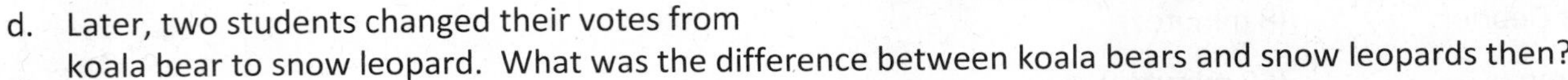

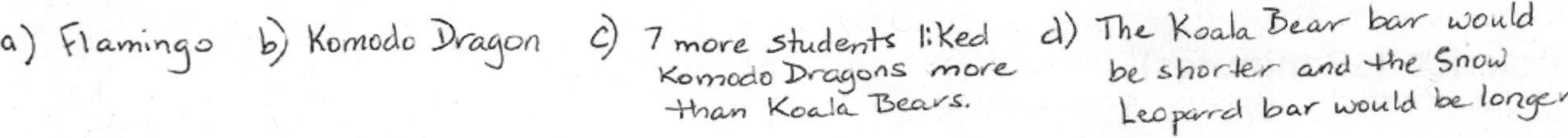

a) Flamingo
b) Komodo Dragon
c) 7 more students liked Komodo Dragons more than Koala Bears.
d) The Koala Bear bar would be shorter and the Snow Leopard bar would be longer.

Note: Project or draw this graph on the board. This problem reviews yesterday's Concept Development, where students learned to read and interpret a bar graph. It leads into today's lesson, where students create bar graphs to represent new data sets.

Concept Development (35 minutes)

Materials: (T) Graph from Application Problem, 2 pieces of chart paper (see list below) (S) Template 3 (blank graphs), colored pencils or crayons, personal white board

Our Birthdays

Spring Mar., Apr., May	Summer June, July, Aug.	Fall Sept., Oct., Nov.	Winter Dec., Jan., Feb.
8	6	2	9

Chart 1

Note: Prior to the lesson, prepare two tables:

- Chart 1: Our Birthdays labeled with the seasons of the year and the months that comprise each season
- Chart 2: Favorite Books labeled with three titles

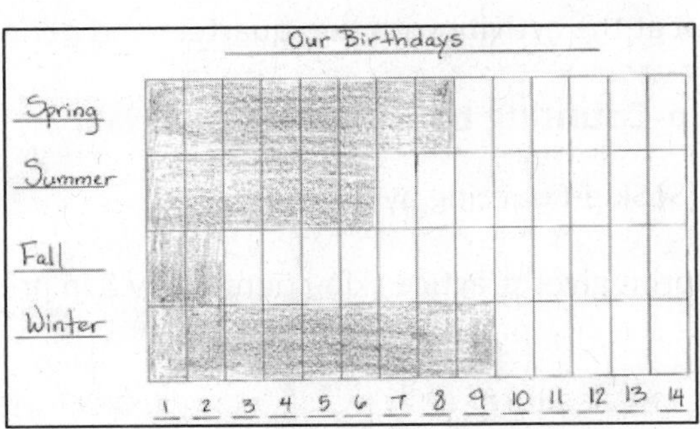

Template 3

Part 1: Complete the bar graph using the table Our Birthdays. Then ask and answer questions using the data.

Post the table entitled *Our Birthdays*, conduct a class survey, and record the results. Note that some students may not know their birthday, so have the information readily available. Then, distribute Template 3.

T: Now that we have new data, let's create a bar graph that represents the information.

T: We're going to use the horizontal graph at the top of your page. What information do we need to fill in first? Discuss with your partner.

S: We have to write the title. → We have to label the categories with the names of the seasons. → We need to put the number scale below the graph.

T: You are all correct! Let's fill in those elements. (Model as students do the same.)

T: Now fill in the bars to match the table. (Pause.)

Favorite Books		
The Miraculous Journey of Edward Tulane	Click, Clack, Moo: Cows That Type	Zen Shorts
11	9	5

Chart 2

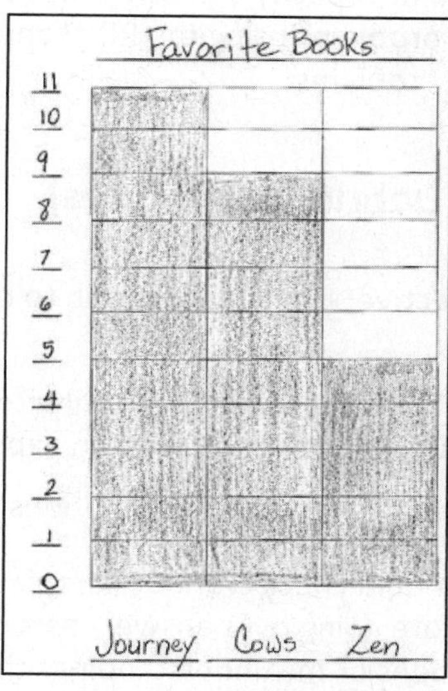

Template 3

Pose questions such as those below, and have students write their answers on their personal boards. Then, invite students to pose comparison questions to the class based on the bar graph.

- Do we know who has a birthday in the fall by reading this graph? What do we know about fall birthdays?
- How many fewer students have birthdays in the summer than in the winter?
- How many more students have a birthday in the spring and the fall than in the winter?

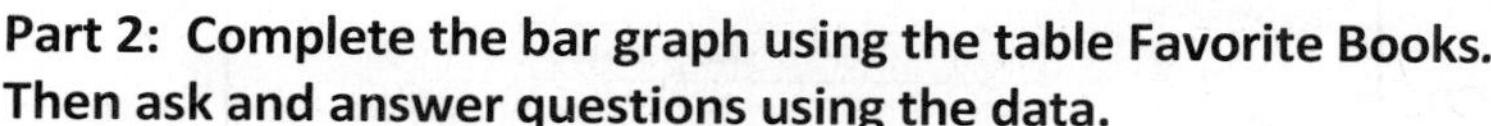

Part 2: Complete the bar graph using the table Favorite Books. Then ask and answer questions using the data.

Repeat the above procedure to generate the new data set.

T: We're going to record our new data on the second graph. Talk with your partner about how these two graphs are similar and different.

S: The first one goes across and the second one goes up and down. → The one on top is horizontal and the bottom one is vertical. → We'll compare how tall the bars are instead of how long they are. → The scale goes on the side instead of on the bottom.

MP.6

T: Ah! Yesterday some of you said the numbers of the scale reminded you of a meter strip, a ruler, or a number line. Those are very good observations.

T: Just as on the ruler the space from 0 to 1 is one length unit, the space from the beginning of the bar to the first line represents a count of 1.

T: We can also turn our scale vertically just like we can turn a ruler vertically to measure height.

T: Let's fill in the scale together, starting at 0. (Model as students do the same.)

NOTES ON MULTIPLE MEANS OF REPRESENTATION:

Use a ruler to provide visual support along with the explicit explanation of how the vertical scale mimics the ruler or number line. Provide a ruler to students who need the extra concrete support of turning the ruler.

MP.6 T: Now, fill in the rest of the graph. Then, ask and answer questions based on the data with a partner.

As students demonstrate proficiency interpreting the data, allow them to move on to the Problem Set. Continue working with any students who need support.

Problem Set (10 minutes)

Students should do their personal best to complete the Problem Set within the allotted 10 minutes. For some classes, it may be appropriate to modify the assignment by specifying which problems they work on first. Some problems do not specify a method for solving. Students solve these problems using the RDW approach used for Application Problems.

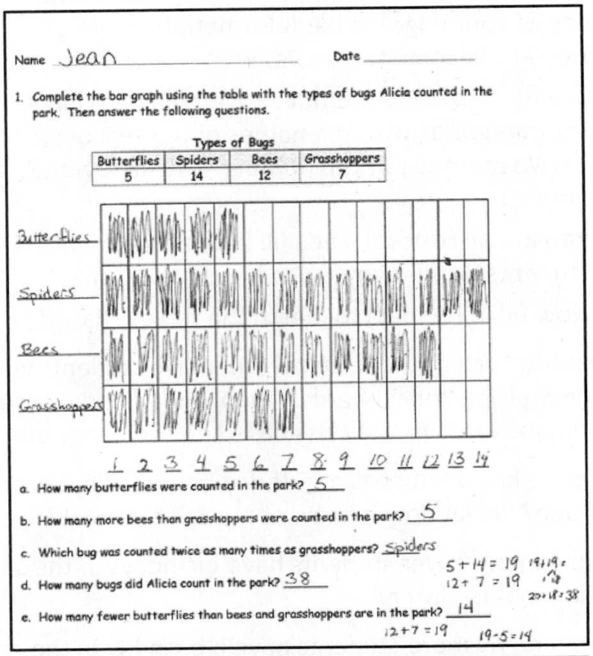

Name Jean Date

1. Complete the bar graph using the table with the types of bugs Alicia counted in the park. Then answer the following questions.

Types of Bugs

Butterflies	Spiders	Bees	Grasshoppers
5	14	12	7

Butterflies
Spiders
Bees
Grasshoppers
1 2 3 4 5 6 7 8 9 10 11 12 13 14

a. How many butterflies were counted in the park? 5

b. How many more bees than grasshoppers were counted in the park? 5

c. Which bug was counted twice as many times as grasshoppers? Spiders

d. How many bugs did Alicia count in the park? 38 5 + 14 = 19 12 + 7 = 19 19 + 19 = 38

e. How many fewer butterflies than bees and grasshoppers are in the park? 14 12 + 7 = 19 19 - 5 = 14

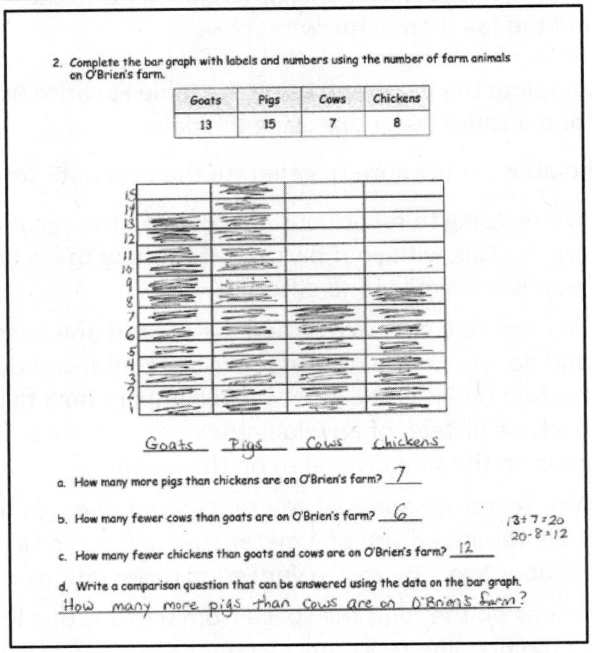

2. Complete the bar graph with labels and numbers using the number of farm animals on O'Brien's farm.

Goats	Pigs	Cows	Chickens
13	15	7	8

1 2 3 4 5 6 7 8 9 10 11 12 13 14 15
Goats Pigs Cows Chickens

a. How many more pigs than chickens are on O'Brien's farm? 7

b. How many fewer cows than goats are on O'Brien's farm? 6

c. How many fewer chickens than goats and cows are on O'Brien's farm? 12 13 + 7 = 20 20 - 8 = 12

d. Write a comparison question that can be answered using the data on the bar graph. How many more pigs than cows are on O'Brien's farm?

Student Debrief (8 minutes)

Lesson Objective: Draw a bar graph to represent a given data set.

The Student Debrief is intended to invite reflection and active processing of the total lesson experience.

Invite students to review their solutions for the Problem Set. They should check work by comparing answers with a partner before going over answers as a class. Look for misconceptions or misunderstandings that can be addressed in the Debrief. Guide students in a conversation to debrief the Problem Set and process the lesson.

You may choose to use any combination of the questions below to lead the discussion.

- Explain to your partner the labels you wrote on your graph before you started to record the data. Is it important to label and write a number scale before you start graphing the data? Why or why not?
- In the bug graph, which problems asked a comparison question? (Problems 1(b), 1(c), and 1(e).) If you used equations to figure out the answer to the comparison questions, what operation did you use? If you did not write an equation, tell your partner how you figured out the answer to Problems 1(b) and 1(e).
- Look at O'Brien's farm bar graph. Did you write a number scale? Where did you put it? Does it

matter if we write the number scale across the bottom or on the side?

- Talk to your partner about how picture and bar graphs help us organize and compare information. Can you think of something in your life where making a graph would help you?
- So far, what has each box or picture represented in our graphs? (One unit. → One animal. → One thing.) Do you think each box always has to be one unit?

Exit Ticket (3 minutes)

After the Student Debrief, instruct students to complete the Exit Ticket. A review of their work will help you assess the students' understanding of the concepts that were presented in the lesson today and plan more effectively for future lessons. You may read the questions aloud to the students.

A # Correct ____

Fill-in the blank.

1	0, 5, __		23	35, __, 45	
2	5, 10, __		24	15, __, 25	
3	10, 15, __		25	40, __, 50	
4	15, 20, __		26	25, __, 15	
5	20, 25, __		27	50, __, 40	
6	25, 30, __		28	20, __, 10	
7	30, 35, __		29	45, __, 35	
8	35, 40, __		30	15, __, 5	
9	40, 45, __		31	40, __, 30	
10	50, 45, __		32	10, __, 0	
11	45, 40, __		33	35, __, 25	
12	40, 35, __		34	__, 10, 5	
13	35, 30, __		35	__, 35, 30	
14	30, 25, __		36	__, 15, 10	
15	25, 20, __		37	__, 40, 35	
16	20, 15, __		38	__, 20, 15	
17	15, 10, __		39	__, 45, 40	
18	0, __, 10		40	50, 55, __	
19	25, __, 35		41	45, 50, __	
20	5, __, 15		42	65, __, 55	
21	30, __, 40		43	55, 60, __	
22	10, __, 20		44	60, 65, __	

B Improvement _____ # Correct _____

Fill-in the blank.

1	5, 10, __		23	15, __, 25	
2	10, 15, __		24	35, __, 45	
3	15, 20, __		25	30, __, 20	
4	20, 25, __		26	25, __, 15	
5	25, 30, __		27	50, __, 40	
6	30, 35, __		28	20, __, 10	
7	35, 40, __		29	45, __, 35	
8	40, 45, __		30	15, __, 5	
9	50, 45, __		31	35, __, 25	
10	45, 40, __		32	10, __, 0	
11	40, 35, __		33	35, __, 25	
12	35, 30, __		34	__, 15, 10	
13	30, 25, __		35	__, 40, 35	
14	25, 20, __		36	__, 20, 15	
15	20, 15, __		37	__, 45, 40	
16	15, 10, __		38	__, 10, 5	
17	0, __, 10		39	__, 35, 30	
18	25, __, 35		40	45, 50, __	
19	5, __, 15		41	50, 55, __	
20	30, __, 40		42	55, 60, __	
21	10, __, 20		43	65, __, 55	
22	35, __, 45		44	__, 60, 55	

Name ______________________________ Date ______________

1. Complete the bar graph using the table with the types of bugs Alicia counted in the park. Then answer the following questions.

Types of Bugs

Butterflies	Spiders	Bees	Grasshoppers
5	14	12	7

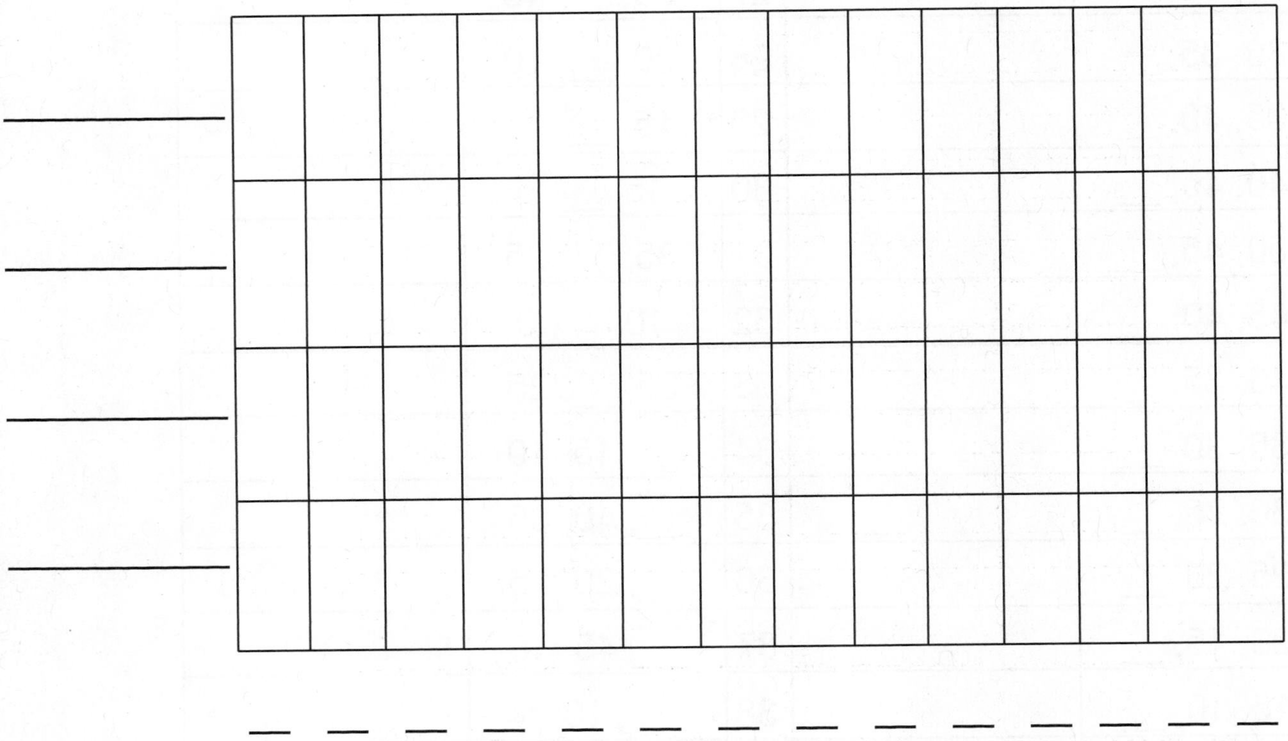

a. How many butterflies were counted in the park? _____

b. How many more bees than grasshoppers were counted in the park? _______

c. Which bug was counted twice as many times as grasshoppers? ______

d. How many bugs did Alicia count in the park? _______

e. How many fewer butterflies than bees and grasshoppers are in the park? ______

2. Complete the bar graph with labels and numbers using the number of farm animals on O'Brien's farm.

Goats	Pigs	Cows	Chickens
13	15	7	8

______ ______ ______ ______

a. How many more pigs than chickens are on O'Brien's farm? ______

b. How many fewer cows than goats are on O'Brien's farm? ______

c. How many fewer chickens than goats and cows are on O'Brien's farm? ______

d. Write a comparison question that can be answered using the data on the bar graph.

____

Name ______________________________ Date ______________

Complete the bar graph using the table with the types of bugs Jeremy counted in his backyard. Then answer the following questions.

Types of Bugs

Butterflies	Spiders	Bees	Grasshoppers
4	8	10	9

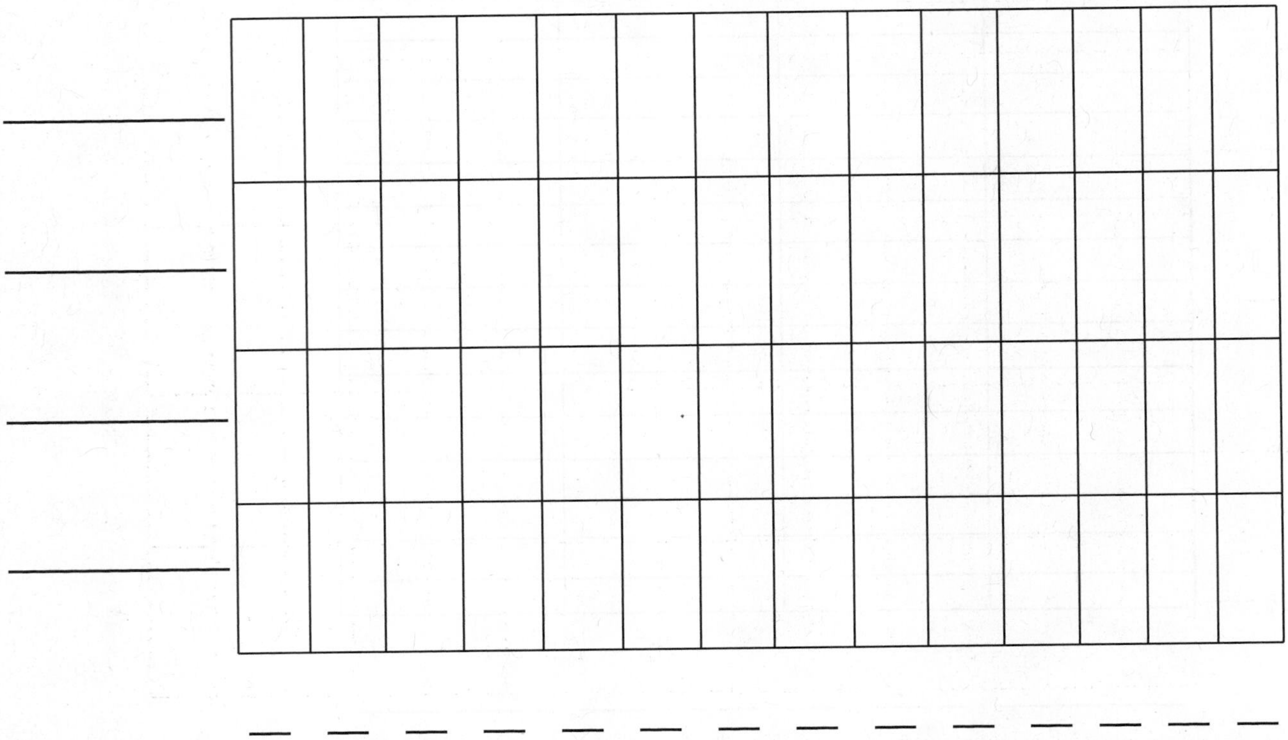

a. How many more spiders and grasshoppers were counted than bees and butterflies?________

b. If 5 more butterflies were counted, how many bugs would have been counted?

______

Name ______________________________ Date ______________

1. Complete the bar graph using the table with the types of reptiles at the local zoo. Then answer the following questions.

Types of Reptiles

Snakes	Lizards	Turtles	Tortoises
13	11	7	8

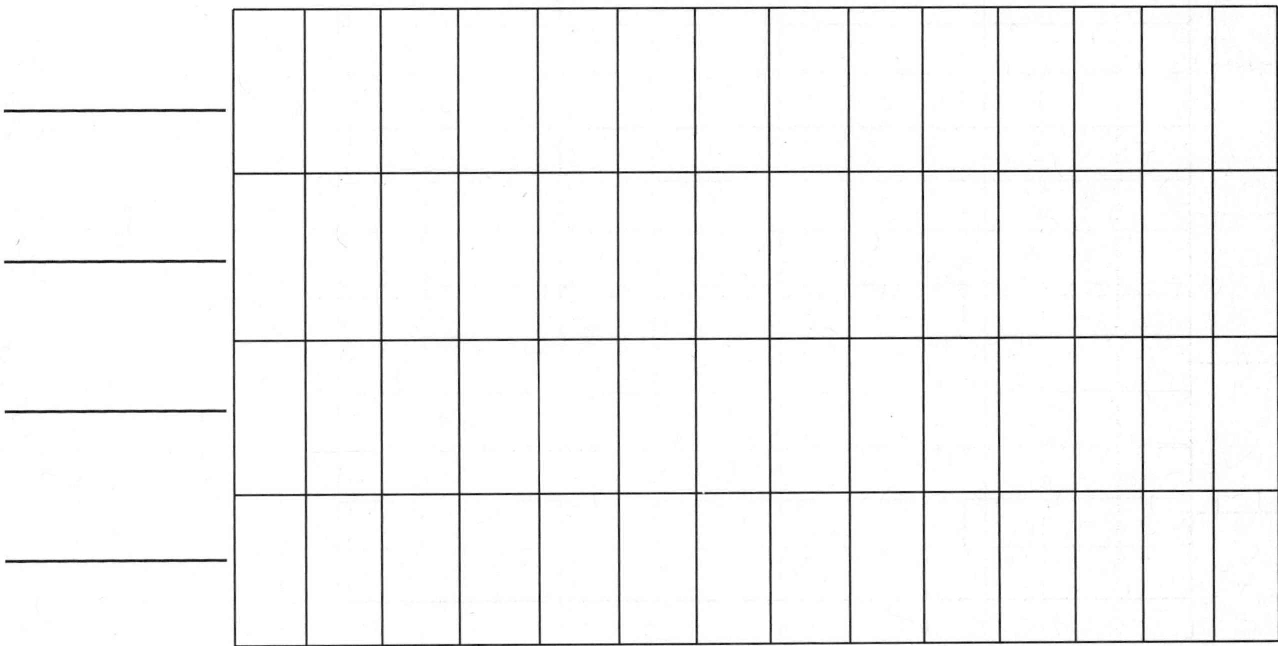

a. How many reptiles are at the zoo? ______

b. How many more snakes and lizards than turtles are at the zoo? _______

c. How many fewer turtles and tortoises than snakes and lizards are at the zoo? ___

d. Write a comparison question that can be answered using the data on the bar graph.

____

2. Complete the bar graph with labels and numbers using the number of underwater animals Emily saw while scuba diving.

Sharks	Stingrays	Starfish	Seahorse
6	9	14	13

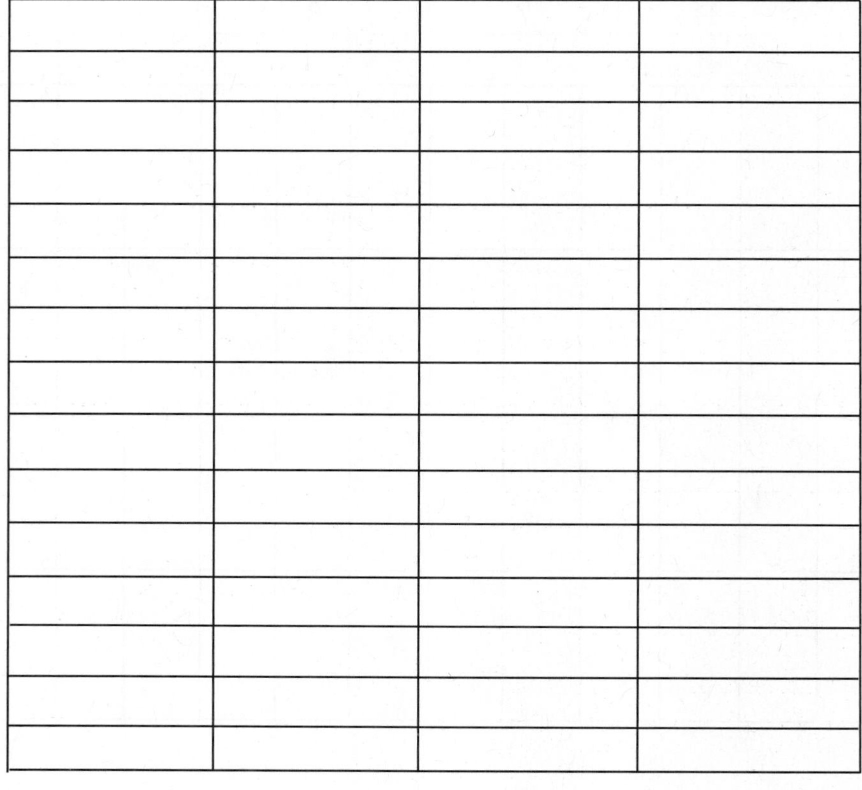

a. How many more starfish than sharks? ___

b. How many fewer stingrays than seahorses? ___

c. Write a comparison question that can be answered using the data on the bar graph.

____

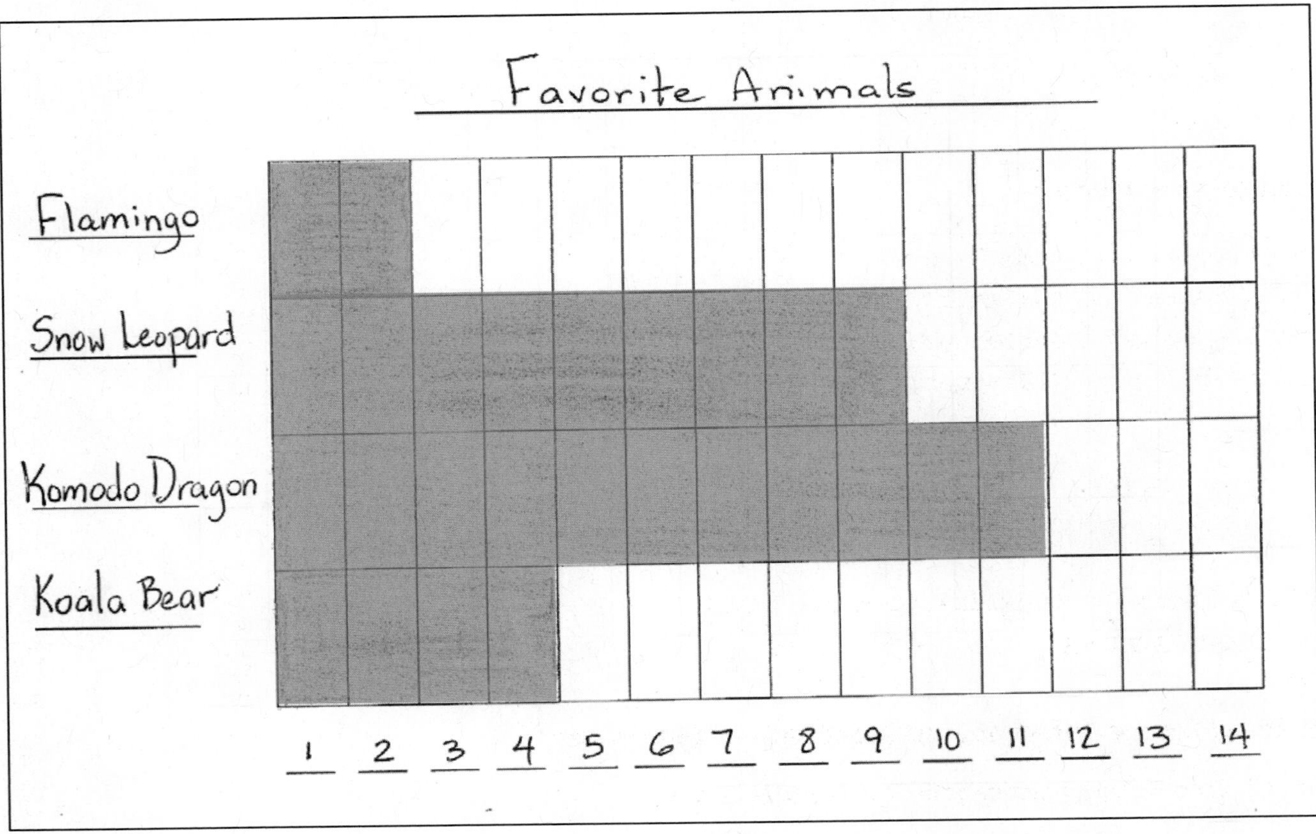
Favorite Animals
Flamingo
Snow Leopard
Komodo Dragon
Koala Bear
1
2
3
4
5
6
7
8
9
10
11
12
13
14

Lesson 5

Objective: Solve word problems using data presented in a bar graph.

Suggested Lesson Structure

Fluency Practice	(10 minutes)
Application Problem	(5 minutes)
Concept Development	(35 minutes)
Student Debrief	(10 minutes)
Total Time	**(60 minutes)**

Fluency Practice (10 minutes)

- Grade 2 Core Fluency Differentiated Practice Sets **2.OA.2** (5 minutes)
- Coin Drop **2.NBT.2, 2.OA.2** (5 minutes)

Grade 2 Core Fluency Differentiated Practice Sets (5 minutes)

Materials: (S) Core Fluency Practice Sets from G2–M7–Lesson 1

Note: During G2–M7–Topic A and for the remainder of the year, each day's fluency includes an opportunity for review and mastery of the sums and differences with totals through 20 by means of the Core Fluency Practice Sets or Sprints. The process is detailed and Practice Sets are provided in G2–M7–Lesson 1.

Coin Drop (5 minutes)

Materials: (T) 2 quarters, 10 dimes, 10 nickels, can

Note: In this activity, students practice adding and subtracting 25, 10, and 5.

T: (Hold up a quarter.) Name my coin.
S: A quarter.
T: How much is it worth?
S: 25 cents.
T: Watch carefully as I drop the quarter and some nickels in my can. Count along in your minds.

Drop in a quarter and some nickels and ask how much money is in the can. Take out some of the nickels and show them. Ask how much money is still in the can. Continue adding and subtracting nickels for a minute or so. Then repeat the activity with a quarter and dimes, a quarter with dimes and nickels, then 2 quarters with dimes and nickels.

Application Problem (5 minutes)

Rita has 19 more pennies than Carlos. Rita has 27 pennies. How many pennies does Carlos have?

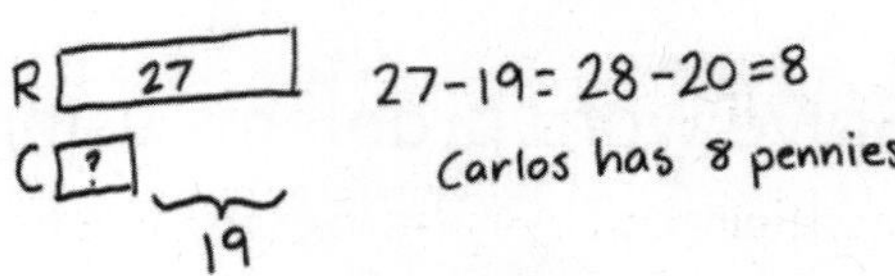

Note: In this problem, the context shifts to money. This leads into today's Concept Development where students work with money data to solve word problems, and segues into problem solving with coins and bills in G2–M7–Topic B. The problem type is *compare with smaller unknown*, one of the more difficult problem types because *more* suggests the wrong operation. Guide students, as needed, to draw a tape diagram to solve.

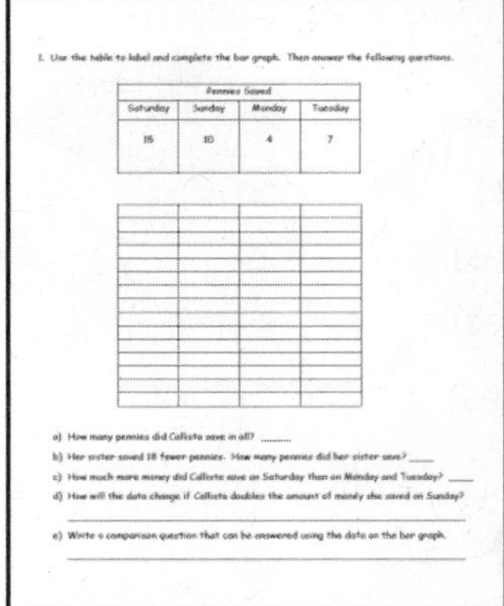

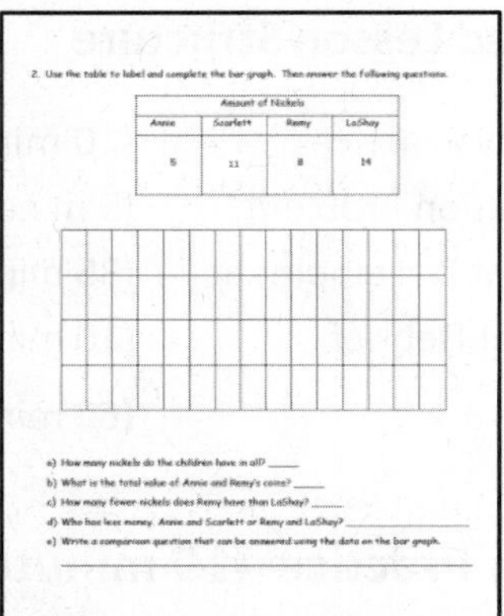

Concept Development (35 minutes)

Materials: (T) Ruler (optional) (S) Lesson Activity Sheets 1 and 2, colored pencils or crayons, Template 4 (blank table, graph, and lines for question)

Note: In G2–M7–Lesson 5, students use money data to solve word problems. Depending on the needs of your students, you may choose to have them work independently, with a partner, or in groups.

MP.6

T: Today we're going to use activity sheets for our lesson. Use the information in the table to complete the graphs, and then use the data to answer the questions.

Pass out Activity Sheets 1 and 2. Circulate to be sure students are labeling their graphs accurately, paying special attention to the count scale. You may wish to remind them with the visual aid of a ruler that the beginning of the scale is 0 and not 1.

Provide support as students work. Invite them to share how they solved as they complete each problem. This is a good opportunity to work with a small group of students who are struggling with graphing or answering questions based on information presented in a graph. It is also a chance to provide extension for students working above grade level. For those students, a good alternative activity might be using Template 4 to design their own survey and table and then creating a graph and questions to represent and interpret the data.

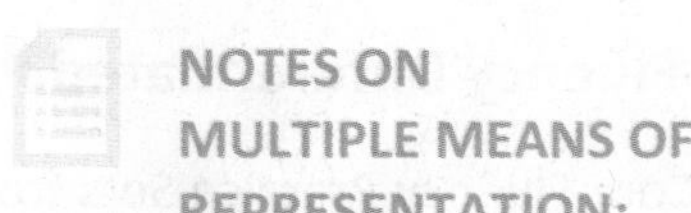

NOTES ON MULTIPLE MEANS OF REPRESENTATION:

Some students may find it visually challenging to fill in and read the graphs. Enlarge the activity sheet, or provide these students with Template 1 (G2–M7–Lesson 2), which leaves space between the bars. Also, have students use different colors to further distinguish the bars.

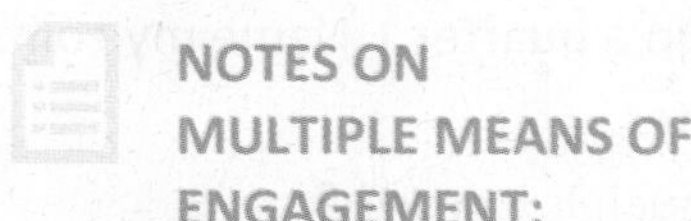

NOTES ON MULTIPLE MEANS OF ENGAGEMENT:

Activate multiple senses by playing music to create a soothing atmosphere. Allow flexible grouping and allow students to move around and check their work and ask questions of those not in their pair or group.

As students successfully complete their work, allow them to move on to the Problem Set.

Problem Set (10 minutes)

Students should do their personal best to complete the Problem Set within the allotted 10 minutes. For some classes, it may be appropriate to modify the assignment by specifying which problems they work on first. Some problems do not specify a method for solving. Students solve these problems using the RDW approach used for Application Problems.

Name Autumn Date

1. Complete the bar graph with labels and numbers using the table with the number of dimes each student has in their pocket. Then answer the following questions.

Number of Dimes

Emily	Andrew	Thomas	Ava
8	12	6	13

Emily, Andrew, Thomas, Ava

1 2 3 4 5 6 7 8 9 10 11 12 13

a. How many more dimes does Andrew have than Emily? 4

b. How many fewer dimes does Thomas have than Ava and Emily? 15 13+8 = 21 21 - 6 = 15

c. i. Circle the pair with more dimes, Emily and Ava or Andrew and Thomas.

ii. How many more? 3 8+13 = 21 12+6 = 18 21 - 18 = 3

d. What is the total number of dimes if all the students combine all their money? 39 8+12 = 20 13+6 = 19 20+19 = 39

2. Complete a bar graph with labels and numbers using the number of dimes each student donated.

Madison	Robin	Benjamin	Miguel
12	10	15	13

1 2 3 4 5 6 7 8 9 10 11 12 13 14 15

Madison Robin Benjamin Miguel

a. How much many more dimes did Miguel donate than Robin? 3

b. How many fewer dimes did Madison donate than Robin and Benjamin? 13 10 + 15 = 25 25 - 12 = 13

c. How many more dimes are needed for Miguel to donate the same as Benjamin and Madison? 14 15+12 = 27 27 - 13 = 14

d. How many dimes were donated? 50 12+10 = 22 15+13 = 28 22 + 28 = 20+30 = 50

Student Debrief (10 minutes)

Lesson Objective: Solve word problems using data presented in a bar graph.

The Student Debrief is intended to invite reflection and active processing of the total lesson experience.

Invite students to review their solutions for the Problem Set. They should check work by comparing answers with a partner before going over answers as a class. Look for misconceptions or misunderstandings that can be addressed in the Debrief. Guide students in a conversation to debrief the Problem Set and process the lesson.

You may choose to use any combination of the questions below to lead the discussion.

- Look at Emily's dimes in the Problem Set. How many dimes would Emily have if you doubled her dimes? (16.) How would we record 16 in the graph? (We would have to make more boxes. Or, we could make each unit box's value 2 instead of 1.)
- In each graph you completed today, you were asked to find the total amount of coins recorded in the graph. Tell your partner if you figured out the answer in your head or with paper and pencil. Share the calculation strategy you used.
- Think about a question you could ask our class that you could turn into a bar graph. Tell your partner what question you would ask. What would you title your graph? What would the categories be labeled?

Exit Ticket (3 minutes)

After the Student Debrief, instruct students to complete the Exit Ticket. A review of their work will help you assess the students' understanding of the concepts that were presented in the lesson today and plan more effectively for future lessons. You may read the questions aloud to the students.

1. Use the table to label and complete the bar graph. Then answer the following questions.

Pennies Saved			
Saturday	Sunday	Monday	Tuesday
15	10	4	7

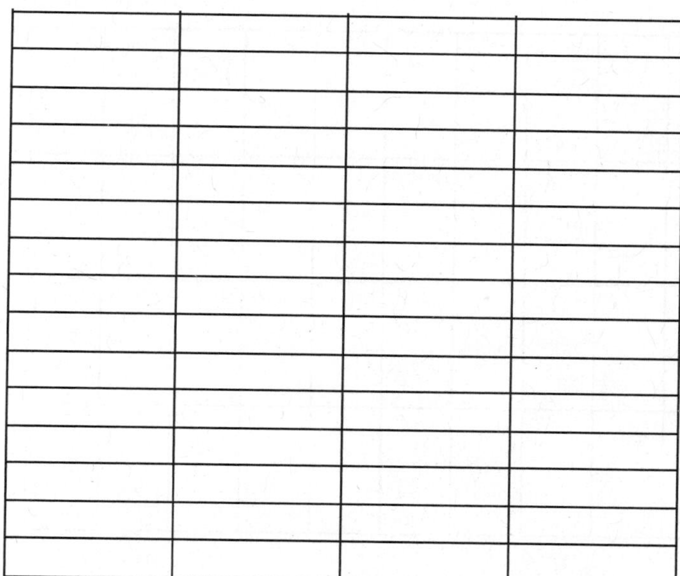

a) How many pennies did Callista save in all? ______

b) Her sister saved 18 fewer pennies. How many pennies did her sister save? _____

c) How much more money did Callista save on Saturday than on Monday and Tuesday? _____

d) How will the data change if Callista doubles the amount of money she saved on Sunday?

____

e) Write a comparison question that can be answered using the data on the bar graph.

____

2. Use the table to label and complete the bar graph. Then answer the following questions.

Amount of Nickels			
Annie	Scarlett	Remy	LaShay
5	11	8	14

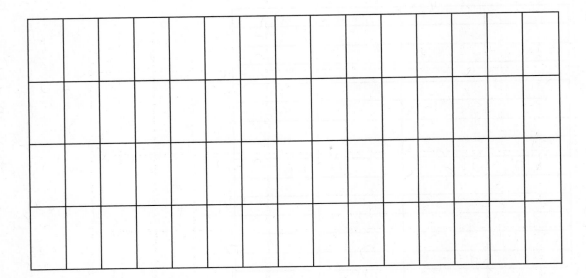

a) How many nickels do the children have in all? ______

b) What is the total value of Annie and Remy's coins? ______

c) How many fewer nickels does Remy have than LaShay? ______

d) Who has less money, Annie and Scarlett or Remy and LaShay? ____________________

e) Write a comparison question that can be answered using the data on the bar graph.

____

Name ______________________________ Date ______________

1. Complete the bar graph with labels and numbers using the table with the number of dimes each student has in their pocket. Then answer the following questions.

Number of Dimes

Emily	Andrew	Thomas	Ava
8	12	6	13

a. How many more dimes does Andrew have than Emily? _____

b. How many fewer dimes does Thomas have than Ava and Emily? ______

c. i. Circle the pair with more dimes, Emily and Ava or Andrew and Thomas.

ii. How many more? ______

d. What is the total number of dimes if all the students combine all their money?

_____

2. Complete a bar graph with labels and numbers using the number of dimes each student donated.

Madison	Robin	Benjamin	Miguel
12	10	15	13

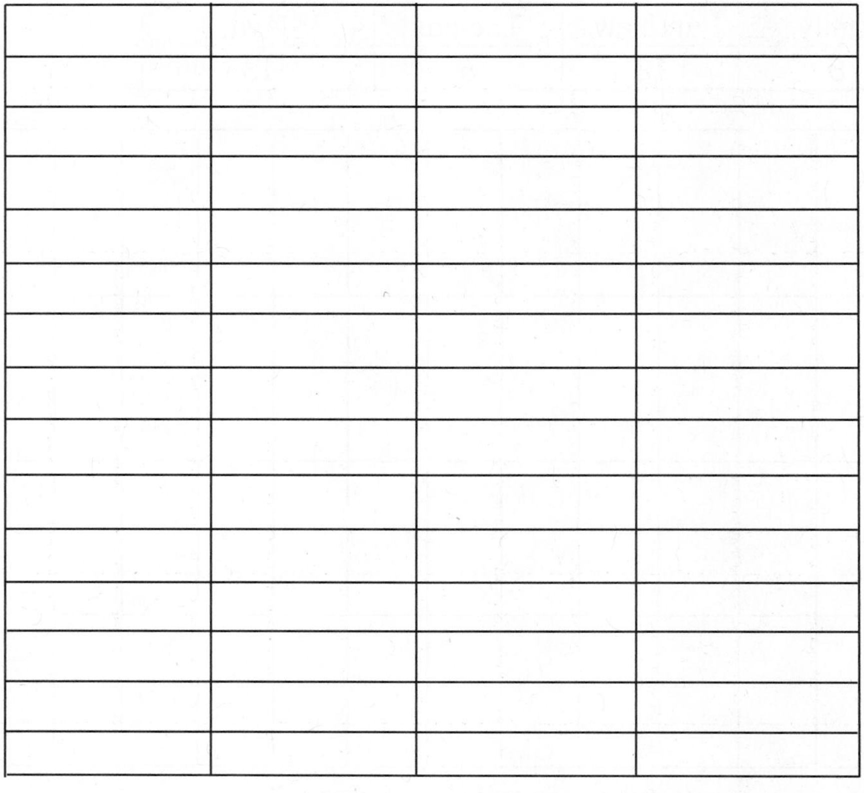

______ ______ ______ ______

a. How much many more dimes did Miguel donate than Robin? ________

b. How many fewer dimes did Madison donate than Robin and Benjamin? _____

c. How many more dimes are needed for Miguel to donate the same as Benjamin and Madison? __________

d. How many dimes were donated? ______

Name ______________________________ Date ______________

Complete the bar graph with labels and numbers using the information in the table. Then answer the following questions.

Number of Dimes

Lacy	Sam	Stefanie	Amber
6	11	9	14

a. How many more dimes does Amber have than Stefanie? _____

b. How many dimes will Sam and Lacy need to save to equal Stefanie and Amber?

____

Name ____________________________ Date ________________

1. Complete the bar graph with labels and numbers using the table with the name of nickels each student has in their piggy bank. Then answer the following questions.

Number of Nickels

Justin	Melissa	Meghan	Douglas
13	9	12	7

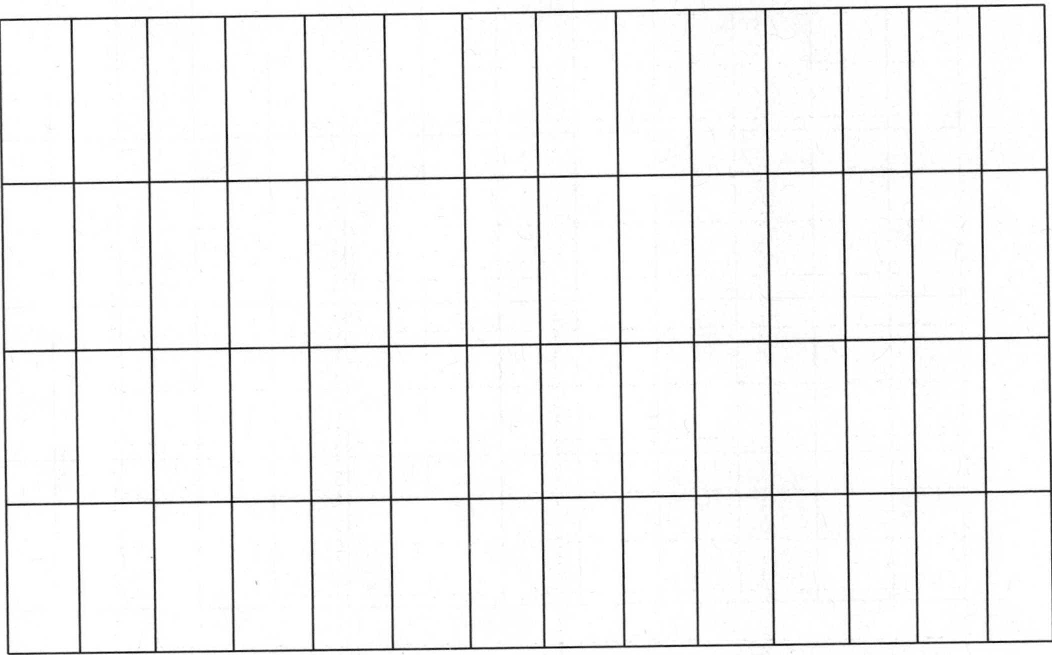

a. How many more nickels does Meghan have than Melissa? ______

b. How many fewer nickels does Douglas have than Justin? ______

c. i. Circle the pair that has more nickels, Justin and Melissa or Douglas and Meghan.

ii. How many more? ______

d. What is the total number of nickels if all the students combine all their money?______

2. Complete a bar graph with labels and numbers using information in the table.

Dimes Donated

Kylie	Tom	John	Shannon
12	10	15	13

__________ __________ __________ __________

a. How many dimes did Shannon donate? _________

b. How many fewer dimes did Kylie donate than John and Shannon? ______

c. How many more dimes are needed for Tom to donate the same as Shannon and Kylie? ___________

d. How many dimes were donated in total? __________

1. Design a survey and collect the data.
2. Label and fill in the table.
3. Use the table to label and complete the bar graph.
4. Write questions based on the graph, then let students use your graph to answer them.

a) ____

b) ____

c) ____

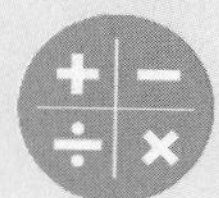

Topic B

Problem Solving with Coins and Bills

2.NBT.5, **2.MD.8**, 2.NBT.2, 2.NBT.6

Focus Standard:	2.NBT.5	Fluently add and subtract within 100 using strategies based on place value, properties of operations, and/or the relationship between addition and subtraction.
	2.MD.8	Solve word problems involving dollar bills, quarters, dimes, nickels, and pennies, using $ and ¢ symbols appropriately. *Example: If you have 2 dimes and 3 pennies, how many cents do you have?*
Instructional Days:	8	
Coherence -Links from:	G1–M6	Place Value, Comparison, Addition and Subtraction to 100
-Links to:	G3–M1	Properties of Multiplication and Division and Solving Problems with Units of 2–5 and 10
	G3–M2	Place Value and Problem Solving with Units of Measure

In Topic B, students solve problems involving coins and bills. They begin at the concrete level in Lesson 6, using play money to review the different coin values from Grade 1. Beginning with the largest coin value (often the quarter), students count the total value of a group of coins, applying their knowledge of addition strategies (**2.NBT.5**) and skip-counting by fives and tens when there are multiple nickels or dimes.

Lesson 7 builds upon this foundation as students find the total value of a group of coins in the context of simple addition and subtraction word problem types with the result unknown (**2.MD.8**). For example, "Carla has 2 dimes, 1 quarter, 1 nickel, and 3 pennies. How many cents does she have?" Likewise, "Carla has 53¢ and gives a dime to her friend. How many cents does she have left?" To solve the *add to or take from with result unknown* word problem types, students might use the RDW process to draw, write the corresponding number sentence, and write a statement with the solution, just as they have been doing throughout the year with word problems in varied contexts.

Similarly, in Lesson 8, students apply their understanding of place value strategies and skip-counting to find the total value of a group of bills within $100, again in the context of addition and subtraction word problems. As in Lesson 6, students arrange bills from greatest to least, count on to find the total, and write a number sentence to represent the total value of the bills, sometimes adding up to four two-digit numbers. They solve problems such as, "Raja has $85 in his pocket. Two $5 bills fall out. How many dollars are in his pocket now?" or, "If Raja has 6 one dollar bills, 4 ten dollar bills, and 3 five dollar bills, how many dollars does he have?" Students may write number sentences in any number of ways. One student might skip-count mentally and make a ten, thinking 4 tens make 40 and 3 fives make 15 and then writing 40 + 15 + 6 = 40 + 20 + 1 = 61. Another might correctly write 10 + 10 + 10 +10 + 5 + 5 + 5 + 6 = 40 + 15 + 6 = 55 + 6 = 61. Students are encouraged to think flexibly and to apply learned solution strategies.

In Lessons 9 and 10, different combinations of coins are manipulated to make the same total value, for example, "Estella has 75¢ to buy a yo-yo. How many different ways could she pay for it?" Seventy-five cents might be recorded with 3 quarters or shown with 2 quarters, 2 dimes, and 5 pennies. Students work cooperatively to explain their reasoning and solution strategies. In Lesson 10, multiple ways are found to represent the same quantity, with the added complexity of using the fewest number of coins (e.g., 67¢ equals 2 quarters, 1 dime, 1 nickel, and 2 pennies.) Students see that just as they changed 10 ones for 1 ten in Modules 4 and 5, they can also change coins of a lesser value for coins of a greater value (e.g., 2 nickels = 1 dime).

Students focus on making change from one dollar in Lessons 11 and 12, using the understanding that $1 has the same value as 100 pennies. In Lesson 11, students learn how to make change from one dollar using counting on, simplifying strategies (e.g., the arrow way), and the relationship between addition and subtraction. They represent the part–whole relationship using a number bond and by writing a number sentence, often using the related addition to solve (e.g., $1 – 45¢ = ____ or 45¢ + ____ = 100¢), as shown at right.

45¢ + ____ = 100¢

100 → 45, ?

45 →(+5) 50 →(+50) 100

5 + 50 = 55¢

In Lesson 12, students use play money to act out scenarios with a partner. For example, "Michael bought an apple for 45¢. He gave the cashier $1. How much change did he receive?" They focus on making a ten, counting up, and skip-counting with fives and tens to solve. For example, one student might move coins and say, "45, 50, 60, 70, 80, 90, 100," while another might start by counting up to 50 with pennies and then skip-count by fives. While efficiency is noted, students can make change in a variety of ways.

In the final lesson of Topic B, students solve two-step addition and subtraction word problems with abstract drawings and equations with the unknown in various positions. For example, "Devon found 98¢ in her piggy bank. She counted 1 quarter, 8 pennies, 3 dimes, and some nickels. How many nickels did she find?" After

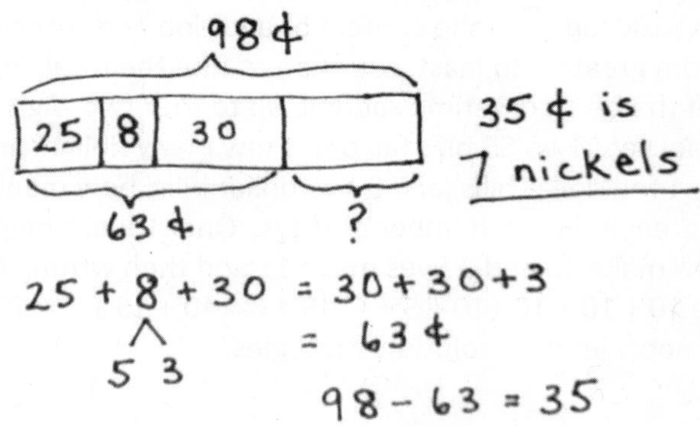

making a tape diagram, one student's first step might involve adding the given coins from greatest to least and skip-counting, while another might bond the quarter with 5 pennies to make the next ten before counting on, as shown above. Students synthesize their understanding of place value, making a ten, and skip-counting strategies to solve a variety of problem types embedded within the two-step problems

A Teaching Sequence Towards Mastery of Problem Solving with Coins and Bills

Objective 1: **Recognize the value of coins and count up to find their total value. (Lesson 6)**

Objective 2: **Solve word problems involving the total value of a group of coins. (Lesson 7)**

Objective 3: **Solve word problems involving the total value of a group of bills. (Lesson 8)**

Objective 4: **Solve word problems involving different combinations of coins with the same total value. (Lessons 9)**

Objective 5: **Use the fewest number of coins to make a given value. (Lessons 10)**

Objective 6: **Use different strategies to make a dollar or make change from $1. (Lesson 11)**

Objective 7: **Solve word problems involving different ways to make change from $1. (Lesson 12)**

Objective 8: **Solve two-step word problems involving dollars or cents with totals within $100 or $1. (Lesson 13)**

Lesson 6

Objective: Recognize the value of coins and count up to find their total value.

Suggested Lesson Structure

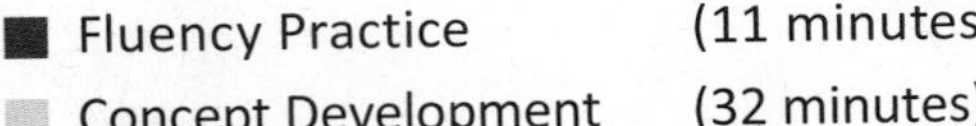

Fluency Practice	(11 minutes)
Concept Development	(32 minutes)
Application Problem	(7 minutes)
Student Debrief	(10 minutes)
Total Time	**(60 minutes)**

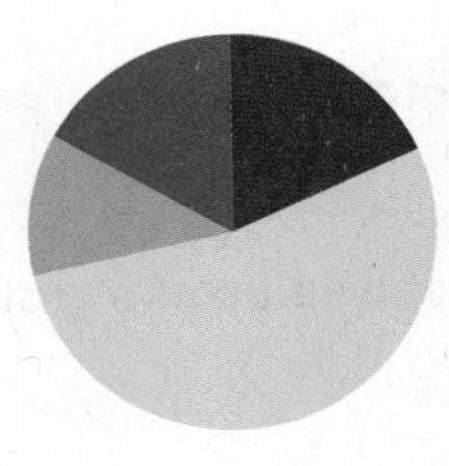

Fluency Practice (11 minutes)

- Grade 2 Core Fluency Differentiated Practice Sets **2.OA.2** (5 minutes)
- Decomposition Tree **2.NBT.5** (6 minutes)

Grade 2 Core Fluency Differentiated Practice Sets (5 minutes)

Materials: (S) Core Fluency Practice Sets from G2–M7–Lesson 1

Note: During G2–M7–Topic B and for the remainder of the year, each day's fluency includes an opportunity for review and mastery of the sums and differences with totals through 20 by means of the Core Fluency Practice Sets or Sprints. The process is detailed and Practice Sets are provided in G2–M7–Lesson 1.

Decomposition Tree (6 minutes)

Materials: (S) Decomposition Tree Template

Note: Students are given 90 seconds to decompose a specified amount in as many ways as they can. This fluency allows students to work at their own skill level and decompose amounts in a multitude of ways in a short amount of time

T: (Post a blank Deco Tree.) I'm going to think of a way to break 50 cents into two parts. I know 2 quarters make 50 cents and each quarter is worth 25 cents.

T: Watch me as I track our thinking on this Deco Tree. It is called a Deco Tree because we are decomposing the number at the top. The tree is like a number bond because the sum of the two parts is equal to the whole.

50¢

1 quarter	1 quarter
25¢	25¢
0¢	50¢
40¢	10¢
30¢	20¢
35¢	15¢
4 dimes	1 dime
49 pennies	1 penny
5 nickels	5 nickels

T: Raise your hand when you have another way to break 50 cents into two parts.

S: 0¢ and 50¢. → 40¢ and 10¢. → 30¢ and 20¢. → 35¢ and 15¢. → 4 dimes and 1 dime. → 49 pennies and 1 penny. → 5 nickels and 5 nickels.

T: (Write each correct student response on the posted Deco Tree.)

T: Great! You are on a roll! Now let's see what you can do on your own. (Distribute tree template.)

T: You are going to break apart 60¢ on your own tree for 90 seconds. Make as many pairs as you can. GO!

S: (Work for 90 seconds.)

T: Now exchange your tree with your partner and check each other's work. (Allow students 30–45 seconds to check.)

T: Return each other's papers. Did you see another way to make 60¢ on your partner's paper? (Allow students to share for another 30 seconds.)

T: Turn your paper over. Let's break apart 60¢ for another minute.

Concept Development (32 minutes)

Materials: (T) Personal white board, bag with the following play money coins: 4 quarters, 20 nickels, 10 dimes, 10 pennies (S) Personal white board, bag with the following play money coins: 4 quarters, 20 nickels, 10 dimes, 10 pennies

Note: Call students to sit in a circle in the communal area. This Concept Development assumes that students know the names of coins and their values based on lessons taught in Grade 1. If this is not the case, add time in the beginning of the lesson to review the names and values of the coins and omit the Application Problem.

Part 1: Count coins in isolation.

T: Let's count some money!

T: (Hold up a penny.) This coin is called a...?

S: Penny!

T: What is its value?

S: 1 cent!

T: (Hold up a nickel.) This coin is called a...?

S: Nickel!

T: What is its value?

S: 5 cents!

T: (Hold up a dime.) This coin is called a...?

S: Dime!

T: What is its value?

S: 10 cents!

T: (Hold up a quarter.) This coin is called a...?

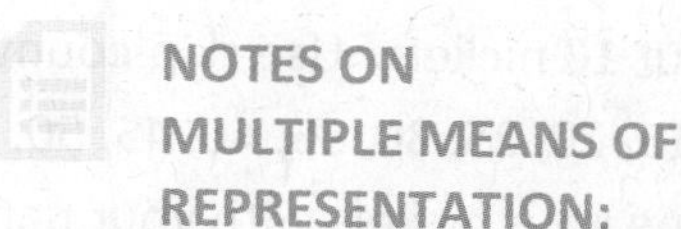

Support English language learners by highlighting the names and values of the coins. Post a chart with a picture, the name, and the value of the coins for reference. Practice saying the names and the values of the coins with them. Students who need more practice can use interactive technology such as the one found at http://www.ixl.com/math/grade-2/names-and-values-of-common-coins.

S: Quarter!

T: What is its value?

S: 25 cents!

T: Use your personal boards to write an addition sentence that shows the value of 3 nickels. (Pause.) Tell me the number sentence.

S: 5 + 5 + 5 = 15.

T: What coin do each of the fives represent in your number sentence?

S: A nickel!

T: Let's do the same with these 3 dimes.

T: Use your personal boards to write an addition sentence showing the value of 3 dimes. (Pause.) Tell me the number sentence.

S: 10 + 10 + 10 = 30.

T: What coin do each of the tens represent in your number sentence?

S: A dime.

5 + 5 + 5 = 15

10 + 10 + 10 = 30

25 + 25 + 25 = 75

T: (Show 3 quarters.) Use your personal boards to write an addition sentence showing the value of 3 quarters. (Pause.) Tell me the number sentence.

S: 25 + 25 + 25 = 75.

T: Let's look at our number sentences. (Point to 5 + 5 + 5 = 15, 10 + 10 + 10 = 30, and 25 + 25 + 25 = 75.) Each shows the value of 3 coins. Which sentence represents the sum of which coin? Review with your partner.

S: (Share.)

T: Take out 10 nickels. Use skip-counting to find the value of the nickels.

S: 5, 10, 15, 20, 25, 30, 35, 40, 45, 50.

T: Combine your nickels with your partner. Together, skip-count to find the value of your nickels.

S: 5, 10, 15 ...100.

Support students and listen for misconceptions. Repeat process with dimes.

T: Take out 1 nickel and 5 dimes. Skip-count starting with value of the nickel.

S: 5, 15, 25, 35, 45, 55.

T: Exchange your nickel for a quarter. Skip-count starting with the value of the quarter.

S: 25, 35, 45, 55, 65, 75.

Listen carefully to students as students skip-count by 10 starting from a number other than zero. Provide additional examples as needed to solidify understanding.

Part 2: Count mixed groups of coins starting with the largest value coin.

T: (Take 2 dimes and 3 pennies out of your bag and lay them down on a personal board for the students to see.)

T: Turn and talk: What is the total value of my coins?

S: 23 cents!

T: Let's count the money together. Start with the dimes.

S: 10, 20, 21, 22, 23.

T: Let's count again. This time start with the pennies.

S: 1, 2, 3, 13, 23.

T: Which was easier? Why?

S: Counting the dimes first. → If we count the dimes first, we can count by tens. Then we add the ones.

T: So, it was easier to start with the largest coin value. Let's try that with the next problem.

MP.4

T: (Take out 1 quarter, 1 nickel, and 1 penny.) Turn and talk: What is the total value of my coins and how do you know?

S: 25 cents plus 5 more is 30 cents, plus 1 more is 31. → The quarter and the nickel make 30, plus the penny is 31.

T: Write a number sentence to show the value of 1 quarter, 1 nickel, and 1 penny.

S: (Write 25 + 5 + 1 = 31.)

T: It's so much easier to add 5 to 25 than add 25 to 6! That's why I generally start counting the total value of coins from the largest coin.

Give students time to practice counting mixed groups with the following amounts:

- 1 quarter, 1 dime, 1 penny
- 1 quarter, 2 nickels, 1 dime
- 1 quarter, 2 pennies, 1 dime
- 1 quarter, 2 dimes, 1 nickel
- 2 quarters, 2 dimes, 1 nickel
- 2 quarters, 3 dimes
- 2 quarters, 5 dimes

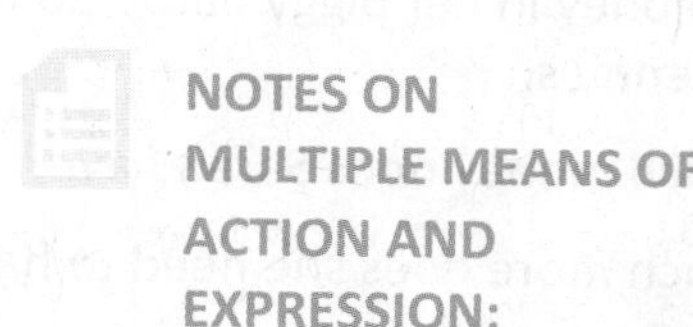

NOTES ON
MULTIPLE MEANS OF
ACTION AND
EXPRESSION:

Challenge above grade level students by asking them to assist by writing a few strings of different amounts using combinations of coins and to provide equations showing the values of those amounts.

Part 3: Count mixed groups of coins by making ten.

T: (Take out 1 quarter, 3 dimes, 1 nickel, and 2 pennies.) Turn and talk: How much money do we have here, and how do you know?

S: 25, 35, 45, 55, 60, 61, 62. → 25 cents plus 30 more is 55 cents, plus 5 more is 60, plus 2 more is 62. → 25, 30, 40, 50, 60, 61, 62. → The quarter and the nickel make 30. Then I add 30 for the dimes to get 60. Then add the pennies: 60 + 2 = 62.

T: Count the value of the coins for me from largest to smallest.

S: 25, 35, 45, 55, 60, 61, 62.

T: Did anyone count a different way?

S: Yes! I added the quarter and nickel first. Then I added the dimes. The pennies were last.

T: You made ten first. Try counting that way.

S: 25, 30, 40, 50, 60, 61, 62.

T: For me, it is easier to make ten first by adding the nickel to the quarter. See if you agree using the following sets of coins. Try finding the total value of the coins by making a ten first and then by not making a ten first.

Write the following amounts on the board:

- 1 quarter, 2 pennies, 1 nickel, 2 dimes
- 1 quarter, 1 penny, 3 nickels, 1 dime

Problem Set (10 minutes)

Students should do their personal best to complete the Problem Set within the allotted 10 minutes. For some classes, it may be appropriate to modify the assignment by specifying which problems they work on first. Some problems do not specify a method for solving. Students solve these problems using the RDW approach used for Application Problems.

Application Problem (7 minutes)

Note: This Application Problem follows the Concept Development because it provides practice for material taught during the Concept Development.

Sarah is saving money in her piggy bank. So far, she has 3 dimes, 1 quarter, and 8 pennies.

a. How much money does Sarah have?

b. How much more does she need to have a dollar?

(10) (10) (10) = 30

(25) = 25

(1) (1) (1) (1) (1) (1) (1) (1) = 8

$30 \xrightarrow{+25} 55 \xrightarrow{+5} 60 \xrightarrow{+3} 63$

a) Sarah has 63 cents

b) $63 \xrightarrow{+7} 70 \xrightarrow{+30} 100$

She needs 37 more cents to make 1 dollar.

Student Debrief (10 minutes)

Lesson Objective: Recognize the value of coins and count up to find their total value.

The Student Debrief is intended to invite reflection and active processing of the total lesson experience.

Invite students to review their solutions for the Problem Set. They should check work by comparing answers with a partner before going over answers as a class. Look for misconceptions or misunderstandings that can be addressed in the Debrief. Guide students in a conversation to debrief the Problem Set and process the lesson.

You may choose to use any combination of the questions below to lead the discussion.

- Look at the first page of your Problem Set. Tell your partner about how the coins are laid out in each row. Where did you start counting? Why did you start there? (Some students might count left to right or right to left, save the dimes for last, or count randomly.) Tell your partner your counting path and why it is a good way to find the value of the coins.
- Look at the second page. Tell your partner about how the coins are laid out in each box. How is it different from the first page? Which one was the easiest to find the value for? Why?
- Did anyone use an addition equation to find the value of the coins? Did skip-counting help you to add faster?
- How can we use what we know about sorting to help us find the value of coins? Could we use a table to help us find the value of a group of coins?

Name Michelle Date

Count or add to find the total value of each group of coins.
Write the value.

1.	8¢
2.	14¢
3.	25¢
4.	19¢
5.	31¢
6.	36¢
7.	52¢

Exit Ticket (3 minutes)

After the Student Debrief, instruct students to complete the Exit Ticket. A review of their work will help you assess the students' understanding of the concepts that were presented in the lesson today and plan more effectively for future lessons. You may read the questions aloud to the students.

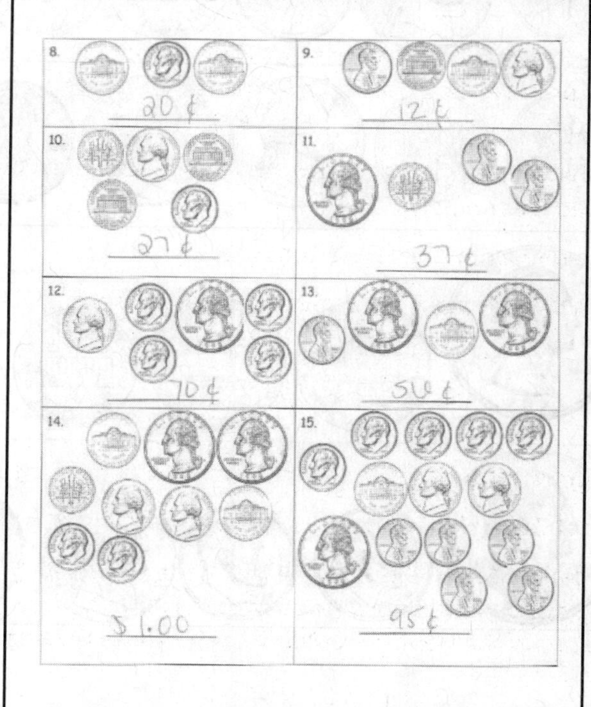

8. 20¢	9. 12¢
10. 27¢	11. 37¢
12. 70¢	13. 56¢
14. $1.00	15. 95¢

Name ______________________ Date ____________

Count or add to find the total value of each group of coins.
Write the value.

1. 	______
2. 	______
3. 	______
4. 	______
5. 	______
6. 	______
7. 	______

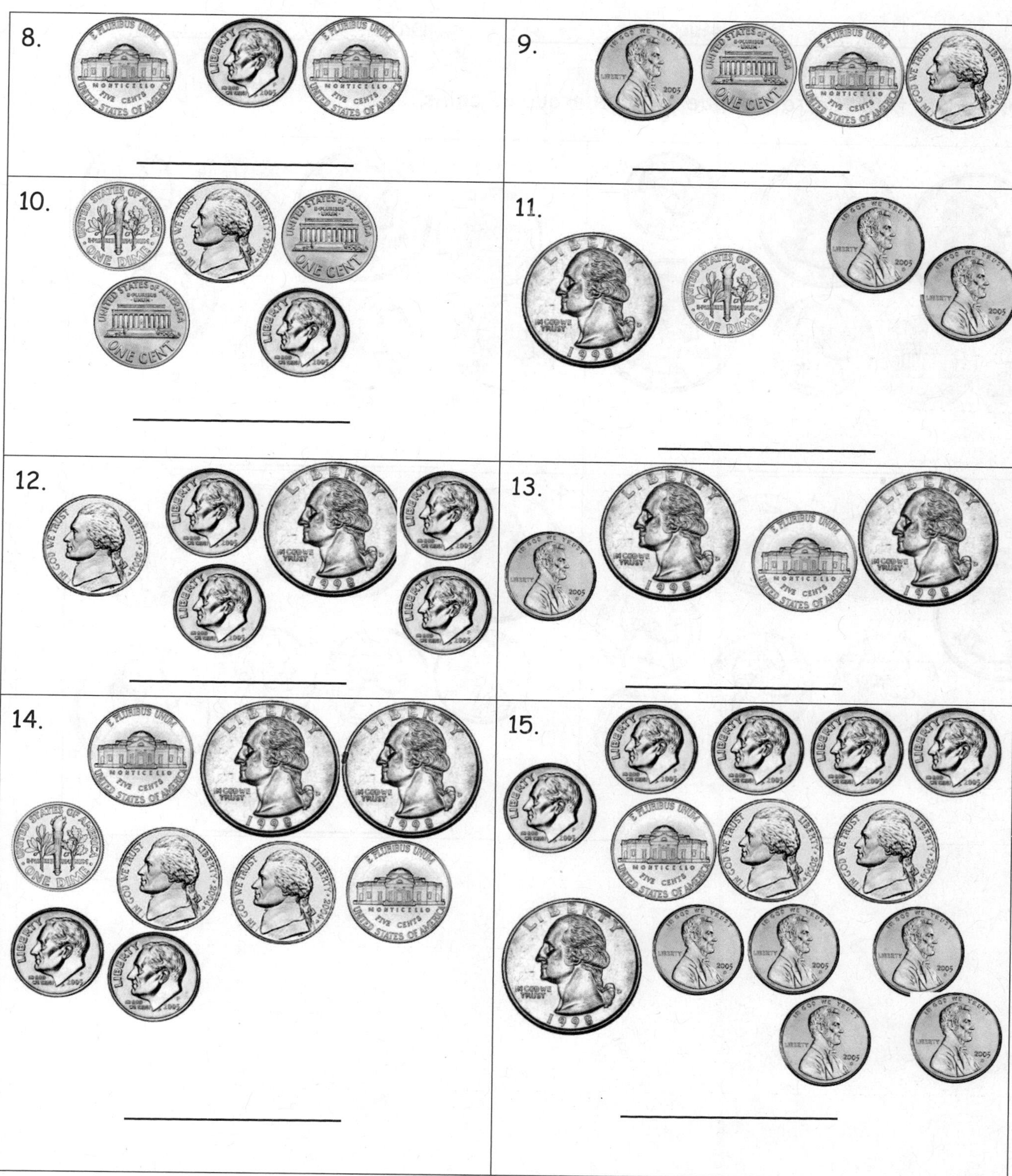
8.
9.
10.
11.
12.
13.
14.
15.

Name ______________________________ Date ______________

Count or add to find the total value of each group of coins.

1. ______________

2. ______________

3. ______________

4. ______________

Name ______________________________ Date ________________

Count or add to find the total value of each group of coins.
Write the value.

1.		________
2.		________
3.		________
4.		________
5.		________
6.		________
7.		________

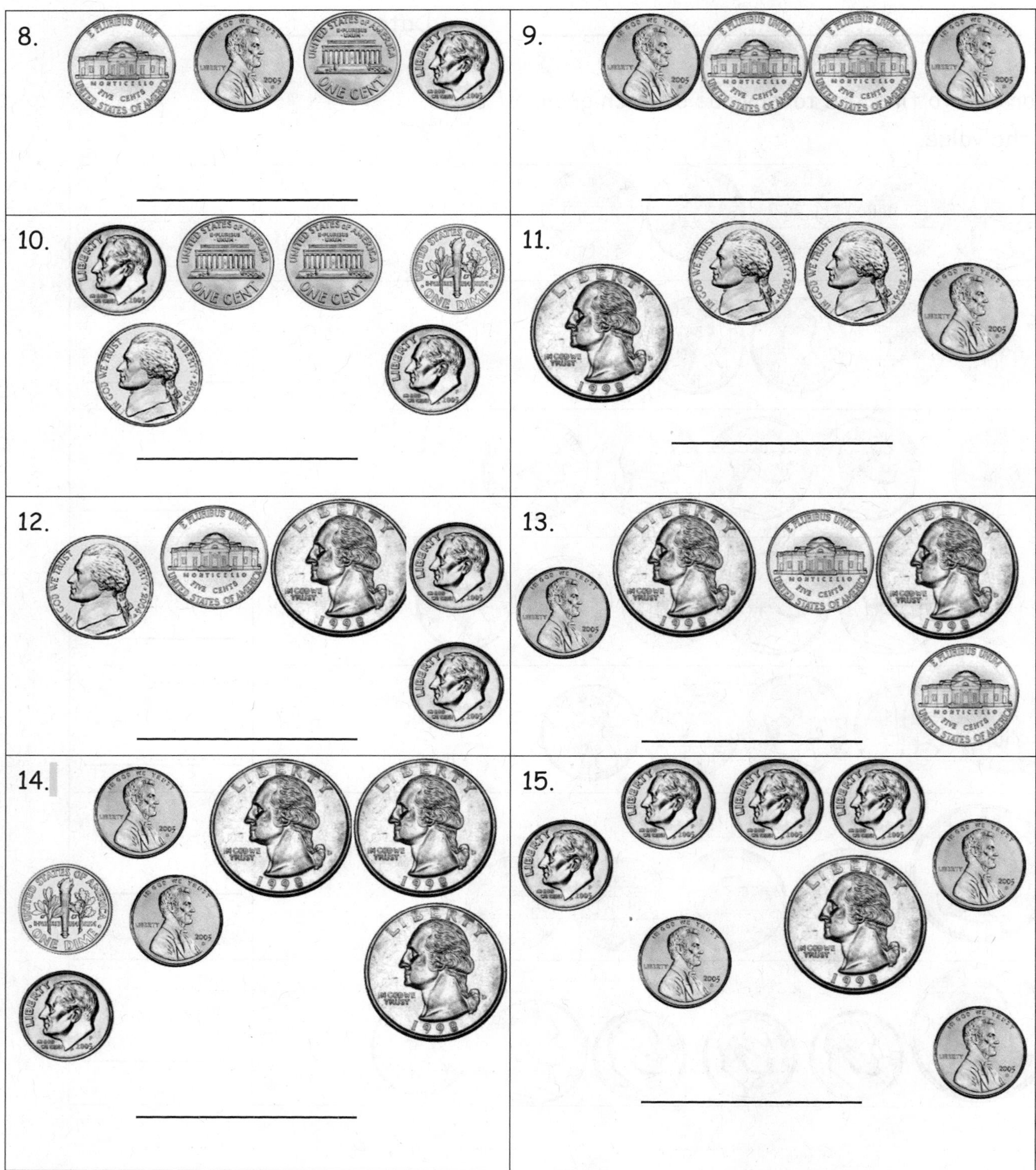
8.
9.
10.
11.
12.
13.
14.
15.

Lesson 7

Objective: Solve word problems involving the total value of a group of coins.

Suggested Lesson Structure

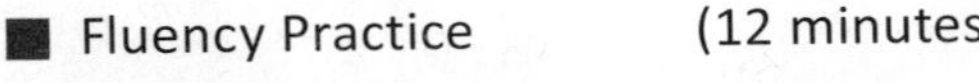

Fluency Practice	(12 minutes)
Application Problem	(5 minutes)
Concept Development	(33 minutes)
Student Debrief	(10 minutes)
Total Time	**(60 minutes)**

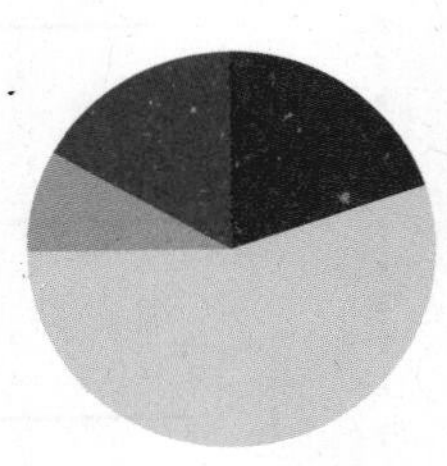

Fluency Practice (12 minutes)

- Skip-Count by \$5 and \$10 Between 85 and 205 **2.NBT.2** (3 minutes)
- Sprint: Subtraction Across a Ten **2.OA.2** (9 minutes)

Skip-Count by \$5 and \$10 Between 85 and 205 (3 minutes)

Materials: (T) 20 ten dollar bills, 10 five dollar bills

Note: Bring students to an area where you can lay the bills on the carpet or central location. Students apply their knowledge of skip-counting by fives and tens to counting bills in preparation for solving word problems with bills in the next lesson.

T: (Lay out \$85 in bills so that all the students can see.) What is the total value of the bills?
S: \$85.
T: Count in your head as I change the value. (Lay down ten dollar bills to make 95, 105, 115.)
T: What is the total value of the bills now?
S: \$115.
T: (Remove ten dollar bills to make 105, 95.) What is the total value of the bills now?
S: \$95.
T: (Add more ten dollar bills to make 105, 115, 125, 135, 145, 155, 165, 175, 185.) What is the total value of the bills?
S: \$185.
T: (Lay down five dollar bills to make 190, 195, 200.) What is the total value of the bills?
S: \$200

Continue to count up and back by 5 and 10, crossing over the hundred and where you notice students struggling.

Sprint: Subtraction Across a Ten (9 minutes)

Materials: (S) Subtraction Across a Ten Sprint

Note: This Sprint gives practice with the grade level fluency of subtracting within 20.

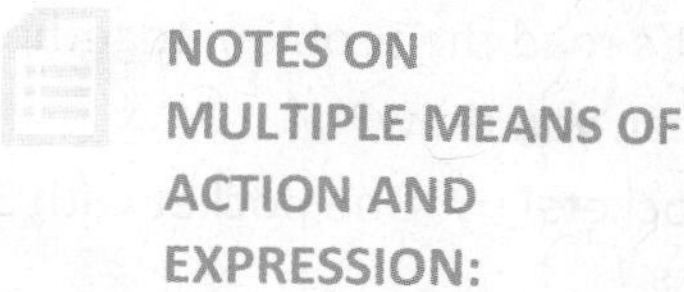

NOTES ON MULTIPLE MEANS OF ACTION AND EXPRESSION:

Challenge above grade level students by asking them to find other ways to show the same value (65 cents) as presented in the Application Problem. Students can use manipulatives to show their results or use paper and pencil to show how many different combinations of coins can make 65 cents.

Application Problem (5 minutes)

Danny has 2 dimes, 1 quarter, 3 nickels, and 5 pennies.

a. What is the total value of Danny's coins?

b. Show two different ways that Danny might add to find the total.

Note: The following problem is designed to encourage students to think flexibly when adding coins. While some may order coins from greatest to least and count on, others may skip-count, and still others may look to make a ten. These strategies will be used to problem solve during today's lesson.

(25) (10) (10) (5) (5) (5)
(1) (1) (1) (1) (1)

25 + 20 + 15 + 5 = ____
25 + 20 + 20 = 65¢

25 + 5 + 10 + 10 + 5 + 5 + 5 = ____
30 + 20 + 15 = 65¢

Concept Development (33 minutes)

Materials: (T) Play money coins, personal white board
(S) Personal white boards

Remind students to use the RDW process when solving word problems with money. Emphasize the importance of re-reading and adjusting.

- Read the problem.
- Draw and label.
- Write number sentences.
- Write a statement.

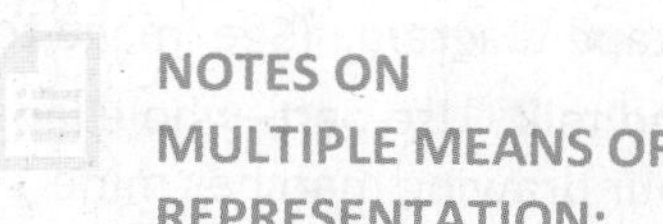

NOTES ON MULTIPLE MEANS OF REPRESENTATION:

At the beginning of the lesson, support English language learners by pointing to visuals of the coins while reading Problem 1 out loud to the class. Pictures of quarters, dimes, nickels, and pennies should have the name of coin printed clearly so that students can learn them more quickly. Post the visuals on the word wall so that students needing extra support can refer to them.

Part 1: Solve a *put together with total unknown* problem.

Ignacio has 3 dimes and 2 nickels in one pocket and 1 quarter and 7 pennies in another pocket. How much money is in Ignacio's pockets?

T: What do we do first when we see a word problem?

S: Read it.

T: Yes, let's read the problem together. (Read aloud.)

T: What can you draw?

S: Two pockets! → One pocket with 3 dimes and 2 nickels and another pocket with 1 quarter and 7 pennies.

T: Great! Get going. I'll give you a minute to draw quietly. When I give the signal, talk to your partner about how your drawing matches the story.

T: (Allow students time to draw. Signal.) Turn and talk: Look at your drawing. What are you trying to find? (See example drawings to the right.)

MP.2

S: We need to find out how much Ignacio has in both pockets. → We need to find the total value of the coins. → We need to find the total in Pocket 1 and the total in Pocket 2, then add them.

T: Go ahead and do that. Write a number sentence and statement to match your work. (Pause to allow students time to work.) Explain to your partner how you solved.

S: For the first pocket I just skip-counted by tens, then fives: 10, 20, 30, 35, 40 cents. → For the first pocket, I added the 2 nickels first to make ten. And then I added on 3 more tens to get 40 cents. → A quarter is 25 cents, and then you can count on 7 cents, so 26, 27, 28, ...32 cents in Pocket 2. → In the second pocket, I drew a number bond to make a ten, so 25 + 5 is 30, plus 2 is 32 cents.

T: What's your number sentence?

S: 40 + 32 = 72.

T: And the statement of your solution?

S: Ignacio has 72 cents in his pockets.

T: Yes! Look how we can also represent this problem with a tape diagram. (See image to the right.)

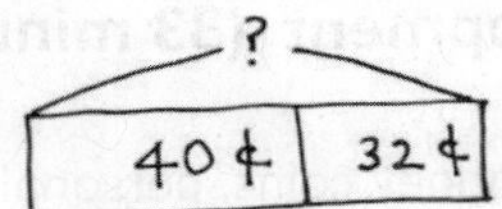

T: Turn and talk. Use part–whole language to describe how your drawing matches mine.

S: Your bar has two parts, and I drew two pockets. → We both added the two parts to find the total. → Our parts have the same amount of money in them.

T: Exactly! Let's try a more challenging problem. You're ready for it!

Repeat the process with the following *put together with result unknown* problem adjusting the level of support as appropriate for the students:

Tamika has 12 pennies and 2 quarters in her new piggy bank. She puts in 4 nickels, 1 dime, and 4 more pennies. How much money does Tamika have in her piggy bank altogether?

NOTES ON MULTIPLE MEANS OF ENGAGEMENT:

Provide struggling students with the chance to continue using coin manipulatives and part–whole templates for their personal boards. This provides extra scaffolding to help them transition to drawing tape diagrams.

Circulate and support students as they use the RDW process to complete the problem independently. Encourage flexible thinking. Check student drawings and problem-solving strategies.

The following questions may be used to check for student understanding:

- What did you draw to show the story?
- What number sentence did you write to match your drawing?

Part 2: Solve a two-step word *put together with total unknown* and *take from with result unknown* word problem.

On Monday, Reese gives 2 dimes and 3 nickels to her sister. On Tuesday, she gives her sister 1 quarter, 1 dime, and 4 pennies. If Reese started with 94 cents, how much money does she have now?

T: Let's read the problem together.

T/S: (Read aloud.)

T: What can you draw first?

S: Two groups of coins, one for Monday and one for Tuesday.

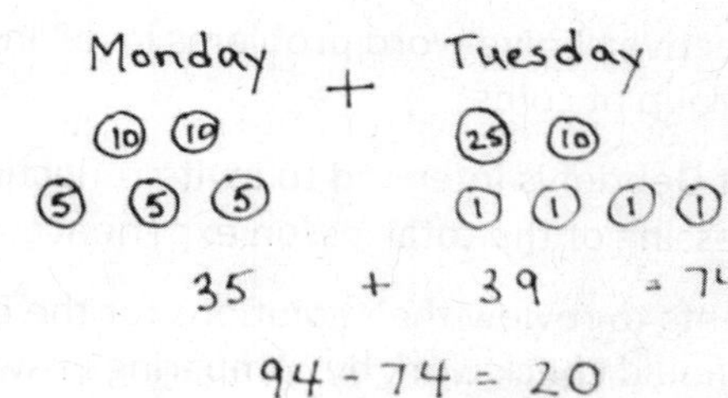

T: Great! Get to work. I'll give you a minute to draw quietly. When I give the signal, talk to your partner about how your drawing matches the story. (Allow students time to draw. See examples to the right.)

T: Turn and talk: Look at your drawing. What are you trying to find?

S: We need to find the total value of all the coins Reese gave to her sister. Then, we need to subtract the total from 94 cents. → We need to add the two groups of coins first, but then we need to subtract to see how much she has left.

T: Go ahead and do that. Write a number sentence and statement to match your work. (Pause to allow students time to work.) Explain to your partner how you solved.

S: First, I added the money from Monday and Tuesday. Then, I subtracted 74¢ from 94¢ to get 20¢. → I used the make a ten strategy to make it easy. 35 + 39 = 34 + 1 + 39 = 34 + 40 = 74.

T: (Circulate to provide support and check for understanding.)

T: What were your number sentences?

S: First, I added, so 20 + 15 + 25 + 10 + 4 = 74. → My second one was 94 – 74 = 20.

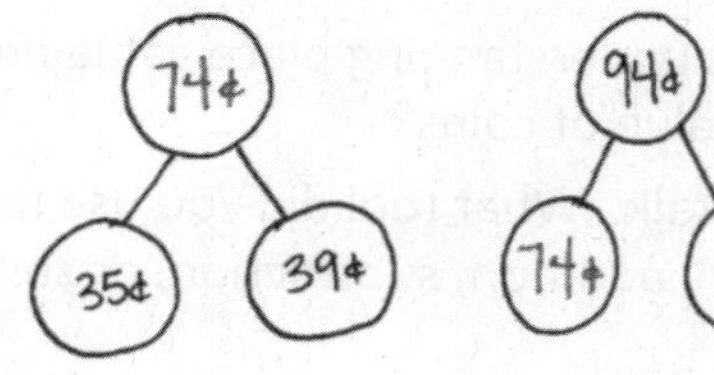

T: And statement of your solution?

S: Reese has 74 cents now.

T: Watch how we can also represent this situation with a number bond.

T: Turn and talk. Use part–whole language to describe how your drawing matches mine.

S: Since Reese started with 94 cents, that's the whole. → We know that she gave her sister a total of 74 cents; that's one part. → We know the whole and the part she gave her sister, and we found the part Reese has left.

T: You're on a roll! Now it's your turn to solve.

Problem Set (10 minutes)

Students should do their personal best to complete the Problem Set within the allotted 10 minutes. For some classes, it may be appropriate to modify the assignment by specifying which problems they work on first. Some problems do not specify a method for solving. Students solve these problems using the RDW approach used for Application Problems.

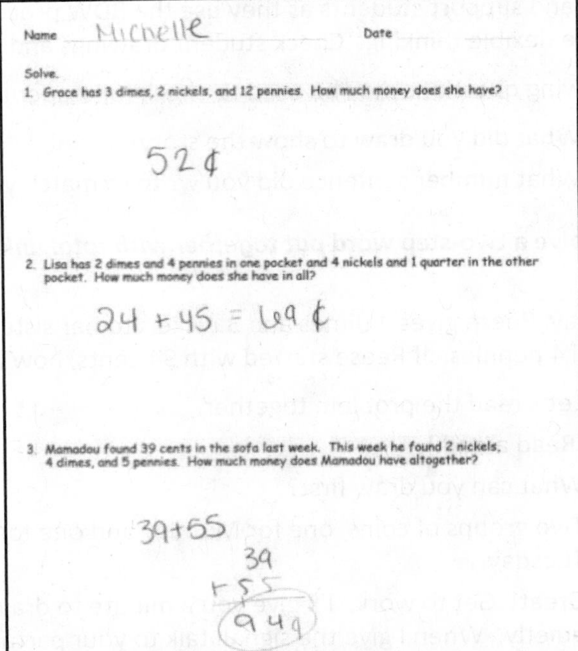

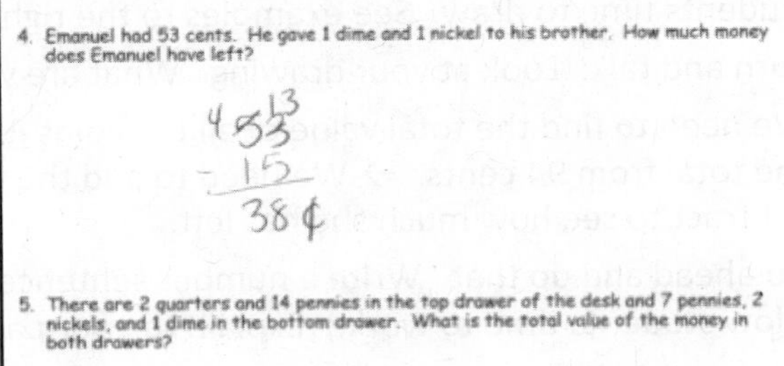

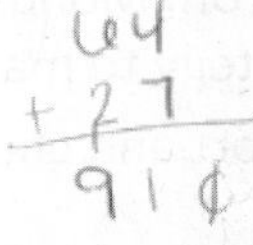

Student Debrief (10 minutes)

Lesson Objective: Solve word problems involving the total value of a group of coins.

The Student Debrief is intended to invite reflection and active processing of the total lesson experience.

Invite students to review their solutions for the Problem Set. They should check work by comparing answers with a partner before going over answers as a class. Look for misconceptions or misunderstandings that can be addressed in the Debrief. Guide students in a conversation to debrief the Problem Set and process the lesson.

You may choose to use any combination of the questions below to lead the discussion.

- Look at the first problem in the Problem Set. Talk with your partner about how you thought about and counted the pennies. How could you think about the nickels to make it easier to find their value?
- How does understanding place value help you to find the value of coins?
- Turn and talk. What tool did you use to solve Problem 4, addition, subtraction, or something else?
- Explain to your partner using part–whole language how you figured out how much money Ricardo had left in Problem 6. If you used a model or an equation show it to your partner.
- How are number bonds and the part–whole tape models the same? How are they different? Are there certain math problems where it is better to use one over the other?

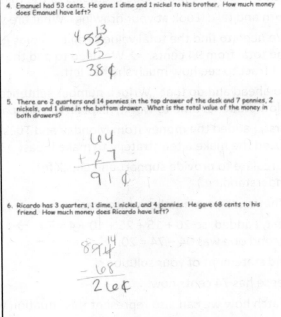

Exit Ticket (3 minutes)

After the Student Debrief, instruct students to complete the Exit Ticket. A review of their work will help you assess the students' understanding of the concepts that were presented in the lesson today and plan more effectively for future lessons. You may read the questions aloud to the students.

A # Correct ______

Subtract.

1	10 - 3 =		23	11 - 9 =	
2	11 - 3 =		24	12 - 9 =	
3	12 - 3 =		25	17 - 9 =	
4	10 - 2 =		26	10 - 8 =	
5	11 - 2 =		27	11 - 8 =	
6	10 - 5 =		28	12 - 8 =	
7	11 - 5 =		29	16 - 8 =	
8	12 - 5 =		30	10 - 6 =	
9	14 - 5 =		31	13 - 6 =	
10	10 - 4 =		32	15 - 6 =	
11	11 - 4 =		33	10 - 7 =	
12	12 - 4 =		34	13 - 7 =	
13	13 - 4 =		35	14 - 7 =	
14	10 - 7 =		36	16 - 7 =	
15	11 - 7 =		37	10 - 8 =	
16	12 - 7 =		38	13 - 8 =	
17	15 - 7 =		39	14 - 8 =	
18	10 - 6 =		40	17 - 8 =	
19	11 - 6 =		41	10 - 9 =	
20	12 - 6 =		42	13 - 9 =	
21	14 - 6 =		43	14 - 9 =	
22	10 - 9 =		44	18 - 9 =	

B

Improvement _____ # Correct _____

Subtract.

1	10 - 2 =		23	11 - 7 =	
2	11 - 2 =		24	12 - 7 =	
3	10 - 4 =		25	16 - 7 =	
4	11 - 4 =		26	10 - 9 =	
5	12 - 4 =		27	11 - 9 =	
6	13 - 4 =		28	12 - 9 =	
7	10 - 3 =		29	18 - 9 =	
8	11 - 3 =		30	10 - 5 =	
9	12 - 3 =		31	13 - 5 =	
10	10 - 6 =		32	10 - 6 =	
11	11 - 6 =		33	13 - 6 =	
12	12 - 6 =		34	14 - 6 =	
13	15 - 6 =		35	10 - 7 =	
14	10 - 5 =		36	13 - 7 =	
15	11 - 5 =		37	15 - 7 =	
16	12 - 5 =		38	10 - 8 =	
17	14 - 5 =		39	13 - 8 =	
18	10 - 8 =		40	14 - 8 =	
19	11 - 8 =		41	16 - 8 =	
20	12 - 8 =		42	10 - 9 =	
21	17 - 8 =		43	16 - 9 =	
22	10 - 7 =		44	17 - 9 =	

Name ______________________________ Date ______________

Solve.

1. Grace has 3 dimes, 2 nickels, and 12 pennies. How much money does she have?

2. Lisa has 2 dimes and 4 pennies in one pocket and 4 nickels and 1 quarter in the other pocket. How much money does she have in all?

3. Mamadou found 39 cents in the sofa last week. This week he found 2 nickels, 4 dimes, and 5 pennies. How much money does Mamadou have altogether?

4. Emanuel had 53 cents. He gave 1 dime and 1 nickel to his brother. How much money does Emanuel have left?

5. There are 2 quarters and 14 pennies in the top drawer of the desk and 7 pennies, 2 nickels, and 1 dime in the bottom drawer. What is the total value of the money in both drawers?

6. Ricardo has 3 quarters, 1 dime, 1 nickel, and 4 pennies. He gave 68 cents to his friend. How much money does Ricardo have left?

Name ____________________ Date ____________

Solve.

1. Greg had 1 quarter, 1 dime, and 3 nickels in his pocket. He found 3 nickels on the sidewalk. How much money does Greg have?

2. Robert gave Sandra 1 quarter, 5 nickels, and 2 pennies. Sandra already had 3 pennies and 2 dimes. How much money does Sandra have now?

Name ______________________________ Date ____________

Solve.

1. Owen has 4 dimes, 3 nickels, and 16 pennies. How much money does he have?

2. Eli found 1 quarter, 1 dime, and 2 pennies in his desk and 16 pennies and 2 dimes in his backpack. How much money does he have in all?

3. Carrie had 2 dimes, 1 quarter, and 11 pennies in her pocket. Then she bought a soft pretzel for 35 cents. How much money did Carrie have left?

4. Ethan had 67 cents. He gave 1 quarter and 6 pennies to his sister. How much money does Ethan have left?

5. There are 4 dimes and 3 nickels in Susan's piggy bank. Nevaeh has 17 pennies and 3 nickels in her piggy bank. What is the total value of the money in both piggy banks?

6. Tison had 1 quarter, 4 dimes, 4 nickels, and 5 pennies. He gave 57 cents to his cousin. How much money does Tison have left?

Lesson 8

Objective: Solve word problems involving the total value of a group of bills.

Suggested Lesson Structure

Fluency Practice	(12 minutes)
Application Problem	(6 minutes)
Concept Development	(32 minutes)
Student Debrief	(10 minutes)
Total Time	**(60 minutes)**

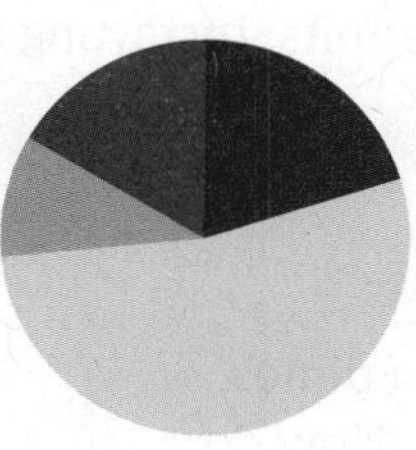

Fluency Practice (12 minutes)

- Sprint: Adding Across a Ten **2.OA.2** (9 minutes)
- More and Less **2.NBT.5** (3 minutes)

Sprint: Adding Across a Ten (9 minutes)

Materials: (S) Adding Across a Ten Sprint

Note: This Sprint gives practice with the grade level fluency of adding within 20.

More and Less (3 minutes)

Note: In this activity, students practice adding and subtracting coins. Because the addition of the value of a quarter may still be challenging for some, the use of a signal to invite a choral response is suggested.

T: The value of one dime more than a quarter is...?

S: 35 cents.

T: Give the number sentence using cents as the unit.

S: 25 cents + 10 cents = 35 cents.

T: Wait for the signal. The value of 1 quarter more than 35 cents is...? (Signal when students are ready.)

S: 60 cents!

T: Give the number sentence.

S: 35 cents + 25 cents = 60 cents.

T: The value of 1 quarter more than 60 cents is...?

S: 85 cents.

T: Give the number sentence.

S: 60 cents + 25 cents = 85 cents.

T: The value of a dime and nickel more than 85 cents is...?

S: 100 cents. → 1 dollar!

T: Give the number sentence.

S: 85 cents + 15 cents = 100 cents.

Continue to repeat this line of questioning as time permits, restarting at zero after reaching 100 cents.

Application Problem (6 minutes)

Kiko's brother says that he will trade her 2 quarters, 4 dimes, and 2 nickels for a one dollar bill. Is this a fair trade? How do you know?

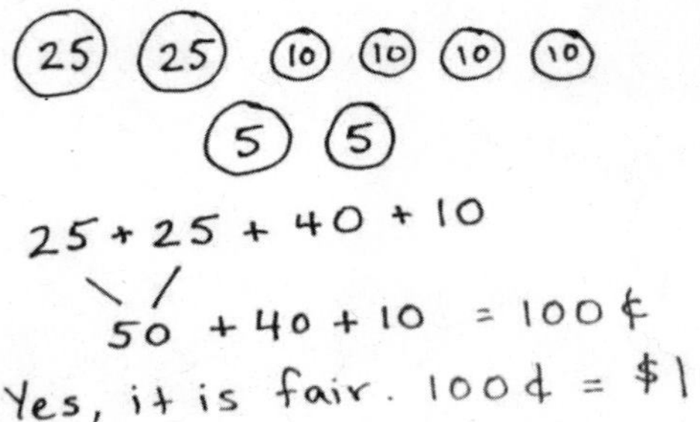

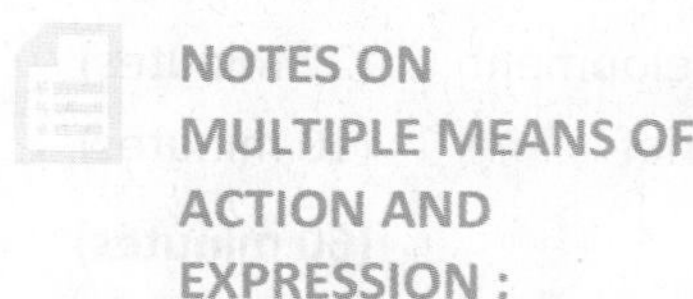

NOTES ON MULTIPLE MEANS OF ACTION AND EXPRESSION:

Scaffold the Application Problem for students who are below grade level as well as for students with disabilities by providing them with coins to use. Work with students one step at a time while they add up the value of the coins: "What is the value of a quarter? 2 quarters? 1 dime, 2 dimes, 3 dimes, 4 dimes? Two nickels equal how much? Let's add them all up together."

Note: The following problem affords students the chance to practice ordering coins from greatest to least and then finding the total. It also asks students to make a judgment call based on their solution. The comparison to $1 serves as a bridge to today's lesson with dollar bills.

Concept Development (32 minutes)

Materials: (T) Play money dollar bills (S) Personal white boards

Part 1: Solve a *put together with total unknown* type problem.

Alyssa has 5 five dollar bills, 12 one dollar bills, and 3 ten dollar bills in her wallet. How much money is in her wallet?

T: What do we do first when we see a word problem?

S: Read the whole thing.

T: Yes, let's read the problem together.

T/S: (Read aloud.)

T: What can you draw?

S: All the dollar bills. → 3 ten dollar bills, 5 five dollar bills, and 12 one dollar bills.

T: Great! I'll give you about one minute to draw quietly. When I give the signal, talk to your partner about how your drawing (shown on the right) matches the story.

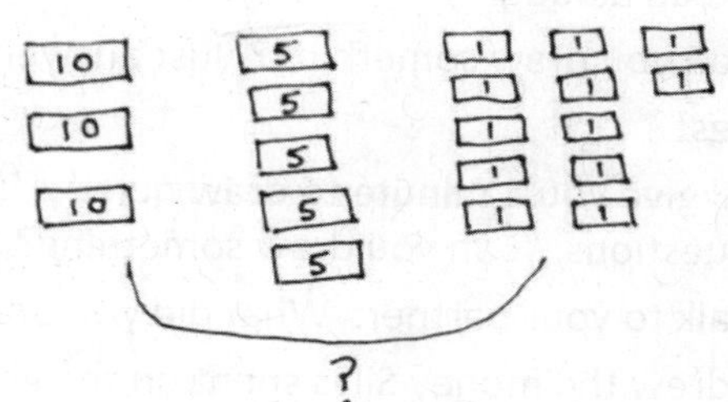

T: Turn and talk: Look at your drawing. What are you trying to find?

S: I need to find out how much money Alyssa has in her wallet. → I need to find the total value of the dollar bills. → I need to find the total value of the tens, then fives, then ones. Then, add.

T: Go ahead and do that. Write a number sentence and a statement to match your work. (Pause to allow students time to work.) Explain to your partner how you solved and how your number sentence matches your drawing.

S: I put the money in order from greatest to least. Then, I skip-counted by tens first: 10, 20, 30. Then I added on and skip-counted by fives: 35, 40, 45, 50, 55. Then I added 12 ones, and I got 67. → I thought, 10 plus 10 is 20, and 20 plus 10 is 30. Then I counted on each 5, so 35, 40, 45, 50, 55. Then I added on 12 ones.

T: What's your number sentence?

S: 30 + 25 + 12 = 67. →
10 + 10 + 10 + 5 + 5 + 5 + 5 + 5 + 12 = 67.

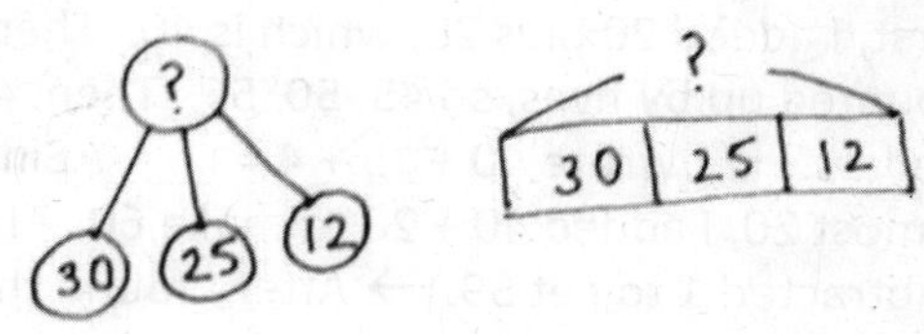

T: And the statement of your solution?

S: Alyssa has 67 dollars in her wallet.

T: Yes! Look how we can also represent this problem with a tape diagram or number bond (see figure on the right).

T: Turn and talk. Use part–whole language to describe how your drawing matches mine and how it is different than mine.

S: I combined three parts to find the whole thing. → We both have question marks for the whole, since we need to find it. → I added three parts, too, the ten dollar bills, five dollar bills, and one dollar bills! → My drawing was a lot more work!

T: Do both drawings make sense?

S: Yes!

T: Whose might be more efficient?

S: Yours!

T: The important thing is that a drawing makes sense, but as we solve more problems, sometimes we do see more efficient ways to draw.

Part 2: Solve a *take from with result unknown* type problem.

Silas uses 2 twenty dollar bills, 3 five dollar bills, and 4 one dollar bills on a gift for his aunt. He is going to save the rest. If Silas started with $80, how much will he save?

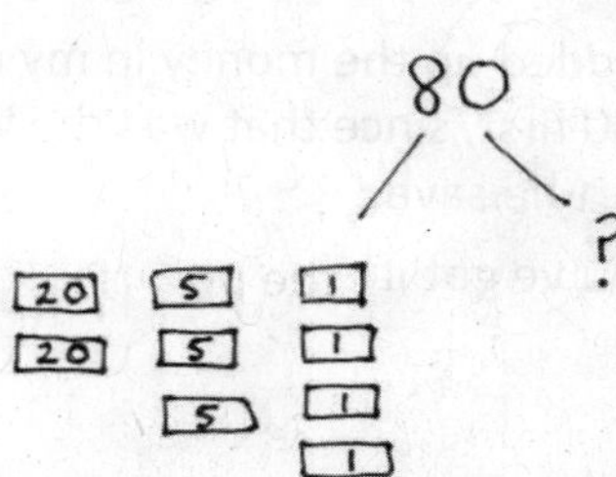

T: Let's read the problem together.

T/S: (Read aloud.)

T: Can you draw something? Just answer yes or no.

S: Yes!

T: I'll give you a minute to draw quietly. (Circulate to support by rereading and repeating the simple questions, "Can you draw something? What can you draw?")

T: Talk to your partner. What did you draw?

S: I drew the money Silas spent on the gift and a question mark for the money he saved. → I drew 2 twenty dollar bills, 3 five dollar bills, and 4 one dollar bills. → I started with 80 and made two arms like a number bond with all the money he spent in one part. (See drawing on previous page.)

T: Turn and talk: Look at your drawing. What are you trying to find?

MP.2

S: First, I am trying to find out how much Silas spent altogether by adding. → I need to find the total value of all the bills. Then, I need to subtract from $80 to see how much he'll save.

T: Good analysis. Now, write a number sentence and a statement to match your work. (Pause while students work.) Explain to your partner how you solved.

S: First, I added 20 plus 20, which is 40. Then, I skip-counted up by fives, so 45, 50, 55. Then, 4 more is 59 dollars. → I wrote 40 + 15 + 4 = ____. Since 15 + 4 is almost 20, I added 40 + 20 to make 60. Then, I subtracted 1 to get 59. → After I found the total, $59, I used compensation to subtract. I changed 80 – 59 to 81 – 60, which is $21. → To find how much Silas saved, I wrote 59 + ___ = 80. I counted up 21 more using the arrow way.

T: I see many of you wrote two number sentences. First, you found the total Silas spent on the gift. From there, you found out how much he saved. Nice work!

T: How much did Silas save? Tell me in a statement.

S: Silas saved 21 dollars.

T: Some of you also represented this situation with a part–whole model (shown on the right).

T: Use part–whole language to describe how your drawing matches your friend's.

S: I added up the money in my drawing to get $59, which is one part in your number bond. → I drew $80 first, since that was the whole amount Silas started with. → I had a question mark, too, for the part he saved.

T: You've got it!

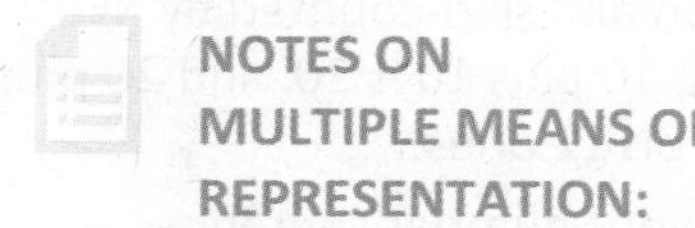

NOTES ON MULTIPLE MEANS OF REPRESENTATION:

Facilitate English language learners' ability to talk to a partner by providing sentence starters:

- Silas spent ____ dollars. I know because ___.
- I need to find ___.
- I drew ___ to match the story.
- I used the ____ strategy to find how much money Deste has.

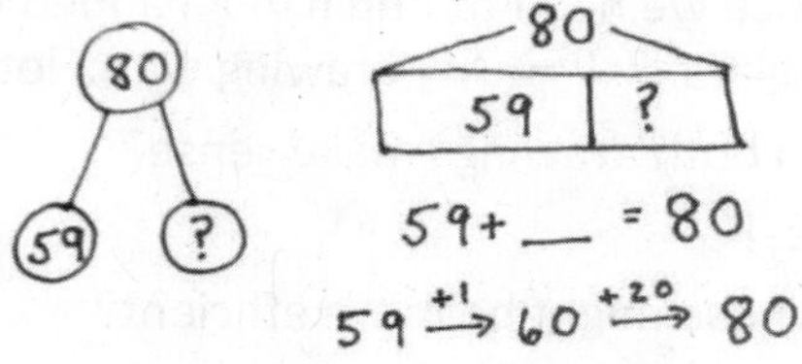

Part 3: Solve a *compare with smaller unknown* type problem.

Deste has 4 ten dollar bills and 6 five dollar bills. She has $25 dollars more than Kirsten. How much money does Kirsten have?

T: Let's read the problem together.

T/S: (Read aloud.)

T: What do we do after we have read?

S: Draw.

T: Great! Get going.

T: Look at your drawing. What are you trying to find? Turn and talk.

S: I'm trying to find out how much money Kirsten has. → I'm trying to find out Kirsten's total money. I know it's $25 less than Deste's.

T: Write a number sentence and a statement to match your work. (Pause to allow students time to work.) Explain to your partner how you solved and how your number sentence matches the story.

S: First, I skip-counted in my head by tens and fives to get Deste's total: 10, 20, 30, 40, 45, 50, ...70. → I knew that if Deste has $25 more, then Kirsten has $25 less. I subtracted 70 – 25. Then, I added 5 to both numbers and made it an easier problem. (See image below.) → I drew a tape diagram, but I wrote *? + 25 = 70*. I counted up 5 to 30 and then added on 40 more, so 45 dollars.

T: How much money does Kirsten have? Tell me in a statement.

S: Kirsten has 45 dollars.

T: The words *more* and *less* in a word problem can be tricky. Let's look back at the problem to be sure our drawing matches the story. (Point while working through the problem.)

T: How much money does Deste have?

S: 70 dollars.

T: Does our drawing show that?

S: Yes.

T: Who has more money?

S: Deste!

T: Does our drawing show that?

S: Yes!

T: How much more money does Deste have than Kristen?

S: $25.

T: Does our drawing show that?

S: Yes!

T: Explain to your partner how you know Deste has more than Kristen.

S: Deste has $70, and that's $25 more than $45. → Kirsten's total should be $25 less than Deste's total. $45 is $25 less than $70.

T: The tricky thing for me is that the problem says Deste has more, but we subtract to find the amount of money Kristen has!

D $70
K ? $25
70 – 25 = ?
75 – 30 = 45
Kirsten has 45 dollars.

Problem Set (10 minutes)

Students should do their personal best to complete the Problem Set within the allotted 10 minutes. For some classes, it may be appropriate to modify the assignment by specifying which problems they work on first. Some problems do not specify a method for solving. Students solve these problems using the RDW approach used for Application Problems.

Name Michelle Date

Solve.

1. Patrick has 1 ten-dollar bill, 2 five-dollar bills and 4 one-dollar bills. How much money does he have?

$24.

2. Susan has 2 five-dollar bills and 3 ten-dollar bills in her purse and 11 one-dollar bills in her pocket. How much money does she have in all?

$51

3. Raja has $60. He gave 1 twenty-dollar bill and 3 five-dollar bills to his cousin. How much money does Raja have left?

5 10 − 35 = $25

4. Michael has 4 ten-dollar bills and 7 five-dollar bills. He has 3 more ten-dollar bills, and 2 more five-dollar bills than Tamara. How much money does Tamara have?

75 − 40 = $35

5. Antonio had 4 ten-dollar bills, 5 five-dollar bills, and 16 one-dollar bills. He put $70 of that money in his bank account. How much money was not put in his bank account?

$81 − 70 = $11

6. Mrs. Clark has 8 five-dollar bills and 2 ten-dollar bills in her wallet. She has 1 twenty-dollar bill, and 12 one-dollar bills in her purse. How much more money does she have in her wallet than in her purse?

60 − 32

5 10 − 32 = $28

Student Debrief (10 minutes)

Lesson Objective: Solve word problems involving the total value of a group of bills.

The Student Debrief is intended to invite reflection and active processing of the total lesson experience.

Invite students to review their solutions for the Problem Set. They should check work by comparing answers with a partner before going over answers as a class. Look for misconceptions or misunderstandings that can be addressed in the Debrief. Guide students in a conversation to debrief the Problem Set and process the lesson.

You may choose to use any combination of the questions below to lead the discussion.

- Look at Problem 2 on your Problem Set. Talk to your partner about how you thought about the one dollar bills when figuring out how much money Susan had. Did you use what you know about place value to help you?
- What strategy did you use in Problem 4 to compare Michael and Tamara's money? (Number bond, tape diagram, pictures, equations.)
- Let's read Problem 6 together. When it asked how much more money is in her wallet than in her purse, did you think add or subtract? Talk to your partner. (Discuss comparison problems and how not to be tricked by the word *more*.)
- Let's read Problem 5 together. Talk to your partner. How did your drawing help you know what you were trying to find? (Without a drawing labeled with a question mark for the unknown, students might miss that they are finding what

Antonio did *not* put in his bank account.)

- Explain to your partner a good way to think about dollars when the problem asks you to count many different bills. How do your organize them so they are easier to count?

Exit Ticket (3 minutes)

After the Student Debrief, instruct students to complete the Exit Ticket. A review of their work will help you assess the students' understanding of the concepts that were presented in the lesson today and plan more effectively for future lessons. You may read the questions aloud to the students.

A # Correct _____

Add.

1	9 + 2 =		23	4 + 7 =	
2	9 + 3 =		24	4 + 8 =	
3	9 + 4 =		25	5 + 6 =	
4	9 + 7 =		26	5 + 7 =	
5	7 + 9 =		27	3 + 8 =	
6	10 + 1 =		28	3 + 9 =	
7	10 + 2 =		29	2 + 9 =	
8	10 + 3 =		30	5 + 10 =	
9	10 + 8 =		31	5 + 8 =	
10	8 + 10 =		32	9 + 6 =	
11	8 + 3 =		33	6 + 9 =	
12	8 + 4 =		34	7 + 6 =	
13	8 + 5 =		35	6 + 7 =	
14	8 + 9 =		36	8 + 6 =	
15	9 + 8 =		37	6 + 8 =	
16	7 + 4 =		38	8 + 7 =	
17	10 + 5 =		39	7 + 8 =	
18	6 + 5 =		40	6 + 6 =	
19	7 + 5 =		41	7 + 7 =	
20	9 + 5 =		42	8 + 8 =	
21	5 + 9 =		43	9 + 9 =	
22	10 + 6 =		44	4 + 9 =	

B Improvement _____ # Correct _____

Add.

1	10 + 1 =		23	5 + 6 =	
2	10 + 2 =		24	5 + 7 =	
3	10 + 3 =		25	4 + 7 =	
4	10 + 9 =		26	4 + 8 =	
5	9 + 10 =		27	4 + 10 =	
6	9 + 2 =		28	3 + 8 =	
7	9 + 3 =		29	3 + 9 =	
8	9 + 4 =		30	2 + 9 =	
9	9 + 8 =		31	5 + 8 =	
10	8 + 9 =		32	7 + 6 =	
11	8 + 3 =		33	6 + 7 =	
12	8 + 4 =		34	8 + 6 =	
13	8 + 5 =		35	6 + 8 =	
14	8 + 7 =		36	9 + 6 =	
15	7 + 8 =		37	6 + 9 =	
16	7 + 4 =		38	9 + 7 =	
17	10 + 4 =		39	7 + 9 =	
18	6 + 5 =		40	6 + 6 =	
19	7 + 5 =		41	7 + 7 =	
20	9 + 5 =		42	8 + 8 =	
21	5 + 9 =		43	9 + 9 =	
22	10 + 8 =		44	4 + 9 =	

Name ______________________________ Date ______________

Solve.

1. Patrick has 1 ten dollar bill, 2 five dollar bills, and 4 one dollar bills. How much money does he have?

2. Susan has 2 five dollar bills and 3 ten dollar bills in her purse, and 11 one dollar bills in her pocket. How much money does she have in all?

3. Raja has $60. He gave 1 twenty dollar bill and 3 five dollar bills to his cousin. How much money does Raja have left?

4. Michael has 4 ten dollar bills and 7 five dollar bills. He has 3 more ten dollar bills and 2 more five dollar bills than Tamara. How much money does Tamara have?

5. Antonio had 4 ten dollar bills, 5 five dollar bills, and 16 one dollar bills. He put $70 of that money in his bank account. How much money was not put in his bank account?

6. Mrs. Clark has 8 five dollar bills and 2 ten dollar bills in her wallet. She has 1 twenty dollar bill and 12 one dollar bills in her purse. How much more money does she have in her wallet than in her purse?

Name ______________________________ Date ______________

Solve.

1. Josh had 3 five dollar bills, 2 ten dollar bills, and 7 one dollar bills. He gave Suzy 1 five dollar bill and 2 one dollar bills. How much money does Josh have left?

2. Jeremy has 3 one dollar bills and 1 five dollar bill. Jessica has 2 ten dollar bills and 2 five dollar bills. Sam has 2 ten dollar bills and 4 five dollar bills. How much money do they have together?

Name ______________________________ Date ______________

Solve.

1. Mr. Chang has 4 ten dollar bills, 3 five dollar bills, and 6 one dollar bills. How much money does he have in all?

2. At her yard sale, Danielle got 1 twenty dollar bill and 5 one dollar bills last week. This week she got 3 ten dollar bills and 3 five dollar bills. What is the total amount she got for both weeks?

3. Patrick has 2 fewer ten dollar bills than Brenna. Patrick has $64. How much money does Brenna have?

4. On Saturday, Mary Jo received 5 ten dollar bills, 4 five dollar bills, and 17 one dollar bills. On Sunday, she received 4 ten dollar bills, 5 five dollar bills, and 15 one dollar bills. How much more money did Mary Jo receive on Saturday than on Sunday?

5. Alexis has $95. She has 2 more five dollar bills, 5 more one dollar bills, and 2 more ten dollar bills than Kasai. How much money does Kasai have?

6. Kate had 2 ten dollar bills, 6 five dollar bills, and 21 one dollar bills before she spent $45 on a new outfit. How much money was not spent?

Lesson 9

Objective: Solve word problems involving different combinations of coins with the same total value.

Suggested Lesson Structure

Fluency Practice	(10 minutes)
Application Problem	(7 minutes)
Concept Development	(33 minutes)
Student Debrief	(10 minutes)
Total Time	**(60 minutes)**

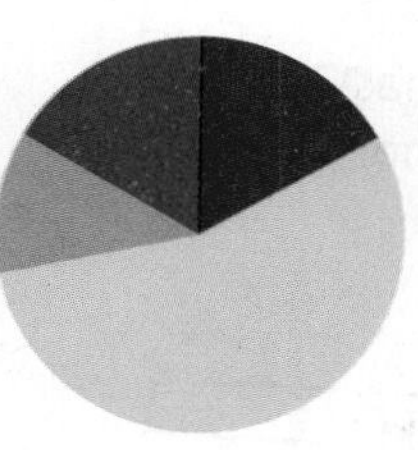

Fluency Practice (10 minutes)

- Grade 2 Core Fluency Differentiated Practice Sets **2.OA.2** (5 minutes)
- Decomposition Tree **2.NBT.5** (5 minutes)

Grade 2 Core Fluency Differentiated Practice Sets (5 minutes)

Materials: (S) Core Fluency Practice Sets from G2–M7–Lesson 1

Note: During G2–M7–Topic B and for the remainder of the year, each day's fluency includes an opportunity for review and mastery of the sums and differences with totals through 20 by means of the Core Fluency Practice Sets or Sprints. The process is detailed and Practice Sets are provided in G2–M7– Lesson 1.

Decomposition Tree (5 minutes)

Materials: (S) Decomposition Tree Template (from G2–M7–Lesson 6)

Note: Students are given 90 seconds to decompose a specified amount in as many ways as they can. This fluency allows students to work at their own skill level and decompose amounts in a multitude of ways in a short amount of time. When decomposing the number a second time, students are more likely to try other representations that they saw on their partner's paper.

T: (Distribute tree template.)

T: You are going to break apart 75¢ on your Deco Tree for 90 seconds. Do as many problems as you can. Go!

S: (Work for 90 seconds.)

T: Now exchange your tree with your partner and check each other's work carefully.

T: (Allow students 30–45 seconds check.) Return each other's papers. Did you see another way to make 75¢ on your partner's paper?

S: (Share for 30 seconds.)

T: Turn your paper over. Let's break apart 75¢ for another minute.

Application Problem (7 minutes)

Clark has 3 ten dollar bills and 6 five dollar bills. He has 2 more ten dollar bills and 2 more five dollar bills than Shannon. How much money does Shannon have?

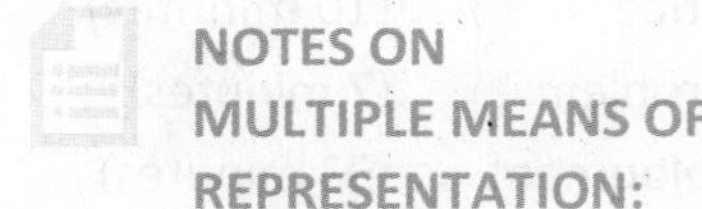

Comparison problems present a comprehension challenge to some students, including English Language Learners. These students will benefit from acting out the Application Problem first. They can then make connections through drawing and, finally, with a number sentence.

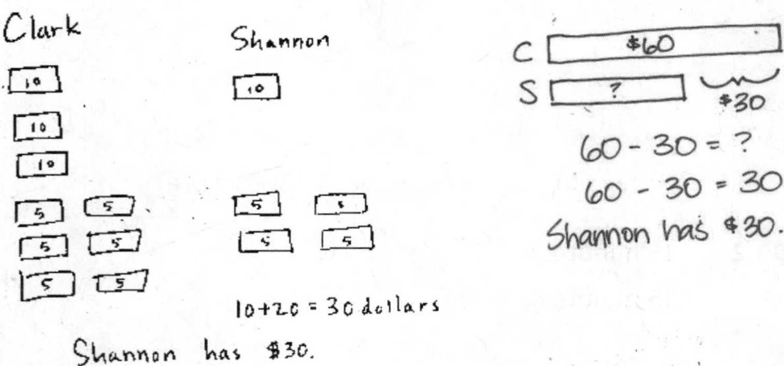

Note: Allow students who are able to work independently and offer guidance to students who need support.

Concept Development (33 minutes)

Materials: (T) 1 dime, 3 nickels, 5 pennies, 2 personal white boards (S) Personal white board, bag with the following coins: 4 quarters, 10 nickels, 10 dimes, 10 pennies

Assign partners before beginning instruction.

Part 1: Manipulate different combinations of coins to make the same total value.

T: (Show 1 dime and 5 pennies on one mat and 3 nickels on another mat.)

T: What is the value of the coins on this mat? (Point to the dime and pennies.)

S: 15 cents!

T: What is the value of the coins on this mat? (Point to the nickels.)

S: 15 cents!

T: So, the values are equal?

S: Yes!

T: How can that be? The coins are different!

S: That one is 10 cents and 5 more. The other is 5 + 5 + 5, so they are both 15 cents. → Three nickels is 15 cents. A dime and 5 pennies is also 15 cents.

T: Aha! So we used different coins to make the same value?

S: Yes!

T: Let's try that! I will say an amount and you work with your partner to show the amount in two different ways.

T: With your partner, show 28 cents two different ways.

S: (Arrange coins on their mats while discussing with their partners.)

T: How did you make 28 cents?

S: I used a quarter and 3 pennies. My partner used 2 dimes and 8 pennies. → I also used a quarter and 3 pennies, but my partner used 2 dimes, 1 nickel, and 3 pennies.

Repeat the above sequence with the following amounts: 56 cents, 75 cents, and 1 dollar.

Part 2: Manipulate different combinations of coins in the context of word problems.

Problem 1: Tony gets 83¢ change back from the cashier at the corner store. What coins might Tony have received?

T: Read the problem to me, everyone.

S: (Read chorally.)

T: Can you draw something?

S: Yes!

T: Do that. (Allow students time to work.)

T: How did you show Tony's change?

S: I drew 8 dimes and 3 pennies. → I made 50¢ using 2 quarters, then added 3 dimes to make 80¢, and then added 3 pennies to make 83¢. → I used 3 quarters, 1 nickel, and 3 pennies.

T: Write your coin combinations and the total value below your drawing. If you used 8 dimes and 3 pennies, write that underneath like this. (Model writing the coin combination with the total value on the board, e.g., 8 dimes, 3 pennies = 83 cents.)

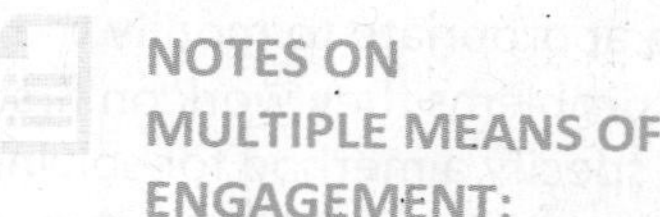

NOTES ON MULTIPLE MEANS OF ENGAGEMENT:

Challenge above grade level students to show you 83¢ two ways: using the least number of coins and using the greatest number of coins. Ask your students to explain how they came up with their solutions and how it is possible for both solutions to have the same value.

T: Now pretend that the cashier has run out of quarters. Draw Tony's change in another way without using quarters. Write your coin combination and total value below.

S: Mine still works! → I traded each of my quarters for 2 dimes and a nickel. Now I have 7 dimes, 2 nickels, and 3 pennies. → I didn't use a quarter before, but this time I used 6 dimes and 4 nickels instead of 7 dimes and 2 nickels to show 80 cents.

Problem 2: Carla has 4 dimes, 1 quarter, and 2 nickels to spend at the snack stand. Peyton has 3 coins, but he has the same amount of money to spend. What coins must Peyton have? How do you know?

T: Read the problem to me, everyone.

S: (Read chorally.)

T: Can you draw something?

S: Yes!

T: Time to draw! (Allow students time to work.)

T: What did you draw?

S: 4 dimes, 1 quarter, and 2 nickels. → A tape diagram with one part 40 cents, one part 25 cents, and one part 10 cents.

T: What is the value of Carla's money?

S: 75 cents.

MP.6 T: Show your partner how you found or can find three coins that make 75¢. (Allow time for sharing.) What coins did Peyton have?

S: 3 quarters.

T: How do you know?

S: We added 25 + 25 + 25 to make 75. → We couldn't make 75¢ with three coins if we used dimes, nickels, or pennies.

Problem Set (10 minutes)

Students should do their personal best to complete the Problem Set within the allotted 10 minutes. For some classes, it may be appropriate to modify the assignment by specifying which problems they work on first. Some problems do not specify a method for solving. Students solve these problems using the RDW approach used for Application Problems.

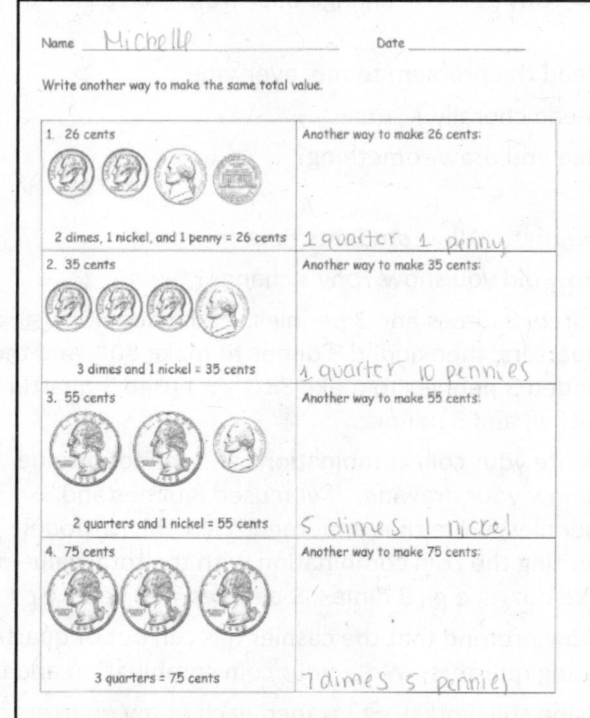

Name Michelle Date

Write another way to make the same total value.

1. 26 cents 2 dimes, 1 nickel, and 1 penny = 26 cents	Another way to make 26 cents: 1 quarter 1 penny
2. 35 cents 3 dimes and 1 nickel = 35 cents	Another way to make 35 cents: 1 quarter 10 pennies
3. 55 cents 2 quarters and 1 nickel = 55 cents	Another way to make 55 cents: 5 dimes 1 nickel
4. 75 cents 3 quarters = 75 cents	Another way to make 75 cents: 7 dimes 5 pennies

Student Debrief (10 minutes)

Lesson Objective: Solve word problems involving different combinations of coins with the same total value.

The Student Debrief is intended to invite reflection and active processing of the total lesson experience.

Invite students to review their solutions for the Problem Set. They should check work by comparing answers with a partner before going over answers as a class. Look for misconceptions or misunderstandings that can be addressed in the Debrief. Guide students in a conversation to debrief the Problem Set and process the lesson.

You may choose to use any combination of the questions below to lead the discussion.

- Look at your partner's coin combinations for 26 cents. Did you use the same combinations as your partner? Are there more combinations that you and your partner did not think of?

- Look at Problem 2, 35 cents. With your partner, think about how you could make 35 cents using the least number of coins. How could you make 35 cents using the largest number of coins?
- Can you think of other math skills we have learned where the same value can be represented in different ways?
- With your partner, find all the different coin combinations for 15 cents.

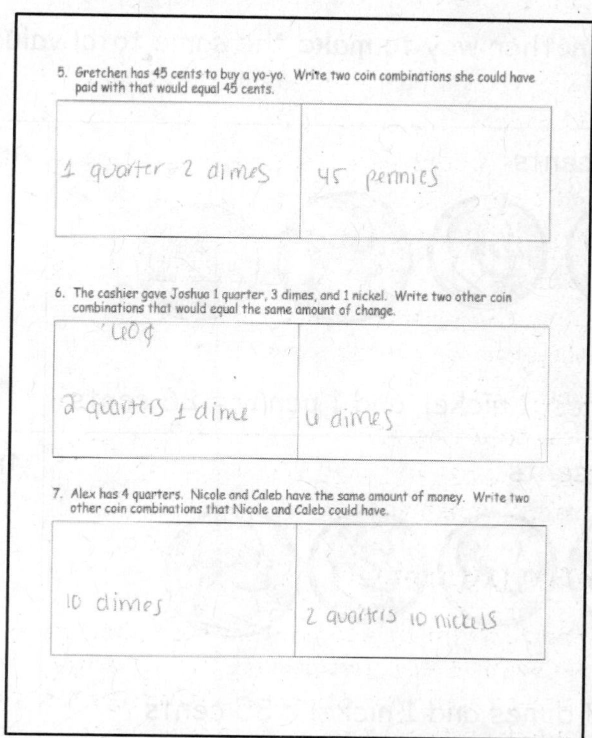

5. Gretchen has 45 cents to buy a yo-yo. Write two coin combinations she could have paid with that would equal 45 cents.

1 quarter 2 dimes	45 pennies

6. The cashier gave Joshua 1 quarter, 3 dimes, and 1 nickel. Write two other coin combinations that would equal the same amount of change.

60¢ 2 quarters 1 dime	6 dimes

7. Alex has 4 quarters. Nicole and Caleb have the same amount of money. Write two other coin combinations that Nicole and Caleb could have.

10 dimes	2 quarters 10 nickels

Exit Ticket (3 minutes)

After the Student Debrief, instruct students to complete the Exit Ticket. A review of their work will help you assess the students' understanding of the concepts that were presented in the lesson today and plan more effectively for future lessons. You may read the questions aloud to the students.

Name ______________________________ Date ______________

Write another way to make the same total value.

1. 26 cents     2 dimes, 1 nickel, and 1 penny = 26 cents	Another way to make 26 cents:
2. 35 cents    3 dimes and 1 nickel = 35 cents	Another way to make 35 cents:
3. 55 cents    2 quarters and 1 nickel = 55 cents	Another way to make 55 cents:
4. 75 cents    3 quarters = 75 cents	Another way to make 75 cents:

5. Gretchen has 45 cents to buy a yo-yo. Write two coin combinations she could have paid with that would equal 45 cents.

6. The cashier gave Joshua 1 quarter, 3 dimes, and 1 nickel. Write two other coin combinations that would equal the same amount of change.

7. Alex has 4 quarters. Nicole and Caleb have the same amount of money. Write two other coin combinations that Nicole and Caleb could have.

Name ______________________________ Date ______________

1. Smith has 88 pennies in his piggy bank. Write two other coin combinations he could have that would equal the same amount.

Name ________________________ Date ____________

Draw coins to show another way to make the same total value.

1. 25 cents    1 dime and 3 nickels = 25 cents	Another way to make 25 cents:
2. 40 cents    4 dimes = 40 cents	Another way to make 40 cents:
3. 60 cents    2 quarters and 1 nickel = 60 cents	Another way to make 60 cents:
4. 80 cents    3 quarters and 1 nickel = 80 cents	Another way to make 80 cents:

5. Samantha has 67 cents in her pocket. Write two coin combinations she could have that would equal the same amount.

6. The store clerk gave Jeremy 2 quarters, 3 nickels, and 4 pennies. Write two other coin combinations that would equal the same amount of change.

7. Chelsea has 10 dimes. Write two other coin combinations she could have that would equal the same amount.

Lesson 10

Objective: Use the fewest number of coins to make a given value.

Suggested Lesson Structure

Fluency Practice	(10 minutes)
Application Problem	(6 minutes)
Concept Development	(34 minutes)
Student Debrief	(10 minutes)
Total Time	**(60 minutes)**

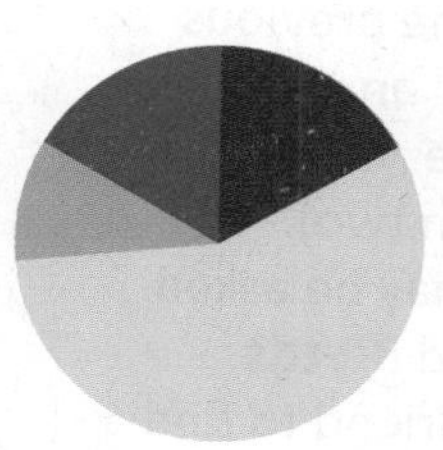

Fluency Practice (10 minutes)

- Grade 2 Core Fluency Differentiated Practice sets **2.OA.2** (5 minutes)
- Decomposition Tree **2.NBT.5** (5 minutes)

Grade 2 Core Fluency Differentiated Practice Sets (5 minutes)

Materials: (S) Core Fluency Practice Sets from G2–M7–Lesson 1

Note: During G2–M7–Topic B and for the remainder of the year, each day's fluency includes an opportunity for review and mastery of the sums and differences with totals through 20 by means of the Core Fluency Practice Sets or Sprints. The process is detailed and Practice Sets are provided in G2–M7–Lesson 1.

Decomposition Tree (5 minutes)

Materials: (S) Decomposition Tree Template (from G2–M7–Lesson 6)

Note: Today, students decompose 95 cents, applying their work from earlier in the topic.

T: (Distribute tree template.)

T: You are going to break apart 95¢ on your Deco Tree for 90 seconds. Do as many problems as you can. Go!

S: (Work for 90 seconds.)

T: Now exchange your tree with your partner and check each other's work. (Allow students 30–45 seconds to check.)

T: Return each other's papers. Did you see another way to make 95¢ on your partner's paper? (Allow students to share for another 30 seconds.)

T: Turn your paper over. Let's break apart 95¢ for another minute.

Application Problem (6 minutes)

Andrew, Brett, and Jay all have 1 dollar in change in their pockets. They each have a different combination of coins. What coins might each boy have in his pocket?

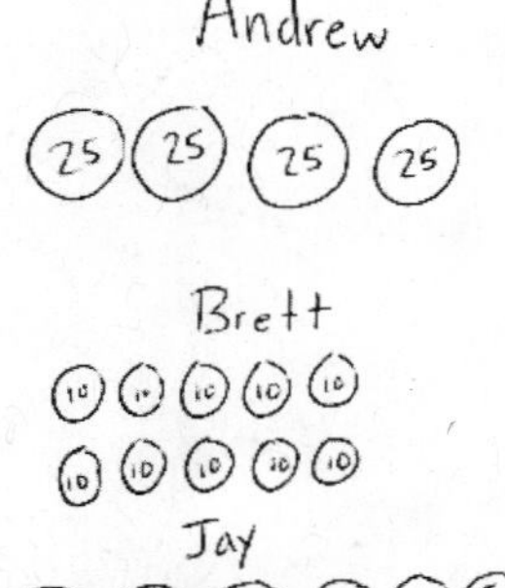

Note: This Application Problem provides practice from the previous day's lesson and includes an extension (showing three combinations rather than two). To differentiate, students may be asked only to show Andrew and Brett's coins and then talk to a friend to find a different combination that could be Jay's.

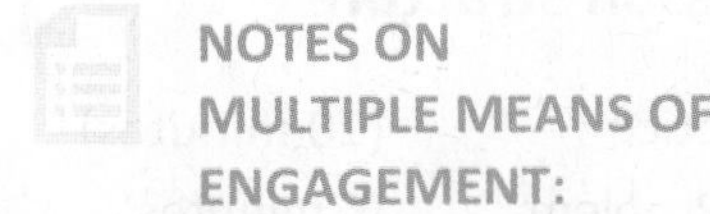

NOTES ON MULTIPLE MEANS OF ENGAGEMENT:

Scaffold the Application Problem for students with disabilities and those who are working below grade level by providing them with coins.

Concept Development (34 minutes)

Materials: (S) Personal white board, small plastic bag with 4 quarters, 10 dimes, 10 nickels, and 10 pennies

Assign partners.

Part 1: Find the fewest number of coins.

T: With your partner, show 50 cents in two ways.

S: (Arrange coins on work mats.)

T: Turn and talk with a partner group near you: How did you make 50 cents?

S: I counted 5 dimes 10, 20, 30, 40, 50. → I used 2 quarters. 25 + 25 = 50. → I used 1 quarter and 5 nickels.

T: If you were giving someone 50 cents, which combination of coins do you think they would rather have?

S: Probably 2 quarters because it's easy to hold. → Two quarters are easier to carry because they're only 2 coins.

T: It is easier if we carry fewer coins, so when we give someone change we try to give the fewest coins possible.

T: With your partner, show 40 cents with as few coins as possible.

S: (Arrange coins on work mats.)

T: How did you make 40 cents?

S: I used 4 dimes. → I used 1 quarter and 3 nickels. → I used 1 quarter, 1 dime, and 1 nickel.

T: Which way uses the fewest coins?

S: 1 quarter, 1 dime, and 1 nickel.

T: What strategies did you use to determine the fewest number of coins?

S: I didn't use pennies. → I used a dime instead of 2 nickels. → I tried to use a quarter because it is worth the most.

T: Yes, to use the fewest coins we want to use coins with the greatest possible value.

Part 2: Use the fewest coins by changing coins for higher value coins.

T: This time, everyone count out 35 cents using 3 dimes and 1 nickel.

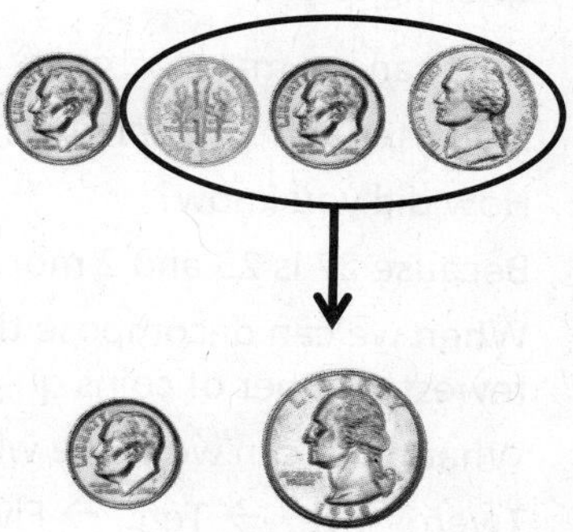

S: (Count change.)

T: How many coins do you have?

S: 4!

T: Can we exchange to have fewer coins?

S: Yes!

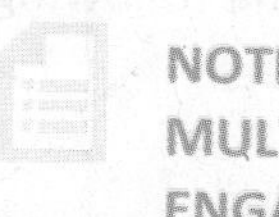

T: Tell your partner: What coins can you exchange so you have fewer coins?

S: 2 dimes and 1 nickel for 1 quarter!

T: Do that!

S: (Exchange coins.)

T: And how many coins do you have on your mat?

S: 2!

T: That is a lot fewer! Can we make any other exchange?

S: No!

T: Now, everyone count out 60 cents using 4 dimes and 4 nickels.

S: (Count change.)

T: How many coins do you have?

S: 8!

T: Look at your coins. Tell your partner any way you can exchange for a coin with a greater value.

S: I can change these 4 nickels for 2 dimes. → I can change 2 dimes and 1 nickel for 1 quarter. → I have 60 cents; if I put one dime aside I can switch the rest for 2 quarters.

T: Yes. Any time we have 50 cents we can use 2 quarters!

T: How can we change our coins for two quarters?

S: Change 4 dimes and 2 nickels for 2 quarters. → Change 4 nickels and 3 dimes for 2 quarters.

T: Make the change.

T: Now how many coins do you have now?

NOTES ON MULTIPLE MEANS OF ENGAGEMENT:

English language learners will benefit throughout the lesson from having sentence starters to help them talk with a partner:

- I changed (exchanged) ____ for ____.
- I added five cents more by using ____.
- I made 30 cents by using ____.

S: 3!

T: Can we exchange any more coins?

S: No!

T: That means we have shown our value with the fewest number of coins possible.

Part 3: Exploring to use the fewest number of coins for a given total.

T: How can we make 27 cents using the fewest number of coins possible?

S: 1 quarter and 2 pennies.

T: How did you know?

S: Because 27 is 25 and 2 more. → A quarter is very close to 27 cents.

T: When we can decompose the total into parts we know are coins with a greater value, we can get the fewest number of coins quickly!

T: What parts can we make with coins of higher value?

S: Twenty-five. → Ten. → Five.

MP.2

T: Let's try another. With your partner, show 60 cents with the fewest number of coins possible by decomposing 60 into as many twenty-fives as you can, and then tens, and then fives.

S: (Make 60 cents.)

T: How did you decompose 60 to show it in coins?

S: I know that 60 is 50 + 10 and 50 is 2 quarters. → I know that 60 is 30 + 30, so I made 2 thirties with a quarter and a nickel each. Then I switched the 2 nickels for a dime!

T: What is another way we could have made 60 cents? Turn and talk.

S: Six dimes because 10, 20, 30, 40, 50, 60. → Two quarters and 2 nickels because 30 + 30 is 60.

Repeat the above process with the following sequence: 43 cents, 80 cents, and 1 dollar.

Problem Set (10 minutes)

Students should do their personal best to complete the Problem Set within the allotted 10 minutes. For some classes, it may be appropriate to modify the assignment by specifying which problems they work on first. Some problems do not specify a method for solving. Students solve these problems using the RDW approach used for Application Problems.

Student Debrief (10 minutes)

Lesson Objective: Use the fewest number of coins to make a given value.

The Student Debrief is intended to invite reflection and active processing of the total lesson experience.

Invite students to review their solutions for the Problem Set. They should check work by comparing answers with a partner before going over answers as a class. Look for misconceptions or misunderstandings that can be addressed in the Debrief. Guide students in a conversation to debrief the Problem Set and process the lesson.

You may choose to use any combination of the questions below to lead the discussion.

- Compare your Problem Set with your partner's. What coin was always included when showing an amount with the fewest coins? Why did this happen?
- Yesterday, when we showed the same amount in different ways, did you always use the same coins as your partner? (No, there were lots of combinations.) Why did this happen?
- When you want to use the fewest possible coins, what is a good strategy to use?
- Look at Problem 8 on your Problem Set. Talk to your partner about how you thought about 56 cents to figure out how to make it with the least number of coins possible.
- Can you think of why you would want to use the fewest number of coins possible? (Because it is more convenient to carry and count. Because it is more efficient.)

Name Michelle Date

1. Kayla showed 30 cents two ways. Circle the way that uses the fewest coins.

A. B.

What two coins from A were changed for one coin in B?

2 nickels into 1 dime

2. Show 20¢ two ways. Use the fewest possible coins on the right below.

	Fewest coins
4 nickels	2 dimes

3. Show 35¢ two ways. Use the fewest possible coins on the right below.

	Fewest coins
3 dimes 1 nickel	1 quarter 1 dime

4. Show 46¢ two ways. Use the fewest possible coins on the right below.

	Fewest coins
4 dimes 1 nickel 1 penny	1 quarter 2 dimes 1 penny

5. Show 73¢ two ways. Use the fewest possible coins on the right below.

	Fewest coins
7 dimes 3 pennies	2 quarters 2 dimes 3 pennies

6. Show 85¢ two ways. Use the fewest possible coins on the right below.

	Fewest coins
2 quarters 3 dimes 1 nickel	3 quarters 1 dime

7. Kayla gave three ways to make 56¢. Circle the correct ways to make 56¢ and star the way that uses the fewest coins.

a. 2 quarters and 6 pennies
b. 5 dimes, 1 nickel, and 1 penny
c. 4 dimes, 2 nickels, and 1 penny

8. Write a way to make 56¢ that uses the fewest possible amount of coins.

2 quarters 1 nickel 1 penny

Exit Ticket (3 minutes)

After the Student Debrief, instruct students to complete the Exit Ticket. A review of their work will help you assess the students' understanding of the concepts that were presented in the lesson today and plan more effectively for future lessons. You may read the questions aloud to the students.

Name ______________________________ Date ____________

1. Kayla showed 30 cents two ways. Circle the way that uses the fewest coins.

a.	b.

What two coins from (a) were changed for one coin in (b)?

____

2. Show 20¢ two ways. Use the fewest possible coins on the right below.

	Fewest coins:

3. Show 35¢ two ways. Use the fewest possible coins on the right below.

	Fewest coins:

4. Show 46¢ two ways. Use the fewest possible coins on the right below.

	Fewest coins:

5. Show 73¢ two ways. Use the fewest possible coins on the right below.

	Fewest coins:

6. Show 85¢ two ways. Use the fewest possible coins on the right below.

	Fewest coins:

7. Kayla gave three ways to make 56¢. Circle the correct ways to make 56¢, and star the way that uses the fewest coins.
   a. 2 quarters and 6 pennies
   b. 5 dimes, 1 nickel, and 1 penny
   c. 4 dimes, 2 nickels, and 1 penny

8. Write a way to make 56¢ that uses the fewest possible amount of coins.

Name ______________________________ Date ______________

1. Show 36 cents two ways. Use the fewest possible coins on the right below.

	Fewest coins:

2. Show 74 cents two ways. Use the fewest possible coins on the right below.

	Fewest coins:

Name ______________________________ Date ______________

1. Tara showed 30 cents two ways. Circle the way that uses the fewest coins.

a.	b.

What coins from (a) were changed for one coin in (b)?

____

2. Show 40¢ two ways. Use the fewest possible coins on the right below.

	Fewest coins:

3. Show 55¢ two ways. Use the fewest possible coins on the right below.

	Fewest coins:

4. Show 66¢ two ways. Use the fewest possible coins on the right below.

	Fewest coins:

5. Show 80¢ two ways. Use the fewest possible coins on the right below.

	Fewest coins:

6. Show $1 two ways. Use the fewest possible coins on the right below.

	Fewest coins:

7. Tara made a mistake when asked for two ways to show 91¢. Circle her mistake, and explain what she did wrong.

	Fewest coins:
3 quarters, 1 dime, 1 nickel, 1 penny	9 dimes, 1 penny

____

____

____

Lesson 11

Objective: Use different strategies to make $1 or make change from $1.

Suggested Lesson Structure

- Fluency Practice (12 minutes)
- Application Problem (6 minutes)
- Concept Development (32 minutes)
- Student Debrief (10 minutes)

Total Time (60 minutes)

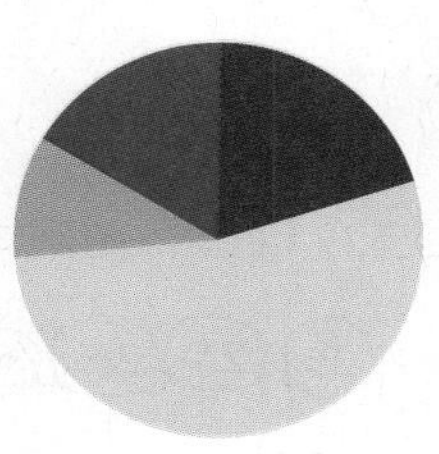

Fluency Practice (12 minutes)

- Sprint: Subtraction from Teens **2.OA.2** (9 minutes)
- Coin Exchange **2.NBT.5** (3 minutes)

Sprint: Subtraction from Teens (9 minutes)

Materials: (S) Subtraction from Teens Sprint

Note: Students practice subtraction from teens in order to gain mastery of the sums and differences within 20.

Coin Exchange (3 minutes)

Materials: (S) Personal white boards

Note: In this activity, students review G2–M7–Lesson 10 by exchanging change combinations for the fewest coins.

T: I have 2 dimes and a nickel. How much do I have?
S: 25 cents.
T: On your boards, show me at least one more way to make the same amount.
T: (Allow students time to work.) Show me your boards. (Review their boards.)
T: Which way uses the fewest coins?
S: 1 quarter.
T: I have 4 dimes and 2 nickels. How much do I have?
S: 50 cents.
T: On your boards, show me at least one more way to

make the same amount.

T: Which way uses the fewest coins?

S: 2 quarters.

Continue with the following possible sequence: 7 nickels, 6 dimes, 7 nickels, and 2 dimes.

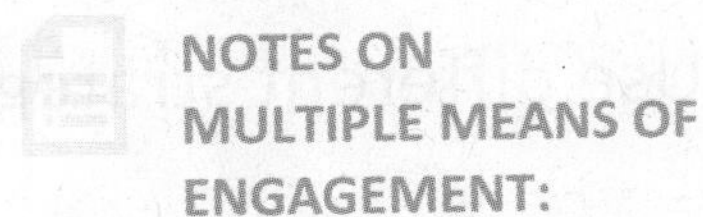

NOTES ON MULTIPLE MEANS OF ENGAGEMENT:

Scaffold the Application Problem for English language learners by giving them coins. They can use the manipulatives to solve and share their solution.

Application Problem (6 minutes)

Tracy has 85 cents in her change purse. She has 4 coins. Which coins are they?

How much more money will Tracy need if she wants to buy a bouncy ball for $1?

Note: The purpose of this Application Problem is twofold. First, it reviews the concept of representing a quantity using the fewest number of coins. Second, it serves as a bridge to today's lesson about making change from $1.

(25) (25) (25) (10)

25 + 25 + 25 + 10 = 85¢ Tracy has 3 quarters and 1 dime.

50 + 25 + 10

85 + ___ = 100 Tracy needs 15¢.

85 →(+5) 90 →(+10) 100

Concept Development (32 minutes)

Materials: (T) Various coins, dollar bill, sealed envelope with a quarter, nickel, and 4 pennies (S) Personal white boards

Part 1: Make a dollar from a given amount.

T: I have 35 cents in my hand. (Show 1 quarter and 1 dime.)

T: How much more do I need to have 100 cents or a dollar? Talk to your partner.

S: You can add a nickel, which will be 40 cents. Then, add another dime, to make 50, and then add 2 quarters, because that's another 50. → You can add 5 to make a ten, then add on 60. So, you need 65 cents more. → You can subtract 35 from a hundred. 100 – 30 is 70, 70 – 5 is 65.

T: I can write a number sentence like this: 35¢ + _____ = 100¢. Then, I can solve by counting up by coins (as shown at right).

T: So, 35 cents plus what equals 100 cents?

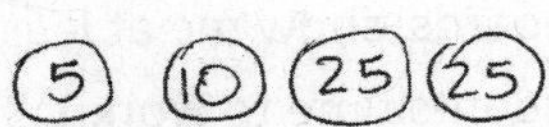

5¢ + 10¢ + 50¢ = 65¢

S: 65 cents!

T: Can I also write a number sentence like this? (Write 35 + _____ = 100 on the board.)

S: Yes, 100 cents is just shown as the number 100. → We know that we are talking about cents. → One dollar can be the whole, too. → We're counting up to a dollar. That is the same as 100 cents or just a hundred.

T: (Hold up a dollar bill.) I have a dollar in my hand in **change**. What do you know about change?

S: It's the money you get back at the store. → If you buy something and it costs less than what you give the cashier, you get change. → If you buy a something for 50 cents, but you only have a dollar, you'll get change.

T: Yes. The cashier takes your money and keeps the part to pay for your things. She gives you back the part that is left over. The left over money is your change.

T: Now that you know about change, let's solve a problem where we make change from a dollar.

T: I'll give Student A 28 cents (count out a quarter and 3 pennies). On your personal boards, write a number sentence to represent how much I have left. For now, let's represent $1 as either 100 or 100 cents so that all our units are the same. (Pause.)

T: Show me.

S: (Show 100¢ – 28¢ = _____. → 28¢ + ______ = 100¢. → 100 – 28 = _____. → 100 cents – 28 cents = _____.)

T: Which of your suggestions uses addition to find the missing part?

S: 28¢ + ______ = 100¢.

T: Solve using the arrow way to add on or count up (as shown on right). Then, share your work with a partner.

$28 \xrightarrow{+2} 30 \xrightarrow{+20} 50 \xrightarrow{+50} 100$

T: How much will I have left?

$100 - 28 = \boxed{72}$

S: 72 cents!

T: Yes! Let's check this by counting up. Start with 28 cents. Let's add the dimes, then the pennies: 38, 48, 58, 68, 78, 88, 98, 99, 100. What do we have now?

S: A dollar!

T: Let's try some more problems with making change from a dollar.

Part 2: Make change from a dollar.

T: I'm holding some coins in my hand. (Hide 83 cents in hand.)

T: Student B has 1 dime, 1 nickel, and 2 pennies in her hand. What is the value of her coins?

S: 17 cents.

T: Together, we have $1. Talk to your partner. How much money is hiding in my hand? Use part–whole language as you talk.

S: I know that one part is hiding and the other part is 17¢. → I know that $1 is the whole. → I know that if 17¢ is one part, I can add another part to make $1.

T: On your personal boards, draw a number bond to show what you know. (See figure to the right.)

T: We agree that the whole is $1, and one part is 17¢. Now, write an equation from the number bond. (Provide work time.) Show me.

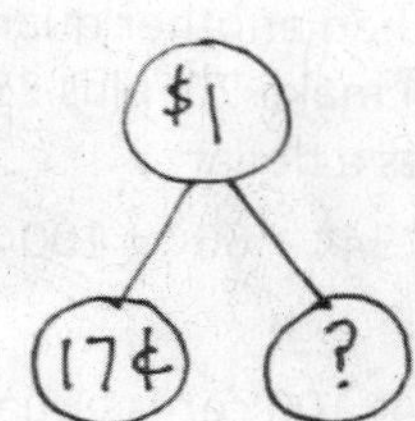

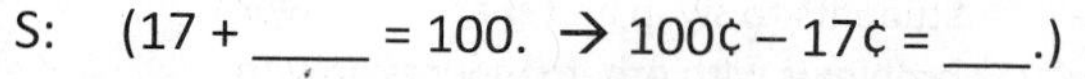
S: (17 + _____ = 100. → 100¢ – 17¢ = ____.)

T: Let's see if you were right! (Open hand for students to count coins.) I'm holding 3 dimes, 2 quarters, 3 pennies. Draw it on your boards, find the total, and circle your answer. (Provide work time.) Show me.

S: (Show 83 cents.)

T: If I had a dollar, and I wanted to buy something that cost 83 cents, how much change should I receive?

S: 17 cents!

T: Turn and talk. What coins would I probably get?

S: A dime, a nickel, and 2 pennies. → Three nickels and 2 pennies.

T: Let's try another situation. Yesterday, I had $1 in coins, and then I spent some on some candy. The cashier gave me 66¢ in change. (Count on with 2 quarters, 1 dime, 1 nickel, 1 penny.) How much did I spend?

T: Can you draw something?

S: Yes!

T: Do that.

T: (Provide work time.) Turn and talk: Look at your drawing. What are you trying to find?

S: We need to find out how much the candy cost. → We have the whole and a part. We need to find the missing part.

T: Write a number sentence and statement to match your work. (Pause while students work.) Explain to your partner how you solved.

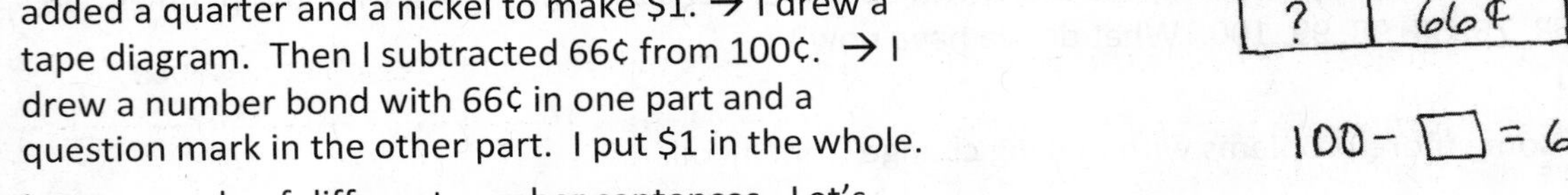

S: I drew 66¢. Then I added 4 pennies to make 70. Then I added a quarter and a nickel to make $1. → I drew a tape diagram. Then I subtracted 66¢ from 100¢. → I drew a number bond with 66¢ in one part and a question mark in the other part. I put $1 in the whole.

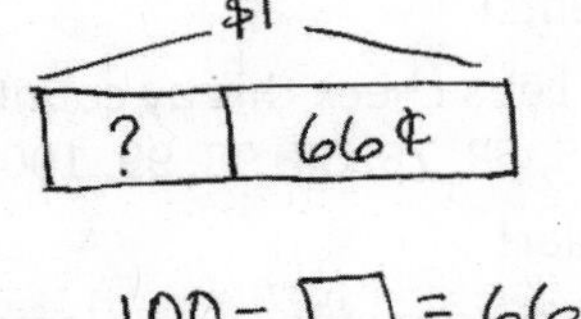

T: I see a couple of different number sentences. Let's share them.

S: 100 – ____ = 66. → 66¢ + ____ = 100¢. → 100 cents – 66 cents = ____ cents. → ____ + 66 cents = 1 dollar.

T: So, the answer is...?

S: 34 cents!

T: These are the coins the cashier kept. (Show a quarter, a nickel, and 4 pennies.) Turn and talk. Count up from 66 to see if together they make a dollar.

S: Sixty-six plus 4 makes 70, and then a nickel makes 75, and then another quarter makes a dollar. → Sixty-six and 4 make 70, plus 25 is 95, and then another nickel makes a dollar.

T: Does 34¢ + 66¢ = 100¢?

S: Yes!

T: And, is 100 cents equal to a dollar?

S: Yes!

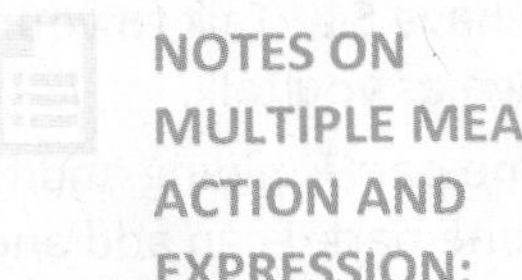

NOTES ON MULTIPLE MEANS OF ACTION AND EXPRESSION:

Challenge students who are performing above grade level to write their own word problems to contextualize the numbers and operations in the lesson. Encourage students to swap and share their word problems with other students or with the class.

T: I think you're ready to work through a few problems with a partner.

Part 3: Choose your own strategy to solve.

Instruct partners to solve the following problems on their personal boards:

- 100 – 45 = ____
- 100¢ – 29¢ = ____
- ____ + 72 cents = 100 cents

Then, instruct students to explain their solution strategies to a partner. Circulate and listen in on student conversations to check for understanding. Then, invite students to complete the Problem Set independently.

Problem Set (10 minutes)

Students should do their personal best to complete the Problem Set within the allotted 10 minutes. For some classes, it may be appropriate to modify the assignment by specifying which problems they work on first. Some problems do not specify a method for solving. Students solve these problems using the RDW approach used for Application Problems.

Student Debrief (10 minutes)

Lesson Objective: Use different strategies to make $1 or make change from $1.

The Student Debrief is intended to invite reflection and active processing of the total lesson experience.

Invite students to review their solutions for the Problem Set. They should check work by comparing answers with a partner before going over answers as a class. Look for misconceptions or misunderstandings that can be addressed in the Debrief. Guide students in a conversation to debrief the Problem Set and process the lesson.

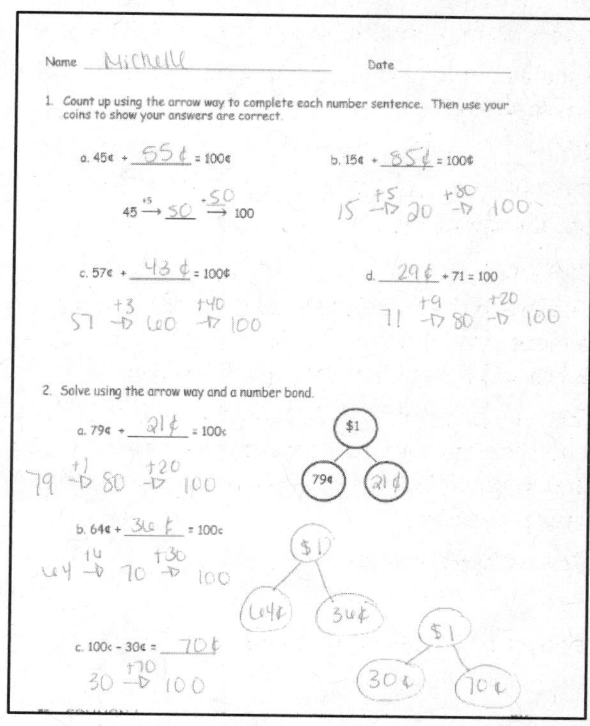

You may choose to use any combination of the questions below to lead the discussion.

- Look at your Problem Set and compare your coin choices with your partner's when you solved each problem the arrow way. Did you make the same coin choices as your partner? Is one of your ways easier to get to $1?
- When we are using the arrow way, are friendly numbers important? Show your partner one problem on your Problem Set where you used a friendly number.

- Look at the second page of the Problem Set. Explain to your partner the strategy you used to figure out the two parts that made $1.
- Look at the second page of the Problem Set. Point to where you see the $1 in each money equation. Use part–whole language to tell your partner about each part of the money equation.
- Explain to your partner how you would think about the two parts that make a dollar as an addition problem. How would you think about it as a subtraction problem?

3. Solve.

a. 67¢ + 33¢ = 100¢
33 →(+7) 40 →(+60) 100
($1 → ? and 33¢)

b. 100¢ − 55¢ = 45¢
55 →(+5) 60 →(+40) 100
($1 → 55¢ and 45¢)

c. 100¢ − 28¢ = 72¢
28 →(+2) 30 →(+70) 100
($1 → 72¢ and 28¢)

d. 100¢ − 43¢ = 57¢
43 →(+7) 50 →(+50) 100
($1 → 57¢ and 43¢)

e. 100¢ − 19¢ = 81¢
19 →(+1) 20 →(+80) 100
($1 → 81¢ and 19¢)

Exit Ticket (3 minutes)

After the Student Debrief, instruct students to complete the Exit Ticket. A review of their work will help you assess the students' understanding of the concepts that were presented in the lesson today and plan more effectively for future lessons. You may read the questions aloud to the students.

A # Correct ______

Subtract.

1	11 - 10 =		23	19 - 9 =	
2	12 - 10 =		24	15 - 6 =	
3	13 - 10 =		25	15 - 7 =	
4	19 - 10 =		26	15 - 9 =	
5	11 - 1 =		27	20 - 10 =	
6	12 - 2 =		28	14 - 5 =	
7	13 - 3 =		29	14 - 6 =	
8	17 - 7 =		30	14 - 7 =	
9	11 - 2 =		31	14 - 9 =	
10	11 - 3 =		32	15 - 5 =	
11	11 - 4 =		33	17 - 8 =	
12	11 - 8 =		34	17 - 9 =	
13	18 - 8 =		35	18 - 8 =	
14	13 - 4 =		36	16 - 7 =	
15	13 - 5 =		37	16 - 8 =	
16	13 - 6 =		38	16 - 9 =	
17	13 - 8 =		39	17 - 10 =	
18	16 - 6 =		40	12 - 8 =	
19	12 - 3 =		41	18 - 9 =	
20	12 - 4 =		42	11 - 9 =	
21	12 - 5 =		43	15 - 8 =	
22	12 - 9 =		44	13 - 7 =	

B Improvement _____ # Correct _____

Subtract.

1	11 - 1 =		23	16 - 6 =	
2	12 - 2 =		24	14 - 5 =	
3	13 - 3 =		25	14 - 6 =	
4	18 - 8 =		26	14 - 7 =	
5	11 - 10 =		27	14 - 9 =	
6	12 - 10 =		28	20 - 10 =	
7	13 - 10 =		29	15 - 6 =	
8	18 - 10 =		30	15 - 7 =	
9	11 - 2 =		31	15 - 9 =	
10	11 - 3 =		32	14 - 4 =	
11	11 - 4 =		33	16 - 7 =	
12	11 - 7 =		34	16 - 8 =	
13	19 - 9 =		35	16 - 9 =	
14	12 - 3 =		36	20 - 10 =	
15	12 - 4 =		37	17 - 8 =	
16	12 - 5 =		38	17 - 9 =	
17	12 - 8 =		39	16 - 10 =	
18	17 - 7 =		40	18 - 9 =	
19	13 - 4 =		41	12 - 9 =	
20	13 - 5 =		42	13 - 7 =	
21	13 - 6 =		43	11 - 8 =	
22	13 - 9 =		44	15 - 8 =	

Name ______________________________ Date ______________

1. Count up using the arrow way to complete each number sentence. Then use your coins to show your answers are correct.

a. 45¢ + ________ = 100¢

45 $\xrightarrow{+5}$ ____ $\xrightarrow{+\_\_\_}$ 100

b. 15¢ + ________ = 100¢

c. 57¢ + ________ = 100¢

d. ________ + 71 = 100

2. Solve using the arrow way and a number bond.

a. 79¢ + ________ = 100¢

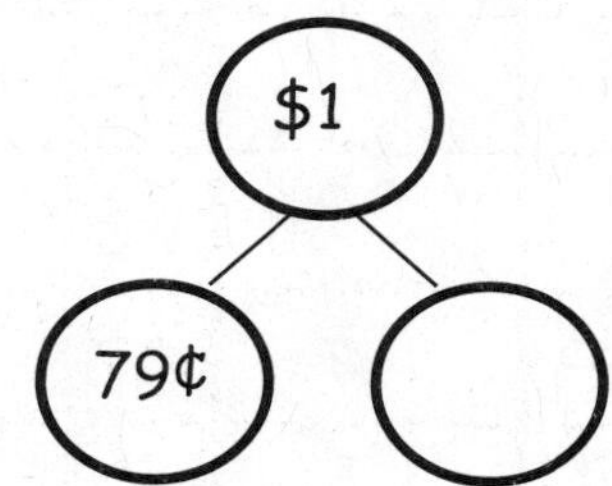

b. 64¢ + ________ = 100¢

c. 100¢ - 30¢ = ________

3. Solve.

a. ________ + 33¢ = 100¢

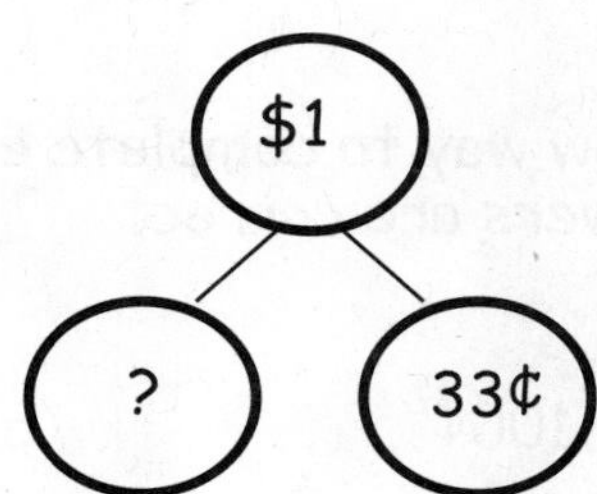

b. 100¢ - 55¢ = ________

c. 100¢ - 28¢ = ________

d. 100¢ - 43¢ = ________

e. 100¢ - 19¢ = ____________

Name ______________________________ Date ________________

Solve.

1. 100¢ - 46¢ = ________

2. ________ + 64¢ = 100¢

3. ________ + 13 cents = 100 cents

Name ______________________________ Date ______________

1. Count up using the arrow way to complete each number sentence. Then use coins to check your answers, if possible.

a. 25¢ + ________ = 100¢

b. 45¢ + ________ = 100¢

$25 \xrightarrow{+5}$ ____ $\xrightarrow{+\_\_\_}$ 100

c. 62¢ + ________ = 100¢

d. ________ + 79 = 100

2. Solve using the arrow way and a number bond.

a. 19¢ + ________ = 100¢

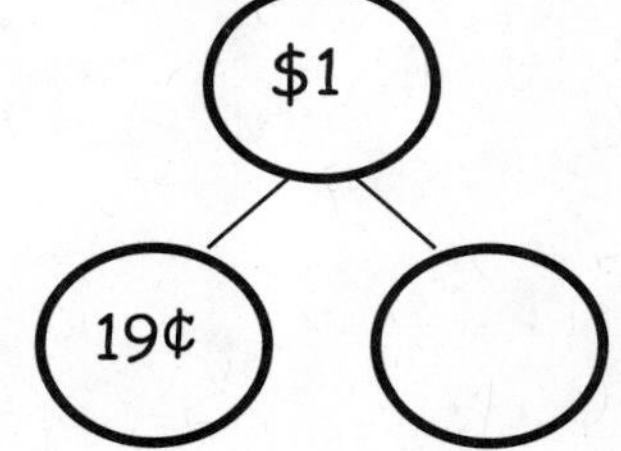

b. 77¢ + ________ = 100¢

c. 100 – 53 = ________

3. Solve.

a. ________ + 38¢ = 100¢

b. 100¢ - 65¢ = ________

c. 100 - 41 = ________

d. 100¢ - 27¢ = ________

e. 100¢ - 14¢ = ________

Lesson 12

Objective: Solve word problems involving different ways to make change from $1.

Suggested Lesson Structure

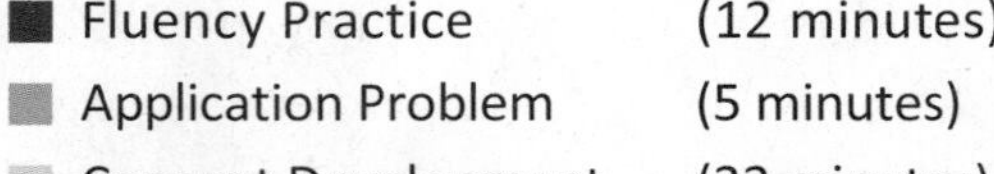

- Fluency Practice (12 minutes)
- Application Problem (5 minutes)
- Concept Development (33 minutes)
- Student Debrief (10 minutes)

Total Time (60 minutes)

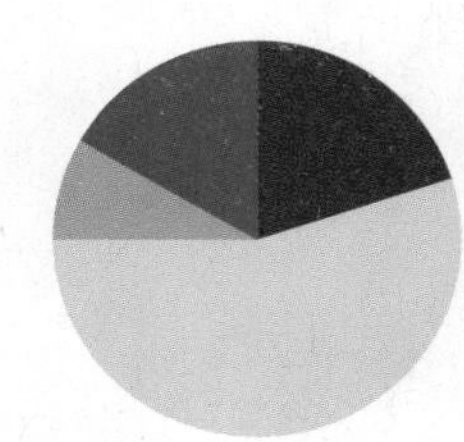

Fluency Practice (12 minutes)

- Sprint: Adding Across a Ten **2.OA.2** (9 minutes)
- Making $1 **2.NBT.5** (3 minutes)

Sprint: Adding Across a Ten (9 minutes)

Materials: (S) Adding Across a Ten Sprint

Note: This Sprint gives practice with the grade level fluency of adding within 20.

Making $1 (3 minutes)

Note: Students review making $1 by counting up with *change unknown* problems as review of previous lesson concepts.

T: (Post 45 cents + ______ = 100 cents.) Read the problem. How many cents are in $1?
S: 100 cents.
T: I have 45 cents. What is the next ten cents I can make?
S: 50 cents.
T: 45 cents needs how much more to make 50 cents?
S: 5 cents.
T: 50 cents need how much more to make 100 cents?
S: 50 cents.
T: 45 cents and what make 1 dollar?
S: 55 cents.

Continue with the following possible sequence: 28 cents, 73 cents, and 14 cents.

NOTES ON MULTIPLE MEANS OF ENGAGEMENT:

Scaffold the Application Problem for students with disabilities and those who are still having difficulties with part–whole relationships by providing a number bond template and helping them fill it out: "Is 24 cents a part or the whole? How many pennies equal $1?"

Application Problem (5 minutes)

T: We can write 100 cents as $1 in our number sentence.

Richie has 24 cents. How much more money does he need to make $1?

Note: This *add to with change unknown* type problem serves as a bridge from yesterday's lesson, where students used simplifying strategies to make change from $1 but always represented the dollar as 100 cents within number sentences. Use this problem as a chance to introduce that students may write $1 – 24¢ = ___ or 24¢ + ___ = $1.

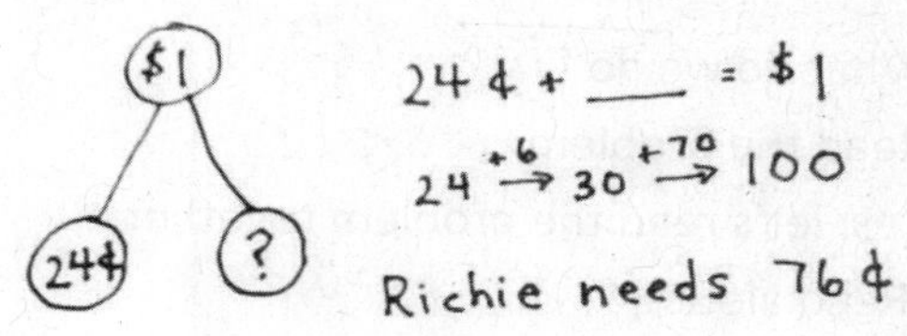

Concept Development (33 minutes)

Materials: (T) Chart with problem-solving steps (S) Personal white boards

Part 1: Solve a *take from with result unknown* type problem.

Shay buys a balloon for 57 cents. She hands the cashier 1 dollar. How much change will she receive?

T: What do we do first?

S: Read the problem.

T: Yes, let's read the problem together.

T/S: (Read aloud.)

T: I'll give you a minute to draw quietly. When I give the signal, talk to your partner about how your drawing (as shown) matches the story. (Signal.)

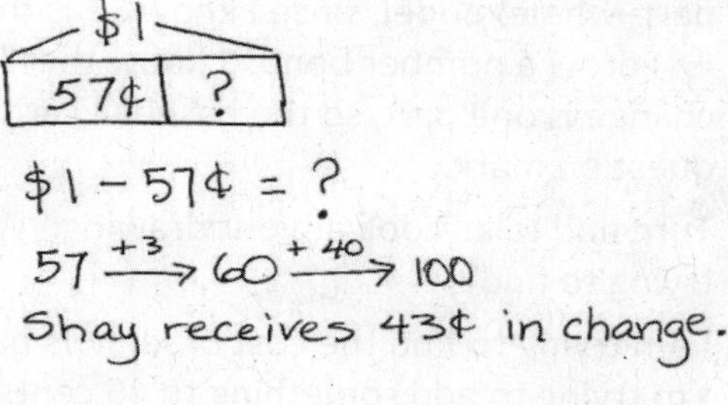

S: Since 57 cents is part of 1 dollar, I drew a number bond. (See figure at right). → I drew a tape diagram with the total and a part. The question mark will be for the change.

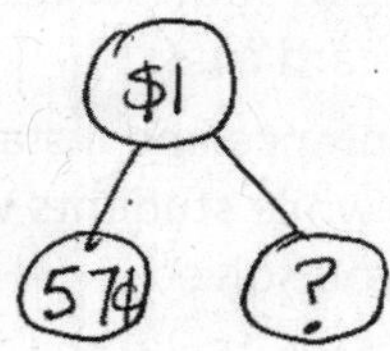

T: Look at your drawing. What are you trying to find?

S: I am trying to find out how much change Shay will get back.

T: Go ahead and do that. Write a number sentence and statement to match your work. (Pause while students work.) Explain to your partner how you solved the problem.

S: I thought of the related addition: 57¢ + ____ = $1. Then, I used the arrow way to count on. (See figure above). → I wrote 100 – 57 = ____. I took away 1 from both numbers to make it easier to

solve without renaming, so 99 – 56 = 43.

T: What's the statement of your solution?

S: Shay receives 43 cents in change.

T: Reread the problem to yourself. Does your answer make sense? How do you know?

S: Yes, because if I add the cost of the balloon and the change, I get 100 cents. → My answer makes sense, because 57 + 43 = 100. 57¢ + 43¢ = $1. I wrote it our new way we learned today and it's true because a dollar is the same as 100 cents.

T: That's right! I think you're ready for a challenge. Here we go....

Part 2: Solve a *take from with change unknown* type problem.

Jamie buys a baseball card. He gives the cashier 1 dollar. Jamie gets 2 dimes, 1 quarter, and 1 penny in change. How much did Jamie's baseball card cost?

T: What do we do first?

S: Read the problem.

T: Yes, let's read the problem together.

T/S: (Read aloud.)

T: I'll give you a minute to draw quietly. When I give the signal, talk to your partner about how your drawing matches the story. (See figure at right.)

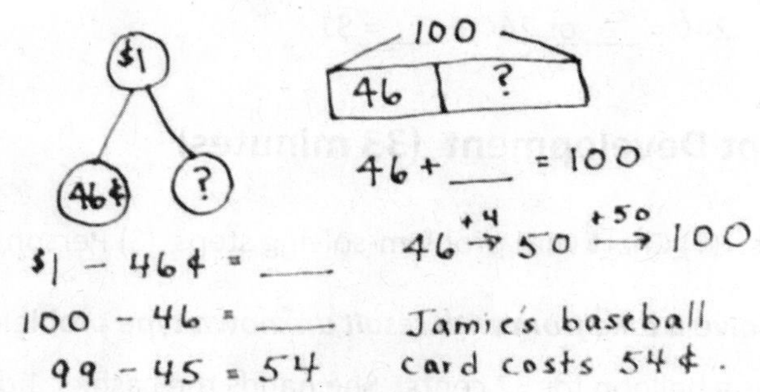

T: I drew Jamie's change: 2 dimes, 1 quarter, and 1 penny. (See figure at right.) → I drew a part–whole model, since I know $1 is the total. → I drew a number bond. I know that Jamie's change is one part, so the baseball card is the question mark.

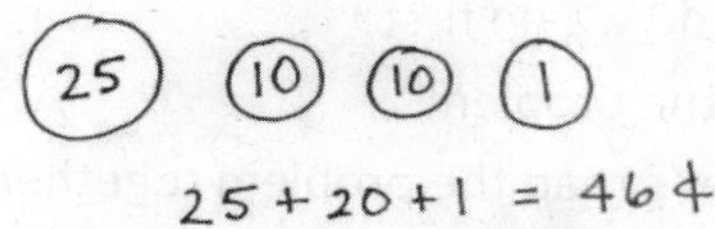

T: Turn and talk: Look at your drawing. What are you trying to find?

MP.1

S: I am trying to find the cost of Jamie's baseball card. → I'm trying to add something to 46 cents to make one dollar. → I'm trying to subtract from $1 to find how much the baseball card costs.

T: Write a number sentence and a statement to match your work. (Pause while students work.) Explain to your partner how you solved.

S: First, I added, 25 + 10 = 35. 35 + 10 = 45, plus 1 more equals 46. → I added the quarter, then the two dimes, and then the penny. I wrote 25 + 20 + 1 = 46. 25 + 20 is 45; then 1 more is 46. → After I added, I subtracted 100 – 46, to get the other part. I took one away from both numbers to make it a simpler problem, so 99 – 45 = 54. → I thought of addition: 46 + ____ = 100. Then,

NOTES ON MULTIPLE MEANS OF EXPRESSION:

Support your English language learners' language growth as well as their mathematical learning by using their background knowledge. For instance, for native Spanish speakers, connect the English words *quarter, part, and whole* with the Spanish *cuarto, parte, and todo.*

MP.1

I used the arrow way to count on.

T: What's the statement of your solution?

T: Jamie's baseball card costs 54 cents.

T: Reread the problem to yourself. Does your answer make sense? How do you know?

S: Yes, because if I add Jamie's change to the cost of the baseball card it equals $1. → My answer makes sense, because 46¢ + 54¢ = $1.

T: Yes! Now, work through this next one, and discuss it with a partner.

Part 3: Solve a multi-step *take from with result unknown* type problem.

Penelope wants to buy a toy whistle that costs $1. She has 15 pennies, 2 nickels, 2 dimes, and 1 quarter. How much more money does Penelope need to buy the whistle?

Bonus: If Penelope's brother gives her the rest of the money to buy the whistle, what different combinations of coins might he give her?

T: Follow these steps with your partner. (Read and post steps.)

- Read the problem.
- Draw a picture or model.
- Write a number sentence and statement to match your work.
- Reread the problem. Check to see if your answer makes sense.

T: (Circulate and provide support as needed.)

T: So, how much more money does Penelope need to buy the whistle? Make a statement.

S: Penelope needs 30 more cents to buy the whistle.

T: I saw you working hard on that bonus question. Which combinations of coins might Penelope's brother give her?

S: 1 quarter and 1 nickel. → 3 dimes. → 10 pennies and 2 dimes.

T: Nice work! Off to the Problem Set.

Problem Set (10 minutes)

Students should do their personal best to complete the Problem Set within the allotted 10 minutes. For some classes, it may be appropriate to modify the assignment by specifying which problems they work on first. Some problems do not specify a method for solving. Students solve these problems using the RDW approach used for Application Problems.

Student Debrief (10 minutes)

Lesson Objective: Solve word problems involving different ways to make change from $1.

The Student Debrief is intended to invite reflection and active processing of the total lesson experience.

Invite students to review their solutions for the Problem Set. They should check work by comparing answers with a partner before going over answers as a class. Look for misconceptions or misunderstandings that can be addressed in the Debrief. Guide students in a conversation to debrief the Problem Set and process the lesson.

You may choose to use any combination of the questions below to lead the discussion.

- What is another way we can think about $1? (As 100¢.)
- Look at your Problem Set. In each problem there are cents and 1 dollar. Talk to your partner about how these units are the same. How are these units different?
- Look at Problem 2, where Abby is buying a banana. (Write $1 – 35¢ = ___ on the board.) Did anyone use a subtraction sentence like this one with their model? Talk to your partner about why we can take 35 cents away from 1 dollar.
- When you think about trading $1 for 100¢ does it remind you about what you know about place value and changing units in a place value chart?
- Look at Problem 5 on the Problem Set. How many problems did you have to solve to find the answer?

Name Michelle Date

Solve using the arrow way, a number bond, or a tape diagram.

1. Jeremy had 80 cents. How much more money does he need to have $1?

80 +20→ 100 20¢

2. Abby bought a banana for 35 cents. She gave the cashier $1. How much change did she receive?

35 +5→ 40 +60→ 100 65¢

3. Joseph spent 75 cents of his dollar at the arcade. How much money does he have left?

$1; 75¢, 25¢ 25¢

4. The notepad Elise wants costs $1. She has 4 dimes and 3 nickels. How much more money does she need to buy the notepad?

55 +5→ 60 +40→ 100 45¢

5. Dane saved 26 cents on Friday and 35 cents on Monday. How much more money will he need to save to have saved $1?

35 + 26 = 61; $1; 61, 39

6. Daniel had exactly $1 in change. He lost 6 dimes and 3 pennies. What coins might he have left?

63¢; $1

37¢

He could have 1 quarter, 1 dime, and 2 pennies.

Exit Ticket (3 minutes)

After the Student Debrief, instruct students to complete the Exit Ticket. A review of their work will help you assess the students' understanding of the concepts that were presented in the lesson today and plan more effectively for future lessons. You may read the questions aloud to the students.

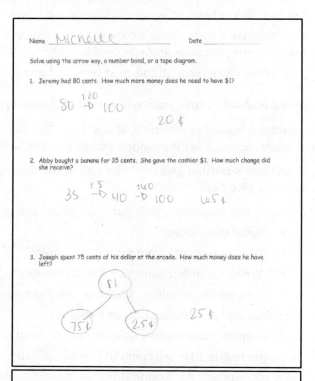

A # Correct ______

Add.

1	9 + 2 =		23	4 + 7 =	
2	9 + 3 =		24	4 + 8 =	
3	9 + 4 =		25	5 + 6 =	
4	9 + 7 =		26	5 + 7 =	
5	7 + 9 =		27	3 + 8 =	
6	10 + 1 =		28	3 + 9 =	
7	10 + 2 =		29	2 + 9 =	
8	10 + 3 =		30	5 + 10 =	
9	10 + 8 =		31	5 + 8 =	
10	8 + 10 =		32	9 + 6 =	
11	8 + 3 =		33	6 + 9 =	
12	8 + 4 =		34	7 + 6 =	
13	8 + 5 =		35	6 + 7 =	
14	8 + 9 =		36	8 + 6 =	
15	9 + 8 =		37	6 + 8 =	
16	7 + 4 =		38	8 + 7 =	
17	10 + 5 =		39	7 + 8 =	
18	6 + 5 =		40	6 + 6 =	
19	7 + 5 =		41	7 + 7 =	
20	9 + 5 =		42	8 + 8 =	
21	5 + 9 =		43	9 + 9 =	
22	10 + 6 =		44	4 + 9 =	

B Improvement _____ # Correct _____

Add.

1	10 + 1 =		23	5 + 6 =	
2	10 + 2 =		24	5 + 7 =	
3	10 + 3 =		25	4 + 7 =	
4	10 + 9 =		26	4 + 8 =	
5	9 + 10 =		27	4 + 10 =	
6	9 + 2 =		28	3 + 8 =	
7	9 + 3 =		29	3 + 9 =	
8	9 + 4 =		30	2 + 9 =	
9	9 + 8 =		31	5 + 8 =	
10	8 + 9 =		32	7 + 6 =	
11	8 + 3 =		33	6 + 7 =	
12	8 + 4 =		34	8 + 6 =	
13	8 + 5 =		35	6 + 8 =	
14	8 + 7 =		36	9 + 6 =	
15	7 + 8 =		37	6 + 9 =	
16	7 + 4 =		38	9 + 7 =	
17	10 + 4 =		39	7 + 9 =	
18	6 + 5 =		40	6 + 6 =	
19	7 + 5 =		41	7 + 7 =	
20	9 + 5 =		42	8 + 8 =	
21	5 + 9 =		43	9 + 9 =	
22	10 + 8 =		44	4 + 9 =	

Name ______________________________ Date ______________

Solve using the arrow way, a number bond, or a tape diagram.

1. Jeremy had 80 cents. How much more money does he need to have $1?

2. Abby bought a banana for 35 cents. She gave the cashier $1. How much change did she receive?

3. Joseph spent 75 cents of his dollar at the arcade. How much money does he have left?

4. The notepad Elise wants costs $1. She has 4 dimes and 3 nickels. How much more money does she need to buy the notepad?

5. Dane saved 26 cents on Friday and 35 cents on Monday. How much more money will he need to save to have saved $1?

6. Daniel had exactly $1 in change. He lost 6 dimes and 3 pennies. What coins might he have left?

Name ____________________________ Date ______________

Solve using the arrow way, a number bond, or a tape diagram.

1. Jacob bought a piece of gum for 26 cents and a newspaper for 61 cents. He gave the cashier $1. How much money did he get back?

Name ______________________________ Date ______________

Solve using the arrow way, a number bond, or a tape diagram.

1. Kevin had 100 cents. He spent 3 dimes, 3 nickels, and 4 pennies on a balloon. How much money does he have left?

2. Colin bought a post card for 45 cents. He gave the cashier $1. How much change did he receive?

3. Eileen spent 75 cents of her dollar at the market. How much money does she have left?

4. The puzzle Casey wants costs $1. She has 6 nickels, 1 dime, and 11 pennies. How much more money does she need to buy the puzzle?

5. Garret found 19 cents in the sofa and 34 cents under his bed. How much more money will he need to find to have $1?

6. Kelly has 38 fewer cents than Molly. Molly has $1. How much money does Kelly have?

7. Mario has 41 more cents than Ryan. Mario has $1. How much money does Ryan have?

Lesson 13

Objective: Solve two-step word problems involving dollars or cents with totals within $100 or $1.

Suggested Lesson Structure

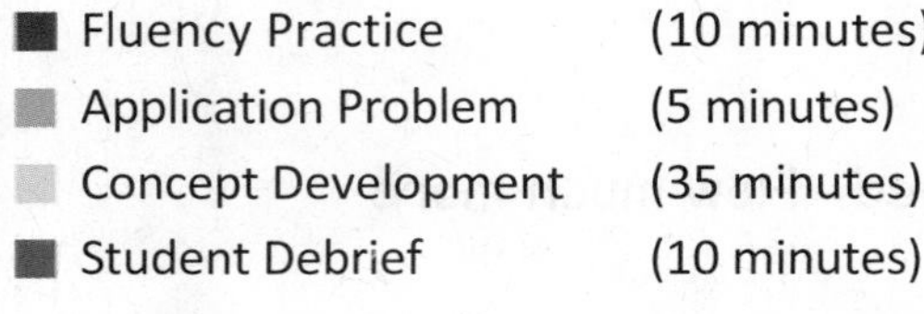

■ Fluency Practice	(10 minutes)
■ Application Problem	(5 minutes)
■ Concept Development	(35 minutes)
■ Student Debrief	(10 minutes)
Total Time	**(60 minutes)**

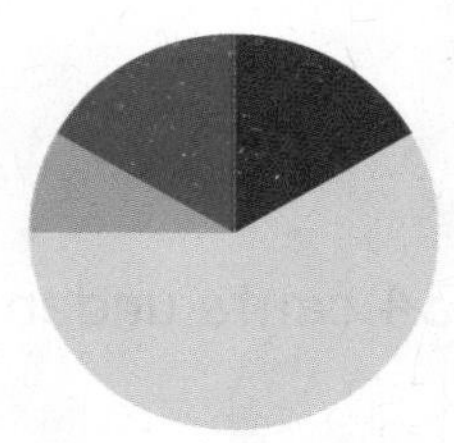

Fluency Practice (10 minutes)

- Grade 2 Core Fluency Differentiated Practice sheets **2.OA.2** (5 minutes)
- Decomposition Tree **2.NBT.5** (5 minutes)

Grade 2 Core Fluency Differentiated Practice Sets (5 minutes)

Materials: (S) Core Fluency Practice Sets from G2–M7–Lesson 1

Note: During G2–M7–Topic B and for the remainder of the year, each day's fluency includes an opportunity for review and mastery of the sums and differences with totals through 20 by means of the Core Fluency Practice Sets or Sprints. The process is detailed and Practice Sets are provided in G2–M7–Lesson 1.

Decomposition Tree (5 minutes)

Materials: (S) Decomposition Tree Template

Note: Students are given 90 seconds to decompose a dollar.

T: (Distribute tree template.)

T: You are going to break apart $1 on your Deco Tree for 90 seconds. Do as many problems as you can. Go!

S: (Work for 90 seconds.)

T: Now exchange your tree with your partner and check each other's work. (Allow students 30–45 seconds to check.)

T: Return each other's papers. Did you see another way to make $1 on your partner's paper? (Allow students to share for another 30 seconds.)

T: Turn your paper over. Let's break apart $1 for another minute.

Application Problem (5 minutes)

Dante had some money in a jar. He puts 8 nickels into the jar. Now he has 100 cents. How much money was in the jar at first?

Note: In this *add to with start unknown* problem, students must pay close attention to the question, as they may incorrectly jump to the conclusion that they should subtract 100 – 8. Ask questions that guide students towards seeing that 100 cents equals 20 nickels, or guide them towards calculating the value of 8 nickels, and subtracting that from 100.

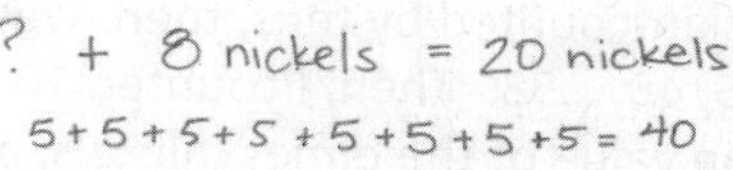

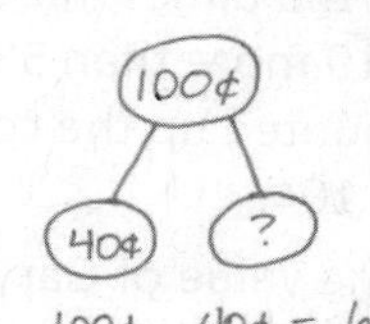

100¢ – 40¢ = 60¢

Dante had 60¢ at first.

NOTES ON MULTIPLE MEANS OF ACTION AND EXPRESSION:

Support students with disabilities and those who are performing below grade level by talking them through the Application Problem one step at a time: "How much money did Dante put in the jar? How much does he have now? Are nickels and cents the same unit? Can we add or subtract different units? What can we do to make them the same unit so that we can solve the problem?" And, if necessary, "What is the value of 8 nickels?"

Concept Development (35 minutes)

Materials: (T) Document camera (if available)
(S) Personal white boards

Part 1: Solve an *add to with change unknown* type problem.

Gary has 2 dimes, 5 nickels, and 13 pennies. His brother gives him one more coin. Now he has 68 cents. What coin did his brother give him?

T: What do we do first when we see a word problem?

S: Read it.

T: Yes, let's read the problem together.

T/S: (Read aloud.)

T: What can you draw?

S: Gary's coins. → We can draw 2 dimes, 5 nickels, 13 pennies, and a question mark coin. → A tape diagram.

T: Great! Do it. (Pause while students draw.)

T: Turn and talk: Look at your drawing. What are you trying to find?

S: The value of the coin Gary's brother gave him. → We need to find the value of the question mark coin.

T: Go ahead and do that. Write a number sentence and statement to match your work. (Allow students time to work.) Explain to your partner how you solved the problem.

S: I skip-counted by tens, then fives, then ones: 10, 20, 25, 30, 35, 40, 45, 46, ...58. Then, I counted 10 more to get to 68. → First, I found the value of the dimes, nickels, and pennies. 20 + 25 + 13 = 58. I know 68 is 10 more than 58, so the coin is a dime. → First, I counted up the coins I know and got 58¢. 68¢ – 58¢ = 10¢.

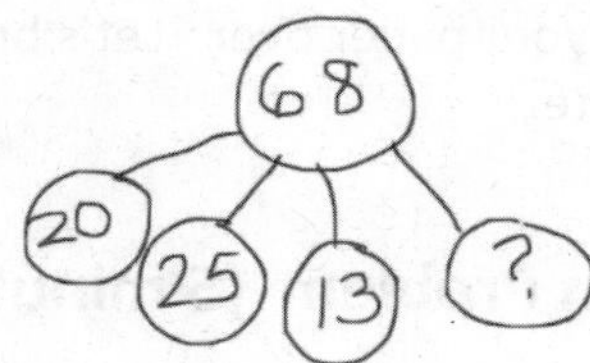

T: What was the value of Gary's money before his brother gave him a coin?

S: 58¢.

T: What's your number sentence?

S: 58¢ + ___ = 68¢. → 68¢ – 58¢ = 10¢.

T: And, what is the statement of your solution?

S: Gary's brother gave him a dime.

T: Yes! Look how we can also represent this problem with a number bond (pictured above to the right).

T: Turn and talk. Use part–whole language to describe how your drawing matches mine.

S: My tape diagram shows two parts and a whole. → Your diagram shows each coin as a different part. That's how I added to find the value of Gary's coins.

T: Great work! Let's do another one.

NOTES ON MULTIPLE MEANS OF ACTION AND EXPRESSION:

At times, students can discuss what they will draw before drawing. At other times, they might go ahead and draw. Use professional judgment to adapt to varying circumstances.

Part 2: Solve a two-step problem.

Hailey bought a pretzel stick for a dime and a nickel. She also bought a juice box for 18 cents more than the pretzel stick. How much did she spend on the pretzel and juice box?

T: What do we do first when we see a word problem?

S: Read it.

T: Yes, let's read the problem together.

T/S: (Read aloud.)

T: What can you draw?

S: The juice box and pretzel stick. → I'm going to write how much they cost, too. → A tape diagram for both.

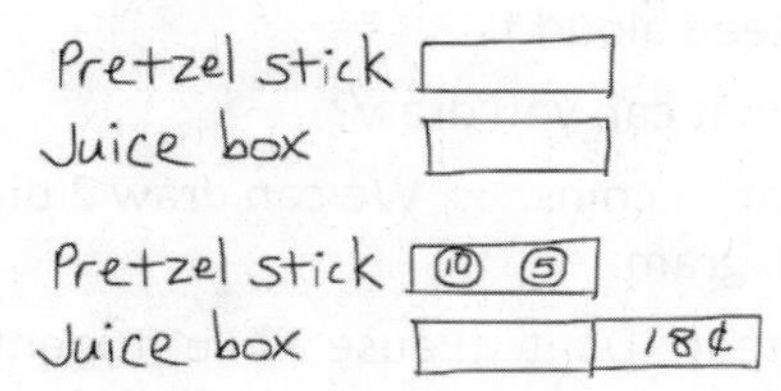

T: Go ahead and draw. (Pause while students draw.)

T: Turn and talk: Look at your drawing. What are you trying to find?

S: How much Hailey spent on the pretzel and juice box. → First, you need to know how much the juice box cost.

T: Go ahead and do that. Write a number sentence and statement to match your work. (Allow students time to work.) Explain to your partner how you solved.

S: I made two tape diagrams that were the same size. Then, I made the juice box tape diagram longer to show the extra 18¢. → I added 15¢ + 18¢ = 33¢ to find out the cost of the juice box. → To find the total, I added 30 + 10 + 3 + 5 = 48.

T: How much did the juice box cost?

S: 33 cents!

T: What's your number sentence to find the total?

S: 15¢ + 33¢ = 48¢.

T: And, what is the statement of your solution?

S: Hailey spent 48¢ on the pretzel and juice.

T: Terrific! Let's work on one more problem together.

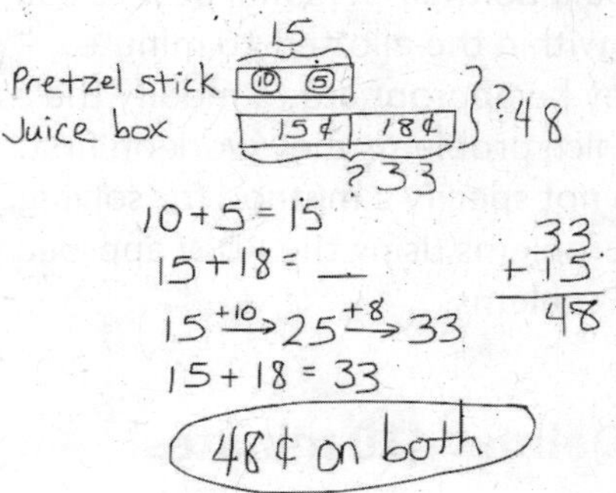

Part 3: Solve a *take from with start unknown* type problem.

Wendell bought a game at the store for $16. He had 2 five dollar bills and 4 one dollar bills left over. How much money did he have before buying the game?

T: Read the problem to me, everyone.

S: (Read chorally.)

T: Can you draw something?

S: Yes!

T: Do that. (Provide work time.)

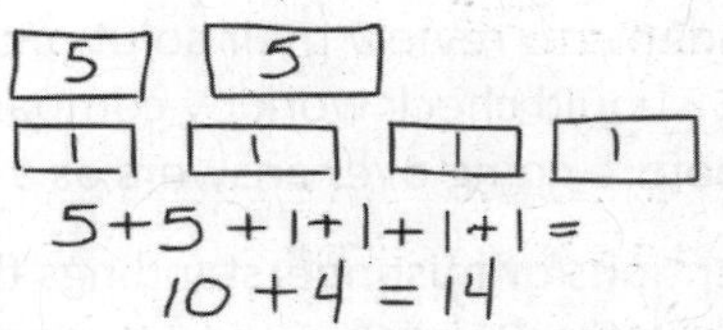

T: Turn and talk: Look at your drawing. What are you trying to find?

S: The amount of money he had before he bought the game. → We need to find the value of his change to know.

T: Go ahead and do that. Write a number sentence and statement to match your work. (Allow students time to work.) Explain to your partner how you solved.

S: First, I drew Wendell's bills and counted by fives and ones. He got $14 in change. → I drew a number bond. The cost of the game is one part and the change is the other part. I made 16 + 14 into 10 + 10 + 6 + 4. That's 3 tens, or 30. → I added $16 + $10 + $4 = $30.

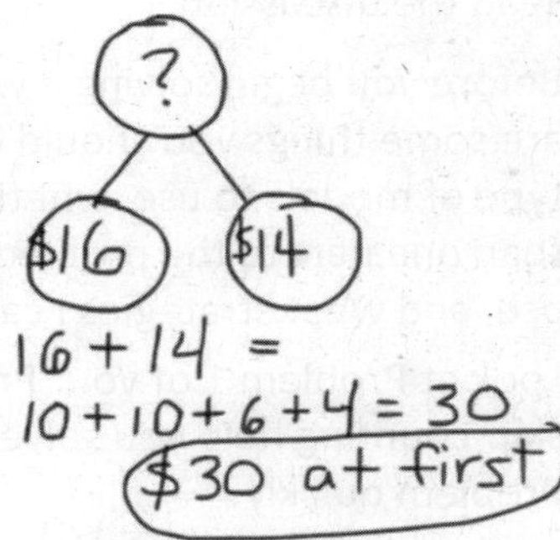

T: What was the value of Wendell's change?

S: $14.

T: What's your number sentence?

S: $16 + $14 = $30.

T: And, what is the statement of your solution?

S: Wendell had $30 at first.

T: Great. You're now ready to work on the Problem Set. Remember the strategies we have been practicing.

Problem Set (10 minutes)

Students should do their personal best to complete the Problem Set within the allotted 10 minutes. For some classes, it may be appropriate to modify the assignment by specifying which problems they work on first. Some problems do not specify a method for solving. Students solve these problems using the RDW approach used for Application Problems.

Name Michelle Date

Solve with a tape diagram and number sentence.

1. Josephine has 3 nickels, 4 dimes, and 12 pennies. Her mother gives her 1 coin. Now Josephine has 92 cents. What coin did her mother give her?

2. Christopher has 3 ten-dollar bills, 3 five-dollar bills, and 12 one-dollar bills. Jenny has $19 more than Christopher. How much money does Jenny have?

3. Isaiah started with 2 twenty-dollar bills, 4 ten-dollar bills, 1 five-dollar bill, and 7 one-dollar bills. He spent 73 dollars on clothes. How much money did he have left?

4. Jackie bought a sweater at the store for $42. She had 3 five dollar bills and 6 one dollar bills left over. How much money did she have before buying the sweater?

5. Akio found 18 cents in his pocket. He found 6 more coins in his other pocket. Altogether he has 73 cents. What were the 6 coins he found in his other pocket?

6. Mary found 98 cents in her piggy bank. She counted 1 quarter, 8 pennies, 3 dimes, and some nickels. How many nickels did she count?

Student Debrief (10 minutes)

Lesson Objective: Solve two-step word problems involving dollars or cents with totals within $100 or $1.

The Student Debrief is intended to invite reflection and active processing of the total lesson experience.

Invite students to review their solutions for the Problem Set. They should check work by comparing answers with a partner before going over answers as a class. Look for misconceptions or misunderstandings that can be addressed in the Debrief. Guide students in a conversation to debrief the Problem Set and process the lesson.

You may choose to use any combination of the questions below to lead the discussion.

- Before you begin solving a word problem what are some things you should think about? (What type of models to use, whether there is more than one part to the problem, what operations to use, and what strategies I can use to help me.)
- Look at Problem 1 of your Problem Set. Could skip-counting help you solve one part of the problem quickly?
- Look at Problem 2. Tell your partner what you did first. Take your partner through your entire solution path.
- Talk to your partner about the models you used to solve word problems today. Share with your partner how you used a model on your Problem Set.
- Share your strategy for figuring out the coins Akio found in his pocket.

Exit Ticket (3 minutes)

After the Student Debrief, instruct students to complete the Exit Ticket. A review of their work will help you assess the students' understanding of the concepts that were presented in the lesson today and plan more effectively for future lessons. You may read the questions aloud to the students.

Name ______________________________ Date ____________

Solve with a tape diagram and number sentence.

1. Josephine has 3 nickels, 4 dimes, and 12 pennies. Her mother gives her 1 coin. Now Josephine has 92 cents. What coin did her mother give her?

2. Christopher has 3 ten dollar bills, 3 five dollar bills, and 12 one dollar bills. Jenny has $19 more than Christopher. How much money does Jenny have?

3. Isaiah started with 2 twenty dollar bills, 4 ten dollar bills, 1 five dollar bill, and 7 one dollar bills. He spent 73 dollars on clothes. How much money did he have left?

4. Jackie bought a sweater at the store for $42. She had 3 five dollar bills and 6 one dollar bills left over. How much money did she have before buying the sweater?

5. Akio found 18 cents in his pocket. He found 6 more coins in his other pocket. Altogether he has 73 cents. What were the 6 coins he found in his other pocket?

6. Mary found 98 cents in her piggy bank. She counted 1 quarter, 8 pennies, 3 dimes, and some nickels. How many nickels did she count?

Name ____________________________ Date ____________

Solve with a tape diagram and number sentence.

1. Gary went to the store with 4 ten dollar bills, 3 five dollar bills, and 7 one dollar bills. He bought a sweater for $26. What bills did he leave the store with?

Name ______________________________ Date ______________

1. Kelly bought a pencil sharpener for 47 cents and a pencil for 35 cents. What was her change from $1?

2. HaeJung bought a pretzel for 3 dimes and a nickel. She also bought a juice box. She spent 92 cents. How much was the juice box?

3. Nolan has 1 quarter, 1 nickel, and 21 pennies. His brother gave him 2 coins. Now, he has 86 cents. What 2 coins did his brother give him?

4. Monique saved 2 ten dollar bills, 4 five dollar bills, and 15 one dollar bills. Harry saved has $16 more than Monique. How much money does Harry have?

5. Ryan went shopping with 3 twenty dollar bills, 3 ten dollar bills, 1 five dollar bill, and 9 one dollar bills. He spent 59 dollars on a video game. How much money did he have left?

6. Heather had 3 ten dollar bills and 4 five dollar bills left after buying a new pair of sneakers for $29. How much money did she have before buying the sneakers?

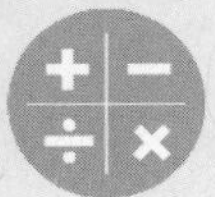

Topic C

Creating an Inch Ruler

2.MD.1

Focus Standard:	2.MD.1	Measure the length of an object by selecting and using appropriate tools such as rulers, yardsticks, meter sticks, and measuring tapes.
Instructional Days:	2	
Coherence -Links from:	G1–M3	Ordering and Comparing Length Measurements as Numbers
-Links to:	G3–M7	Geometry and Measurement Word Problems

Topic C reinforces the measurement concepts and skills learned in Module 2 while focusing on customary units. In Lesson 14, students use an inch tile to measure various objects using iteration. By connecting to prior learning, students deepen their understanding of a length unit, seeing again that just as it was with the centimeter cube, the length unit is the distance from one end of the tile (or cube) to the other or from one hash mark to the next.

In Lesson 15, students create inch rulers using the same process as they did in Module 2 to create centimeter rulers, using the mark and advance technique with inch tiles to record each length unit with a hash mark. Whereas in Module 2 students made rulers 30 centimeters long and related 100 centimeters to a new unit, the meter (supporting work with the base ten system), they now relate 12 inches to a new unit, foot (supporting their work with arrays by recognizing that a new unit can be made with any value). They then use their inch rulers to measure and compare objects around the classroom (**2.MD.1**). Through practice, the foundational concept that the zero point on a ruler is the beginning of the total length and each number on the ruler indicates the number of length units from zero is reinforced.

A Teaching Sequence Towards Mastery of Creating an Inch Ruler

Objective 1: Connect measurement with physical units by using iteration with an inch tile to measure. (Lesson 14)

Objective 2: Apply concepts to create inch rulers; measure lengths using inch rulers. (Lesson 15)

Lesson 14

Objective: Connect measurement with physical units by using iteration with an inch tile to measure.

Suggested Lesson Structure

■ Fluency Practice	(10 minutes)
■ Application Problem	(8 minutes)
■ Concept Development	(32 minutes)
■ Student Debrief	(10 minutes)
Total Time	**(60 minutes)**

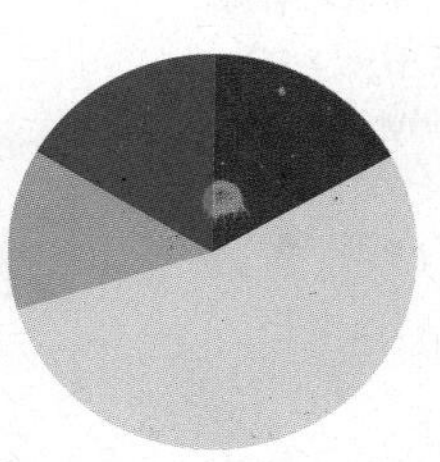

Fluency Practice (10 minutes)

- Subtraction Fact Flash Cards **2.OA.2** (5 minutes)
- Grade 2 Core Fluency Differentiated Practice Sets **2.OA.2** (5 minutes)

Subtraction Fact Flash Cards (5 minutes)

Materials: (T) Flash Cards Set 1

Note: This is a teacher-directed, whole-class activity. By practicing subtraction facts, students gain mastery of differences within 20.

Grade 2 Core Fluency Differentiated Practice Sets (5 minutes)

Materials: (S) Core Fluency Practice Sets from G2–M7–Lesson 1

Note: During G2–M7–Topic C and for the remainder of the year, each day's fluency includes an opportunity for review and mastery of the sums and differences with totals through 20 by means of the Core Fluency Practice Sets or Sprints. The process is detailed and Practice Sets are provided in G2–M7–Lesson 1.

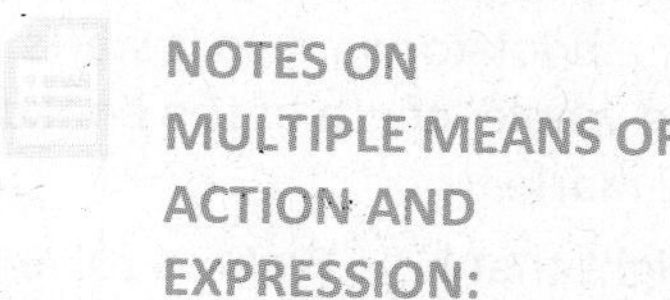

NOTES ON MULTIPLE MEANS OF ACTION AND EXPRESSION:

Invite English language learners to demonstrate understanding by explaining the problem in their native language or by acting it out using books and a bookshelf in class. Extend this invitation to any students who need such support.

Application Problem (8 minutes)

Frances is moving the furniture in her bedroom. She wants to move the bookcase to the space between her bed and the wall, but she is not sure it will fit.

Talk with your partner: What could Frances use as a measurement tool if she doesn't have a ruler? How could she use it?

Show your thinking on your personal board using pictures, numbers, or words.

Frances can put the book at one end of the bookcase and mark where the book ends. Then she moves the book forward so it's right on the mark. She keeps doing that to find the total length. Then she does that between the wall and the bed.

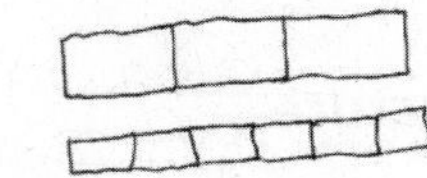

She can use any size book but it'll be faster if she uses a big book because she won't have to mark and move it as many times.

Note: Today's problem is designed to activate prior knowledge of measurement (the focus of G2–Module 2), in particular, the concept of using iteration with one physical unit to measure, in anticipation of the Concept Development.

Concept Development (32 minutes)

Materials: (T) 1 inch tile, 1 centimeter cube (S) Personal white board with Application Problem work, 1 inch tile, Problem Set

Note: Today's Concept Development draws upon measurement concepts and skills learned in G2–Module 2. Students refresh and apply their knowledge about these concepts, but now they will use an inch tile instead of a centimeter cube.

Call students to bring their Application Problem work and sit in a circle on the carpet. Invite them to share their thinking.

T: When talking about our story problem, someone mentioned the mark-and-move-forward strategy. Could you explain that a little more if Frances uses a book as a measurement tool?

S: She could put the book down at the beginning of the bookcase and mark where it ends and then move the book forward so it starts on that mark and mark where it ends again. She keeps doing that until the whole length of the bookcase is measured. → She can't leave any space between the book and the mark.

T: How might that help Frances solve her problem?

S: If the bookcase is 5 books long and the space between the wall and the bed is 4 books long, she knows the bookcase won't fit. → If she measures the bookcase and can fit the same number of books or more, then she knows it will fit.

T: Does the size of the book matter?

S: No, but she has to use the same size book to measure the bookcase and the space. → If she uses a small book she'll have to move it a lot of times to measure. → If she uses a larger book, she'll cover the space faster.

T: You remembered all of the important ideas!

T: (Hold up the centimeter cube.) Take a moment to remember how we used this earlier in the year. What is it called? How did we use it? (Allow students time to share with a partner.)

S: It's a centimeter cube! → We used it to measure things. → Sometimes we used more than one cube, and sometimes we used just one. → We did mark-and-move-forward, and we had to be careful not to leave any space in between. → We used it to make a ruler!

T: Today we're going to look at a different unit of measurement, the **inch**.

T: (Hold up an inch tile alongside the centimeter cube.) How does the size of the inch tile compare to the size of the centimeter cube?

S: The inch tile is bigger!

T: Can we use the inch tile to measure in the same way that we used the centimeter cube?

S: Yes!

Project or draw a 4-inch line on the board. Put a hash mark at the beginning and end of the line.

T: Watch how I use the inch tile to measure this line. I put the tile at the beginning of the line on the hash mark and make another mark where the tile ends. Then, I move the tile forward and place the edge right on top of the mark. (Demonstrate step by step until the total length of the line is measured.)

T: Talk with your partner: What do you notice about the spaces between the hash marks?

S: They're all the same length.

T: Exactly! How many inch tiles long is my line?

S: 4 inch tiles long.

T: Correct! What happens if my line isn't exactly 4 inch tiles long? Discuss with your partner.

S: If it's a half or more of a tile longer, you round up, so it would be 5 inch tiles long. → If it's less than half of a tile, you'd round down and say 4 inch tiles long. → You could try centimeter cubes to get a closer measurement.

T: Yes! We can round units of measure just like we round numbers. (Demonstrate on the board by extending and shortening the line and measuring.)

T: Now, it's your turn! We're going to use the Problem Set for the rest of the lesson.

NOTES ON MULTIPLE MEANS OF REPRESENTATION:

Some students may mistakenly count the hash marks and give an answer of 5 inch tiles. Visually demonstrate to them that the space from the beginning of the line to the first mark is 1 length unit by placing a tile there. Have students count as each subsequent space is filled with the tile.

Pass out the Problem Set and 1 inch tile per student.

T: Use your inch tile and the mark and move forward strategy to measure the objects listed on the Problem Set. Round to the nearest inch and record each measurement in the table.

Note: This activity provides an opportunity to work with a small group that needs support with any aspects of today's lesson.

Problem Set (10 minutes)

Students should do their personal best to complete the Problem Set within the allotted 10 minutes. For some classes, it may be appropriate to modify the assignment by specifying which problems they work on first. Some problems do not specify a method for solving. Students solve these problems using the RDW approach used for Application Problems.

Name Samantha Date

1. Measure the objects below with an inch tile. Record the measurements in the table provided.

Object	Measurement
Pair of scissors	5 inches
Marker	6 inches
Pencil	7 inches
Eraser	2 inches
Length of worksheet	11 inches
Width of worksheet	8 inches
Length of desk	17 inches
Width of desk	23 inches

Student Debrief (10 minutes)

Lesson Objective: Connect measurement with physical units by using iteration with an inch tile to measure.

The Student Debrief is intended to invite reflection and active processing of the total lesson experience.

Invite students to review their solutions for the Problem Set. They should check work by comparing answers with a partner before going over answers as a class. Look for misconceptions or misunderstandings that can be addressed in the Debrief. Guide students in a conversation to debrief the Problem Set and process the lesson.

You may choose to use any combination of the questions below to lead the discussion.

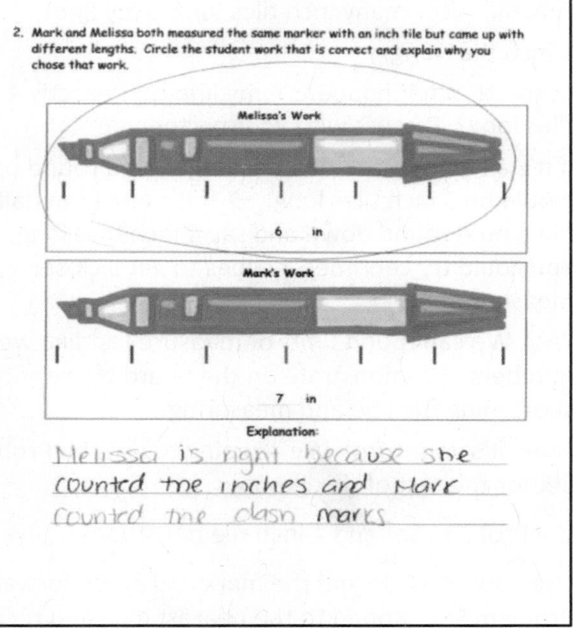

2. Mark and Melissa both measured the same marker with an inch tile but came up with different lengths. Circle the student work that is correct and explain why you chose that work.

Melissa's Work

6 in

Mark's Work

7 in

Explanation:

Melissa is right because she counted the inches and Mark counted the dash marks

- Look at the things you measured in your Problem Set. Talk to your partner about how attending to precision was particularly important today. (Using iteration and hash marks calls for precise work.)
- Did your measurement of each item in your Problem Set come out to the same number of inch tiles as your partner? If not, see if you can figure out why. (Counting hash marks instead of length unit, rounding incorrectly.)
- Talk to your partner about why Melissa and Mark came up with different measurements for the marker.
- We remembered about using centimeter cubes and practiced using inch tiles today. How is using larger length units helpful? Remember our bookcase problem. How are larger length units less precise?
- When is using smaller units helpful? Which of the items on your worksheet would you prefer to measure with inch tiles? With centimeter tiles? Why?

- When you are thinking about measuring how would you decide on which length unit to use?

Exit Ticket (3 minutes)

After the Student Debrief, instruct students to complete the Exit Ticket. A review of their work will help you assess the students' understanding of the concepts that were presented in the lesson today and plan more effectively for future lessons. You may read the questions aloud to the students.

Note: The homework requires students to have an inch tile to measure. Consider sending home 1-inch squares of paper instead of plastic tiles.

Name ______________________________ Date ______________

1. Measure the objects below with an inch tile. Record the measurements in the table provided.

Object	Measurement
Pair of scissors	
Marker	
Pencil	
Eraser	
Length of worksheet	
Width of worksheet	
Length of desk	
Width of desk	

2. Mark and Melissa both measured the same marker with an inch tile but came up with different lengths. Circle the student work that is correct and explain why you chose that work.

Melissa's Work

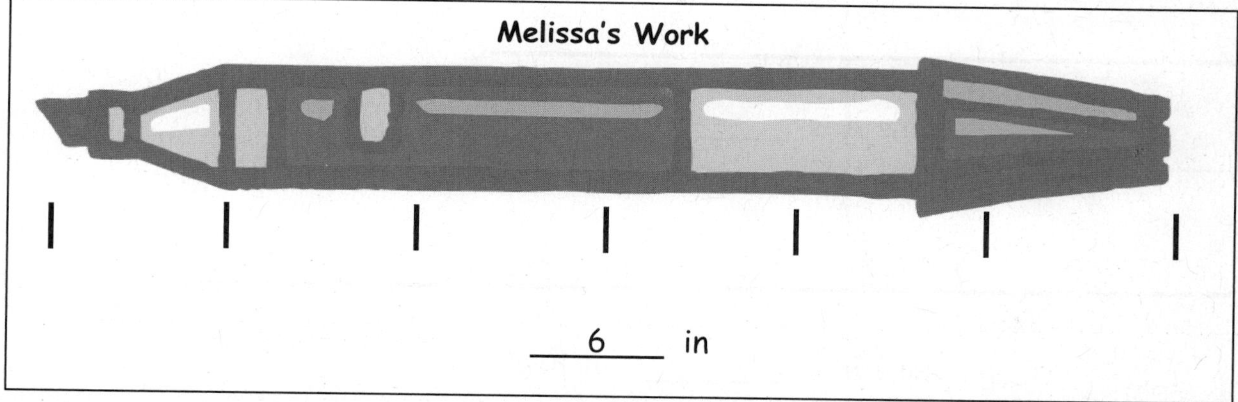

6 in

Mark's Work

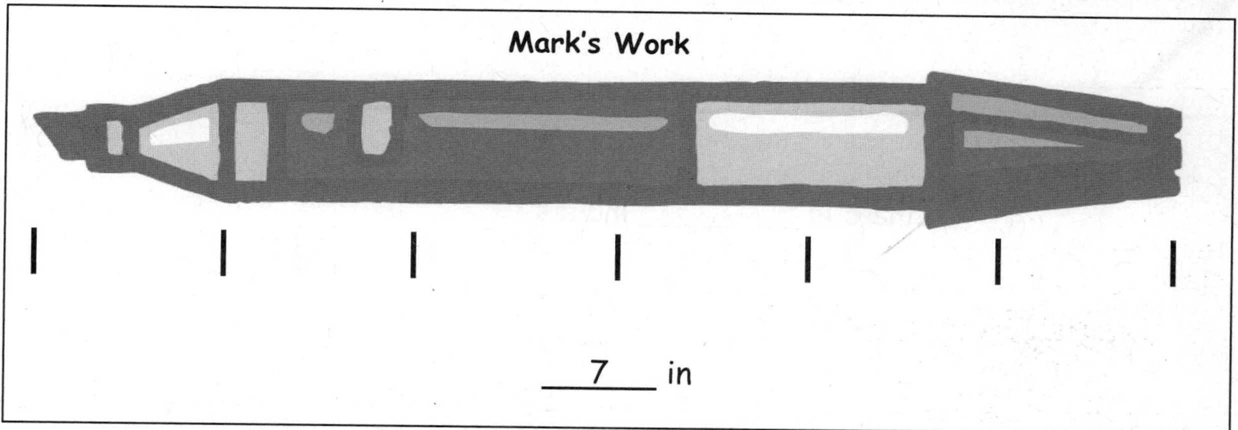

7 in

Explanation:

____

____

____

Name ______________________________ Date ______________

Measure the lines below with an inch tile.

Line A

Line A is ________ inches

Line B

Line B is ________ inches

Line C

Line C is ________ inches

Name ______________________________ Date ______________

1. Measure these objects found in your home with an inch tile. Record the measurements in the table provided.

Object	Measurement
Length of a kitchen fork	
Height of a juice glass	
Length across the center of a plate	
Length of the refrigerator	
Length of a kitchen drawer	
Height of a can	
Length of a picture frame	
Length of a remote control	

2. Norberto begins measuring his pen with his inch tile. He marks off where each tile ends. After two times, he decides this process is taking too long and starts to guess where the tile would end and then marks it.

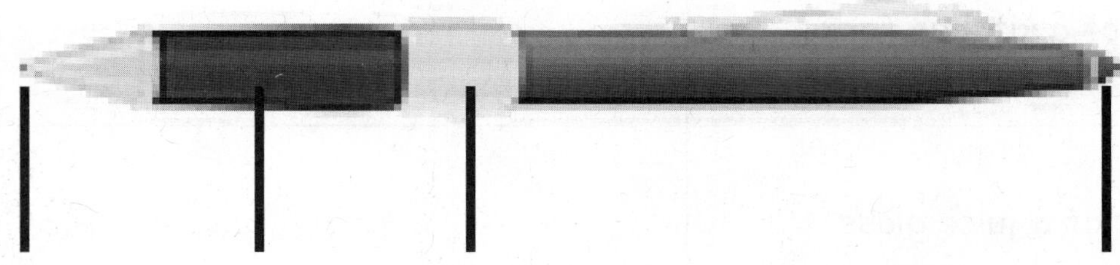

Explain why Norberto's answer will not be correct.

____

____

____

3. Use your inch tile to measure the pen. How many inch tiles long is the pen?

11 - 1	11 - 2
11 - 3	11 - 4
11 - 5	11 - 6
11 - 7	11 - 8
11 - 9	12 - 3

12 - 4	12 - 5
12 - 6	12 - 7
12 - 8	12 - 9
13 - 4	13 - 5
13 - 6	13 - 7

13 - 8	13 - 9
14 - 5	14 - 6
14 - 7	14 - 8
14 - 9	15 - 6
15 - 7	15 - 8

15 - 9	16 - 7
16 - 8	16 - 9
17 - 8	17 - 9
18 - 9	19 - 11
20 - 19	20 - 1

20 - 18	20 - 2
20 - 17	20 - 3
20 - 16	20 - 4
20 - 15	20 - 5
20 - 14	20 - 6

20 - 13	20 - 7
20 - 12	20 - 8
20 - 11	20 - 9
20 - 10	

Lesson 15

Objective: Apply concepts to create inch rulers; measure lengths using inch rulers.

Suggested Lesson Structure

■ Fluency Practice	(11 minutes)
■ Application Problem	(5 minutes)
■ Concept Development	(34 minutes)
■ Student Debrief	(10 minutes)
Total Time	**(60 minutes)**

Fluency Practice (11 minutes)

- Sprint: Adding and Subtracting by 2 **2.OA.2** (9 minutes)
- Subtraction Fact Flash Cards **2.OA.2** (2 minutes)

Sprint: Adding and Subtracting by 2 (9 minutes)

Materials: (S) Adding and Subtracting by 2 Sprint

Note: Students practice adding and subtracting by 2 in order to gain mastery of the sums and differences within 20.

Subtraction Fact Flash Cards (2 minutes)

Materials: (T) Flash Cards Set 1

Note: By practicing subtraction facts, students will gain mastery of differences within 20.

This can be a teacher-directed, whole-class activity or an opportunity for students to work in pairs. The teacher can hold the cards and use choral response or distribute the cards and have students pair up to question each other.

Application Problem (5 minutes)

Materials: (S) Small object approximately 6 inches long or less, 9 lima beans, 3 toothpicks per pair

The lima bean is smaller so the number of units is bigger.

Edwin and Tina have the same toy truck. Edwin says his is 4 toothpicks long. Tina says hers is 12 lima beans long. How can they both be right?

Work with a partner to measure your object. Partner A, measure with lima beans. Partner B, measure with toothpicks. Use words or pictures to explain how Edwin and Tina can both be right.

Note: This problem gives students a hands-on opportunity to reason through the relationship between the size and number of length units: the smaller the length unit, the larger the number of units, and the larger the length unit, the smaller the number of units. This anticipates the comparison between centimeters and inches that students will explore in G2–M7–Lesson 18.

Concept Development (34 minutes)

Materials: (S) 12-inch long × 2-inch wide strip of tag board or sentence strip, paper or math journal, 1 inch tile, 2-inch paper clip, 3 × 5 index card

Pass out tag board and inch tiles.

T: Yesterday we used a 1-inch tile to measure the length of various objects. Today we're going to create a tool that will help us measure inches in a more efficient way.

T: Remember how we made centimeter rulers earlier in the year? Let's make an inch ruler today!

T: Watch how I make the first hash mark on my ruler. (Demonstrate placing the tile at the left end of the tag board, drawing the line, and writing 1 above it.)

T: Now you do the same.

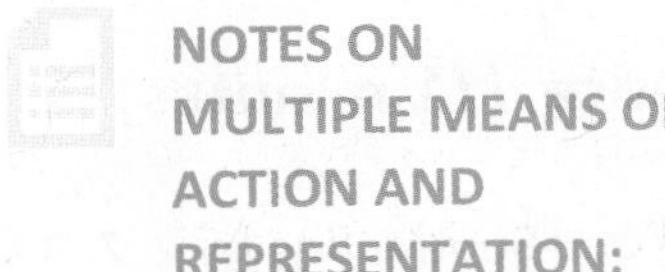

NOTES ON MULTIPLE MEANS OF ACTION AND REPRESENTATION:

Glue a toothpick or Wikki Stix to represent each of the hash marks for blind or visually impaired students, enabling them to feel the length units on their ruler.

Circulate to ensure that all students are marking their rulers correctly.

T: What does the number 1 mean?

S: It's one length unit. → It's where the length unit ends. → It's the space you have measured so far.

T: Yes. And what do we call this length unit that we're using?

S: An inch!

T: Yes. And where should 0 go on our rulers?

S: At the very beginning of the ruler. → Before the number 1.

T: Let's write 0 at the left edge of the ruler. (Model as students do the same.)

T: What does the 0 mean?

S: It means you haven't measured anything yet. → It's where you start to measure.

T: So, when we put our tile at the edge of the ruler and then marked the end of the tile with the hash

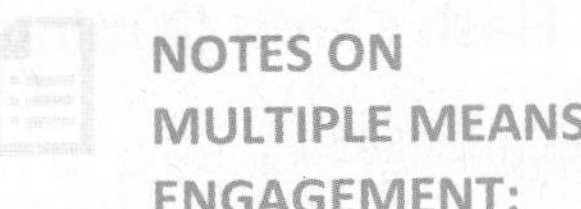

NOTES ON MULTIPLE MEANS OF ENGAGEMENT:

Some students will have a deeper understanding of concepts of measurement. Give them the opportunity to explain to their peers, using words, drawings, or actions, their understanding of notions such as why there can be no gaps or overlaps when creating their rulers.

mark, we actually measured 1 inch.

T: You're going to finish making your rulers now. Each time you move your tile forward, be sure to put it down right on top of the line. Why is it important not to have any gaps between the tiles?

S: Our measurements would all be different. → The length units have to be equal.

T: Correct! Remember to write each number directly above the hash marks as you go.

Support students who need assistance, and allow those who show mastery to complete their rulers independently. Early finishers can explore measuring objects around the room. When all students have finished, distribute the paper, paper clips, and index cards.

T: What is the last number on your ruler?

S: 12!

T: So, this ruler measures 12 what?

S: 12 inches!

T: Yes! And, 12 inches make a larger unit called a **foot**.

T: Everyone say this with me: 12 inches equal 1 foot.

S: (Repeat.)

T: Show your partner how to measure your paper clip with the ruler. (Watch for misconceptions.)

T: How long is the paper clip?

S: 2 inches.

T: So, the number 2 means the number of inches so far. The end of this paper clip is where 2 length units, in this case, inches, end.

T: Now, on your paper, use your ruler to draw a line that is 2 inches long. (Pause.)

T: Lay your paper clip along the line you drew. What do you notice?

S: They're the same length!

T: Tell your partner: How many more inches would we need to add to make a foot? How do you know?

S: Two inches plus 10 inches equal 12 inches and 12 inches equal 1 foot.

T: Now measure the length of the index card. Check your answer with a partner. (Allow students time to check answers.)

T: How long is the index card?

S: 5 inches.

T: So, the card is the same length as the space between 0 and 5 on your ruler. It is the same length as 5 inches.

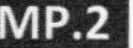

T: Use your ruler to draw a line that is 5 inches long. Then, lay your index card along the line and compare the two lengths.

S: They're both 5 inches long. → They're the same length.

T: 5 inches plus how many inches equal 1 foot?

S: 7 inches!

T: So, a foot is composed of 12 inches, just as a unit of ten is composed of 10...?

S: Ones!

T: And a unit of one hundred is composed of 10…?

S: Tens!

T: A dollar is composed of 100…?

S: Cents!

T: How many inches equal one foot? Give me a complete sentence.

S: 12 inches equal 1 foot!

T: Why is it more efficient to use a ruler than to measure using inch tiles?

S: You can measure all at once instead of going 1 plus 1 plus 1. → Everybody has rulers, but I only see inch tiles in school. → It takes a lot longer to mark and move forward than to just use a ruler. → On the ruler, the inches all stay together in the same place, so it's like all the inch tiles are connected, which is easier to use.

T: That's a great way to think of the ruler! And I'd much rather measure my desk with a ruler than with a single inch tile!

If any students need more support measuring or drawing lines of equal length, repeat the procedure to measure the width of the index card and draw a line of equal length. Otherwise, as students demonstrate proficiency using the ruler to measure and draw lines of equal lengths, allow them to move on to the Problem Set.

Problem Set (10 minutes)

Students should do their personal best to complete the Problem Set within the allotted 10 minutes. For some classes, it may be appropriate to modify the assignment by specifying which problems they work on first. Some problems do not specify a method for solving. Students solve these problems using the RDW approach used for Application Problems.

Name Samantha Date

Use your ruler to measure the length of the objects below in inches. Using your ruler, draw a line the same length as each object.

1. a. A pencil is 7 inches.
   b. Draw a line that is the same length as the pencil.

2. a. An eraser is 2 inches.
   b. raw a line that is the same length as the eraser.

3. a. A crayon is 3 inches.
   b. draww a line that is the same length as the crayon.

4. a. A marker is 6 inches.
   b. Draw a line that is the same length as the marker.

5. a. What is the longest item that you measured? a pencil
   b. How long is the longest item? 7 inches
   c. How long is the shortest item? 2 inches
   d. What is the difference in length between the longest and the shortest items? 5 inches.
   e. Draw a line that is the same as the length you found in d.

Student Debrief (10 minutes)

Lesson Objective: Apply concepts to create inch rulers; measure lengths using inch rulers.

The Student Debrief is intended to invite reflection and active processing of the total lesson experience.

Invite students to review their solutions for the Problem Set. They should check work by comparing answers with a partner before going over answers as a class. Look for misconceptions or misunderstandings that can be addressed in the Debrief. Guide students in a conversation to debrief the Problem Set and process the lesson.

You may choose to use any combination of the questions below to lead the discussion.

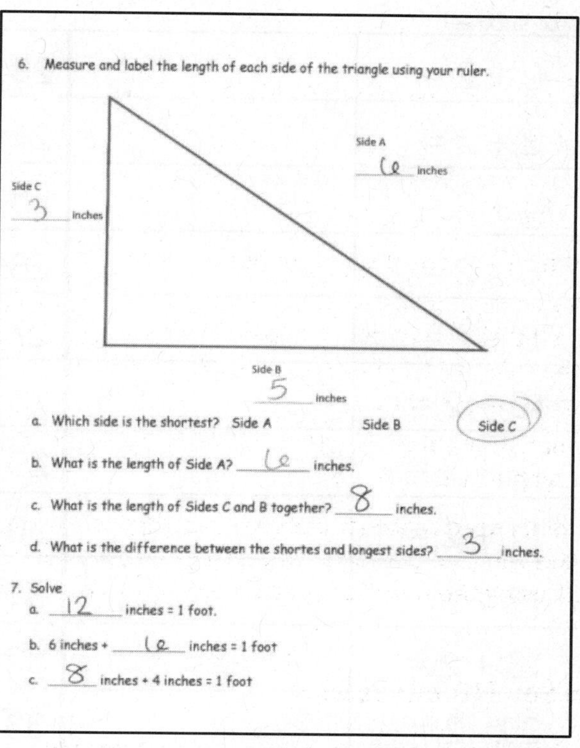

6. Measure and label the length of each side of the triangle using your ruler.

Side A 6 inches

Side C 3 inches

Side B 5 inches

a. Which side is the shortest? Side A Side B (Side C)

b. What is the length of Side A? 6 inches.

c. What is the length of Sides C and B together? 8 inches.

d. What is the difference between the shortes and longest sides? 3 inches.

7. Solve

a. 12 inches = 1 foot.

b. 6 inches + 6 inches = 1 foot

c. 8 inches + 4 inches = 1 foot

- Look at the things you measured on your Problem Set. Did you have to round to the nearest inch on any of the items? Was it easier to measure objects or the lines on the triangle? Why? (Lines, because there is a definite starting and ending point. → Objects are three-dimensional. → The triangle was harder because I had to keep turning my ruler.)
- When you compared the length of two objects on your Problem Set, did you use an equation? What operation did you use in your equation?
- Look at Problem 3 on your Problem Set. What are the two length units in these problems? (Inches and a foot.) Talk to your partner about how these units are related. Can you think of other units that are related like this? (Dollar and cents, tens and ones, hours and minutes, days and hours, etc.)
- When we add 9 and 6, many of us make ten and add five more. What about if we add 9 inches and 6 inches? Would we make ten? How many does 9 need to make a foot? How many extra inches would there be? So, 9 + 6 = 1 ten 5 ones, and 9 inches + 6 inches = 1 foot 3 inches. Explain to your partner how you might add 8 inches and 7 inches making a foot first.

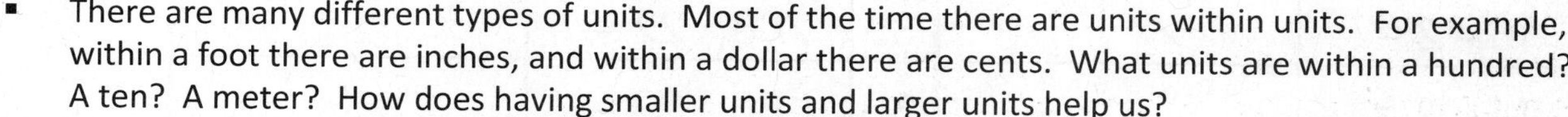

- There are many different types of units. Most of the time there are units within units. For example, within a foot there are inches, and within a dollar there are cents. What units are within a hundred? A ten? A meter? How does having smaller units and larger units help us?
- Think about when we were making our inch rulers today. Tell your partner exactly what the length unit was on our rulers. Will length units always be an inch?

Exit Ticket (3 minutes)

After the Student Debrief, instruct students to complete the Exit Ticket. A review of their work will help you assess the students' understanding of the concepts that were presented in the lesson today and plan more effectively for future lessons. You may read the questions aloud to the students.

A

\# Correct ______

Add or subtract.

1	0 + 2 =		23	2 + 4 =	
2	2 + 2 =		24	2 + 6 =	
3	4 + 2 =		25	2 + 8 =	
4	6 + 2 =		26	2 + 10 =	
5	8 + 2 =		27	2 + 12 =	
6	10 + 2 =		28	2 + 14 =	
7	12 + 2 =		29	2 + 16 =	
8	14 + 2 =		30	2 + 18 =	
9	16 + 2 =		31	0 + 22 =	
10	18 + 2 =		32	22 + 22 =	
11	20 - 2 =		33	44 + 22 =	
12	18 - 2 =		34	66 + 22 =	
13	16 - 2 =		35	88 - 22 =	
14	14 - 2 =		36	66 - 22 =	
15	12 - 2 =		37	44 - 22 =	
16	10 - 2 =		38	22 - 22 =	
17	8 - 2 =		39	22 + 0 =	
18	6 - 2 =		40	22 + 22 =	
19	4 - 2 =		41	22 + 44 =	
20	2 - 2 =		42	66 + 22 =	
21	2 + 0 =		43	888 - 222 =	
22	2 + 2 =		44	666 - 222 =	

B Improvement _____ # Correct _____

Add or subtract.

1	2 + 0 =		23	4 + 2 =	
2	2 + 2 =		24	6 + 2 =	
3	2 + 4 =		25	8 + 2 =	
4	2 + 6 =		26	10 + 2 =	
5	2 + 8 =		27	12 + 2 =	
6	2 + 10 =		28	14 + 2 =	
7	2 + 12 =		29	16 + 2 =	
8	2 + 14 =		30	18 + 2 =	
9	2 + 16 =		31	0 + 22 =	
10	2 + 18 =		32	22 + 22 =	
11	20 - 2 =		33	22 + 44 =	
12	18 - 2 =		34	66 + 22 =	
13	16 - 2 =		35	88 - 22 =	
14	14 - 2 =		36	66 - 22 =	
15	12 - 2 =		37	44 - 22 =	
16	10 - 2 =		38	22 - 22 =	
17	8 - 2 =		39	22 + 0 =	
18	6 - 2 =		40	22 + 22 =	
19	4 - 2 =		41	22 + 44 =	
20	2 - 2 =		42	66 + 22 =	
21	0 + 2 =		43	666 - 222 =	
22	2 + 2 =		44	888 - 222 =	

Name ______________________________ Date ______________

Use your ruler to measure the length of the objects below in inches. Using your ruler, draw a line that is the same length as each object.

1. a. A pencil is ________ inches.
   b. Draw a line that is the same length as the pencil.

2. a. An eraser is ________ inches.
   b. Draw a line that is the same length as the eraser.

3. a. A crayon is ________ inches.
   b. Draw a line that is the same length as the crayon.

4. a. A marker is ________ inches.
   b. Draw a line that is the same length as the marker.

5. a. What is the longest item that you measured? ________________
   b. How long is the longest item? ________________ inches
   c. How long is the shortest item? ________________ inches
   d. What is the difference in length between the longest and the shortest items?
   ________________ inches
   e. Draw a line that is the same as the length you found in (d).

6. Measure and label the length of each side of the triangle using your ruler.

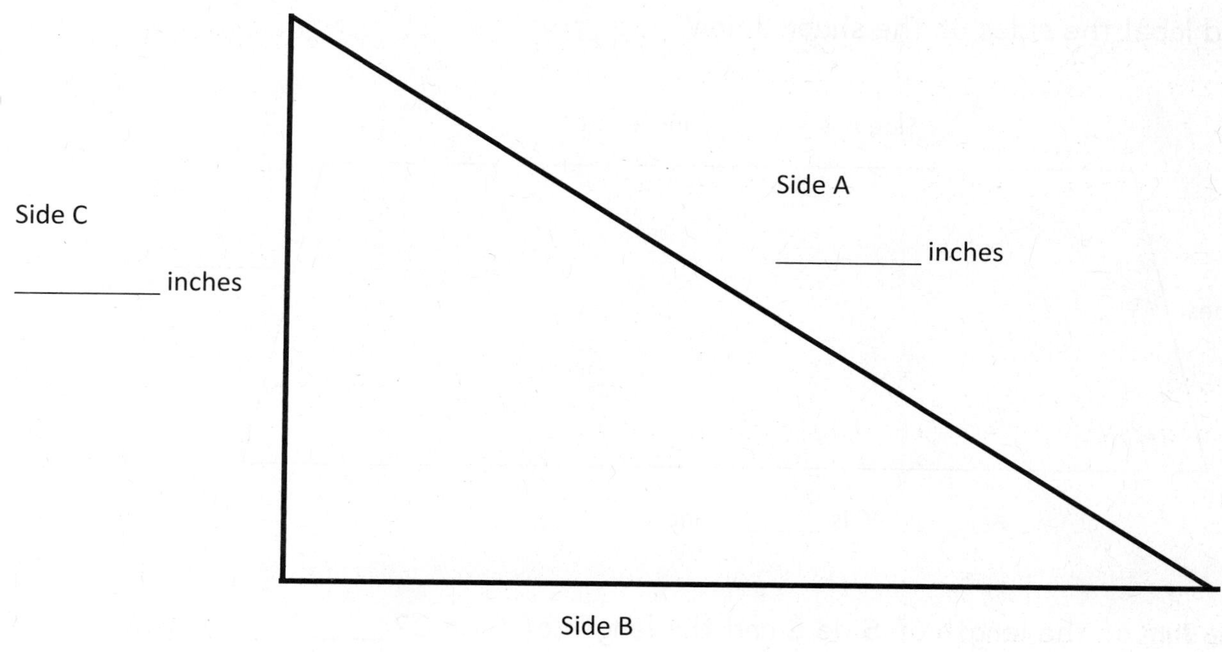

a. Which side is the shortest? Side A Side B Side C

b. What is the length of Side A? __________ inches

c. What is the length of Sides C and B together? ________ inches.

d. What is the difference between the shortest and longest sides? _________ inches

7. Solve.

a. __________ inches = 1 foot

b. 6 inches + __________ inches = 1 foot

c. _______ inches + 4 inches = 1 foot

Name ______________________________ Date ______________

Measure and label the sides of the shape below.

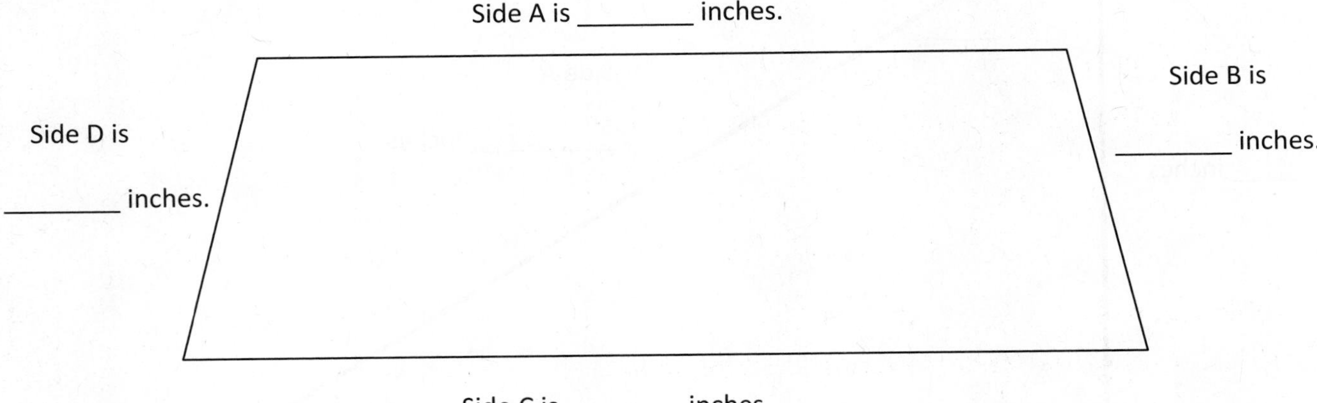
Side A is _______ inches.
Side B is _______ inches.
Side C is _______ inches
Side D is _______ inches.

What is the sum of the length of Side B and the length of Side D? _________ inches

Name ______________________________ Date ______________

Measure the length of each household object with your ruler, and then use your ruler to draw a line equal to the length of each object in the space provided.

1. a. A dinner fork is ________ inches.
   b. Draw a line that is the same length as the fork.

2. a. A tablespoon is ________ inches.
   b. Draw a line that is the same length as the spoon.

Write two other household objects to measure.

3. a. ________________________ is ________ inches.
   b. Draw a line that is the same length as the ____________________.

4. a. ________________________ is ________ inches.
   b. Draw a line that is the same length as the ____________________.

5. a. The longest object was ____________________________.

   b. The shortest object was ___________________________.

   c. The difference between the longest item and the shortest item is ________ inches.

6. Measure and label the length of each side of each shape in inches using your ruler.

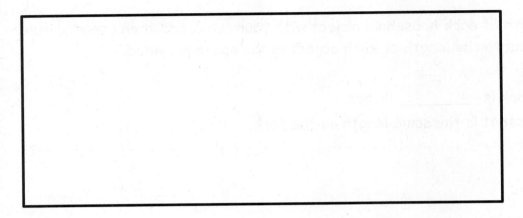

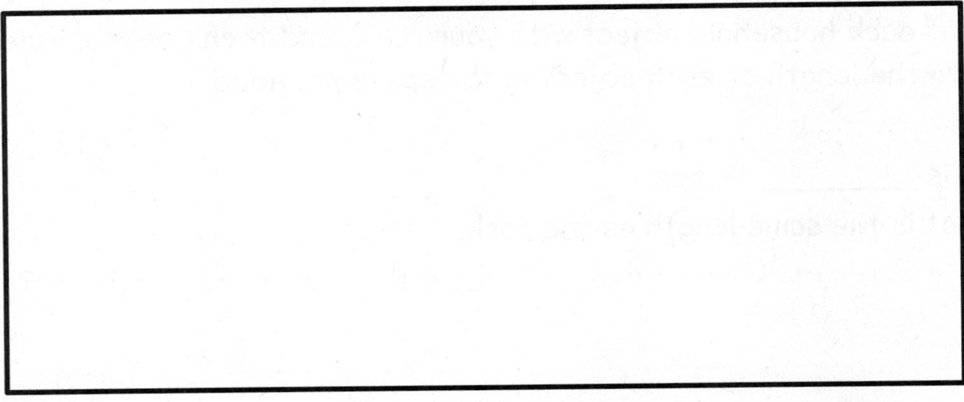

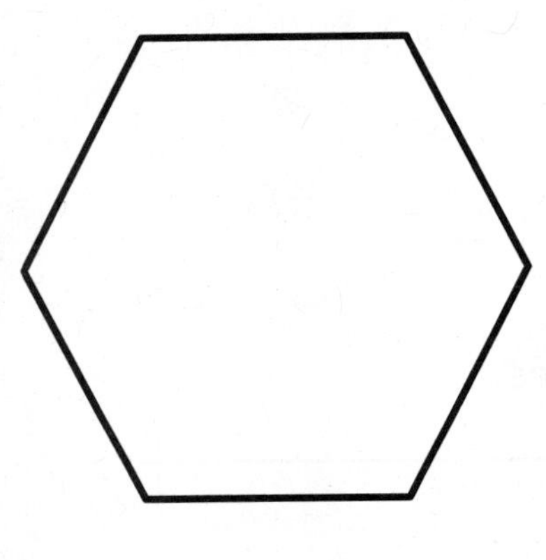

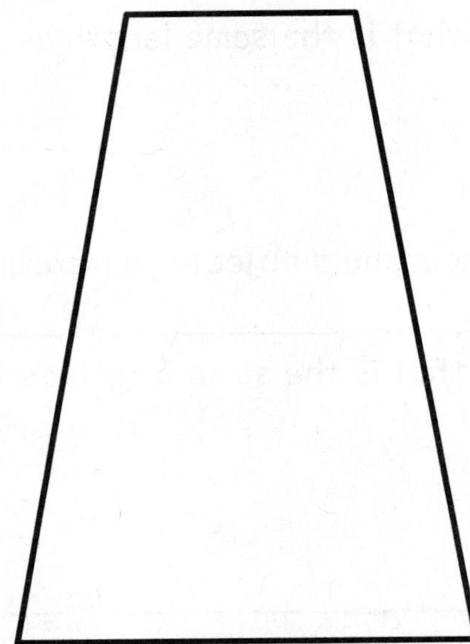

a. The longer side of the rectangle is _______ inches.

b. The shorter side of the rectangle is _______ inches.

c. The longer side of the rectangle is _____ inches longer than the shorter side of the rectangle.

d. The shortest side of the trapezoid is _______ inches.

e. The longest side of the trapezoid is _______ inches.

f. The longest side of the trapezoid is _____ inches longer than the shortest side.

g. Each side of the hexagon is ________ inches.

h. The total length around the hexagon is ________ inches.

1	2	3	4	5

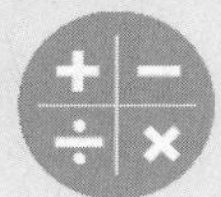

Topic D

Measuring and Estimating Length Using Customary and Metric Units

2.MD.1, 2.MD.2, 2.MD.3, 2.MD.4

Focus Standards:	2.MD.1	Measure the length of an object by selecting and using appropriate tools such as rulers, yardsticks, meter sticks, and measuring tapes.
	2.MD.2	Measure the length of an object twice, using length units of different lengths for the two measurements; describe how the two measurements relate to the size of the unit chosen.
	2.MD.3	Estimate lengths using units of inches, feet, centimeters, and meters.
	2.MD.4	Measure to determine how much longer one object is than another, expressing the length difference in terms of a standard length unit.
Instructional Days:	4	
Coherence -Links from:	G1–M3	Ordering and Comparing Length Measurements as Numbers
	G2–M2	Addition and Subtraction of Length Units
-Links to:	G3–M2	Place Value and Problem Solving with Units of Measure

Topic D builds upon the work students completed in Module 2 with centimeter measures, as students now explore measurement using both customary and metric units. In Lesson 16, students rotate through various centers and measure a variety of objects with inch rulers and yardsticks, strategically choosing the appropriate measurement tool and units for measuring a given object (**2.MD.1**). In doing so, they develop mental images of customary benchmark lengths.

Next, in Lesson 17, students deepen their measurement sense by applying their experiences in Lesson 16 to estimating the lengths of different objects and then checking their estimates by measuring (**2.MD.3**). For example, a student might estimate that a desk is three feet tall and then measure to discover that it is actually three feet, six inches tall.

Then, in Lesson 18, students measure the same objects twice, using both metric and customary units. In this way, they learn that centimeters are smaller than inches, but meters are larger than both feet and yards. This reinforces the understanding that when measuring with a smaller unit, more iterations of that unit are needed to measure the same object than when measuring with a larger unit (**2.MD.2**).

Finally, students compare different lengths using addition and subtraction in Lesson 19. They determine how much longer one object is than another, subtracting the smaller length from the larger one. Problems are

solved in a variety of ways using the relationship between addition and subtraction (e.g., 25 in – 18 in = ____ in, or 18 in + ______ = 25 in), and the differences are expressed using standard length units (e.g., 7 in) (**2.MD.4**).

The work with measurement tools and various length units in Topic D lays the groundwork for problem solving in Topic E, as students use the more abstract tape diagrams to relate addition and subtraction to length.

A Teaching Sequence Towards Mastery of Measuring and Estimating Length Using Customary and Metric Units	
Objective 1:	**Measure various objects using inch rulers and yardsticks.** **(Lesson 16)**
Objective 2:	**Develop estimation strategies by applying prior knowledge of length and using mental benchmarks.** **(Lesson 17)**
Objective 3:	**Measure an object twice using different length units and compare; relate measurement to unit size.** **(Lesson 18)**
Objective 4:	**Measure to compare the differences in lengths using inches, feet, and yards.** **(Lesson 19)**

Lesson 16

Objective: Measure various objects using inch rulers and yardsticks.

Suggested Lesson Structure

Fluency Practice	(11 minutes)
Concept Development	(39 minutes)
Student Debrief	(10 minutes)
Total Time	**(60 minutes)**

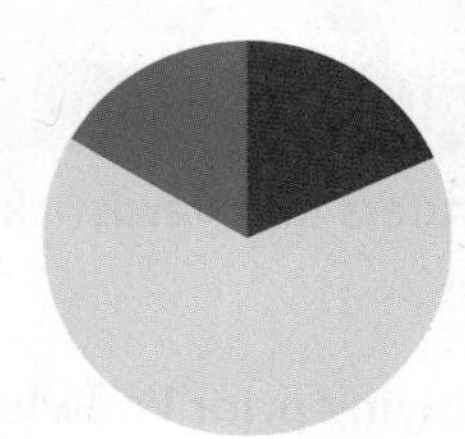

Fluency Practice (11 minutes)

- Sprint: Adding and Subtracting by 3 **2.OA.2** (9 minutes)
- Subtraction Fact Flash Cards **2.OA.2** (2 minutes)

Sprint: Adding and Subtracting by 3 (9 minutes)

Materials: (S) Adding and Subtracting by 3 Sprint

Note: Students practice adding and subtracting by 3 in order to gain mastery of the sums and differences within 20.

Subtraction Fact Flash Cards (2 minutes)

Materials: (T) Flash Cards Set 1

Note: This is a teacher-directed, whole-class activity. By practicing subtraction facts, students will gain mastery of differences within 20.

Concept Development (39 minutes)

Materials: (S) 12-inch ruler, yardstick, Recording Sheet set

Note: In this lesson, the Recording Sheet will serve as the Problem Set.

This Concept Development is designed for students to work in centers, rotating approximately every six minutes. Each group should have roughly five students. To prepare for the lesson, make one copy of the Recording Sheet set per student. Print the Recording Sheets single-sided so that students can work on the back if necessary. Post the directions at each center.

Note that the Application Problem has been omitted from this lesson, and instead, four out of five centers include a word problem related to the measurement task. Students may not have time to solve the word problem at every center, but they should complete at least two out of the four.

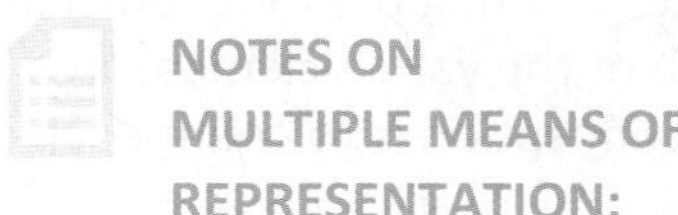

NOTES ON MULTIPLE MEANS OF REPRESENTATION:

Introduce English language learners to all the centers that have been created so that they know what is expected of them at each center. Clarify what they are being asked to measure, e.g., *shin,* and clarify the measuring units they will be using at each center, e.g., inches, feet, and yards.

Center 1: Measure and Compare Shin Lengths

Materials: (S) 12-inch rulers, yardsticks, Center 1 Recording Sheet

Students measure the length of group members' shins and record on a table. Observe how students go about this task. Do they use the most efficient measuring tool? Do they consistently measure from the same points on each person (top of foot to bottom of knee)?

Center 2: Compare Lengths to a Yardstick

Materials: (S) Book, yardstick, Center 2 Recording Sheet

Note: This center would best be located near a desk and classroom door.

Students first estimate how three classroom objects compare to a yardstick and then use a yardstick to measure the objects. The yardstick can be used to measure in different units: inches, feet, or yards. Keep a watchful eye to support students as they navigate the choice of units.

Center 3: Choose the Units to Measure Objects

Materials: (S) 12-inch ruler, yardstick, Center 3 Recording Sheet

At this center, students select the most appropriate unit to measure an object. Encourage students to choose objects with significantly different lengths so that they can gain experience measuring in inches, feet, and yards. Observe how students measure. Are they using a measuring tool that fits with their chosen object? Is it the most efficient measuring unit for the object?

Center 4: Find Benchmarks

Materials: (S) 12-inch ruler, yardstick, Center 4 Recording Sheet

Students identify objects for each of three benchmark lengths: inch, foot, and yard. Through a trial and error process, students develop a more precise understanding of the benchmark length.

NOTES ON MULTIPLE MEANS OF ACTION AND EXPRESSION:

Challenge above grade level students by asking them to help write measurement word problems to exchange with other students and solve. This will extend their learning of the content and also assess their content learning.

Center 5: Choose a Tool to Measure

Materials: (S) 12-inch ruler, yardstick, Center 5 Recording Sheet, math book, pencil, pink eraser

Note: This center would best be located near a rug and

chalkboard or white board.

Students practice selecting the most efficient measuring tool for a given object. Help students remember that every length of the yardstick measures 3 feet when they calculate the length of the rug and chalkboard. (A common misconception is to count each iteration of the yardstick as 1 unit when measuring in feet.)

Student Debrief (10 minutes)

Lesson Objective: Measure various objects using inch rulers and yardsticks.

The Student Debrief is intended to invite reflection and active processing of the total lesson experience.

Invite students to review their solutions for the Problem Set. They should check work by comparing answers with a partner before going over answers as a class. Look for misconceptions or misunderstandings that can be addressed in the Debrief. Guide students in a conversation to debrief the Problem Set and process the lesson.

You may choose to use any combination of the questions below to lead the discussion.

- When you used the 12-inch ruler, how did you label your measurement? (1 foot, 3 inches.) When you used the yardstick, did you have to use two unit labels? Explain why or why not.
- Choose one of the word problems you completed during centers. Explain your solution path to your partner.
- At Center 4, were the objects you chose close to the benchmark lengths? Were the things you chose for a foot, 12 inches long? For the yard, 3 feet long?
- If you didn't have a 12-inch ruler or a yardstick, could you think of a way to measure an object? Would you know about how many inches or feet that object was? Talk to your partner.
- How do you decide which unit to use when measuring?

Exit Ticket (3 minutes)

After the Student Debrief, instruct students to complete the Exit Ticket. A review of their work will help you assess the students' understanding of the concepts that were presented in the lesson today and plan more effectively for future lessons. You may read the questions aloud to the students.

A

Correct ____

Add or subtract.

1	0 + 3 =		23	6 + 3 =	
2	3 + 3 =		24	9 + 3 =	
3	6 + 3 =		25	12 + 3 =	
4	9 + 3 =		26	15 + 3 =	
5	12 + 3 =		27	18 + 3 =	
6	15 + 3 =		28	21 + 3 =	
7	18 + 3 =		29	24 + 3 =	
8	21 + 3 =		30	27 + 3 =	
9	24 + 3 =		31	0 + 33 =	
10	27 + 3 =		32	33 + 33 =	
11	30 - 3 =		33	66 + 33 =	
12	27 - 3 =		34	33 + 66 =	
13	24 - 3 =		35	99 - 33 =	
14	21 - 3 =		36	66 - 33 =	
15	18 - 3 =		37	999 - 333 =	
16	15 - 3 =		38	33 - 33 =	
17	12 - 3 =		39	33 + 0 =	
18	9 - 3 =		40	30 + 3 =	
19	6 - 3 =		41	33 + 3 =	
20	3 - 3 =		42	36 + 3 =	
21	3 + 0 =		43	63 + 33 =	
22	3 + 3 =		44	63 + 36 =	

B Improvement _____ # Correct _____

Add or subtract.

1	3 + 0 =		23	6 + 3 =	
2	3 + 3 =		24	9 + 3 =	
3	3 + 6 =		25	12 + 3 =	
4	3 + 9 =		26	15 + 3 =	
5	3 + 12 =		27	18 + 3 =	
6	3 + 15 =		28	21 + 3 =	
7	3 + 18 =		29	24 + 3 =	
8	3 + 21 =		30	27 + 3 =	
9	3 + 24 =		31	0 + 33 =	
10	3 + 27 =		32	33 + 33 =	
11	30 - 3 =		33	33 + 66 =	
12	27 - 3 =		34	66 + 33 =	
13	24 - 3 =		35	99 - 33 =	
14	21 - 3 =		36	66 - 33 =	
15	18 - 3 =		37	999 - 333 =	
16	15 - 3 =		38	33 - 33 =	
17	12 - 3 =		39	33 + 0 =	
18	9 - 3 =		40	30 + 3 =	
19	6 - 3 =		41	33 + 3 =	
20	3 - 3 =		42	36 + 3 =	
21	0 + 3 =		43	36 + 33 =	
22	3 + 3 =		44	36 + 63 =	

Center 1: Measure and Compare Shin Lengths

Choose a measuring unit to measure the shins of everyone in your group.
Measure from the top of the foot to the bottom of the knee.
I chose to measure using ________________.
Record the results in the table below. Include the units.

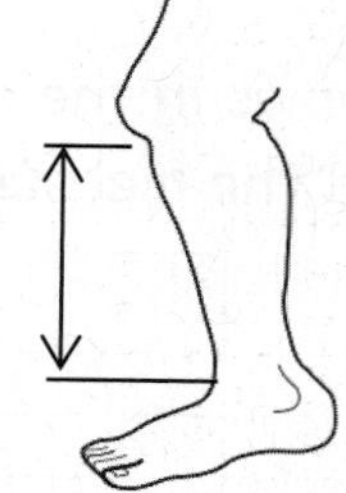

Name	Length of Shin

What is the difference in length between the longest and shortest shins? Write a number sentence and statement to show the difference between the two lengths.

Center 2: Compare Lengths to a Yardstick

Fill in your estimate for each object using the words *more than*, *less than*, or *about the same length as*. Then, measure each object with a yardstick and record the measurement on the chart.

1. The length of a book is ________________ the yardstick.
2. The height of the door is ________________ the yardstick.
3. The length of a student desk is ________________ the yardstick.

Object	Measurement
Length of book	
Height of door	
Length of student desk	

What is the length of 4 student desks pushed together with no gaps in between? Use the RDW process to solve on the back of this paper.

Center 3: Choose the Units to Measure Objects

Name 4 things in the classroom. Circle which unit you would use to measure that item, and record the measurement in the chart.

Object	Length of the Object
	inches/feet/yards
	inches/feet/yards
	inches/feet/yards
	inches/feet/yards

Billy measures his pencil. He tells his teacher it is 7 feet long. Use the back of this paper to explain how you know that Billy is incorrect and how he can change his answer to be correct.

Center 4: Find Benchmarks

Look around the room to find 2 or 3 objects for each benchmark length. Write each object in the chart and record the exact length.

Things that are about an **inch**.	Things that are about a **foot**.	Things that are about a **yard**.
1. _____ inches	1. _____ inches	1. _____ inches
2. _____ inches	2. _____ inches	2. _____ inches
3. _____ inches	3. _____ inches	3. _____ inches

Center 5: Choose a Tool to Measure

Circle what you chose to measure each item. Then measure and record the length in the chart. Circle the unit.

Object	Measurement Tool	Measurement
Length of the rug	12-inch ruler / yardstick	_______ inches/feet
Math book	12-inch ruler / yardstick	_______ inches/feet
Pencil	12-inch ruler / yardstick	_______ inches/feet
Length of the chalkboard	12-inch ruler / yardstick	_______ inches/feet
Pink eraser	12-inch ruler / yardstick	_______ inches/feet

Sera's jump rope is the length of 6 math books. On the back of this paper, make a tape diagram to show the length of Sera's jump rope. Then write a repeated addition sentence using the math book measurement from the chart to find the length of Sera's jump rope.

Name ______________________________ Date ______________

1. Circle the unit you would use to measure each item.

Marker	inch / foot / yard
Height of a car	inch / foot / yard
Birthday card	inch / foot / yard
Soccer field	inch / foot / yard
Length of a computer screen	inch / foot / yard
Height of a bunk bed	inch / foot / yard

Name ______________________________ Date ______________

1. Circle the unit you would use to measure each item.

Height of a door	inch / foot / yard
Math book	inch / foot / yard
Pencil	inch / foot / yard
Length of a car	inch / foot / yard
Length of your street	inch / foot / yard
Paint brush	inch / foot / yard

2. Circle the correct estimate for each object.

   a. The height of a flagpole is more than / less than / about the same as the length of a yardstick.

   b. The width of a door is more than / less than / about the same as the length of a yardstick.

   c. The length of a laptop computer is more than / less than / about the same as the length of a 12-inch ruler.

   d. The length of a cellphone is more than / less than / about the same as the length of a 12-inch ruler.

3. Name 3 things in your classroom. Decide which unit you would use to measure that item. Record it in the chart in a full statement.

Item	Unit
a.	I would use ________________ to measure the length of ______________________________.
b.	
c.	

4. Name 3 things in your home. Decide which unit you would use to measure that item. Record it in the chart in a full statement.

Item	Unit
a.	I would use ________________ to measure the length of ______________________________.
b.	
c.	

Lesson 17

Objective: Develop estimation strategies by applying prior knowledge of length and using mental benchmarks.

Suggested Lesson Structure

Fluency Practice	(10 minutes)
Application Problem	(5 minutes)
Concept Development	(35 minutes)
Student Debrief	(10 minutes)
Total Time	**(60 minutes)**

Fluency Practice (10 minutes)

- Subtraction Fact Flash Cards **2.OA.2** (5 minutes)
- Grade 2 Core Fluency Differentiated Practice Sets **2.OA.2** (5 minutes)

Subtraction Fact Flash Cards (5 minutes)

Materials: (T) Flash Cards Set 1

Note: This is a teacher-directed, whole-class activity. By practicing subtraction facts, students gain mastery of differences within 20 through regular, motivating practice.

Grade 2 Core Fluency Differentiated Practice Sets (5 minutes)

Materials: (S) Core Fluency Practice Sets from G2–M7–Lesson 1

Note: During G2–M7–Topic D and for the remainder of the year, each day's fluency includes an opportunity for review and mastery of the sums and differences with totals through 20 by means of the Core Fluency Practice Sets or Sprints. The process is detailed and Practice Sets are provided in G2–M7–Lesson 1.

Application Problem (5 minutes)

Benjamin measures his forearm and records the length as 15 inches. Then he measures his upper arm and realizes it's the same!

a. How long is one of Benjamin's arms?

b. What is the total length of both Benjamin's arms together?

Note: This Application Problem provides practice of the previous day's concepts. Provide support when needed, but encourage students to solve independently as much as possible.

60 in.
15 in. 15 in. 15 in. 15 in.
30 in. 30 in.

a) 15 + 15 = 30 inches
b) 30 + 30 = 60 inches

Concept Development (35 minutes)

Materials: (T) 2 charts (pictured below), new unused pink eraser

The beginning of this Concept Development provides a structure for students to develop a class list of mental benchmarks. Choose a mental benchmark for each length unit that is meaningful for each individual class.

Part 1: Identify mental benchmarks.

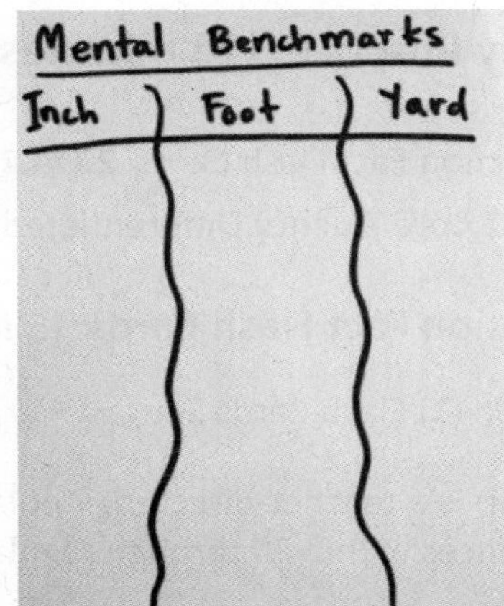

T: Look back at your recording sheets from yesterday's centers. Let's make a list of things we measured that were about the size of a foot. (Record ideas on the chart as students say them.)

S: My math journal was about a foot. It was just a little bit shorter. → The construction paper was exactly a foot. → The homework sheet was a little less than a foot long.

T: What on our list could remind us about the length of a foot?

S: The paper!

T: The length of the paper or the 12-inch ruler can be a mental benchmark for the length of a foot or 12 inches.

T: How about a mental benchmark for a yard? (Chart as students share.)

S: My arms are a yard when I hold them open like this. → I measured my brother's bike at home and it was 3 feet, which is a yard! → The width of our classroom door was exactly a yard!

T: Which item on our list should be our class benchmark for the yard?

S: The width of the door!

T: Look at your recording sheet. Did anyone find something that could be our mental benchmark for an inch?

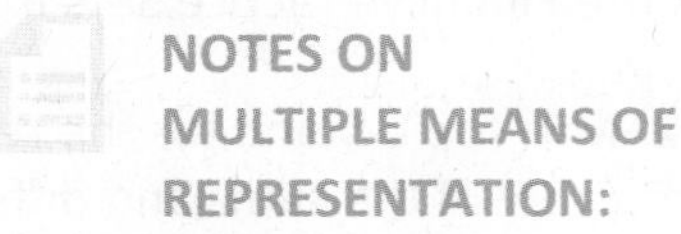

Explain the idea of a mental benchmark by showing a few examples. For instance, demonstrate that width of paper clip is about a centimeter. Explain that having the mental benchmark helps in estimating the length of objects.

S: The middle part of my finger is an inch! → I measured a quarter and it was an inch long.

T: Which one should be our benchmark for an inch?

S: The quarter!

T: Talk to your partner about how it is helpful to understand mental benchmarks when people say things like, "Your new teacher is about 6 feet tall," "Draw a line about 6 inches long," or "The room is about 10 yards long."

S: Then you will know better who might be your new teacher. → Then you will know about how long to draw the line. → Then you can understand the size of the room. → If you understand benchmarks, you can see what people are talking about better.

Part 2: Use mental benchmarks to estimate lengths and check estimations with measurement tools.

T: The width of a quarter is a benchmark for...?

S: An inch.

T: The length of a paper is a benchmark for...?

S: A foot.

T: The width of a door is a benchmark for...?

S: A yard!

T: Let's use mental benchmarks to estimate measurements.

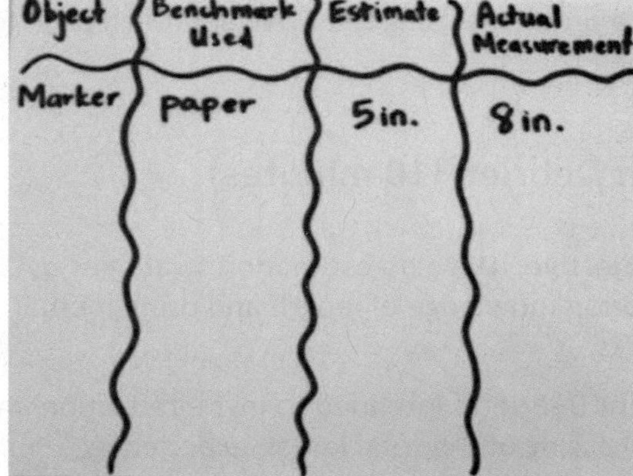

T: Step 1: Use a mental benchmark to think how long something is. Look at this dry erase marker. Turn and talk: How long do you think it is?

S: Shorter than the paper. Maybe 7 inches? → It's longer than a quarter, maybe 5 inches or so.

T: (Record estimates.)

T: Step 2: Let's measure and see how close our estimates are! Which unit should we use?

S: Inches!

P.6

T: (Have a student measure and record the length on the chart.)

S: The actual length of the marker is 8 inches.

T: Were our estimates close to the actual length?

S: Yes! → Mine wasn't that close. → Some were.

T: What strategies can we use so that our estimates are close to the actual length?

S: Think about which benchmark is closest in length to what we are measuring and compare. Is it a little more or a little less, a lot more or a lot less? → Visualize how many times a benchmark makes the same length as the thing you're measuring.

NOTES ON MULTIPLE MEANS OF ACTION AND EXPRESSION:

Before this lesson, find some time to practice estimating and measuring different objects with students with disabilities and those who are performing below grade level. This practice will allow them to participate in the lesson in a more meaningful way and perhaps take the lead in group discussions.

T: Step 1 is...?

S: Estimate using a benchmark!

T: Step 2 is...?

S: Measure to see how close we are.

Repeat the above process with two or three more objects around the room before moving on to the Problem Set.

Problem Set (10 minutes)

Students should do their personal best to complete the Problem Set within the allotted 10 minutes. For some classes, it may be appropriate to modify the assignment by specifying which problems they work on first. Some problems do not specify a method for solving. Students solve these problems using the RDW approach used for Application Problems.

Name Samantha Date

Estimate the length of each item by using a mental benchmark. Then measure the item using feet, inches, or yards.

Item	Mental Benchmark	Estimation	Actual Length
a. Width of the door	door handle to floor	3 ft	about 2 ft
b. Width of the whiteboard or chalkboard	door handle to floor	2 yards	2 yards
c. Height of a desk	door handle to floor	3 ft	2 feet
d. Length of a desk	arm	2 feet	2 feet
e. Length of a reading book	pencil	10 inches	8 inches

Item	Mental Benchmark	Estimation	Actual Length
f. Length of a crayon	pencil	8 inches	7 inches
g. Length of the room	yard stick	4 yards	5 yards
h. Length of a pair of scissors	pencil	8 inches	7 inches
i. Length of the window	ruler	3 feet	4 feet

Student Debrief (10 minutes)

Lesson Objective: Develop estimation strategies by applying prior knowledge of length and using mental benchmarks.

The Student Debrief is intended to invite reflection and active processing of the total lesson experience.

Invite students to review their solutions for the Problem Set. They should check work by comparing answers with a partner before going over answers as a class. Look for misconceptions or misunderstandings that can be addressed in the Debrief. Guide students in a conversation to debrief the Problem Set and process the lesson.

You may choose to use any combination of the questions below to lead the discussion.

- Look at your Problem Set. With a partner, figure out the difference between your estimate of the height of a desk and the actual measure of the height of a desk. Did you include the unit?
- Look at your Problem Set. Were there some estimates and actual length measures that were exactly the same? Why do you think that you were able to guess the right measurement for some items?
- How do mental benchmarks, objects that are about the same length as standard forms of measure like the 12-inch ruler, help when we are comparing length?

- Talk to your partner about why getting good about estimating length could be helpful?
- Sometimes when we measure things, they are not exactly a foot or a yard long. How do we record things that are a foot and a little bit more or a yard and a foot more?

Exit Ticket (3 minutes)

After the Student Debrief, instruct students to complete the Exit Ticket. A review of their work will help you assess the students' understanding of the concepts that were presented in the lesson today and plan more effectively for future lessons. You may read the questions aloud to the students.

Name ______________________________ Date ______________

Estimate the length of each item by using a mental benchmark. Then measure the item using feet, inches, or yards.

Item	Mental Benchmark	Estimation	Actual Length
a. Width of the door			
b. Width of the white board or chalkboard			
c. Height of a desk			
d. Length of a desk			
e. Length of a reading book			

Item	Mental Benchmark	Estimation	Actual Length
f. Length of a crayon			
g. Length of the room			
h. Length of a pair of scissors			
i. Length of the window			

Name ______________________________ Date ______________

Estimate the length of each item by using a mental benchmark. Then measure the item using feet, inches, or yards.

Item	Mental Benchmark	Estimation	Actual Length
a. Length of an eraser			
b. Width of this paper			

Name ____________________ Date ____________

Estimate the length of each item by using a mental benchmark. Then measure the item using feet, inches, or yards.

Item	Mental Benchmark	Estimation	Actual Length
a. Length of a bed			
b. Width of a bed			
c. Height of a table			
d. Length of a table			
e. Length of a book			

Item	Mental Benchmark	Estimation	Actual Length
f. Length of your pencil			
g. Length of a refrigerator			
h. Height of a refrigerator			
i. Length of a sofa			

Lesson 18

Objective: Measure an item twice using different length units and compare; relate measurement to unit size.

Suggested Lesson Structure

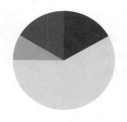

Fluency Practice	(10 minutes)
Application Problem	(5 minutes)
Concept Development	(35 minutes)
Student Debrief	(10 minutes)
Total Time	**(60 minutes)**

Fluency Practice (10 minutes)

- Decomposition Tree **2.OA.2** (5 minutes)
- Grade 2 Core Fluency Differentiated Practice Sets **2.OA.2** (5 minutes)

Decomposition Tree (5 minutes)

Materials: (S) Decomposition Tree Template (from G2–M7–Lesson 6)

Note: Students are given 90 seconds to decompose 20 inches. Students apply knowledge of sums and differences within 20 to length.

T: (Distribute tree template.)

T: You are going to break apart 20 inches on your Deco Tree for 90 seconds. Do as many problems as you can. Go!

S: (Work for 90 seconds.)

T: Now exchange your tree with your partner and check each other's work. (Allow students 30–45 seconds to check.)

T: Return each other's papers. Did you see another way to make 20 inches on your partner's paper? (Allow students to share for another 30 seconds.)

T: Turn your paper over. Let's break apart 20 inches for another minute.

Grade 2 Core Fluency Differentiated Practice Sets (5 minutes)

Materials: (S) Core Fluency Practice Sets from G2–M7–Lesson 1

Note: During G2–M7–Topic D and for the remainder of the year, each day's fluency includes an opportunity for review and mastery of the sums and differences with totals through 20 by means of the Core Fluency Practice Sets or Sprints. The process is detailed and Practice Sets provided in G2–M7–Lesson 1.

Application Problem (5 minutes)

Ezra is measuring things in his bedroom. He thinks his bed is about 2 yards. Is this a reasonable estimate? Explain your answer using pictures, words or numbers.

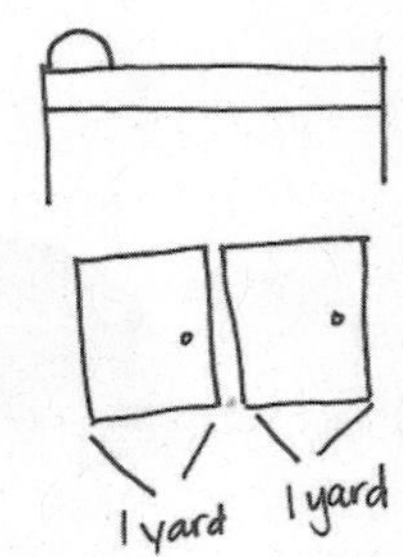

Ezra could be right because the bed could be a little longer than 2 classroom doors and that is 2 yards.

Note: This Application Problem provides practice using benchmarks to estimate measurement. When students finish invite them to share their reasoning either whole group or with partners.

Concept Development (35 minutes)

Materials: (T) Chart for recording measurements as pictured below (S) Centimeter ruler, inch ruler; 1 plain sheet of white paper; bag with an unsharpened pencil, a new crayon, a new eraser

Part 1: Compare centimeters and inches.

Assign Partners A and B.

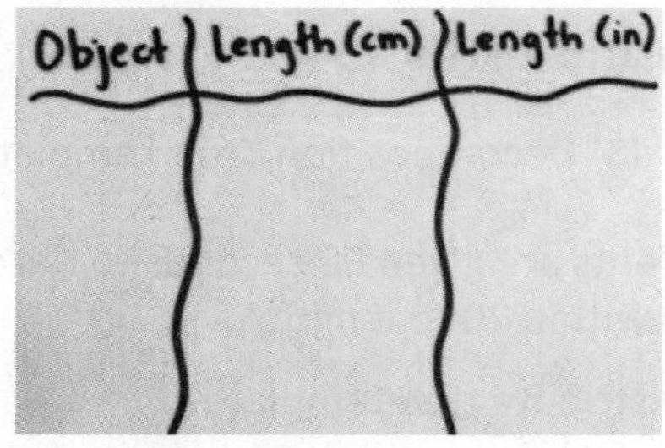

T: Partner A, measure the pencil using the inch ruler. Partner B, measure the pencil using the centimeter ruler.

T: Partner A, how long is the pencil?

S: About 7 inches!

T: (Record answer.) Partner B, how long is the pencil?

S: About 18 centimeters!

T: (Record answer.) Hmm, why do you think the measurements are so different? Turn and talk.

MP.2

S: We used different units to measure. → He measured with an inch ruler, and I used a centimeter ruler.

T: Are both measurements correct?

S: Yes!

T: Let's check and see. Partner A, this time measure the pencil with the centimeter ruler. Partner B, measure the pencil with the inch ruler.

S: (Measure.)

T: Are your measurements the same as your partner's when using the different rulers?

S: Yes!

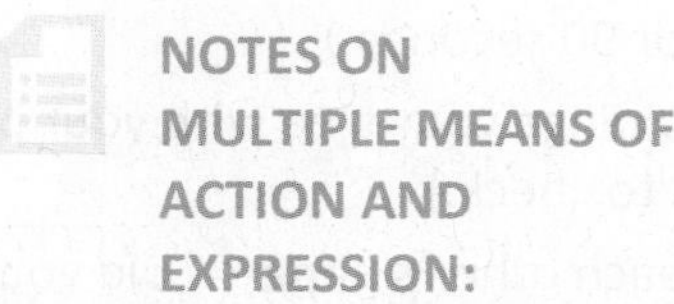

NOTES ON MULTIPLE MEANS OF ACTION AND EXPRESSION:

Scaffold the lesson for English language learners by pointing to the inch ruler and the centimeter ruler while giving directions. Point out the different units on the rulers while asking students which unit is bigger: the inch or the centimeters.

T: Which is longer, a unit of one centimeter or one inch?

S: An inch!

T: That means 7 inches is about the same length as 18 centimeters. Did we use more centimeters or more inches to measure the pencil?

S: More centimeters.

T: Why did we need more centimeters to measure the pencil?

S: Centimeters are smaller, so it takes more of them to cover the length of the pencil.

T: Talk to your partner about why the measurements are different for the same object.

S: Centimeters are smaller than inches. → It takes fewer inches to measure because inches are bigger. → The smaller the unit, the more units it takes to measure the same thing.

Part 2: Measure using centimeters and inches.

Give students time to measure both the objects in their bags and the sides of the white paper using both inches and centimeters. They should stop to record the measurements on the plain paper as they go. Encourage students to replicate your chart to organize their work.

T: What pattern do you see in your measurements using the different rulers?

S: The number of inches is always smaller. → The number of centimeters is always bigger, because a centimeter unit is smaller than an inch unit and it takes more of them when we are measuring.

T: Does this remind you of the time we measured straws with two different size paper clips?

S: Yes!

T: Turn and talk: What do you know about measurement and unit size?

S: The smaller the unit means it takes more of those units when measuring something. → The bigger the unit means you use less of them.

T: Using your rulers, draw two lines on your white paper. Make one line 5 inches and the other 5 centimeters.

T: Before you begin, tell your partner which line will be longer.

S: The 5 inch line!

T: Tell your partner how you know!

S: One inch is longer than 1 centimeter, so 5 inches will be longer than 5 centimeters. → Inches are longer, so the line will be longer too.

T: (Allow students time to draw the two lines.)

T: Were we right? Is the 5-inch line longer than the 5-centimeter line?

S: Yes!

T: Look at your lines. How many centimeters do you think it would take to equal 5 inches? Use your centimeter ruler to check your estimate.

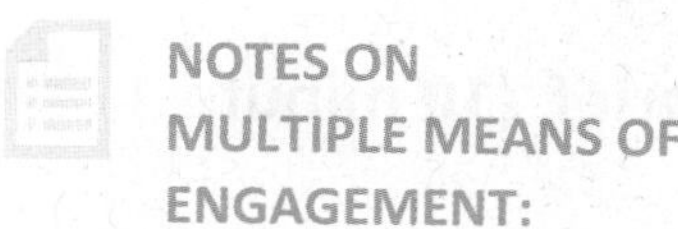

Support students performing below grade level by repeating the activity with different lengths. Ask them to draw lines that are 6 centimeters long and 6 inches long. Repeat until students are sure that the inch line is longer than the centimeter line and can explain that:

- The same number of units will make a longer line when using inches than centimeters.
- It takes more centimeters than inches to measure different objects.

S: (Allow students time to check their estimate.) Thirteen centimeters is about 5 inches.

T: Measure to see about how many inches 5 centimeters is.

S: About 2 inches!

T: How many centimeters would it take to be longer than 5 inches? Would you have to measure again or could you figure it out another way?

S: We wouldn't have to measure again because we know that 13 centimeters is about 5 inches, so to be longer than 5 inches, it can be any number of centimeters more than 13.

Problem Set (10 minutes)

Students should do their personal best to complete the Problem Set within the allotted 10 minutes. For some classes, it may be appropriate to modify the assignment by specifying which problems they work on first. Some problems do not specify a method for solving. Students solve these problems using the RDW approach used for Application Problems.

Name Samantha Date

Measure the lines in inches and centimeters. Round the measurements to the nearest inch or centimeter.

1. 13 cm 5 in

2. 11 cm 4 in

3. 14 cm 6 in

4. 8 cm 3 in

5. Draw lines with the measurements below.
   a. 3 centimeters long
   b. 3 inches long

6.
   a. Did you use more inches or centimeters when measuring the lines above? centimeter
   b. Write a sentence to explain why you used more of that unit. because centimeters are smaller so you need more

7. Thomas and Chris both measured the crayon below but came up with different answers. Explain why both answers are correct.

Thomas: 8 cm
Chris: 3 in

Explanation: one measured in centimeters and one measured in inches so they are both correct

Student Debrief (10 minutes)

Lesson Objective: Measure an item twice using different length units and compare; relate measurement to unit size.

The Student Debrief is intended to invite reflection and active processing of the total lesson experience.

Invite students to review their solutions for the Problem Set. They should check work by comparing answers with a partner before going over answers as a class. Look for misconceptions or misunderstandings that can be addressed in the Debrief. Guide students in a conversation to debrief the Problem Set and process the lesson.

You may choose to use any combination of the questions below to lead the discussion.

- Look at the lines you measured on your Problem Set. Talk to your partner about why it is important to label the length with your chosen unit. Why is it important to label our numbers in math in general?

- Look at Problem 5 on your Problem Set. Are the lines you drew equal in length? Why might somebody think that the lines should be equal?
- Can you think of other times where we have used different units in math?
- When you measured in centimeters and inches, did you ever have to round up or down? How did you do that?
- Talk to your partner about why the unit size matters when we are measuring things.
- Why do we measure using different units? When would you want to measure using a small unit? A large unit?

Exit Ticket (3 minutes)

After the Student Debrief, instruct students to complete the Exit Ticket. A review of their work will help you assess the students' understanding of the concepts that were presented in the lesson today and plan more effectively for future lessons. You may read the questions aloud to the students.

Name ______________________________ Date ______________

Measure the lines in inches and centimeters. Round the measurements to the nearest inch or centimeter.

1.

_______ cm _______ in

2.

_______ cm _______ in

3.

_______ cm _______ in

4.

_______ cm _______ in

5. Draw lines with the measurements below.
   a. 3 centimeters long

   b. 3 inches long

6.
   a. Did you use more inches or more centimeters when measuring the lines above?

   ____

   b. Write a sentence to explain why you used more of that unit.

   ____

   ____

7. Thomas and Chris both measured the crayon below but came up with different answers. Explain why both answers are correct.

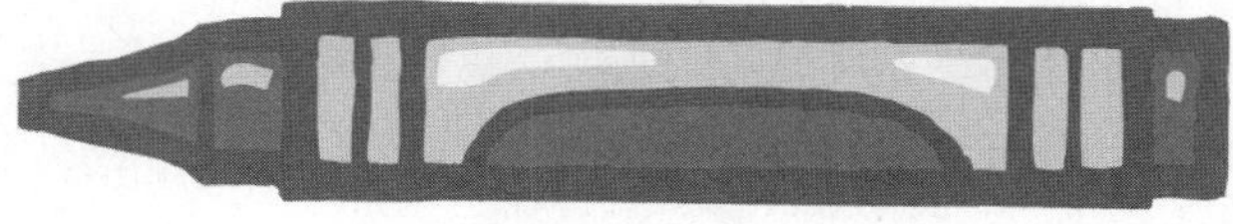

Thomas: ___8___ cm
Chris: ___3___ in

Explanation: ______________________________

____

____

____

Name ______________________________ Date ______________

Measure the lines in inches and centimeters.

1.

_______ cm _______ in

2.

_______ cm _______ in

Name ______________________________ Date ______________

Measure the lines in inches and centimeters. Round the measurements to the nearest inch or centimeter.

1.

_____ cm _____ in

2.

_____ cm _____ in

3.

_____ cm _____ in

4.

_____ cm _____ in

5. a. Draw a line that is 5 centimeters in length.

   b. Draw a line that is 5 inches in length.

6. a. Draw a line that is 7 inches in length.

   b. Draw a line that is 7 centimeters in length.

7. Takeesha drew a line 9 centimeters long. Damani drew a line 4 inches long. Takeesha says her line is longer than Damani's because 9 is greater than 4. Explain why Takeesha might be wrong.

___

___

___

8. Draw a line that is 9 centimeters long and a line that is 4 inches long to prove that Takeesha is wrong.

Lesson 19

Objective: Measure to compare the differences in length using inches, feet, and yards.

Suggested Lesson Structure

■ Fluency Practice	(11 minutes)
■ Concept Development	(24 minutes)
■ Application Problem	(15 minutes)
■ Student Debrief	(10 minutes)
Total Time	**(60 minutes)**

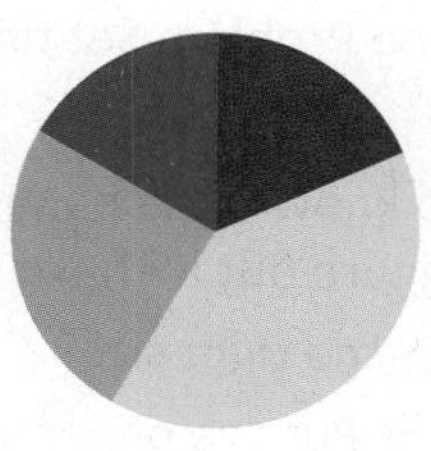

Fluency Practice (11 minutes)

- Subtraction from Tens **2.NBT.5** (2 minutes)
- Sprint: Subtraction Patterns **2.OA.2, 2.NBT.5** (9 minutes)

Subtraction from Tens (2 minutes)

Note: This fluency reviews mental math strategies within 100 and subtraction of 9 or 8 from any number.

T: When I say a basic fact, you add 10 to the whole and continue until I say to stop. So, after 11 – 9, you would solve 21 – 9, then...?

S: 31 – 9, 41 – 9, 51 – 9.

T: Yes, go as high as you can before I give the signal to stop. Let's begin. 11 – 9.

S: (Work.)

T: (Stop them when you see the slowest student has completed at least two problems.)

Continue with the following possible sequence: 12 – 8, 11 – 8, and 13 – 9.

Sprint: Subtraction Patterns (9 minutes)

Materials: (S) Subtraction Patterns Sprint

Note: Students practice subtraction in order to gain mastery of the sums and differences within 20 and see relationships with higher numbers.

Concept Development (24 minutes)

Materials: (T) Piece of butcher paper (30 inches × 18 inches), 1 student desk (18 inches × 24 inches), 12-inch ruler, yardstick, piece of string (7 feet long) (S) Personal white boards

Note: The dialogue below uses hypothetical measurements. The length of the string should be about 10 to 15 feet shorter than the length of the classroom wall. The Application Problem should be completed before sending students off to work on the Problem Set. (The Problem Set time has been added to the Application Problem.)

T: I want to cover this desk in paper. I need to know if the paper is long enough. I need a few extra inches on each side to tape it down. Let's figure out if I have enough paper.

T: What do we need to do to see if the paper is the right size?

S: Measure both the desktop and the paper. → Put the paper on the desk to make sure the paper is longer than the table. → Use a ruler or a yardstick to measure both lengths.

T: Good ideas! Let's measure the desktop and the paper. (Call a student volunteer to measure the paper and another to measure the table.)

MP.5

T: What measurement tool do you think they should use to measure the paper and the table? Why? Talk to your partner.

S: A yardstick, because I can see that the paper and the table are both longer than a 12-inch ruler. → We won't have to measure and advance so many times if we use a yardstick. → We can use the yardstick, but use inches to actually measure.

T: If we use the yardstick, why don't we have to measure in yards? Talk to your partner.

S: We can choose inches, feet, or yards. → We can do what we want. It just depends on what we are measuring. → The yardstick can be used to measure yards, but we only need inches for the table.

S: (Volunteers measure the paper and the table with a yardstick.)

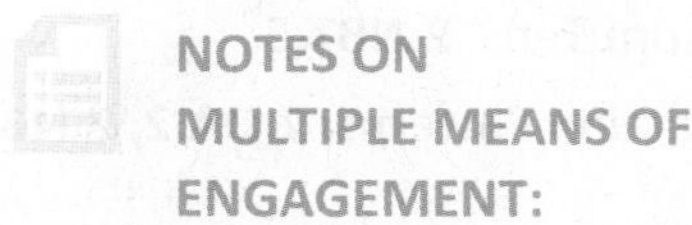

NOTES ON MULTIPLE MEANS OF ENGAGEMENT:

Support the oral practice of English language learners by providing them with sentence frames to help in turn-and-talk with partners: "The ____ is ________longer/shorter than the ______because __________." Post the sentence starters so that they can easily refer to them.

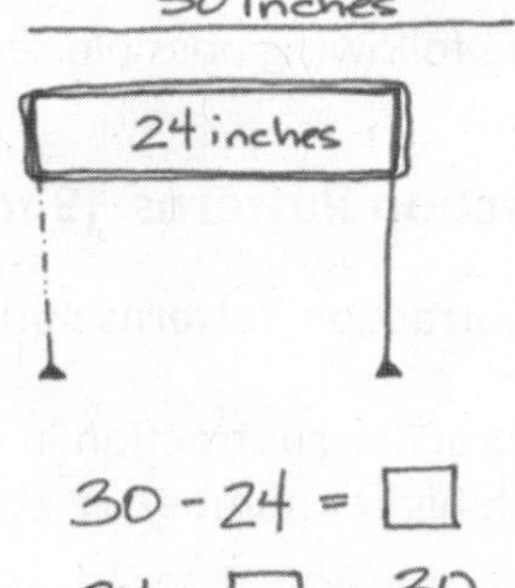

T: How long is the table?

S: 24 inches.

T: (Record measurement.) How long is the paper?

S: 30 inches.

T: (Record measurement.) Which is longer?

S: The paper!

T: Turn and talk. How much longer is the paper, and how do you know?

S: The paper is 6 inches longer because 30 – 24 is 6. → It's 6 inches longer because 24 + 6 = 30.

T: (Record the difference in the two lengths as a number sentence.) Do we have enough paper to cover the table?

S: Yes!

Invite students to measure and compare the lengths of the following objects: journal and pencil, crayon and pink eraser, and marker and scissors. Have them record each length and the difference in lengths as they go. Each time, they should compare the two lengths and describe the difference using a number sentence.

T: Can you help me with one more thing? I would like to use this string to hang our work along the wall. How can we figure out if we have enough string?

S: Measure the string and the wall.

T: Which measurement tool should we use?

S: The yardstick!

T: We know we don't have to measure in yards. What unit should we use this time?

S: Inches! → Feet! → Yards.

T: First, let's measure both lengths in feet so we can more precise than we could be using yards. Inches would be too much! Do you remember what to do if our measurement falls in between the foot hash marks?

S: If it is more than halfway, or 6 inches, to the next foot we will round up, if it is less than halfway we will round down.

T: Good! (Call on a few student volunteers to measure the length of the wall and the length of the string.) While these students are measuring silently, it is everyone's job to tally the number of feet as they go.

T: (Allow students time to measure the string.) How long is the string?

S: 17 feet!

T: (Record measurement.)

T: (Allow students time to measure the wall.) How long is the wall?

S: 32 feet.

T: (Record measurement.)

T: Uh, oh. We need more string. Turn and talk: How can we figure out how much more string we need?

S: Subtract! → Add on from 17 to get to 32.

T: (Write the number sentences on the board as shown to the right.)

T: Count on from 17 to figure out how much more string we need.

S: Seventeen plus 3 is 20, plus 12 more is 32. We need 15 more feet.

$17 + \square = 32$

$32 - 17 = \square$

$17 \xrightarrow{+3} 20 \xrightarrow{+12} 32$

We need 15 feet more.

Repeat this activity, this time measuring the string and wall using yards. Students should again compare the two lengths and describe the difference using a number sentence.

T: What was the difference between the length of the string and the length of the wall when we measured in feet?

S: 15 feet.

T: What was the difference between the length of the string and the length of the wall when we measured in yards?

S: 5 yards.

T: Did the length of the string or the wall change? Why are the differences so different?

S: No! Feet and yards are different. → We used a different unit each time. → Feet are smaller than yards, so we need more of them to cover the same distance.

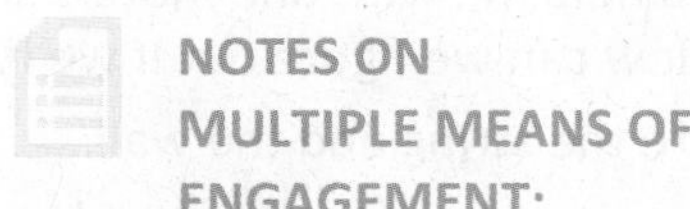

NOTES ON MULTIPLE MEANS OF ENGAGEMENT:

Challenge above grade level students by asking them what would happened if Katia is asked to hang two strings of lights on the building wall. How many more yards of lights will she have to buy? Ask students to explain what strategies they used to find the answer.

Application Problem (15 minutes)

Katia is hanging decorative lights. The strand of lights is 46 feet long. The building wall is 84 feet long. How many more feet of lights does Katia need to buy to equal the length of the wall?

Note: This Application Problem provides practice with comparing the difference between measurements without making the measurement. When students finish, invite them to share their reasoning with either the whole group or with partners.

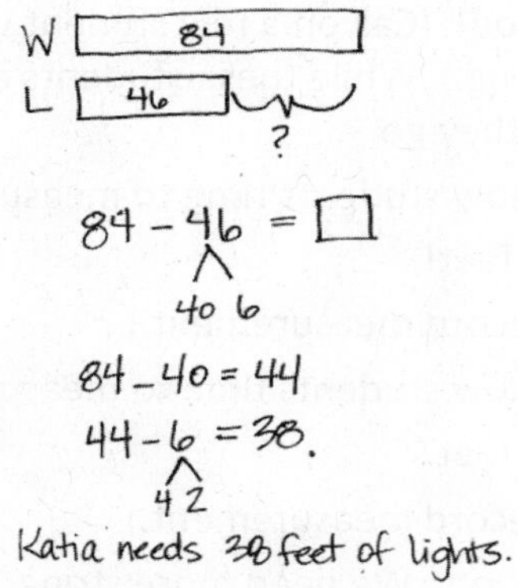

Problem Set (10 minutes)

Students should do their personal best to complete the Problem Set within the allotted 10 minutes. For some classes, it may be appropriate to modify the assignment by specifying which problems they work on first. Some problems do not specify a method for solving. Students solve these problems using the RDW approach used for Application Problems.

Student Debrief (10 minutes)

Lesson Objective: Measure to compare the differences in length using inches, feet, and yards.

The Student Debrief is intended to invite reflection and active processing of the total lesson experience.

Invite students to review their solutions for the Problem Set. They should check work by comparing answers with a partner before going over answers as a class. Look for misconceptions or misunderstandings that can be addressed in the Debrief. Guide students in a conversation to debrief the Problem Set and process the lesson.

You may choose to use any combination of the questions below to lead the discussion.

- When you measured the lines on your Problem Set, did the endpoint fall exactly on an inch hash mark? Talk to your partner about what you did if the endpoints of the lines fell between inch hash marks.
- Look at Problem 4 on your Problem Set. Tell your partner how long Martha's fence is. Did anyone have a measurement smaller than 54 yards? Without doing any calculations, how do you know that this is incorrect?
- Explain to your partner what you did first in Problem 5. What did you do next?
- Today in the lesson when we were measuring and comparing lengths, how did you decide which tool to use? Talk to your partner about when and why you would choose a 12-inch ruler instead of a yardstick, or a yardstick instead of a 12-inch ruler.
- Sometimes we choose to measure in yards, other times in feet, yet others in inches or centimeters. Talk to your partner about when you might measure using each of these units. (Yards for a football field, feet for a wall, inches for a book, centimeters for a bean.)
- What strategies did you use to solve the Application Problem? How many more yards of lights does Katia need?

Name Samantha Date

Measure each set of lines in inches write the length on the line. Complete the comparison sentence.

1. Line A ____________

   Line B ____________

   Line A measured about 5 inches. Line B measured about 2 inches.

   Line A is about 3 inches **longer** than Line B.

2. Line C ____________

   Line D ____________

   Line C measured about 3 inches. Line D measured about 5 inches.

   Line C is about 2 inches **shorter** than Line D.

3. Solve the following problems:

   a. 32 ft. + 55 ft = 87 ft. (87 − 32 = 55)

   b. 68 ft. − 29 ft. = 39 ft. (68 − 29 = 39)

   c. 61 ft. − 43 ft. = 18 ft. (43 + 18 = 61)

4. Tammy and Martha both built fences around their properties. Tammy's fence is 54 yards long. Martha's fence is 29 yards longer than Tammy's.

   Tammy's Fence 54 yards

   Martha's Fence ____ yards

   a. How long is Martha's fence? 83 yards (54 + 29 = 83)

   b. What is the total length of both fences? 137 yards (83 + 54 = 137)

Exit Ticket (3 minutes)

After the Student Debrief, instruct students to complete the Exit Ticket. A review of their work will help you assess the students' understanding of the concepts that were presented in the lesson today and plan more effectively for future lessons. You may read the questions aloud to the students.

A # Correct ____

Subtract.

1	10 - 1 =		23	21 - 6 =	
2	10 - 2 =		24	91 - 6 =	
3	20 - 2 =		25	10 - 7 =	
4	40 - 2 =		26	11 - 7 =	
5	10 - 2 =		27	31 - 7 =	
6	11 - 2 =		28	10 - 8 =	
7	21 - 2 =		29	11 - 8 =	
8	51 - 2=		30	41 - 8 =	
9	10 - 3 =		31	10 - 9 =	
10	11 - 3 =		32	11 - 9 =	
11	21 - 3 =		33	51 - 9 =	
12	61 - 3 =		34	12 - 3 =	
13	10 - 4 =		35	82 - 3 =	
14	11 - 4 =		36	13 - 5 =	
15	21 - 4 =		37	73 - 5 =	
16	71 - 4 =		38	14 - 6 =	
17	10 - 5 =		39	84 - 6 =	
18	11 - 5 =		40	15 - 8 =	
19	21 - 5 =		41	95 - 8 =	
20	81 - 5 =		42	16 - 7 =	
21	10 - 6 =		43	46 - 7 =	
22	11 - 6 =		44	68 - 9 =	

B Improvement _____ # Correct _____

Subtract.

1	10 - 2 =		23	21 - 6 =	
2	20 - 2 =		24	41 - 6 =	
3	30 - 2 =		25	10 - 7 =	
4	50 - 2 =		26	11 - 7 =	
5	10 - 2 =		27	51 - 7 =	
6	11 - 2 =		28	10 - 8 =	
7	21 - 2 =		29	11 - 8 =	
8	61 - 2 =		30	61 - 8 =	
9	10 - 3 =		31	10 - 9 =	
10	11 - 3 =		32	11 - 9 =	
11	21 - 3 =		33	31 - 9 =	
12	71 - 3 =		34	12 - 3 =	
13	10 - 4 =		35	92 - 3 =	
14	11 - 4 =		36	13 - 5 =	
15	21 - 4 =		37	43 - 5 =	
16	81 - 4 =		38	14 - 6 =	
17	10 - 5 =		39	64 - 6 =	
18	11 - 5 =		40	15 - 8 =	
19	21 - 5 =		41	85 - 8 =	
20	91 - 5 =		42	16 - 7 =	
21	10 - 6 =		43	76 - 7 =	
22	11 - 6 =		44	58 - 9 =	

Name ______________________________ Date ______________

Measure each set of lines in inches, and write the length on the line. Complete the comparison sentence.

1. Line A ____

   Line B ______________________

   Line A measured about _____ inches. Line B measured about ______ inches.

   Line A is about ______ inches **longer** than Line B.

2. Line C ______________________________

   Line D ____

   Line C measured about _____ inches. Line D measured about _____ inches.

   Line C is about ______ inches **shorter** than Line D.

3. Solve the following problems:

   a. 32 ft + ________ = 87 ft

   b. 68 ft - 29 ft = ________

   c. ________ - 43 ft = 18 ft

4. Tammy and Martha both built fences around their properties. Tammy's fence is 54 yards long. Martha's fence is 29 yards longer than Tammy's.

Tammy's Fence 54 yards	**Martha's Fence** ________ yards

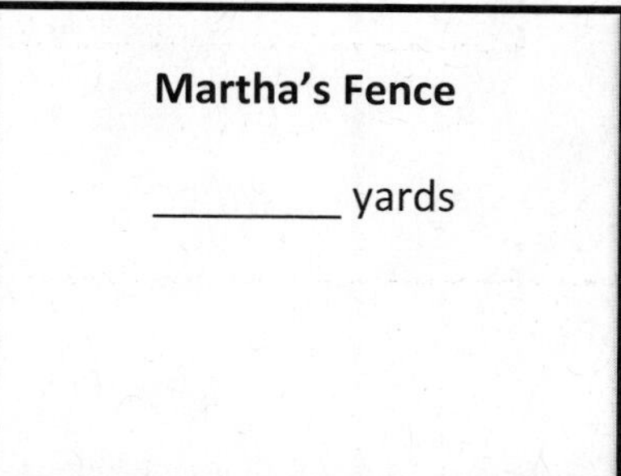

   a. How long is Martha's fence? __________ yards

   b. What is the total length of both fences? __________ yards

Name ______________________________ Date ______________

Line A ____

Line B ____

Line A measured about ____ inches. Line B measured about ____ inches.

Line A is about _____ inches **longer/shorter** than Line B.

Name ______________________________ Date ______________

Measure each set of lines in inches, and write the length on the line. Complete the comparison sentence.

1. Line A ____

   Line B ______________________

   Line A measured about _____ inches. Line B measured about _____ inches.

   Line A is about _____ inches longer than Line B.

2. Line C ___________________________________

   Line D ______________________________

   Line C measured about _____ inches. Line D measured about _____ inches.

   Line C is about _____ inches shorter than Line D.

3. Solve. Check your answers with a related addition or subtraction sentence.

   a. 8 inches – 5 inches = _______ inches

      _______ inches + 5 inches = 8 inches

b. 8 centimeters + ________ centimeters = 19 centimeters

c. 17 centimeters – 8 centimeters = ________ centimeters

d. ________ centimeters + 6 centimeters = 18 centimeters

e. 2 inches + _______ inches = 7 inches

Topic E

Problem Solving with Customary and Metric Units

2.MD.5, 2.MD.6, 2.NBT.2, 2.NBT.4, 2.NBT.5

Focus Standard:	2.MD.5	Use addition and subtraction within 100 to solve word problems involving lengths that are given in the same units, e.g., by using drawings (such as drawings of rulers) and equations with a symbol for the unknown number to represent the problem.
	2.MD.6	Represent whole numbers as lengths from 0 on a number line diagram with equally spaced points corresponding to the numbers 0, 1, 2, ..., and represent whole-number sums and differences within 100 on a number line diagram.
Instructional Days:	3	
Coherence -Links from:	G2–M2	Addition and Subtraction of Length Units
	G2–M3	Place Value, Counting, and Comparison of Numbers to 1,000
-Links to:	G3–M2	Place Value and Problem Solving with Units of Measure

Beginning Topic E, Lesson 20 has students using drawings to compare lengths and writing equations with an unknown to represent problems, just as they did in Module 2 (**2.MD.5**). In this lesson, however, students solve *two-digit* addition and subtraction measurement problems using customary *or* metric units, composing or decomposing a ten if necessary. Just as they made comparisons and found differences using bar graphs in Topic A, students now compare lengths using the tape diagram, essentially a horizontal bar, to solve two-step problems. For example, "Frankie has a 54-inch piece of rope and another piece that is 18 inches shorter than the first. What is the total length of both ropes?" Students also solve problems in the context of geometry to find the missing lengths of a rectangle or the height of a pyramid.

Building upon their understanding of length, students represent whole numbers as lengths on a number line (**2.MD.6**) in Lesson 21. Students identify unknown numbers by using mental benchmarks or reference points (e.g., 5, 10, 25, 50) and intervals of 1, 5, or 10. For example, on a number line with 6 equally spaced segments and endpoints 20 and 50, a student marks the middle segment as 35, realizing that 20 to 35 and 35 to 50 are the same distance, or length. Problems increase in complexity as students use their understanding of place value and the distance between positions to label points. For example, they label 340 as one endpoint when 350 is the midpoint and 360 is the other endpoint.

In Lesson 22, students represent two-digit sums and differences on a number line (**2.MD.6**) and write a number sentence to represent the addition or subtraction situation. For example, they solve the following problems using a number line marked with endpoints 0 and 50, marked intervals of 10, and unmarked intervals of 5. "On a football field, Pepe starts running at the 10 yard line. He runs 25 yards, pauses, and runs 11 more yards. Which yard line is Pepe on now? How far has he run?" In comparison, "Marcel starts running at the 5 yard line. He runs 15 yards, pauses, runs 15 more yards, stumbles, and runs 6 more yards. Which yard line is Marcel on now? How far has he run?" Students show how they solve these problems on the number line with different starting points, and they consider how two different measurement situations can result in the same total and are thus equal to each other (e.g., 25 + 11 = 15 + 15 + 6), as shown below.

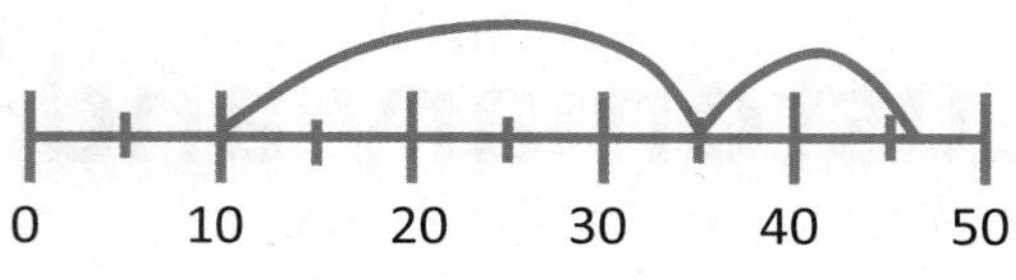

25 + 11 = 36 yards

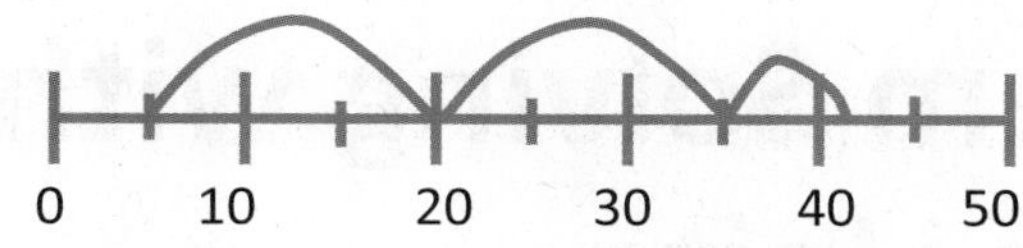

15 + 15 + 6 = 36 yards

A Teaching Sequence Towards Mastery of Problem Solving with Customary and Metric Units	
Objective 1:	**Solve two-digit addition and subtraction word problems involving length by using tape diagrams and writing equations to represent the problem.** **(Lesson 20)**
Objective 2:	**Identify unknown numbers on a number line diagram by using the distance between numbers and reference points.** **(Lesson 21)**
Objective 3:	**Represent two-digit sums and differences involving length by using the ruler as a number line.** **(Lesson 22)**

Lesson 20

Objective: Solve two-digit addition and subtraction word problems involving length by using tape diagrams and writing equations to represent the problem.

Suggested Lesson Structure

■ Fluency Practice	(10 minutes)
■ Concept Development	(40 minutes)
■ Student Debrief	(10 minutes)
Total Time	**(60 minutes)**

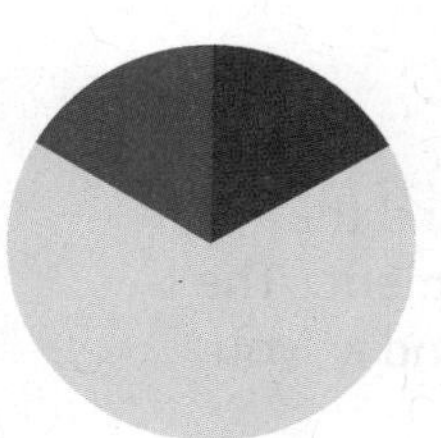

Fluency Practice (10 minutes)

- Compensation **2.NBT.5** (2 minutes)
- Sprint: Subtraction Patterns **2.OA.2, 2.NBT.5** (8 minutes)

Compensation (2 minutes)

Note: This fluency drill reviews the mental math strategy compensation. By making a multiple of 10, students solve a much simpler addition problem. Draw a number bond for the first problem on the board to help students visualize the decomposition.

T: (Write 42 + 19 = ______.) Let's use a mental math strategy to add.
How much more does 19 need to make the next ten?

S: 1 more.

T: Where can 19 get 1 more from?

S: From the 42!

T: Take 1 from 42 and give it to 19. Say the new number sentence, with the answer.

S: 41 + 20 = 61.

T: 37 + 19.

S: 36 + 20 = 56.

42 + 19
41 1
41 + 20 = 61

Continue with the following possible sequence: 29 + 23, 38 + 19, 32 + 19, 24 + 17, and 34 + 19.

Sprint: Subtraction Patterns (8 minutes)

Materials: (S) Subtraction Patterns Sprint

Note: Students practice subtraction in order to gain mastery of the sums and differences within 20 and identify relationships with higher numbers.

Concept Development (40 minutes)

Materials: (S) Personal white board, Problem Set

Note: For today's lesson, the Application Problem and the Problem Set are embedded in the Concept Development. The Problem Set is designed so that there is a "we do" and a "you do" portion.

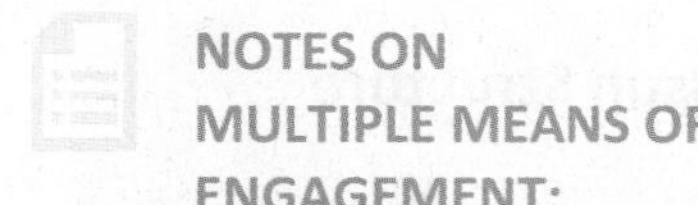

NOTES ON MULTIPLE MEANS OF ENGAGEMENT:

Scaffold the lesson for students who are struggling by using adding machine tape or sentence strips to measure, cut, and compare actual lengths. Students can then measure the difference between how long Mr. Ramos wants his scarf to be and the length of what he's knit so far (19 cm). Make sure that students line up the zero point as they compare the two lengths.

Part 1: Solve a *difference unknown* type problem.

Mr. Ramos has knit 19 inches of a scarf he wants to be 1 yard long. How many more inches of scarf does he need to knit? (This is Problem 1 on the Problem Set.)

T: Let's read through Problem 1 together.

T/S: (Read aloud.)

T: What can we draw?

S: The scarf now and when he is done. → A tape diagram.

T: Great! I'll give you a minute to draw quietly. When I give the signal, talk to your partner about how your drawing matches the story (as shown on right).

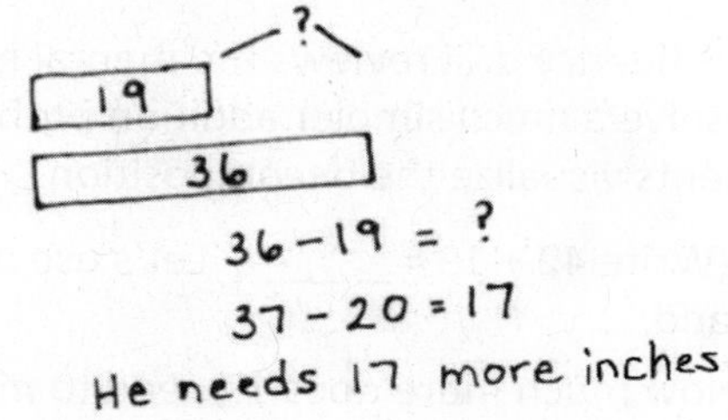

T: Turn and talk: Look at your drawing. What are you trying to find? Put a question mark to show the part we are trying to figure out.

S: (Work.)

T: Why did you put 36 in the tape showing the finished scarf?

S: Because 1 yard is 36 inches. → To find the answer we have to change 1 yard to 36 inches.

T: Yes! We can compare these lengths just like we compared data using bars in our graphs. (Draw the tape diagram on the board.)

T: Now, write a number sentence and statement to match your work. (Pause while students work.) Explain to your partner how you solved.

S: I wrote *19 + ____ = 36*. I counted up 1 to make 20, then added 16 more to reach 36, and 1 and 16 is 17. → I wrote *36 – 19 = ?* I added 1 to both numbers, so I wouldn't have to rename. And 37 – 20 = 17.)

T: Tell your partner the answer in a statement.

S: He needs to knit 17 more centimeters.

T: Use what we have practiced to complete Problem 2 on your Problem Set by yourself.

Let students work independently on the next problem. Have them compare with a partner when they are finished. Circulate to give support to those students who need it.

Part 2: Solve a two-step problem with a *compare with smaller unknown* type problem as one step.

Frankie has a 64-inch piece of rope and another piece that is 18 inches shorter than the first. What is the total length of both ropes? (This is Problem 3 on the Problem Set.)

T: Let's read this problem together.

T: Do we know how long each rope is?

S: No. → We know how long one of the ropes is, 64 inches. → We don't know how long the shorter rope is.

T: That's right. Our first step is to find out the length of the shorter rope to answer the question. Then we can answer the question.

T: What can we draw?

S The ropes. → A tape diagram.

T: Yes. Let's do this one together. First, let's draw a tape diagram that shows how to find the length of the shorter rope. Remember to put a question mark to show what will answer the question.

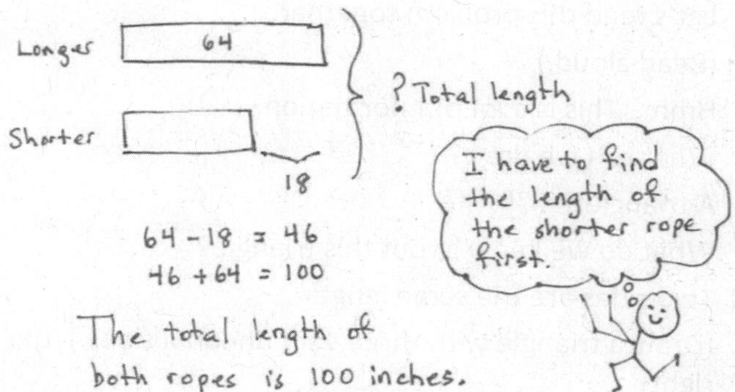

Circulate and guide students to understand that 18 inches is not the length of the shorter rope; rather, it is the difference. Also guide the students to place the question mark not within the tape of the shorter rope, but where it shows the total length of both ropes.

T: Turn and talk: How did you label your drawing? Where did you write the 18? Where did you write your question mark?

S: (Share.)

T: Find the length of the shorter rope by writing an equation and telling the answer to your partner in a statement.

S: (Solve using any number of learned subtraction strategies, and check their answer with a partner.)

T: What is the length of the shorter rope?

S: 46 inches!

T: Did the problem ask how long the shorter rope is?

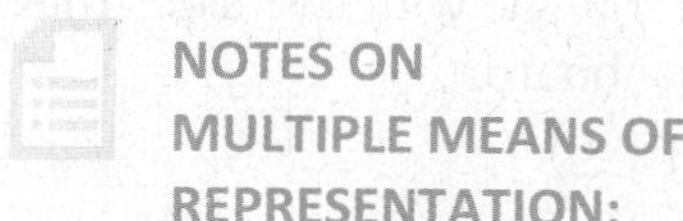

NOTES ON MULTIPLE MEANS OF REPRESENTATION:

English language learners might get confused about the difference between *short* and *shorter*. Use sets of objects to compare short and shorter objects to illustrate the difference between the two words. Have students practice saying the words as they pick out the shorter objects until they are successful in picking out the shorter objects.

S: No.

T: Write a number sentence and statement to answer the question. (Have students share their number sentences and statements once they are finished working.)

T: Excellent. The next problem also has two steps. Work on Problem 4 by yourself. When you are done, explain your solution path to your partner.

Let students work independently on the next problem. Have them compare with a partner when they are finished. Circulate to give support to those students who need it.

Part 3: Solve a *put together* problem involving geometry.

The total length of all three sides of a triangle is 96 feet. The triangle has two sides that are the same length. One of the equal sides measures 40 feet. What is the length of the side that is not equal? (This is Problem 5 on the Problem Set.)

T: Let's read this problem together.

T/S: (Read aloud.)

T: Hmm. This is a lot of information.

T: What can we draw?

S: A triangle!

T: What do we know about this triangle?

S: Two sides are the same length!

T: (Draw a triangle with three very unequal sides.) Did I draw it right?

S: No!

T: Why?

S: It has to have two sides that are equal!

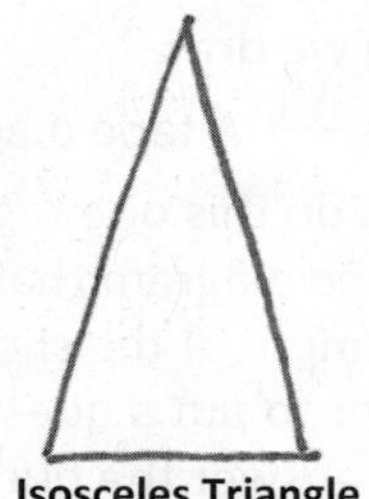

Isosceles Triangle

T: Is this better? (Draw an isosceles triangle.)

S: Yes.

T: Draw a triangle with two sides that are the same length on your personal board.

S: (Draw.)

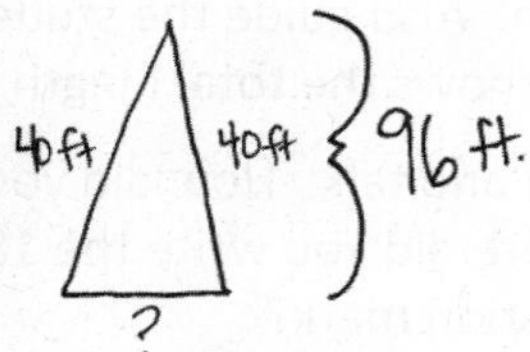

T: Now, let's go back and read the problem and put the information it gives us on our triangle.

T: What does the first part say?

S: All three sides of the triangle put together are 96 feet.

T: Label your drawing to show that the length of the sides of the triangle is 96 feet. Let's not write the units on our drawing for today. Just label it simply as 96.

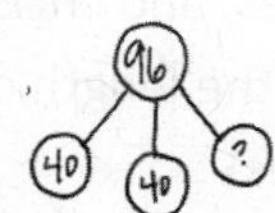

S: (Work.)

T: Good. What is the next piece of information?

S: We know the length of one of the equal sides, 40 feet.

T: Yes. Label 40 on your picture. Since we know the length of one equal side, can we add more information to our picture that wasn't written in the problem?

S: Yes! Since the two sides of the triangle are equal, that means their length is equal also, so the other equal side of the triangle is 40 feet too!

T: Very nice reasoning skills. Sometimes we can figure out more information even if it is not written down in the problem.

T: The last piece of information we have to label on our picture is a question mark to label what we are trying to figure out. What are we trying to figure out?

S: The length of the side of the triangle that is not equal to the others.

T: Good. Do that now.

S: (Work.)

T: What is the length of the missing side of the triangle?

S: 16 feet!

T: What did you do to find that out? Talk to your partner.

S: I subtracted both of the sides we know the length of from 96. → I added the sides we know the length of, then subtracted it from the total 96. → I added the sides and then counted up to 96.

T: Good, all of the solutions I heard involved doing two steps.

T: It's time to try one on your own. Work on Problem 6 on your Problem Set.

Let students work independently on the next problem. Have them compare with a partner when they are finished as you circulate to give support to those students that need it.

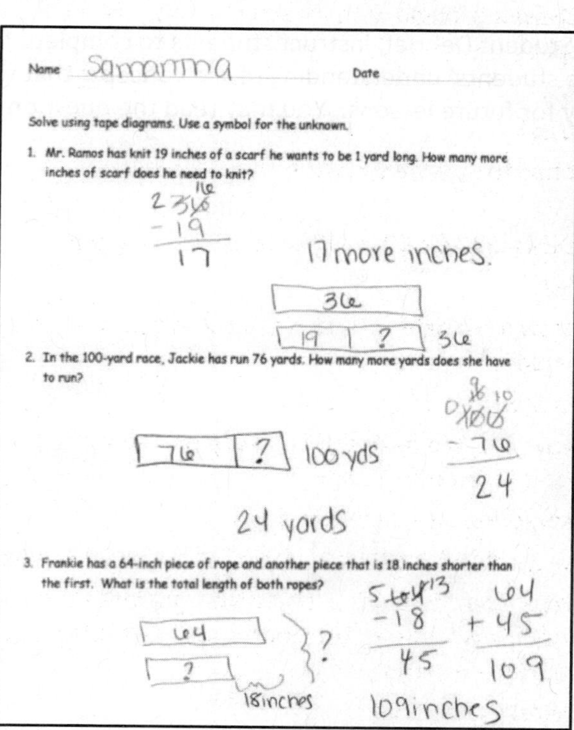
Name Samantha Date

Solve using tape diagrams. Use a symbol for the unknown.

1. Mr. Ramos has knit 19 inches of a scarf he wants to be 1 yard long. How many more inches of scarf does he need to knit?

2. In the 100-yard race, Jackie has run 76 yards. How many more yards does she have to run?

3. Frankie has a 64-inch piece of rope and another piece that is 18 inches shorter than the first. What is the total length of both ropes?

Student Debrief (10 minutes)

Lesson Objective: Solve two-digit addition and subtraction word problems involving length by using tape diagrams and writing equations to represent the problem.

The Student Debrief is intended to invite reflection and active processing of the total lesson experience.

Invite students to review their solutions for the Problem Set. They should check work by comparing answers with a partner before going over answers as a class. Look for misconceptions or misunderstandings that can be addressed in the Debrief. Guide students in a conversation to debrief the Problem Set and process the lesson.

You may choose to use any combination of the questions below to lead the discussion.

- Look at the first page of your Problem Set. How many number sentences did it take to solve Problem 1? How many number sentences did it take to solve Problems 2 and 3? Why is it important to re-read the problem?
- Explain your solution path for Problem 4 to your partner. Did your partner do the same thing as you? Can you understand how your partner got his or her answer?
- Look at the triangle problem. Raise your hand if you used only addition. Raise your hand if you used addition and subtraction. (Discuss both solution paths. First, 40 + 40 = 80. Then, 80 + ___ = 96 or 96 – 80 = ___.)
- Sometimes there is more than one part in our math problems. Tell your partner a math story with more than one part. Use your Problem Set to help you get started.

4. Maria had 96 inches of ribbon. She used 36 inches to wrap a small gift and 48 inches to wrap a larger gift. How much ribbon did she have left?

|36|48|?| 96

36 + 48 = 84

96 − 84 = 12

12 inches

5. The total length of all three sides of a triangle is 96 feet. The triangle has 2 sides that are the same length. One of the equal sides measures 40 feet. What is the length of the side that is not equal?

|40|40|?| 96

96 − 80 = 16

16 feet

6. The length of one side of a square is 4 yards. What is the combined length of all four sides of the square?

|4|?|?|?|

8+8 = 16

16 yards

Exit Ticket (3 minutes)

After the Student Debrief, instruct students to complete the Exit Ticket. A review of their work will help you assess the students' understanding of the concepts that were presented in the lesson today and plan more effectively for future lessons. You may read the questions aloud to the students.

A

Correct ______

Subtract.

1	8 - 1 =		23	41 - 20 =	
2	18 - 1 =		24	46 - 20 =	
3	8 - 2 =		25	7 - 5 =	
4	18 - 2 =		26	70 - 50 =	
5	8 - 5 =		27	71 - 50 =	
6	18 - 5 =		28	78 - 50 =	
7	28 - 5 =		29	80 - 40 =	
8	58 - 5 =		30	84 - 40 =	
9	58 - 7 =		31	90 - 60 =	
10	10 - 2 =		32	97 - 60 =	
11	11 - 2 =		33	70 - 40 =	
12	21 - 2 =		34	72 - 40 =	
13	61 - 2 =		35	56 - 4 =	
14	61 - 3 =		36	52 - 4 =	
15	61 - 5 =		37	50 - 4 =	
16	10 - 5 =		38	60 - 30 =	
17	20 - 5 =		39	90 - 70 =	
18	30 - 5 =		40	80 - 60 =	
19	70 - 5 =		41	96 - 40 =	
20	72 - 5 =		42	63 - 40 =	
21	4 - 2 =		43	79 - 30 =	
22	40 - 20 =		44	76 - 9 =	

B Improvement _____ # Correct _____

Subtract.

1	7 - 1 =		23	51 - 20 =	
2	17 - 1 =		24	56 - 20 =	
3	7 - 2 =		25	8 - 5 =	
4	17 - 2 =		26	80 - 50 =	
5	7 - 5 =		27	81 - 50 =	
6	17 - 5 =		28	87 - 50 =	
7	27 - 5 =		29	60 - 30 =	
8	57 - 5 =		30	64 - 30 =	
9	57 - 6 =		31	80 - 60 =	
10	10 - 5 =		32	85 - 60 =	
11	11 - 5 =		33	70 - 30 =	
12	21 - 5 =		34	72 - 30 =	
13	61 - 5 =		35	76 - 4 =	
14	61 - 4 =		36	72 - 4 =	
15	61 - 2 =		37	70 - 4 =	
16	10 - 2 =		38	80 - 40 =	
17	20 - 2 -		39	90 - 60 =	
18	30 - 2 =		40	60 - 40 =	
19	70 - 2 =		41	93 - 40 =	
20	71 - 2 =		42	67 - 40 =	
21	5 - 2 =		43	78 - 30 =	
22	50 - 20 =		44	56 - 9 =	

Name ______________________________ Date ______________

Solve using tape diagrams. Use a symbol for the unknown.

1. Mr. Ramos has knitted 19 inches of a scarf he wants to be 1 yard long. How many more inches of scarf does he need to knit?

2. In the 100-yard race, Jackie has run 76 yards. How many more yards does she have to run?

3. Frankie has a 64-inch piece of rope and another piece that is 18 inches shorter than the first. What is the total length of both ropes?

4. Maria had 96 inches of ribbon. She used 36 inches to wrap a small gift and 48 inches to wrap a larger gift. How much ribbon did she have left?

5. The total length of all three sides of a triangle is 96 feet. The triangle has two sides that are the same length. One of the equal sides measures 40 feet. What is the length of the side that is not equal?

?

6. The length of one side of a square is 4 yards. What is the combined length of all four sides of the square?

Name ______________________________ Date ______________

Solve using a tape diagram. Use a symbol for the unknown.

1. Jasmine has a jump rope that is 84 inches long. Marie's is 13 inches shorter than Jasmine's. What is the length of Marie's jump rope?

Name ______________________________ Date ______________

Solve using tape diagrams. Use a symbol for the unknown.

1. Luann has a piece of ribbon that is 1 yard long. She cuts off 33 inches to tie a gift box. How many inches of ribbon are not used?

2. Elijah runs 68 yards in a 100 yard race. How many more yards does he have to run?

3. Chris has a 57-inch piece of string and another piece that is 15 inches longer than the first. What is the total length of both strings?

4. Janine knitted 12 inches of a scarf on Friday and 36 inches on Saturday. She wants the scarf to be 72 inches long. How many more inches does she need to knit?

5. The total length of all three sides of a triangle is 120 feet. Two sides of the triangle are the same length. One of the equal sides measures 50 feet. What is the length of the side that is not equal?

6. The length of one side of a square is 3 yards. What is the combined length of all four sides of the square?

Lesson 21

Objective: Identify unknown numbers on a number line diagram by using the distance between numbers and reference points.

Suggested Lesson Structure

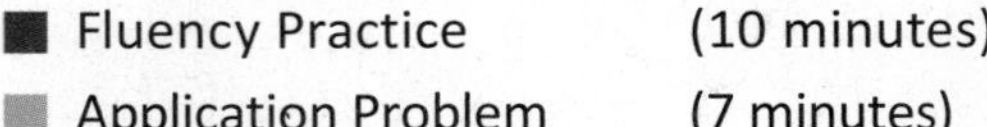

■ Fluency Practice	(10 minutes)
■ Application Problem	(7 minutes)
■ Concept Development	(33 minutes)
■ Student Debrief	(10 minutes)
Total Time	**(60 minutes)**

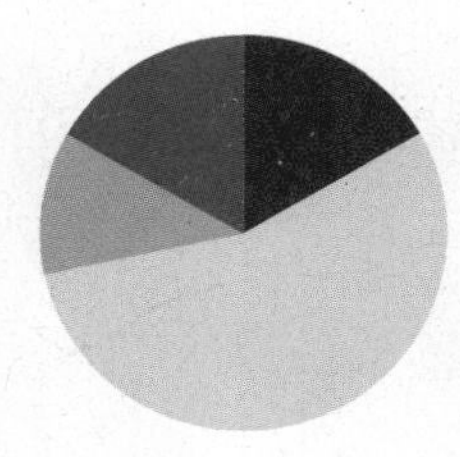

Fluency Practice (10 minutes)

- Roll and Follow the Rule **2.OA.2** (5 minutes)
- Grade 2 Core Fluency Differentiated Practice Sets **2.OA.2** (5 minutes)

Roll and Follow the Rule (5 minutes)

Materials: (S) 1 die per student or pair, math journal or notebook

Note: Give students a base number such as 9. They roll their die to find the "rule." For example, if they roll a 5, they add 5 repeatedly, 9 + 5 = 14, 14 + 5 = 19, 19 + 5 = 24, etc. Students track their number sentences in their notebook and count the total of number sentences they have written after 30 seconds. Continue the process with a different base number and/or operation.

Base numbers for addition: 38, 156, 291. Base numbers for subtraction: 40, 100.

Grade 2 Core Fluency Differentiated Practice Sets (5 minutes)

Materials: (S) Core Fluency Practice Sets from G2–M7–Lesson 1

Note: During G2–M7–Topic E and for the remainder of the year, each day's fluency includes an opportunity for review and mastery of the sums and differences with totals through 20 by means of the Core Fluency Practice Sets or Sprints. The process is detailed and Practice Sets are provided in G2–M7–Lesson 1.

Application Problem (7 minutes)

In order to ride the Mega Mountain rollercoaster, riders must be at least 44 inches tall. Caroline is 57 inches tall. She is 18 inches taller than Addison. How tall is Addison? How many more inches must Addison grow to ride the rollercoaster?

Note: This two-step word problem involving length bridges the work done in the previous lesson with the number line work to follow. Encourage students to use the RDW process to solve and to write equations to represent the problem.

57   18

$57 - 18 = ?$

$18 + \boxed{39} = 57$

$18 \xrightarrow{+40} 58 \xrightarrow{-1} 57$

Addison is 39 in.

$39 + \_\_ = 44$ She must grow 5 in.

Concept Development (33 minutes)

Materials: (T) Standard measuring tape, Helpful Hints chart for Problem 3 (S) 1-meter strip and straightedge (ruler), personal white board

Distribute meter strip and ruler (straightedge) to students.

Problem 1: Identify missing points on a number line with endpoints 30 and 50 and units of 5.

T: What are the endpoints of your meter strip?

S: Zero and 1 meter!

T: 1 meter is how many centimeters?

S: 100 centimeters!

T: Let's change the endpoints. Partner A, put your finger on 30 centimeters. Partner B, put your finger on 50 centimeters.

T: Let's draw a number line to represent this part of the meter strip.

T: Use your meter strip as a ruler to make hash marks at 30 and 50 centimeters on your personal boards.

S: (Draw hash marks.)

T: Now, take away your meter strip and use your straightedge to connect your hash marks with a line.

S: (Draw.)

T: Label the hash mark on the left 30 and the hash mark on the right 50.

T: We have used our meter strip to draw part of a number line. What are the endpoints of our number line? Let's just work with the numbers rather than continue to call the numbers centimeters.

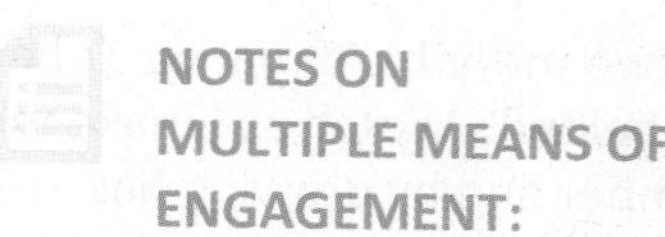

NOTES ON MULTIPLE MEANS OF ENGAGEMENT:

Students who are struggling can continue to use measuring tape for support, marking the intervals with additional paper clips, or sliding their finger along the tape while skip counting. The continued use of the measuring tape will help students to focus more on the conceptual understanding of the activity.

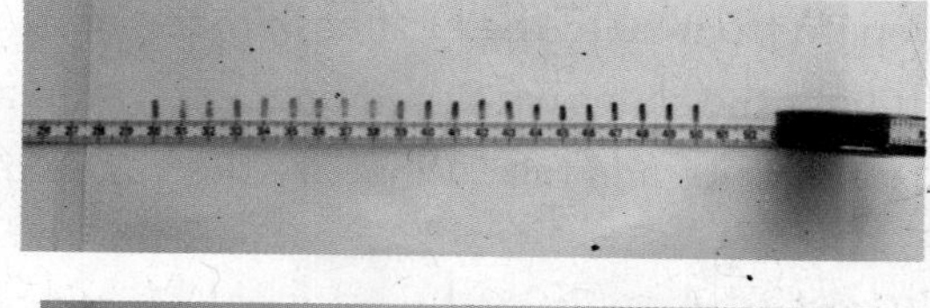

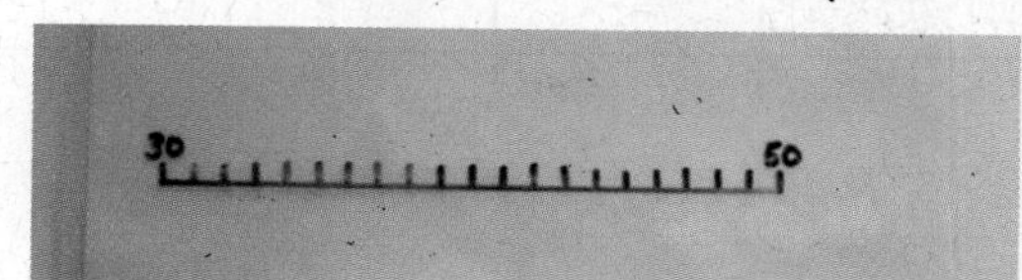

S: 30 and 50.

T: Our left endpoint is often 0. Turn and talk: Where has 0 gone?

S: It didn't disappear; we just aren't using that part of the number line. → If I put my meter strip back, it's about over here.

T: It's like zooming in on a piece of the number line; the numbers to the left and right are not written down, but we could extend this out and see them if we needed or wanted to.

T: Watch as I draw a hash mark in the middle, equal distances from both endpoints. The length between hash marks is a unit. Let's count the units together. (Use your finger to slide on the number line to show two equal units)

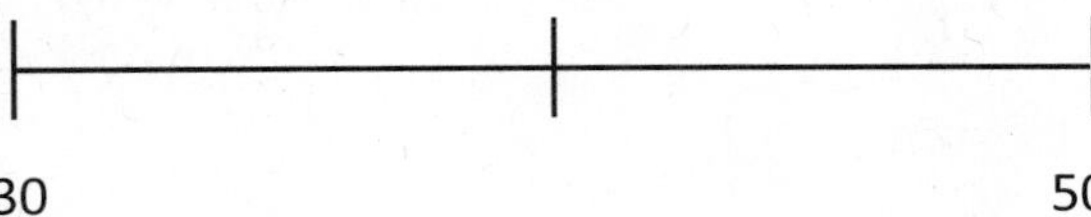

S: (Chorally count.) 1, 2.

T: What number comes right in the middle of 30 and 50?

S: 40!

T: Label the middle hash mark 40 on your number line.

T: (Draw two more hash marks. Label them A and B as shown below). Watch as I make more equal units on my number line by drawing hash marks in the middle between 30 and 40 and between 40 and 50 (Demonstrate.) Make more equal units on your number line. (Allow students time to work.)

T: How many hash marks are on our number line?

S: Five!

T: How many units do we have on our number line now?

S: Four! → Five!

T: The units are the lengths. Put your finger on 30, and let's slide straight from 30 to the next hash mark to count the units. We say "one" after we gone the length from 30 to the next hash mark.

S: (Count the slides with their fingers.) There are 4 units!

NOTES ON MULTIPLE MEANS OF REPRESENTATION:

Support English language learners by having the words *thirty, forty,* and *fifty* with their corresponding numerals posted. ELLs can easily confuse *thirty, forty,* and *fifty* with the pronunciation of *thirteen, fourteen,* and *fifteen*. Posting and referring to the visual will clarify any confusion that might arise.

MP.2

T: Good. Turn and talk: What are the values of Point A and Point B? How do you know? Label them.

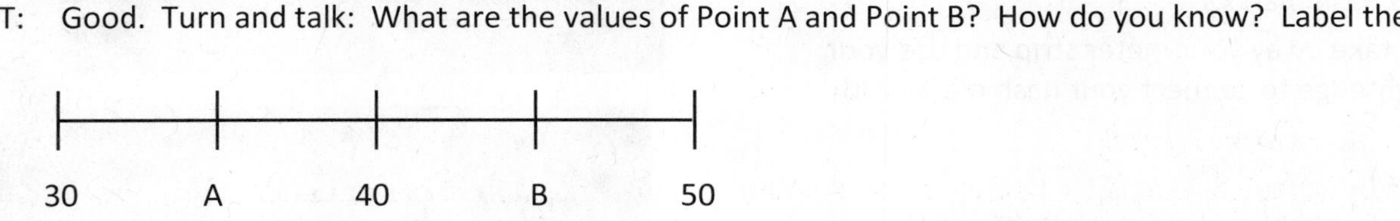

S: If the distance from 30 to 40 is 10, then Point A has to be 35, because it's in the middle. → I figured out that the distance from one hash mark to the next one is 5, so I counted by fives: 30, 35, 40, 45,

50. → Since 40 to 50 has a length of 10, Point B cuts the length in half, so each smaller distance has to be 5.

T: What is the length of each unit?

MP.2 S: 5!

T: What happens when we add the lengths of the units on this part of the meter strip?

S: We get the total distance from 30 to 50. → 5 + 5 + 5 + 5 = 20, which is the total length. → I counted up: 5, 10, 15, 20.

Problem 2: Use the unit length to count up or down to figure out endpoints.

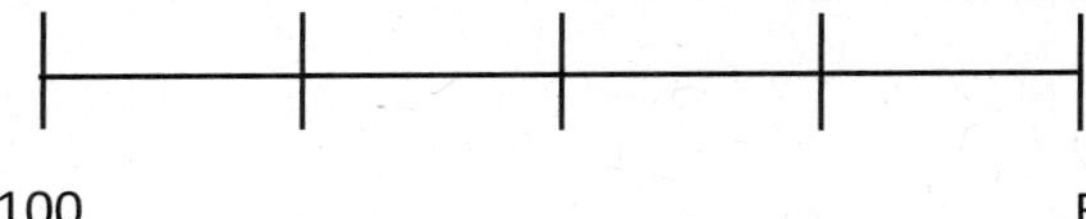

100 E

T: (Draw the number line above on the board.) Look at this number line. How many units are there?

S: Four!

T: If you know each equal unit length is 10, can you figure out the other endpoint, E?

S: Yes. Since we know the beginning endpoint is 100, we can count by tens until I get to E.

T: Good! What is the value of E?

S: 140!

T: Yes, let me label that on my number line. What is the difference in length between endpoints? Tell your partner how you can figure this out.

S: The difference is 40. I counted up by tens for 4 units. → The difference is 40. I subtracted the shorter endpoint from the longer endpoint, 140 – 100 = 40.

T: Good. I'm going to write the difference between endpoints on the side of my number line. (Don't erase from the board because it will be needed to compare with the next number line.)

Problem 3: Vary the position of the unknown on the number line.

T: Now, draw a number line that is just the same as your other one on your personal board with 4 units (5 hash marks) with a right endpoint of 95. Label the left endpoint with an A. Look at the number line on the board if you need help.

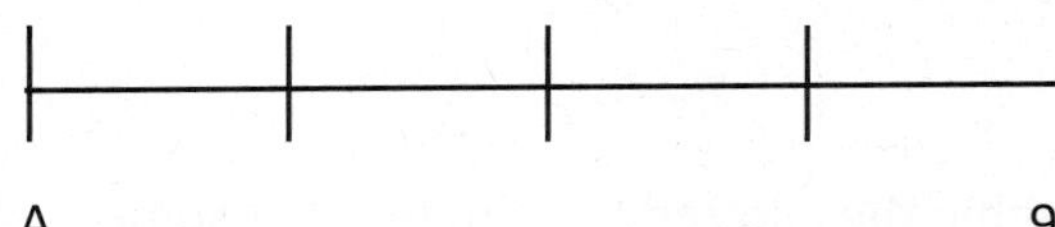

A 95

S: (Draw. Assist as necessary.)

T: If each equal unit length is 10, figure out the starting point, A.

S: (Count backwards from 95 by tens to determine the value of A.)

T: What did you label Point A?

S: 55!

T: Good. Now that we know both endpoints, use one of the strategies we just talked about to find the difference in length between the endpoints on your number line, and then tell your partner.

T: What was the difference on this number line?

S: 40!

T: Now, look at your number line and the one that's on the board. Talk to your partner about what is the same and what is different.

S: The endpoints are different. → Each number line has the same number of units. → Each unit was 10 in both number lines. → The difference between endpoints was the same.

Continue the work using a sequence of problems such as the following to prepare students for the Problem Set:

1. Find the value of Point B on the number line.

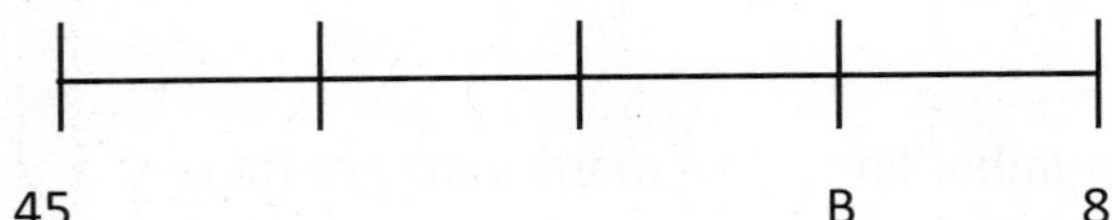

2. Find the value of Point C on the number line. What is the difference between the two endpoints?

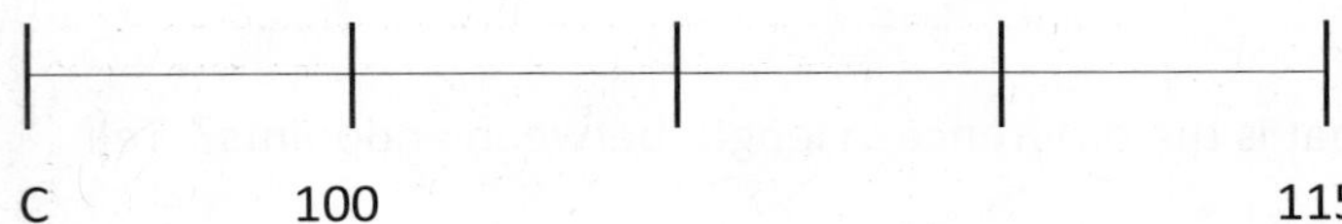

3. Find the value of Point D on the number line. Each hash mark represents a value of 10. What is the distance between the two endpoints?

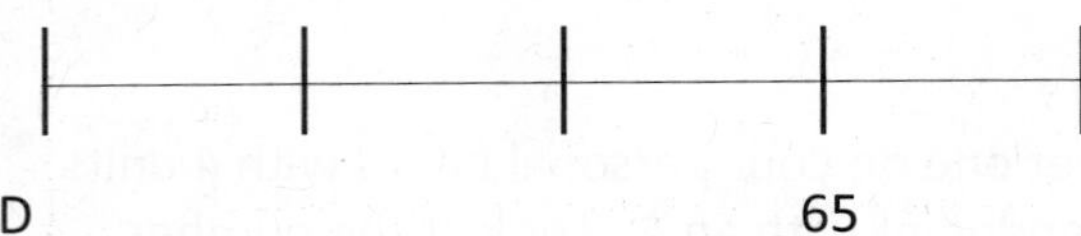

Problem Set (10 minutes)

Students should do their personal best to complete the Problem Set within the allotted 10 minutes. For some classes, it may be appropriate to modify the assignment by specifying which problems they work on first. Some problems do not specify a method for solving. Students solve these problems using the RDW approach used for Application Problems.

Student Debrief (10 minutes)

Lesson Objective: Identify unknown numbers on a number line diagram by using the distance between numbers and reference points.

The Student Debrief is intended to invite reflection and active processing of the total lesson experience.

Invite students to review their solutions for the Problem Set. They should check work by comparing answers with a partner before going over answers as a class. Look for misconceptions or misunderstandings that can be addressed in the Debrief. Guide students in a conversation to debrief the Problem Set and process the lesson.

You may choose to use any combination of the questions below to lead the discussion.

- Look at the first number line on your Problem Set. Count the hash marks. (7.) Count the units. (6.) What do you notice? Look at the second number line and compare how many hash marks to how many units. What do you notice?
- What do we count when we are counting units? (The spaces between the hash marks.) What do the hash marks do on a number line? (Separate the units and tells us where to write the reference points.)
- If you know the value of one unit on a number line do you know the value of all of them?
- Look at the second number line on your Problem Set. Explain to your partner the strategy you used to find the value of each unit.
- Look at Problem 4 on your Problem Set. Explain to your partner how you found the difference between endpoints.
- On a yardstick, can you find two different sections that have the same difference between endpoints?

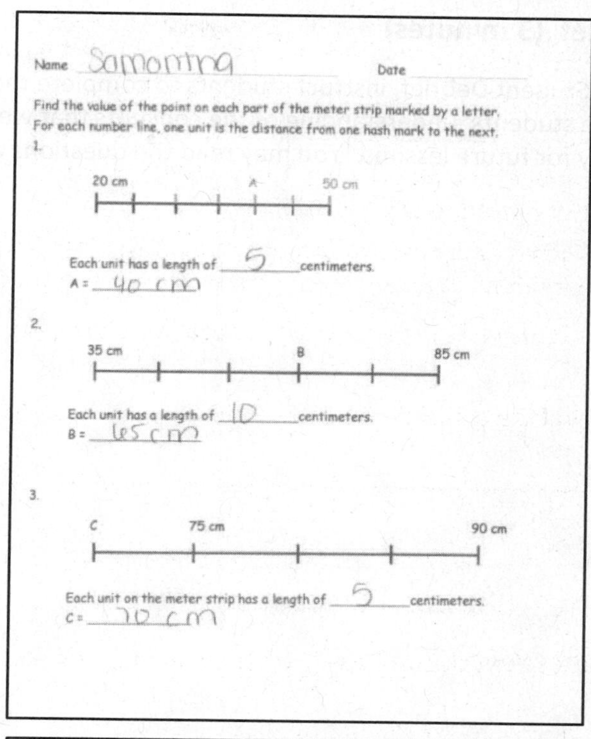

Name Samantha Date

Find the value of the point on each part of the meter strip marked by a letter. For each number line, one unit is the distance from one hash mark to the next.

1. 20 cm A 50 cm

Each unit has a length of 5 centimeters.
A = 40 cm

2. 35 cm B 85 cm

Each unit has a length of 10 centimeters.
B = 65 cm

3. C 75 cm 90 cm

Each unit on the meter strip has a length of 5 centimeters.
C = 70 cm

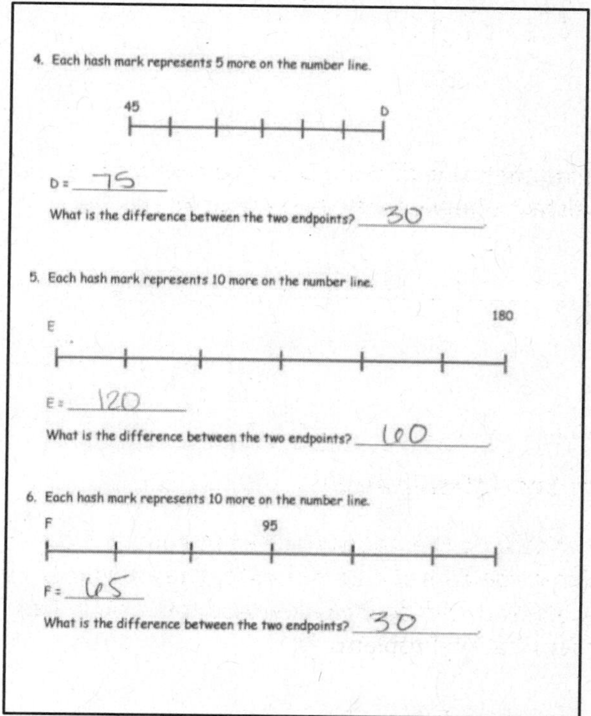

4. Each hash mark represents 5 more on the number line.

45 D

D = 75

What is the difference between the two endpoints? 30

5. Each hash mark represents 10 more on the number line.

E 180

E = 120

What is the difference between the two endpoints? 100

6. Each hash mark represents 10 more on the number line.

F 95

F = 65

What is the difference between the two endpoints? 30

Exit Ticket (3 minutes)

After the Student Debrief, instruct students to complete the Exit Ticket. A review of their work will help you assess the students' understanding of the concepts that were presented in the lesson today and plan more effectively for future lessons. You may read the questions aloud to the students

Name _______________________ Date ___________

Find the value of the point on each part of the meter strip marked by a letter.
For each number line, one unit is the distance from one hash mark to the next.

1.

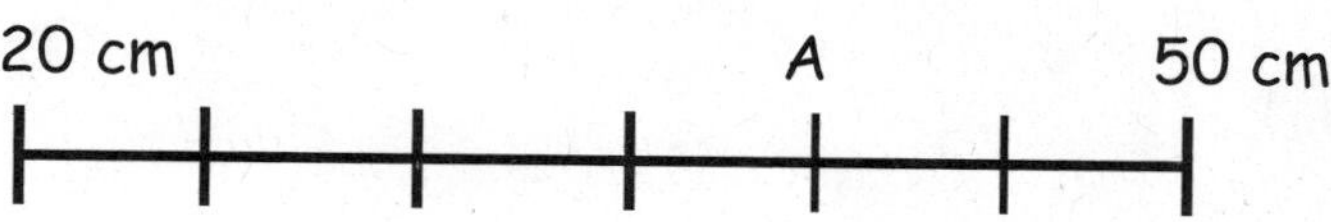

Each unit has a length of __________ centimeters.

A = ______________

2.

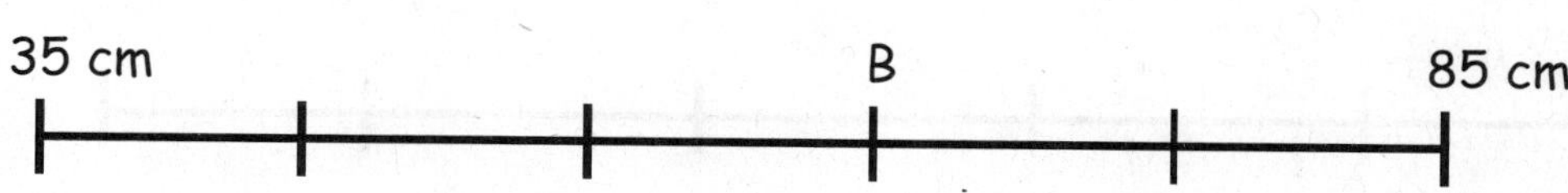

Each unit has a length of __________ centimeters.

B = ______________

3.

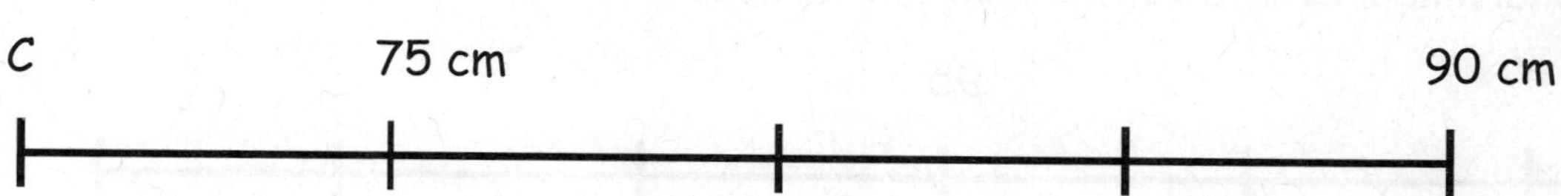

Each unit on the meter strip has a length of __________ centimeters.

C = ______________

4. Each hash mark represents 5 more on the number line.

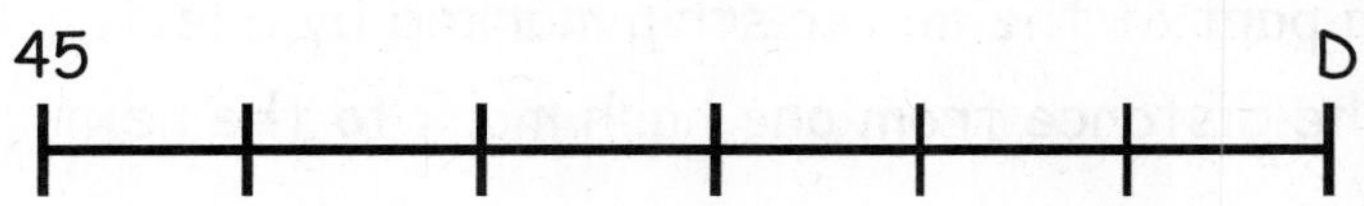

D = ______________

What is the difference between the two endpoints? ______________.

5. Each hash mark represents 10 more on the number line.

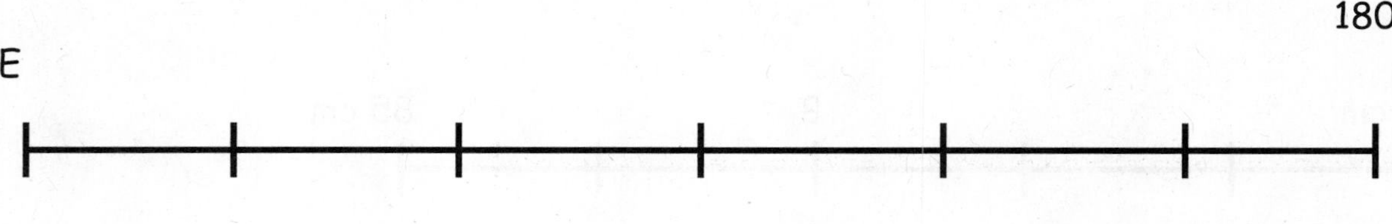

E = ______________

What is the difference between the two endpoints? ______________.

6. Each hash mark represents 10 more on the number line.

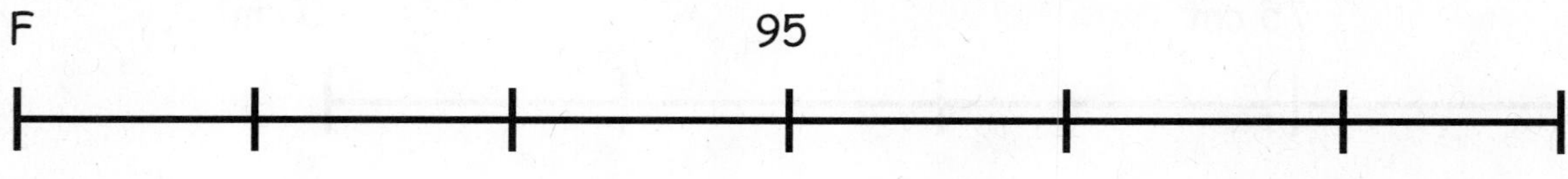

F = ______________

What is the difference between the two endpoints? ______________.

Name ______________________________ Date ______________

Find the value of the point on each number line marked by a letter.

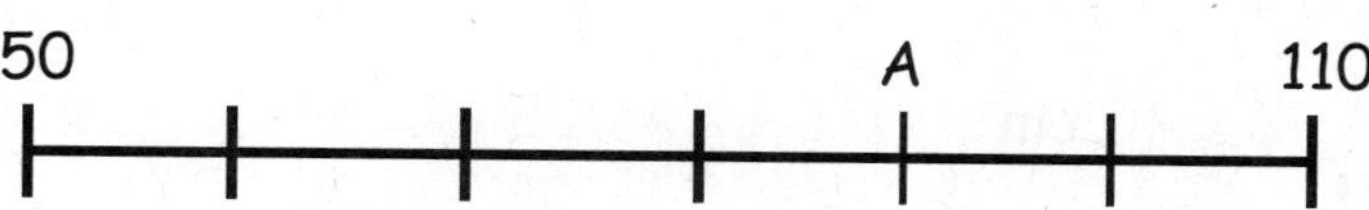

1. Each unit has a length of __________ centimeter.

   A = _____________

23 B 73

2. What is the difference between the two endpoints? _____________.

   B = _____________

Name ______________________________ Date ______________

Find the value of the point on each part of the meter strip marked by a letter.
For each number line, one unit is the distance from one hash mark to the next.

1.

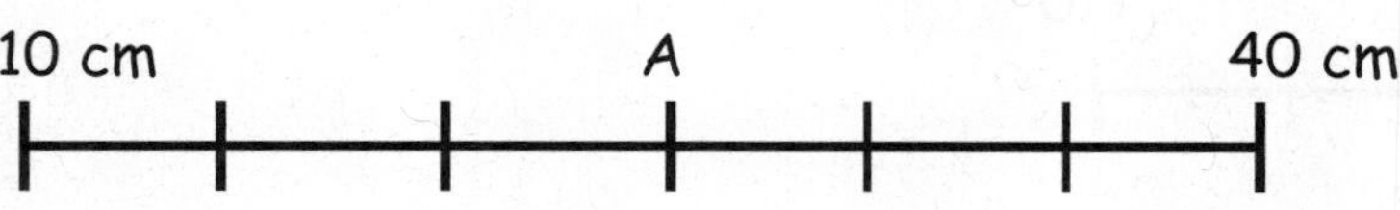

Each unit has a length of __________ centimeters.

A = ____________

2.

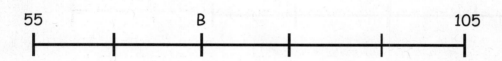

Each unit has a length of __________ centimeters.

B = ____________

3.

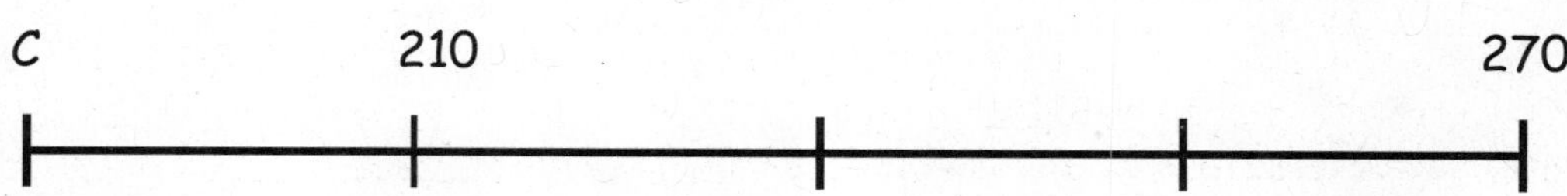

Each unit has a length of __________ centimeters.

C = ____________

4. Each hash mark represents 5 more on the number line.

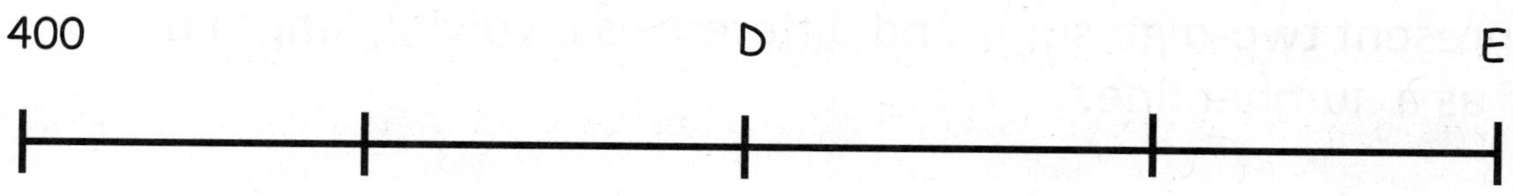

What is the difference between D and E? ________________.

D = ____________

E = ____________

5. Each hash mark represents 10 more on the number line.

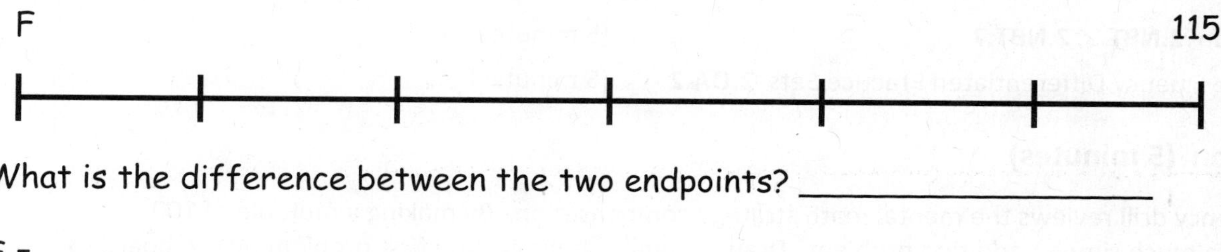

What is the difference between the two endpoints? ________________

F = ____________

6. Each hash mark represents 10 more on the number line.

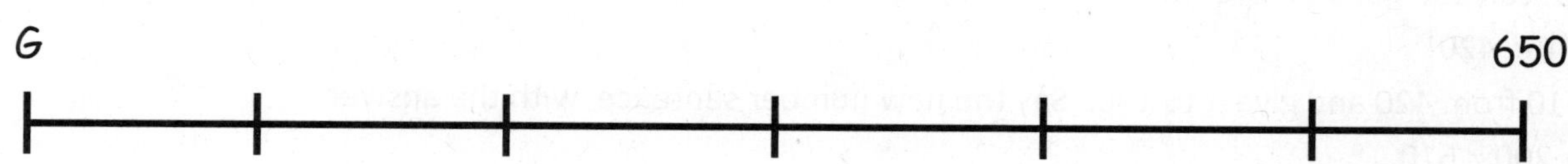

What is the difference between the two endpoints? ________________.

G = ____________

Lesson 22

Objective: Represent two-digit sums and differences involving length by using the ruler as a number line.

Suggested Lesson Structure

Fluency Practice	(10 minutes)
Application Problem	(5 minutes)
Concept Development	(35 minutes)
Student Debrief	(10 minutes)
Total Time	**(60 minutes)**

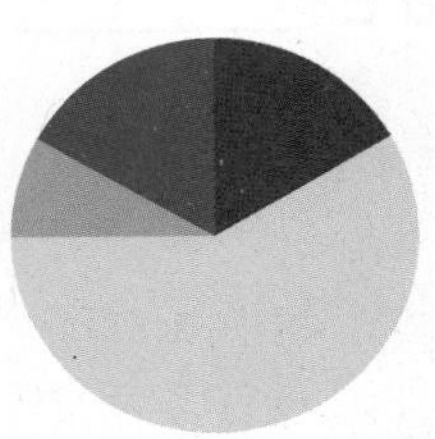

Fluency Practice (10 minutes)

- Compensation **2.NBT.5, 2.NBT.7** (5 minutes)
- Grade 2 Core Fluency Differentiated Practice Sets **2.OA.2** (5 minutes)

Compensation (5 minutes)

Note: This fluency drill reviews the mental math strategy compensation. By making a multiple of 100, students solve a much simpler addition problem. Draw a number bond for the first problem on the board to help students visualize the decomposition.

T: (Write 420 + 190 = _____.) Let's use a mental math strategy to add. How much more does 190 need to make the next hundred?

S: 10 more.

T: Where can 190 get 10 more from?

S: From the 420!

T: Take 10 from 420 and give it to 190. Say the new number sentence, with the answer.

S: 410 + 200 = 610.

T: 370 + 190.

S: 360 + 200 = 560.

Continue with the following possible sequence: 290 + 230, 380 + 190, 320 + 190, 240 + 170, and 340 + 190.

Grade 2 Core Fluency Differentiated Practice Sets (5 minutes)

Materials: (S) Core Fluency Practice Sets from G2–M7–Lesson 1

Note: During G2–M7–Topic E and for the remainder of the year, each day's fluency includes an opportunity for review and mastery of the sums and differences with totals through 20 by means of the Core Fluency Practice Sets or Sprints. The process is detailed and Practice Sets are provided in G2–M7–Lesson 1.

Application Problem (5 minutes)

Liza, Cecilia, and Dylan are playing soccer. Liza and Cecilia are 120 feet apart. Dylan is in between them. If Dylan is standing the same distance from both girls, how many feet is Dylan from Liza?

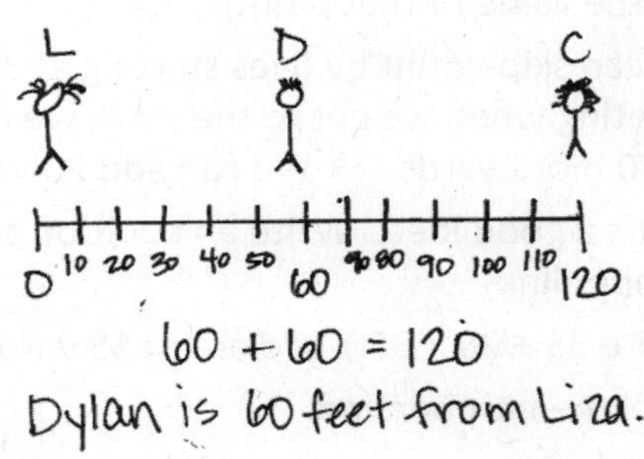

Note: In this problem, students synthesize their understanding of length by finding the middle point on a number line and realizing that the length from 0 to 60 feet is equal to the length from 60 to 120 feet. For example, students might draw a number line and count by tens and then estimate or use trial and error to find the midpoint. They might also simply think of 120 as 12 tens, so 6 tens is the middle point.

Concept Development (35 minutes)

Materials: (S) Number Line Template A and B, personal white board, 1 new pencil

Draw a large number line segment on the board (as shown below). Distribute number line Template A for use in Parts 1 and 2. Instruct students to slide Template A into their personal boards.

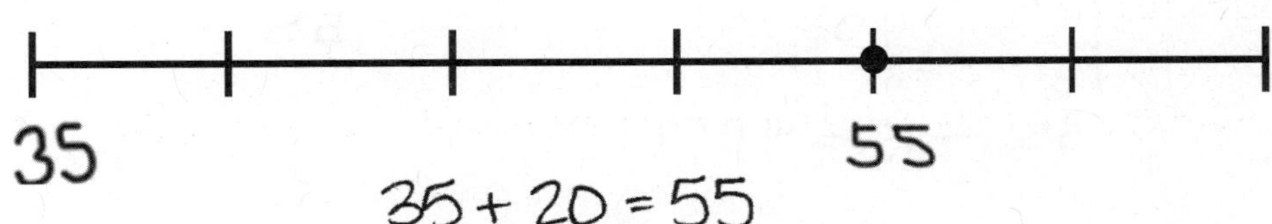

Problem 1: Relate more length on the number line to addition.

T: How can we use the number line to show 20 yards more than 35 yards? Talk to your partner.

S: We can label the left endpoint 35 and then slide 20 more yards counting by fives. → We could count by tens, too.

T: For now, let's say that each unit has a length of 5 yards.

T: Student A, come up and label the endpoint and show us how you slide 20 more yards when each hash mark is a length of 5 yards. Everyone else use the number line in your personal boards to do the same. (Allow students time to work.)

T: So, did we end up at 20 yards?

S: No, because we went more than 35 yards. → No, we counted up 20 more than 35. → Twenty yards was the distance we traveled.

T: Hmm. Let's put a dot where we ended to show 20 more than 35 yards. What do we need to do to figure out the value of that point?

S: We can skip-count by fives starting at 35, but stop counting when we get to the mark we made so we only go 20 more yards. → We can add 20 yards to 35 yards.

NOTES ON MULTIPLE MEANS OF ACTION AND EXPRESSION:

Support English language learners by pointing to the number line segment on the board as you speak. While asking what the distance is between each labeled interval, sweep your finger from 0 to 10, 10 to 20, 20 to 30, etc. Do the same for the smaller intervals.

T: That's a good idea. Write an addition sentence on your board that matches 20 more than 35 on the number line.

S: (Write 35 + 20 = 55.) We are at 55 yards.

T: Label the number line.

Continue giving examples with different units and endpoints (on the left) until students readily write an addition sentence corresponding to more length. Consider using the following suggestions:

- Show 15 more than 45.
- Show 50 more than 60 using units of 10.
- Show 30 more than 85 using units of 5.

Problem 2: Relate less length on the number line to subtraction.

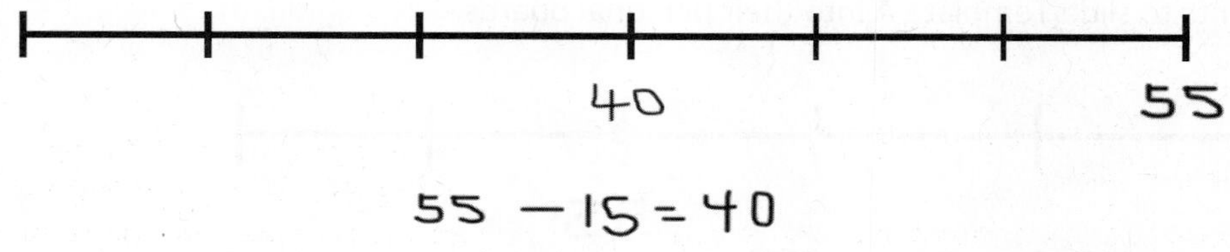

T: How can we use the number line to show 15 feet less than 55 feet? Talk to your partner.

S: We can label the right endpoint 55 and then slide 15 less feet going back. → We could label the left endpoint 55 and then count back as we slide to the right.

T: Both methods are fine, but we just did addition moving to the right. (Demonstrate.) So, now let's do the opposite and move to the left to show subtraction.

MP.6

T: Work on your personal boards to show 15 less than 55. (Allow students time to work.)

T: Where did you end up?

S: At 40!

MP.6 T: Label the number line, and write a subtraction sentence on your board that matches 15 less than 55 on the number line.

Continue giving examples with different units and endpoints (on the right) until students readily write a subtraction sentence corresponding to less length. Consider using the following suggestions:

- Show 15 less than 45.
- Show 20 less than 90 using units of 10.
- Show 30 less than 115 using units of 5.

Problem 3: Relate the length of an object on the number line to subtraction. Use compensation to simplify calculation.

T: Look at our other number line (Template B). This was part of a whole meter strip but it got cut at 49 and 66. These are our endpoints.

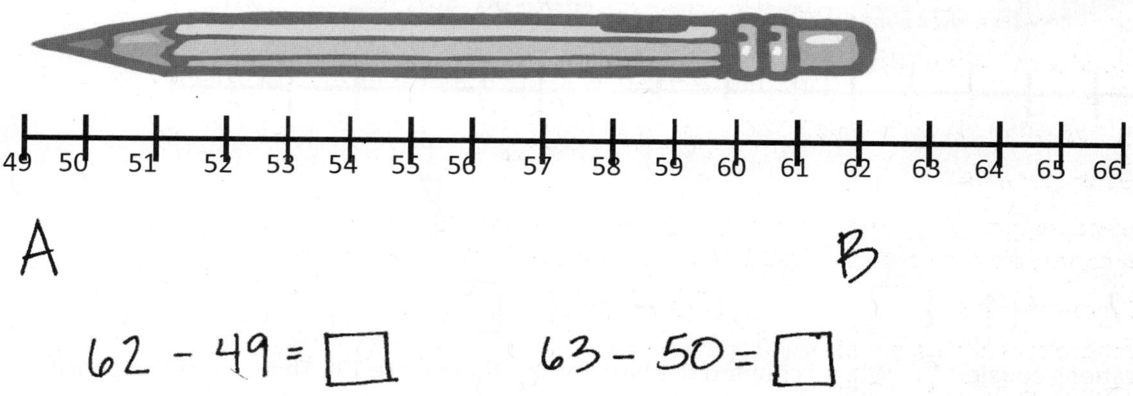

T: Place the end of your pencil at the endpoint of the number line where it says 49.

T: How can we figure out the length of the pencil?

S: We can count the units from the beginning of the pencil to the end. → We can write a subtraction sentence to find the difference.

T: Let's mark the beginning and endpoints of our pencil on the number line. Mark the point on the right A and the point on the right B.

S: (Work.)

T: The length from A to B is the same as the length of the...?

S: Pencil.

T: How can we find the length of the pencil?

S: We can count up from A to B. → We can subtract.

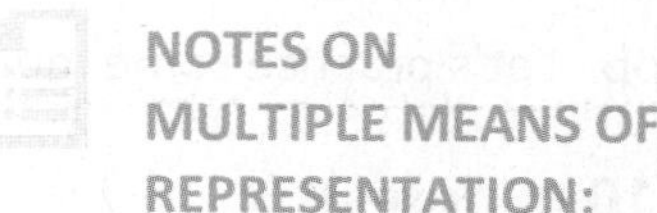

NOTES ON MULTIPLE MEANS OF REPRESENTATION:

Help students who are performing below grade level by demonstrating, one step at a time, how to understand 62 – 49 = 63 – 50 by having them solve each side of the equation. Have students express what 62 – 49 is, and then ask them what 63 – 50 is. Have students write the difference after each step and re-write the whole equation (13 = 13). Ask them to express in their own words what they think the equal sign meant in the original equation.

T: On your personal boards, under the number line, write and solve a subtraction sentence that will tell us the length of the pencil. Don't solve yet. Just leave a blank for the unknown length of the pencil.

S: (Write 62 – 49 = ____.)

T: Hmm. Will the pencil length change if I move it on the number line?

S: No!

T: Could I move the pencil on the number line so that I can write a subtraction sentence that is simpler to solve?

S: Yes! If you move the pencil 1 unit to the right so that the end of the pencil is at the 50 hash mark, your number sentence would be 63 – 50 = ____!

T: Move your pencil, and write the new number sentence. Solve both equations. Count the hash marks to check and see if the length of the pencil is the same as the answers to your equations.

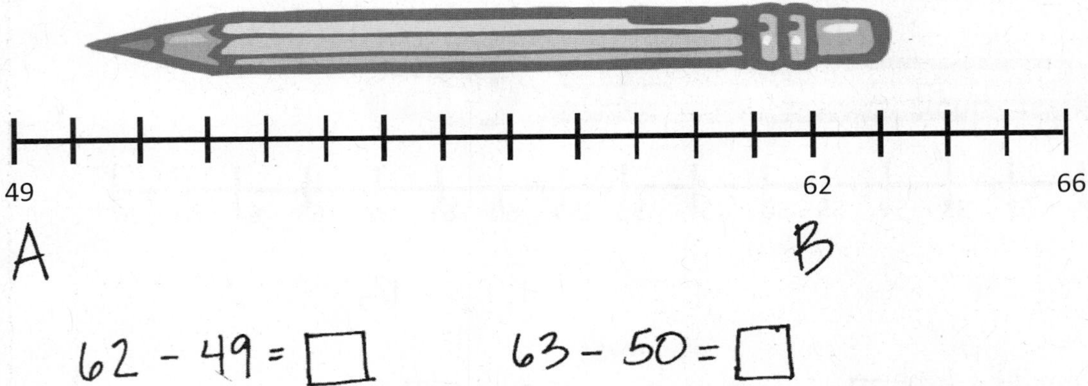

S: Both equations equaled 13. When I counted the hash marks, there were 13. That means the pencil is 13 units long.

T: (Write 62 – 49 = 63 – 50 on the board.) Talk to your partner about what I wrote on the board. Is this true? Why or why not?

T: Great job. Let's practice some more problems like the ones we have done today on our Problem Set.

Problem Set (10 minutes)

Students should do their personal best to complete the Problem Set within the allotted 10 minutes. For some classes, it may be appropriate to modify the assignment by specifying which problems they work on first. Some problems do not specify a method for solving. Students solve these problems using the RDW approach used for Application Problems.

Student Debrief (10 minutes)

Lesson Objective: Represent two-digit sums and differences involving length by using the ruler as a number line.

The Student Debrief is intended to invite reflection and active processing of the total lesson experience.

Invite students to review their solutions for the Problem Set. They should check work by comparing answers with a partner before going over answers as a class. Look for misconceptions or misunderstandings that can be addressed in the Debrief. Guide students in a conversation to debrief the Problem Set and process the lesson.

You may choose to use any combination of the questions below to lead the discussion.

- Look at Problem 1 on your Problem Set. Using your finger and skip-counting, show your partner how you represented 30 more than 65 centimeters on the number line
- Talk to your partner about how Problem 3 on your Problem Set can help you solve Problem 4. (I know the length of each flute will stay the same if I move each flute 1 centimeter to the right, and in doing so, I make a much easier subtraction problem for me to solve. Instead of 71 – 29, I can think 72 – 30!)
- Sometimes we count the units on a ruler or number line to figure out the length of an object. What are some things we have to think about when we use this strategy? (We have to be aware of the length of each unit so we can skip-count if necessary, and we have to be careful to count the jumps and not the hash marks.)
- If you knew the endpoints of an object, could you figure out the length of the object without using a number line or ruler? How?

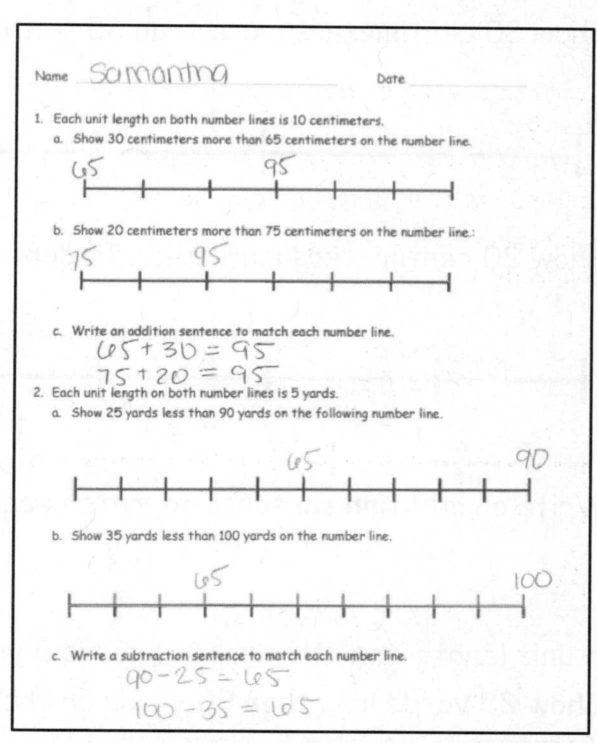

Name Samantha Date

1. Each unit length on both number lines is 10 centimeters.
   a. Show 30 centimeters more than 65 centimeters on the number line.

   65 95

   b. Show 20 centimeters more than 75 centimeters on the number line.

   75 95

   c. Write an addition sentence to match each number line.

   65 + 30 = 95
   75 + 20 = 95

2. Each unit length on both number lines is 5 yards.
   a. Show 25 yards less than 90 yards on the following number line.

   65 90

   b. Show 35 yards less than 100 yards on the number line.

   65 100

   c. Write a subtraction sentence to match each number line.

   90 – 25 = 65
   100 – 35 = 65

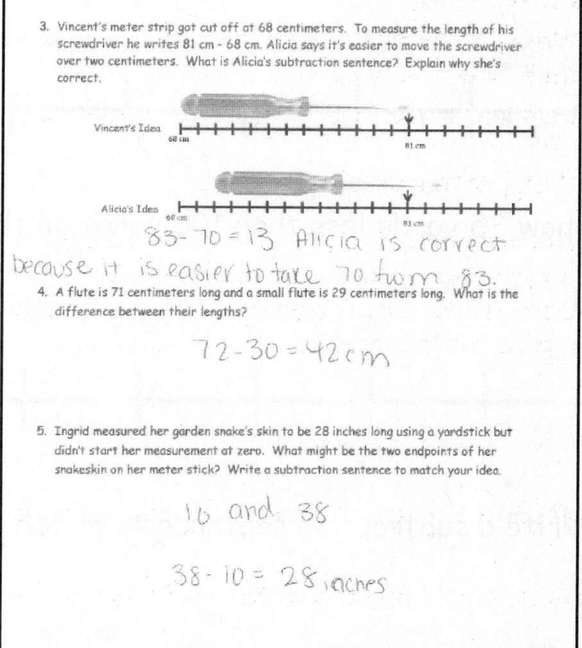

3. Vincent's meter strip got cut off at 68 centimeters. To measure the length of his screwdriver he writes 81 cm - 68 cm. Alicia says it's easier to move the screwdriver over two centimeters. What is Alicia's subtraction sentence? Explain why she's correct.

   Vincent's Idea 68 cm 81 cm

   Alicia's Idea 68 cm 81 cm

   83 – 70 = 13 Alicia is correct because it is easier to take 70 from 83.

4. A flute is 71 centimeters long and a small flute is 29 centimeters long. What is the difference between their lengths?

   72 – 30 = 42 cm

5. Ingrid measured her garden snake's skin to be 28 inches long using a yardstick but didn't start her measurement at zero. What might be the two endpoints of her snakeskin on her meter stick? Write a subtraction sentence to match your idea.

   10 and 38

   38 – 10 = 28 inches

Exit Ticket (3 minutes)

After the Student Debrief, instruct students to complete the Exit Ticket. A review of their work will help you assess the students' understanding of the concepts that were presented in the lesson today and plan more effectively for future lessons. You may read the questions aloud to the students.

Name ______________________________ Date ______________

1. Each unit length on both number lines is 10 centimeters.
   a. Show 30 centimeters more than 65 centimeters on the number line.

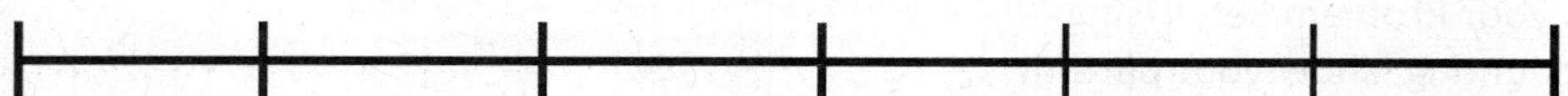

   b. Show 20 centimeters more than 75 centimeters on the number line.

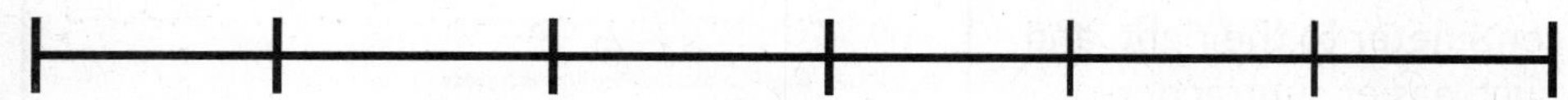

   c. Write an addition sentence to match each number line.

2. Each unit length on both number lines is 5 yards.
   a. Show 25 yards less than 90 yards on the following number line.

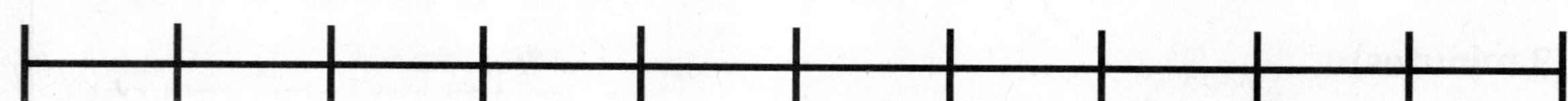

   b. Show 35 yards less than 100 yards on the number line.

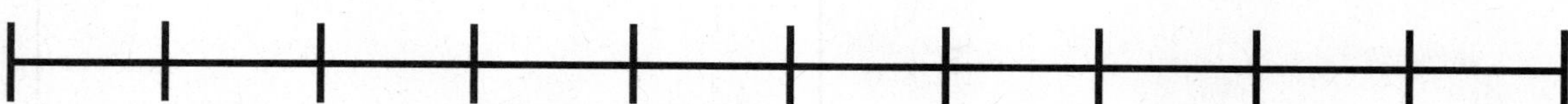

   c. Write a subtraction sentence to match each number line.

3. Vincent's meter strip got cut off at 68 centimeters. To measure the length of his screwdriver, he writes "81 cm – 68 cm." Alicia says it's easier to move the screwdriver over 2 centimeters. What is Alicia's subtraction sentence? Explain why she's correct.

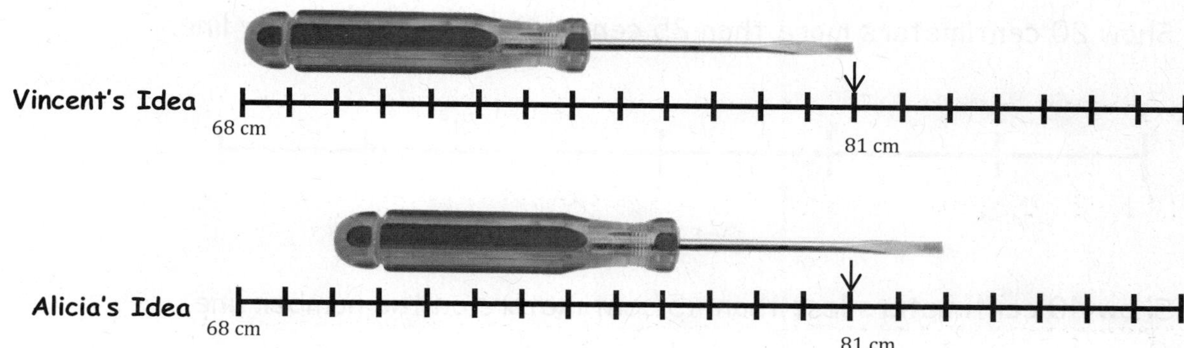

4. A large flute is 71 centimeters long, and a small flute is 29 centimeters long. What is the difference between their lengths?

5. Ingrid measured her garden snake's skin to be 28 inches long using a yardstick, but didn't start her measurement at zero. What might be the two endpoints of her snakeskin on her meter stick? Write a subtraction sentence to match your idea.

Name ______________________________ Date ______________

1. Each unit length on both number lines is 20 centimeters.

   a. Show 20 centimeters more than 25 centimeters on the number line.

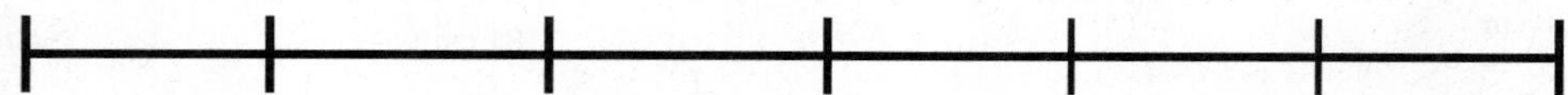

   b. Show 40 centimeters less than 45 centimeters on the number line.

   c. Write an addition or subtraction sentence to match each number line.

Name ______________________________ Date ______________

1. Each unit length on both number lines is 10 centimeters.
   a. Show 20 centimeters more than 35 centimeters on the number line.

   b. Show 30 centimeters more than 65 centimeters on the number line.

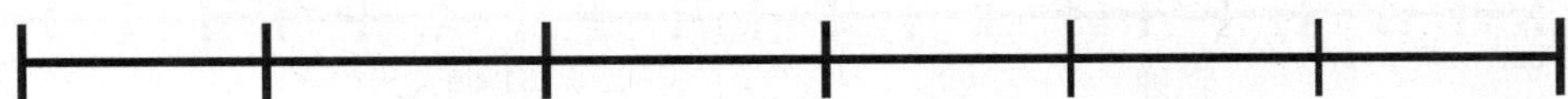

   c. Write an addition sentence to match each number line.

2. Each unit length on both number lines is 5 yards.
   a. Show 35 yards less than 80 yards on the following number line.

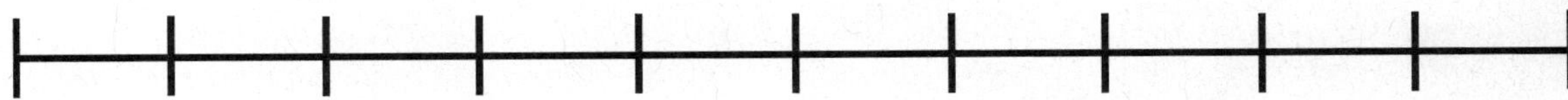

   b. Show 25 yards less than 100 yards on the number line.

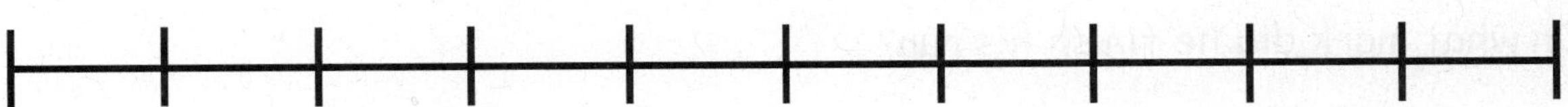

   c. Write a subtraction sentence to match each number line.

3. Laura's meter strip got cut off at 37 centimeters. To measure the length of her screwdriver, she writes "51 cm – 37 cm." Tam says it's easier to move the screwdriver over 3 centimeters. What is Tam's subtraction sentence? Explain why she's correct.

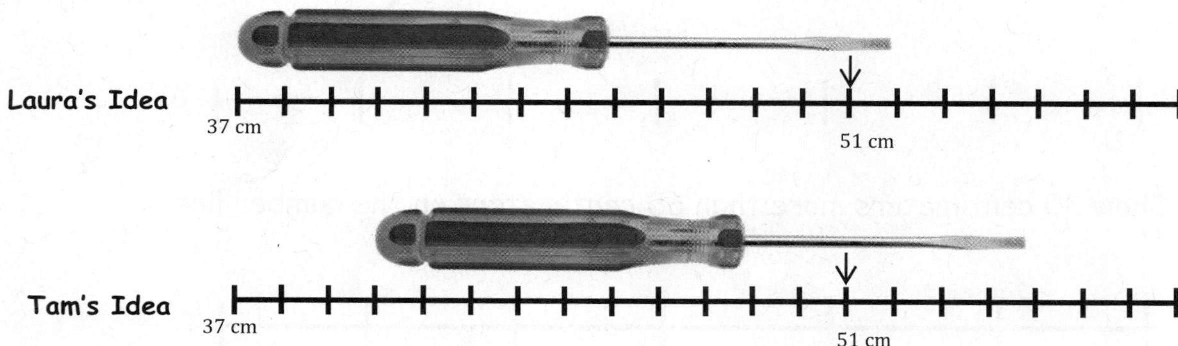

4. Alice measured her belt to be 22 inches long using a yardstick, but she didn't start her measurement at zero. What might be the two endpoints of her belt on her meter stick? Write a subtraction sentence to match your idea.

5. Isaiah ran 100 meters on a 200 meter track. He started running at the 19 meter mark. On what mark did he finish his run?

Template A

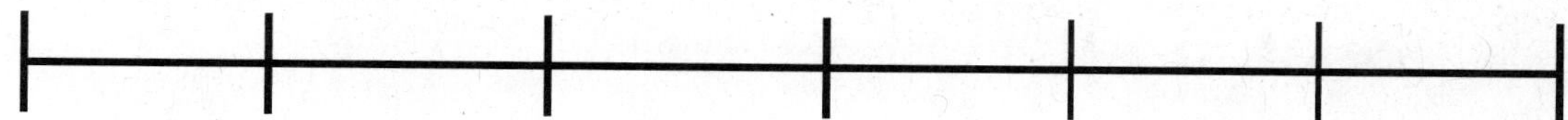

Template B

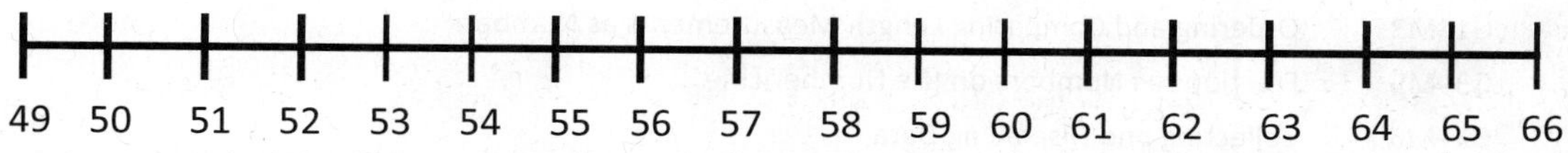

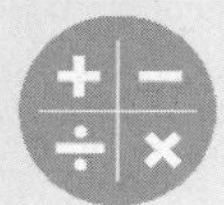

Topic F

Displaying Measurement Data

2.MD.6, 2.MD.9, 2.MD.1, 2.MD.5

Focus Standards:	2.MD.6	Represent whole numbers as lengths from 0 on a number line diagram with equally spaced points corresponding to the numbers 0, 1, 2, ..., and represent whole-number sums and differences within 100 on a number line diagram.
	2.MD.9	Generate measurement data by measuring lengths of several objects to the nearest whole unit, or by making repeated measurements of the same object. Show the measurements by making a line plot, where the horizontal scale is marked off in whole-number units.
Instructional Days:	4	
Coherence -Links from:	G1–M3	Ordering and Comparing Length Measurements as Numbers
-Links to:	G3–M5	Fractions as Numbers on the Number Line
	G3–M6	Collecting and Displaying Data

Building on the work in Topic E, students now connect the process of measuring to displaying data in line plots. In Lesson 23, the students measure their own handspan (i.e., the distance from the tip of the thumb to the tip of the pinky with hand fully extended) as well as those of five friends, rounding the lengths to the nearest whole inch. They then share the data as a class. Using tally marks, students create a table to record and organize the data. Then, in Lesson 24, students display the data from the table as a line plot, relating the horizontal measurement scale in whole centimeters and inches to the number line diagram (**2.MD.9**). Students observe and comment on the patterns they observe in the line plot.

Sit and Reach Distance (cm)	Number of Students
22 cm	1
23 cm	1
25 cm	1
26 cm	2
27 cm	3
28 cm	4
29 cm	3
30 cm	3
31 cm	1
34 cm	1

Finally, in Lessons 25 and 26, students are presented with different data sets, which they represent using line plots (**2.MD.6**). They then discuss the results and learn how to interpret the data. For example, using the table shown, students create a plot and then answer questions such as, "What was the most common distance reached? What was the least common?" They infer and draw conclusions from the data set and representations, discovering that while a table is useful for organizing data, a line plot allows for the visual comparisons of the different quantities.

A Teaching Sequence Towards Mastery of Displaying Measurement Data	
Objective 1:	**Collect and record measurement data in a table; answer questions and summarize the data set. (Lesson 23)**
Objective 2:	**Draw a line plot to represent the measurement data; relate the measurement scale to the number line. (Lesson 24)**
Objective 3:	**Draw a line plot to represent a given data set; answer questions and draw conclusions based on measurement data. (Lessons 25–26)**

Lesson 23

Objective: Collect and record measurement data in a table; answer questions and summarize the data set.

Suggested Lesson Structure

- Fluency Practice (11 minutes)
- Concept Development (39 minutes)
- Student Debrief (10 minutes)

Total Time (60 minutes)

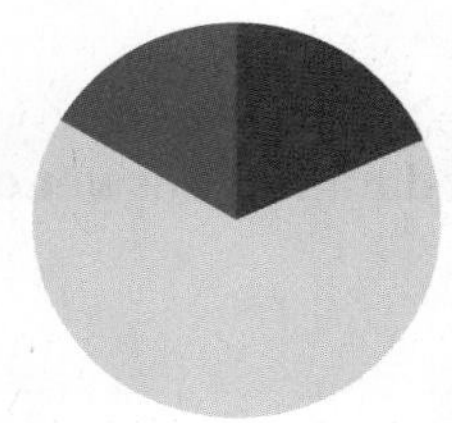

Fluency Practice (11 minutes)

- How Many More Hundreds? **2.NBT.7** (2 minutes)
- Sprint: Adding Across a Ten **2.OA.2** (9 minutes)

How Many More Hundreds? (2 minutes)

Note: Practicing subtracting multiples of a hundred prepares students for the lesson.

T: If I say 300 – 200, you say 100. To say it in a sentence, you say, "100 more than 200 is 300." Ready?
T: 300 – 200.
S: 100.
T: Say it in a sentence.
S: 100 more than 200 is 300.

Continue with the following possible sequence: 405 – 305, 801 – 601, 650 – 350, 825 – 125, and 999 – 299.

Sprint: Adding Across a Ten (9 minutes)

Materials: (S) Adding Across a Ten Sprint

Note: This Sprint gives practice with the grade level fluency of adding within 20.

Concept Development (39 minutes)

Note: The Concept Development today might be time consuming because it involves data collection from the entire class. For this reason and because the lesson itself is within real world context, the Application Problem has been omitted for today.

Materials: (T) Ruler, document projector (if available) (S) Ruler, Problem Set

Part 1: Collect and record data.

T: Everyone hold up your right hand.

S: (Hold up right hands.)

T: How do you know if it's your right or left hand? Turn and talk.

S: Because my left hand makes an L. → I write with my right hand. → I write with my other hand. → I just do.

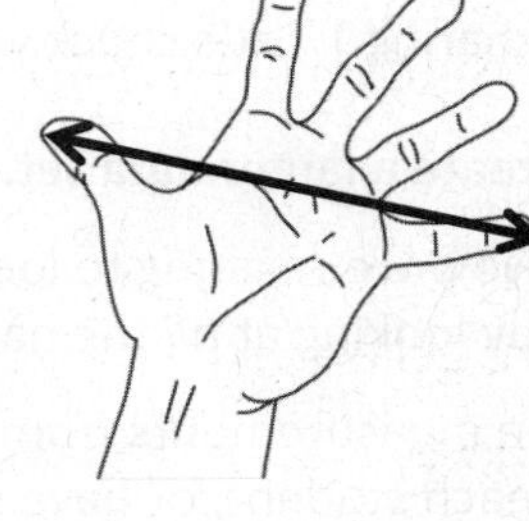

MP.5

T: Now, stretch your fingers all the way out. (Demonstrate.)

T: Talk to a partner. How many inches do you think it is from the tip of your pinky to the tip of your thumb?

S: (Various guesses.)

T: This measurement from the tip of our pinky to the tip of our thumb is called our **handspan**. We will be measuring that today.

T: (Hold ruler with right hand and show ruler against handspan, as in picture at right, mirroring what the students will do.) Look at how I measure my handspan. What are some important things I need to remember when I measure this?

S: Start measuring at zero on the ruler. → Remember what unit you are using. → Notice where your handspan starts and ends.

T: Very good! I just measured my handspan, and it is ____ inches. Even though it was not exactly that many inches, I rounded up to the next whole inch. I would have rounded down if it had been closer to the other inch mark. (Write the measurement on the board.)

Put students in groups of four or five. Hand out Problem Sets and rulers. Project Problem Set or have a copy of the table on the board to fill in.

T: Look at your Problem Set. Notice that the top of the first page has a chart where we can record our measurements in inches. Let's start with my hand measure. (Tally it on your table for students to copy.)

T: Now, work with a partner. Measure your handspan, and have your partner help you make sure your measurement is correct. Then, record your measurement on the line. (Give students time to complete this.)

T: Now switch. When you have finished with your partner, record the handspans of the other people in your group.

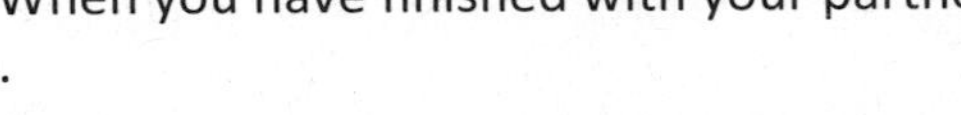

Circulate among the students as they complete this activity.

T: Now, take the data in your chart and fill in the table. Use a tally mark to record each person's measurement in the appropriate box. (Provide work time.)

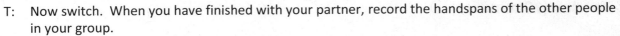

NOTES ON MULTIPLE MEANS OF REPRESENTATION:

Scaffold the lesson for your English language learners by posting key vocabulary after you have introduced it in the lesson. Post terms such as *handspan, table, data,* and *tally marks* with a visual for each that captures its meaning. Having such a reference will help your English language learners to talk with a partner and complete the activities in the lesson.

T: You have now recorded **data** in a table! Real scientists collect and record information like this when they do research.

T: Now that we have this information, we can use it to learn some things. Look at your data set in your table and the questions that are next to it. Count the tally marks to answer the questions.

Circulate among the students and provide support as they complete this activity.

T: Tell your partner what you think the most common handspan will be for the whole class. (Pause for sharing.) Let's check your predictions.

Part 2: Create a larger data set.

T: Now we're going to look at the information we can get by looking at *all* the handspans in our class.

Collect the measurements from each group and make a tally mark for each student, or have students record their own tally mark on the board.

T: Let's count up and answer the questions on our recording sheet. (Add and write the totals of the handspans next to the tallies for each measurement.)

T: Which handspan was the most common in our class?

S: (Various answers.)

T: And the least common?

S: (Various answers.)

T: Now write a comparison question about the class data for your friend to answer. For example, "How many more students' handspan measured 5 inches than measured 8 inches?" (Pause for students to write a question.)

T: Now share your question with a partner, and answer your partner's question. (Provide work time.)

T: Let's listen to and answer some of the questions you came up with about this data set.

Solicit questions from the students and facilitate a discussion about them.

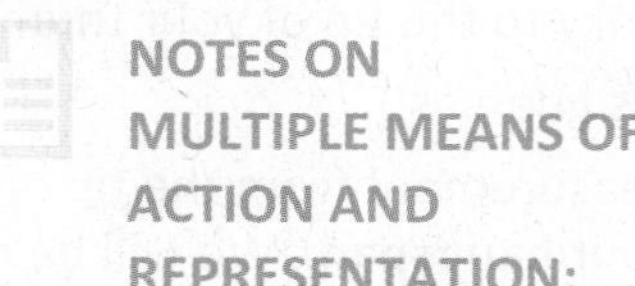

NOTES ON MULTIPLE MEANS OF ACTION AND REPRESENTATION:

Before asking below grade level students to move on to the final activity, ask them to restate what they learned in the last part of the lesson. Ask them guiding questions like, "How did we record our hand span data? What kind of questions did we ask about data?" in order to encourage them to think about and express their learning from the lesson.

Problem Set (5 minutes)

Note: Students will only have 5 minutes to complete this activity. If the first two parts take much time, the second page of the Problem Set may be omitted.

Student Debrief (10 minutes)

Lesson Objective: Collect and record measurement date in a table; answer questions and summarize the data set.

The Student Debrief is intended to invite reflection and active processing of the total lesson experience.

Invite students to review their solutions for the Problem Set. They should check work by comparing answers with a partner before going over answers as a class. Look for misconceptions or misunderstandings that can be addressed in the Debrief. Guide students in a conversation to debrief the Problem Set and process the lesson.

You may choose to use any combination of the questions below to lead the discussion.

- Why doesn't the whole class data set match your individual data sheet?
- Do you think having more or fewer data points is better in science? Why? Turn and talk.
- Why do you think ____ was the most common handspan in our class? If we collected data from all the second-grade classes, do you think this would change? Why or why not?
- What if we collected data in the fifth-grade classroom, do you think ___ will still be the most common handspan? Why or why not?
- Talk to your partner about what you think would happen to our data if we took the handspan of everyone at our school from the kindergartners to the fifth-graders, and even the adults. Why is it good to have as much data as possible?
- When you used the handspan data to make your comparison problem, did you use addition or subtraction? Show your partner your solution to your comparison problem.

Name Samantha Date

1. Measure the lines below in inches. Record the data using tally marks on the table provided.

Line A

Line B

Line C

Line D

Line E

Line F

Line G

Line Length	Number of Lines
Shorter than 5 inches	|||
Longer than 5 inches		
Equal to 5 inches	|||

a. How many more lines are equal to 5 inches than shorter than 5 inches? 0

b. What is the difference between the number of lines that are shorter than 5 inches and those that are longer than 5 inches? 2

c. Ask and answer a compare question that could be answered using the data above.

Question: If 7 more lines were longer than 5 inches how many more would be longer than shorter. 5

Switch papers with a partner. Have you partner answer your question on the back.

Exit Ticket (3 minutes)

After the Student Debrief, instruct students to complete the Exit Ticket. A review of their work will help you assess the students' understanding of the concepts that were presented in the lesson today and plan more effectively for future lessons. You may read the questions aloud to the students.

A # Correct ___

Add.

1	9 + 2 =		23	4 + 7 =	
2	9 + 3 =		24	4 + 8 =	
3	9 + 4 =		25	5 + 6 =	
4	9 + 7 =		26	5 + 7 =	
5	7 + 9 =		27	3 + 8 =	
6	10 + 1 =		28	3 + 9 =	
7	10 + 2 =		29	2 + 9 =	
8	10 + 3 =		30	5 + 10 =	
9	10 + 8 =		31	5 + 8 =	
10	8 + 10 =		32	9 + 6 =	
11	8 + 3 =		33	6 + 9 =	
12	8 + 4 =		34	7 + 6 =	
13	8 + 5 =		35	6 + 7 =	
14	8 + 9 =		36	8 + 6 =	
15	9 + 8 =		37	6 + 8 =	
16	7 + 4 =		38	8 + 7 =	
17	10 + 5 =		39	7 + 8 =	
18	6 + 5 =		40	6 + 6 =	
19	7 + 5 =		41	7 + 7 =	
20	9 + 5 =		42	8 + 8 =	
21	5 + 9 =		43	9 + 9 =	
22	10 + 6 =		44	4 + 9 =	

B Improvement ______ # Correct ______

Add.

1	10 + 1 =		23	5 + 6 =	
2	10 + 2 =		24	5 + 7 =	
3	10 + 3 =		25	4 + 7 =	
4	10 + 9 =		26	4 + 8 =	
5	9 + 10 =		27	4 + 10 =	
6	9 + 2 =		28	3 + 8 =	
7	9 + 3 =		29	3 + 9 =	
8	9 + 4 =		30	2 + 9 =	
9	9 + 8 =		31	5 + 8 =	
10	8 + 9 =		32	7 + 6 =	
11	8 + 3 =		33	6 + 7 =	
12	8 + 4 =		34	8 + 6 =	
13	8 + 5 =		35	6 + 8 =	
14	8 + 7 =		36	9 + 6 =	
15	7 + 8 =		37	6 + 9 =	
16	7 + 4 =		38	9 + 7 =	
17	10 + 4 =		39	7 + 9 =	
18	6 + 5 =		40	6 + 6 =	
19	7 + 5 =		41	7 + 7 =	
20	9 + 5 =		42	8 + 8 =	
21	5 + 9 =		43	9 + 9 =	
22	10 + 8 =		44	4 + 9 =	

Name ______________________________ Date ______________

1. Gather and record group data.

Measure your handspan and record it here: __________

Write your teacher's handspan measure here: __________

Then measure the handspans of the other people in your group and write them here. We will be using the data tomorrow.

Name:	Handspan:

Handspan	Tally of Number of People
3 inches	
4 inches	
5 inches	
6 inches	
7 inches	
8 inches	

What length is the most common? ____________

What length is the least common? ____________

What do you think the most common handspan will be for the whole class? Why?

2. Record class data.

Record the class data using tally marks on the table provided.

Handspan	Tally of Number of People
3 inches	
4 inches	
5 inches	
6 inches	
7 inches	
8 inches	

What length is the most common? _______________

What length is the least common? _______________

Ask and answer a comparison question that can be answered using the data above.

Question: ____

____

Answer: ____

____

Name ______________________________ Date ______________

1. Measure the lines below in inches. Record the data using tally marks on the table provided.

Line A ____

Line B ______________________________

Line C ____

Line D ____

Line E ______________________

Line F __________________________

Line G ____

Line Length	Number of Lines
Shorter than 5 inches	
Longer than 5 inches	
Equal to 5 inches	

a. How many more lines are equal to 5 inches than shorter than 5 inches? ____________

b. What is the difference between the number of lines that are shorter than 5 inches and those that are longer than 5 inches? __________

c. Ask and answer a comparison question that could be answered using the data above.

Question: ____

____

Switch papers with a partner. Have you partner answer your question on the back.

Name ____________________ Date ____________

1. The lines below have been measured for you. Record the data using tally marks on the table provided and answer the questions below.

Line A 5 inches

Line B 6 inches

Line C 4 inches

Line D 6 inches

Line E 3 inches

Line Length	Number of Lines
Shorter than 5 inches	
5 inches or longer	

a. If 8 more lines were measured to be longer than 5 inches and 12 more lines were measured to be shorter than 5 inches, how many tallies would be in the chart?

____

Name _______________ Date _______________

1. Measure your handspan and record it here: __________

   Then measure the handspans of your family members and write them below.

Name: **Handspan:**

_______________ _______________

_______________ _______________

_______________ _______________

_______________ _______________

_______________ _______________

2. Record your data using tally marks on the table provided.

Handspan	Tally of Number of People
3 inches	
4 inches	
5 inches	
6 inches	
7 inches	
8 inches	

a. What length is the most common? __________

b. What length is the least common? __________

c. Ask and answer one comparison question that can be answered using the data above.

Question:

____

____

Answer:

____

____

3. Use your ruler to measure the lines below in inches. Record the data using tally marks on the table provided.

Line A ____

Line B ____

Line C ____

Line D ____

Line E ____________________________

Line F ____________________________________

Line G ____

Line Length	Number of Lines
Shorter than 4 inches	
Longer than 4 inches	
Equal to 4 inches	

a. How many more lines are equal to 4 inches than shorter than 4 inches?

____

What is the difference between the number of lines that are shorter than 4 inches and those that are longer than 4 inches? __________

b. Ask and answer one comparison question that could be answered using the date above.

Question: ____

____

Answer: ____

____

Lesson 24

Objective: Draw a line plot to represent the measurement data; relate the measurement scale to the number line.

Suggested Lesson Structure

■ Fluency Practice	(11 minutes)
■ Application Problem	(7 minutes)
■ Concept Development	(32 minutes)
■ Student Debrief	(10 minutes)
Total Time	**(60 minutes)**

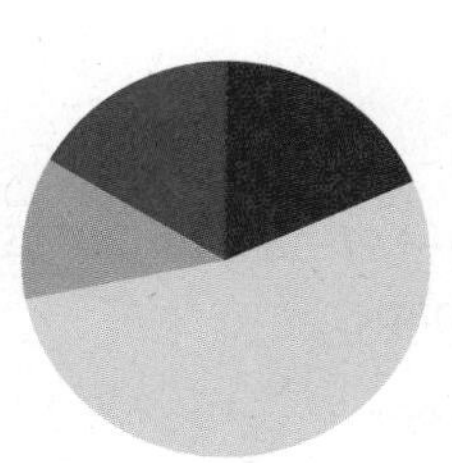

Fluency Practice (11 minutes)

- Find the Difference **2.NBT.5** (2 minutes)
- Sprint: Subtraction Patterns **2.OA.2, 2.NBT.5** (9 minutes)

Find the Difference (2 minutes)

Materials: (S) Personal white boards

Note: Students review using mental strategies to solve subtraction problems.

T: (Write 24 – 16 =_____.) Solve using a mental math strategy and write your answer on the board.

Repeat process and sequence for 34 – 6, 44 – 16, 20 – 5, 21 – 5, 21 – 15, 31 – 25, 22 – 8, 32 – 18, and 42 – 19.

Sprint: Subtraction Patterns (9 minutes)

Materials: (S) Subtraction Patterns Sprint

Note: Students practice subtraction in order to gain mastery of the sums and differences within 20 and identify relationships with higher numbers.

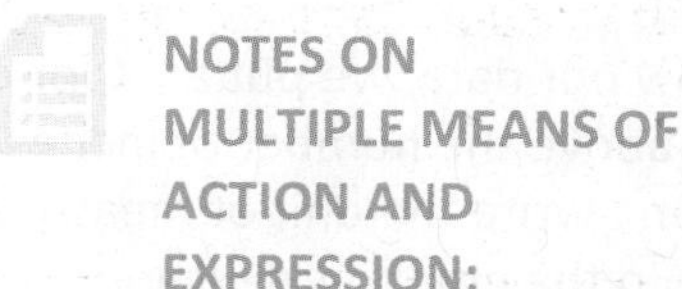

NOTES ON MULTIPLE MEANS OF ACTION AND EXPRESSION:

Challenge above grade level students by asking them to find the value of the coins that Mike, Dennis, and April collected. Ask them to explain in writing how they arrived at their solution.

Application Problem (7 minutes)

Mike, Dennis, and April all collected coins from a parking lot. When they counted up their coins, they found they had 24 pennies, 15 nickels, 7 dimes, and 2 quarters. They put all the pennies into one cup and the other coins in another. Which cup had more coins? How many more?

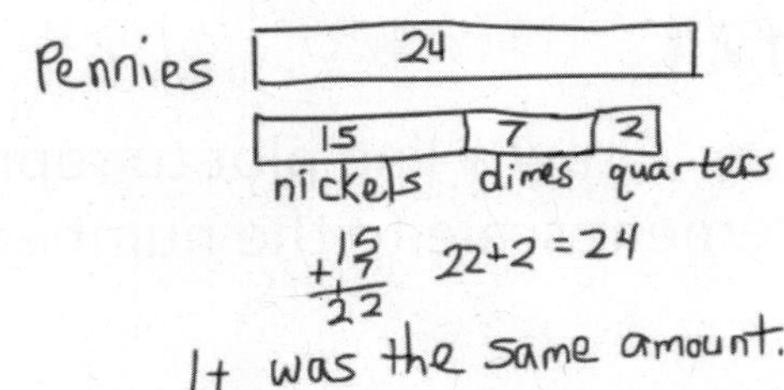

Note: This two-step problem involves data comparisons, which is a skill that will be used by the students in their data work. Encourage students to use the RDW process and make a tape diagram to visualize their work.

Concept Development (32 minutes)

Materials: (T) Data table with student data from G2–M7–Lesson 23 (S) Problem Set from G2–M7–Lesson 23, recording sheet, rulers, centimeter grid paper

Part 1: Plot yesterday's data on a line plot.

Project or show the data from G2–M7–Lesson 23 as shown at right.

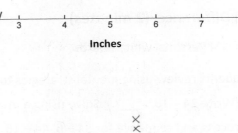

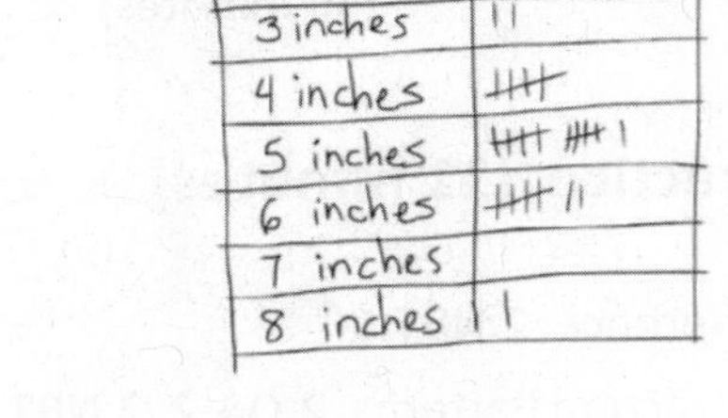

Hand Span	Tally
3 inches	II
4 inches	𝍸
5 inches	𝍸 𝍸 I
6 inches	𝍸 II
7 inches	
8 inches	I

T: This is our data table from yesterday, with all the measurements from our class.

T: (Project or show a number line.) What is this?

S: A number line!

T: Yes. We used the number line to help us with addition and subtraction problems the other day by sliding up and down the number line. We can also use a number line in a different way to show data. (Draw a number line with a range of 3 to 8.)

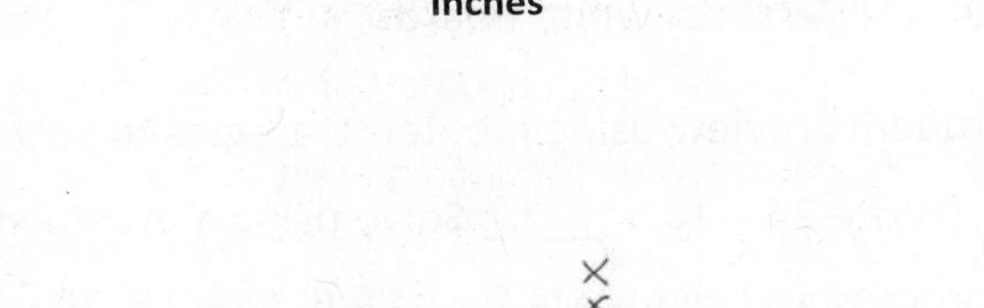

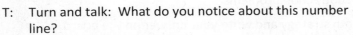

T: Turn and talk: What do you notice about this number line?

S: It goes from 3 to 8. → It doesn't start at 1. → There is a zero and then some slashes and then a 3. → It says *inches.*

T: That's right! Our data doesn't start at 0, so we make two slashes to show that we are skipping some numbers.

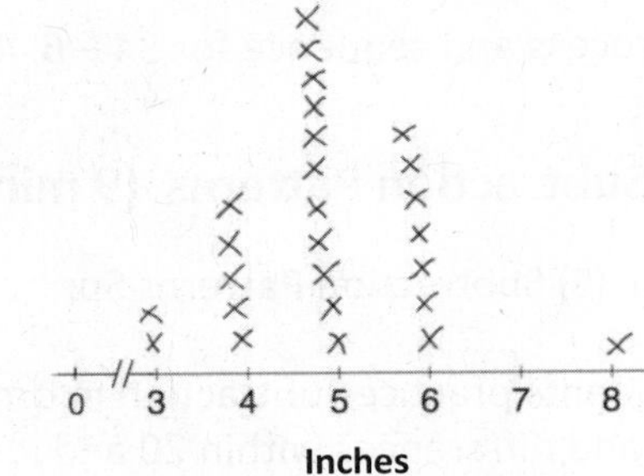

T: To show our data, we put an X for each of our tally marks above the number of inches our handspans were and write the unit of measure. (Demonstrate as shown in the graph at right.)

T: Now it's your turn. (Distribute number line templates.) Transfer the class data from yesterday's tally table onto your number line template. (Circulate among the students as they complete this activity.)

T: You have just made a graph called a **line plot**! Compare your line plots with a partner. What information can you see in your line plot?

S: I see that most people have a 5-inch handspan. → There are a lot more people with a 5- or 6-inch

handspan than 7- or 8-inch handspans. → The starting point of the labels is the shortest measurement, and the endpoint is the longest measurement.

Part 2: Collect, organize, and plot shoe measurements in a table.

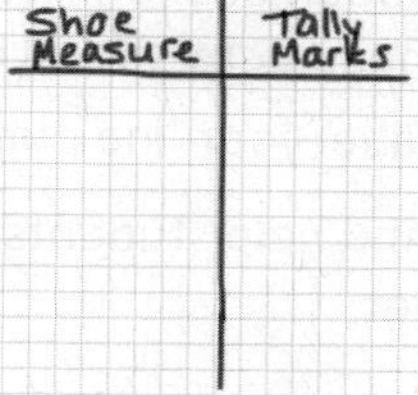

Shoe Measure	Tally Marks
26 cm	I
20 cm	III
21 cm	III
19 cm	I
22 cm	II

T: Let's measure how long our shoes are. This time we're going to use centimeters instead of inches. (Distribute rulers and grid paper.)

T: Measure your shoe length by placing your ruler flat on the bottom of your shoe. Write the centimeter measurement down on the top of your page. (Model how to do this. Allow time for students to measure.)

T: Now we're going to make a collection table for our data. First, make your chart with the labels *shoe measure* and *tally marks.* (Model as shown at right.)

T: Next, record your shoe measurement with make a tally mark next to it. I'm going to write 26 cm (use your own measure) and make the tally mark.

T: Next, collect 9 more shoe measurements from your friends. Just be sure to add a tally mark if you get the same measurement more than once. (Circulate among the students, and facilitate the data collection.)

T: We now have a table with 10 measurements tallied on it. How many of you have 10 different measurements on your collection table? (Acknowledge student responses.)

T: How many of you found at least 5 people with the same shoe measure? (Acknowledge responses.)

Part 3: Reorganize shoe measurement data on a line plot.

T: Let's turn our data into a line plot.

T: This time, instead of a number line that I give you, I'm going to have you create your own line plot using grid paper.

T: Take your ruler and measure the width of one of the boxes on your grid paper. (Pause for students to do this.)

T: What is the measure?

S: 1 centimeter!

MP.4

T: Turn and talk. How might this help make the number line for our line plots?

S: I can use the grids to make it easier to draw my lines. → The centimeter grids are just like the centimeters on my ruler. → We can make our line plots match our rulers. → A ruler is just like a number line!

T: I heard someone say that a ruler is just like a number line! That's true. In this case, though, we don't have to make our number line start at zero.

NOTES ON MULTIPLE MEANS OF REPRESENTATIONS:

Support English language learners by pointing to the number line, the range of 3–8 on the number line, line plot, tally marks, etc., when referring to them during the lesson. Label everything and post on the word wall so that English language learners can refer to them as they do their math work.

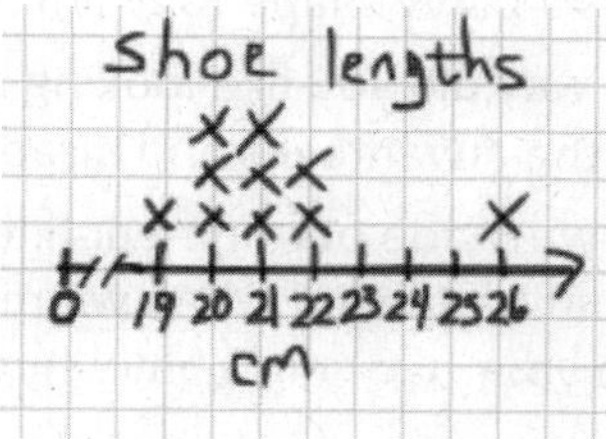

T: Let's draw the number line base. Turn and talk: How do you know how to label your number line?

S: We do it in order from shortest to longest. → We need to go from 19 centimeters to 26 centimeters, the longest. → If we don't have any shoes that measure 23 or 24 centimeters, do we label them, too?

T: Good question. Do we need to label measurements that are between others, even if there are no measurements? Let's do. It shows there were none and that is interesting, too.

S: Label your line plots and mark an X for each tally of the measurements in your graph.

Circulate and help students draw their line plots. As they finish their plots, release them to work on the Problem Set.

Problem Set (10 minutes)

If the Concept Development lesson takes the entire amount of time, use the Problem Set for homework or early finishers instead.

Student Debrief (10 minutes)

Lesson Objective: Draw a line plot to represent the measurement data; relate the measurement scale to the number line.

The Student Debrief is intended to invite reflection and active processing of the total lesson experience.

Invite students to review their solutions for the Problem Set. They should check work by comparing answers with a partner before going over answers as a class. Look for misconceptions or misunderstandings that can be addressed in the Debrief. Guide students in a conversation to debrief the Problem Set and process the lesson.

You may choose to use any combination of the questions below to lead the discussion.

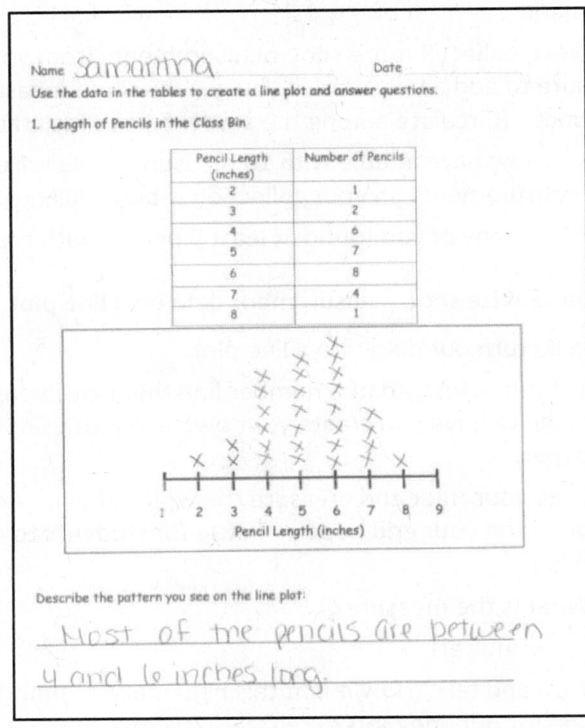

Name Samantha Date

Use the data in the tables to create a line plot and answer questions.

1. Length of Pencils in the Class Bin

Pencil Length (inches)	Number of Pencils
2	1
3	2
4	6
5	7
6	8
7	4
8	1

Describe the pattern you see on the line plot:

Most of the pencils are between 4 and 6 inches long.

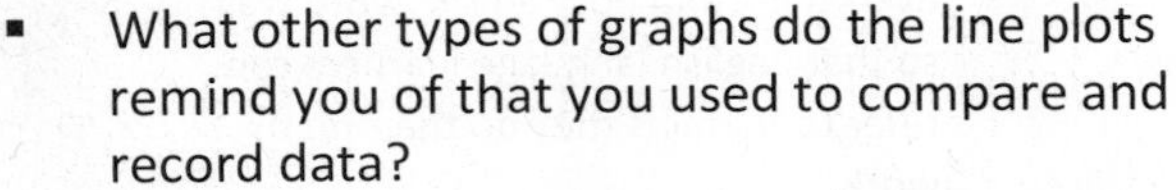

- What other types of graphs do the line plots remind you of that you used to compare and record data?
- Compare the shape of the handspan plot and the shoe plot. What do you notice? Why do you think there is a curvy shape to it starting low, going up, and then coming down again?
- Which way did you like looking at the data, the tally chart, or the line plot? Talk to your partner about the advantages and disadvantages of each.
- When we made our number line for our handspans in the lesson today, why didn't we start at 0 or 1? What happened when we measured our shoes? Did you make a number line that started with 1? Talk to your partner about why or why not.

- Look at the intervals on your number line for the shoe measurement data. Could we have just made intervals at 19, 20, 21, 22, and 26 since those were the only shoe measurements that we had in our class?
- Explain to your partner why we needed to put 23-, 24-, and 25-inch hash marks on the number line even though there was no data for these measurements. (All intervals on a number line must be equal. It helps us to see that there is a gap in shoe sizes and to wonder about it like scientists.)

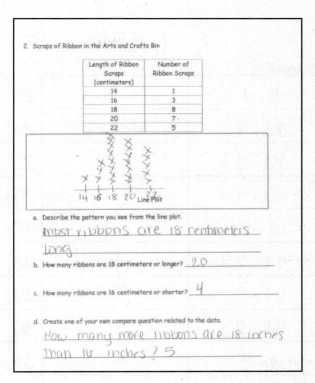

2. Scraps of Ribbon in the Arts and Crafts Bin

Length of Ribbon Scraps (centimeters)	Number of Ribbon Scraps
14	1
16	3
18	8
20	7
22	5

14 16 18 20 22

Line Plot

a. Describe the pattern you see from the line plot.
most ribbons are 18 centimeters long.

b. How many ribbons are 18 centimeters or longer? 20

c. How many ribbons are 16 centimeters or shorter? 4

d. Create one of your own compare question related to the data.
How many more ribbons are 18 inches than 16 inches? 5

Exit Ticket (3 minutes)

After the Student Debrief, instruct students to complete the Exit Ticket. A review of their work will help you assess the students' understanding of the concepts that were presented in the lesson today and plan more effectively for future lessons. You may read the questions aloud to the students.

A # Correct ______

Subtract.

1	3 - 1 =		23	8 - 7 =	
2	13 - 1 =		24	18 - 7 =	
3	23 - 1 =		25	58 - 7 =	
4	53 - 1 =		26	62 - 2 =	
5	4 - 2 =		27	9 - 8 =	
6	14 - 2 =		28	19 - 8 =	
7	24 - 2 =		29	29 - 8 =	
8	64 - 2 =		30	69 - 8 =	
9	4 - 3 =		31	7 - 3 =	
10	14 - 3 =		32	17 - 3 =	
11	24 - 3 =		33	77 - 3 =	
12	74 - 3 =		34	59 - 9 =	
13	6 - 4 =		35	9 - 7 =	
14	16 - 4 =		36	19 - 7 =	
15	26 - 4 =		37	89 - 7 =	
16	96 - 4 =		38	99 - 5 =	
17	7 - 5 =		39	78 - 6 =	
18	17 - 5 =		40	58 - 5 =	
19	27 - 5 =		41	39 - 7 =	
20	47 - 5 =		42	28 - 6 =	
21	43 - 3 =		43	49 - 4 =	
22	87 - 7 =		44	67 - 4 =	

B Improvement _____ # Correct _____

Subtract.

1	2 - 1 =		23	8 - 7 =	
2	12 - 1 =		24	18 - 7 =	
3	22 - 1 =		25	68 - 7 =	
4	52 - 1 =		26	32 - 2 =	
5	5 - 2 =		27	9 - 8 =	
6	15 - 2 =		28	19 - 8 =	
7	25 - 2 =		29	29 - 8 =	
8	65 - 2 =		30	79 - 8 =	
9	4 - 3 =		31	8 - 4 =	
10	14 - 3 =		32	18 - 4 =	
11	24 - 3 =		33	78 - 4 =	
12	84 - 3 =		34	89 - 9 =	
13	7 - 4 =		35	9 - 7 =	
14	17 - 4 =		36	19 - 7 =	
15	27 - 4 =		37	79 - 7 =	
16	97 - 4 =		38	89 - 5 =	
17	6 - 5 =		39	68 - 6 =	
18	16 - 5 =		40	48 - 5 =	
19	26 - 5 =		41	29 - 7 =	
20	46 - 5 =		42	38 - 6 =	
21	23 - 3 =		43	59 - 4 =	
22	67 - 7 =		44	77 - 4 =	

Recording sheet for first activity. Copy and cut as many slips as you need for the class.

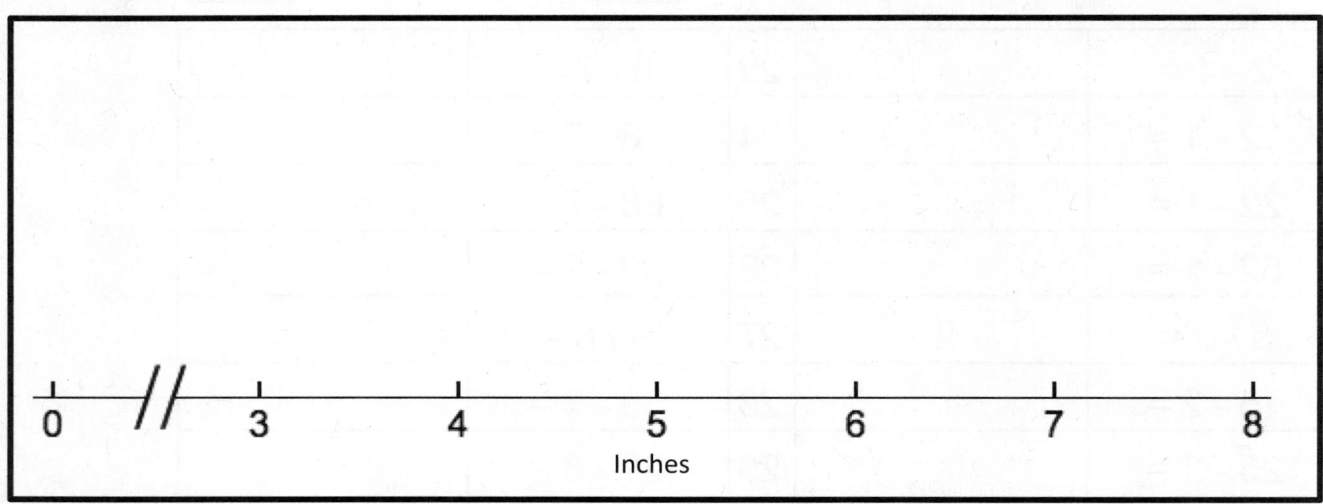

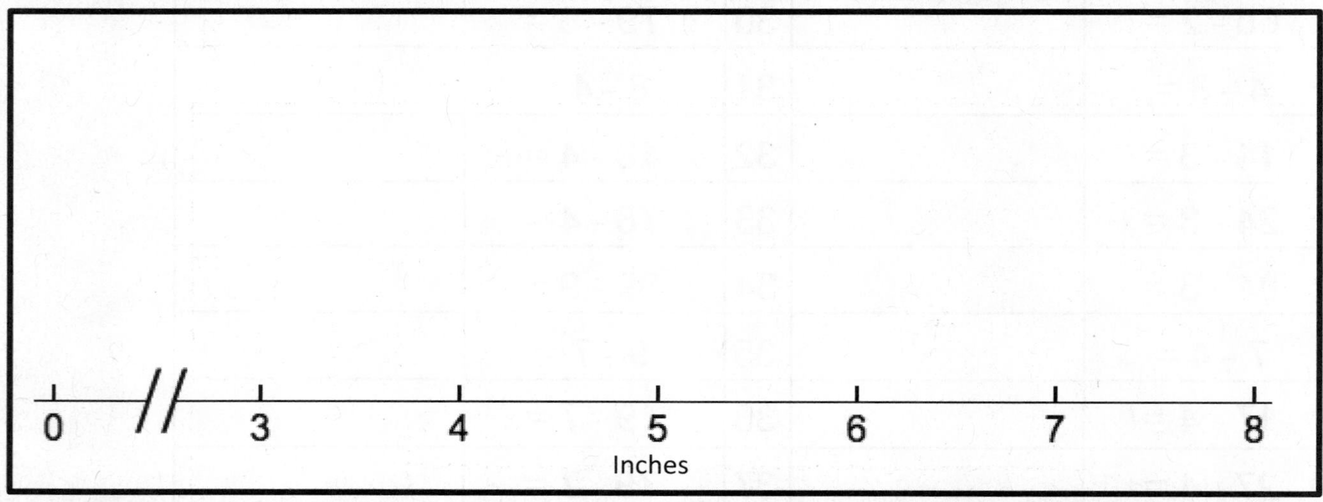

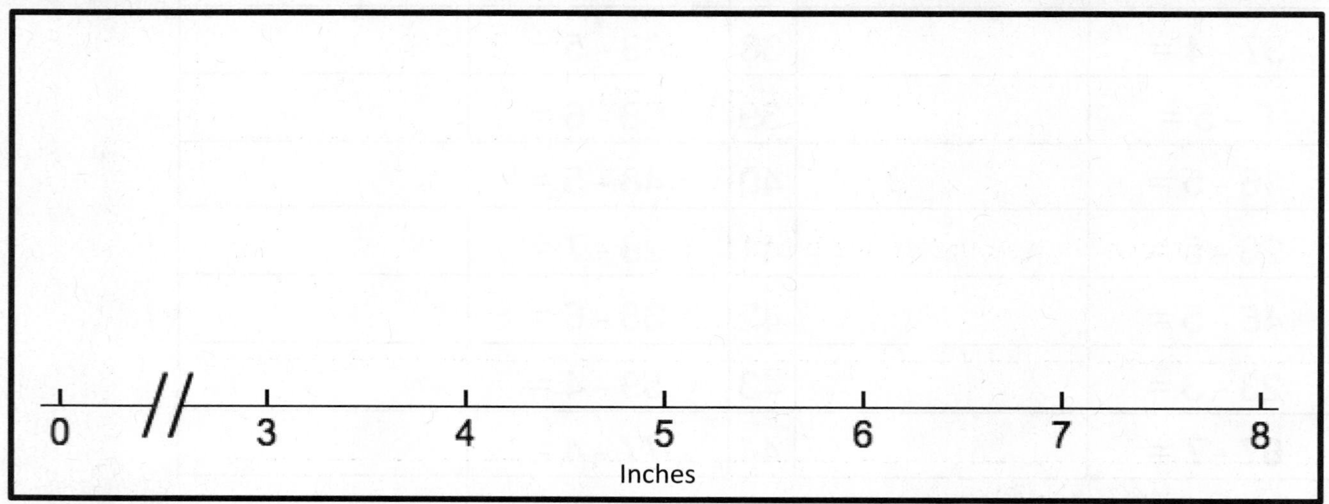

Name ____________________ Date ________

Use the data in the tables to create a line plot and answer questions.

1. Length of Pencils in the Class Bin

Pencil Length (inches)	Number of Pencils
2	1
3	2
4	6
5	7
6	8
7	4
8	1

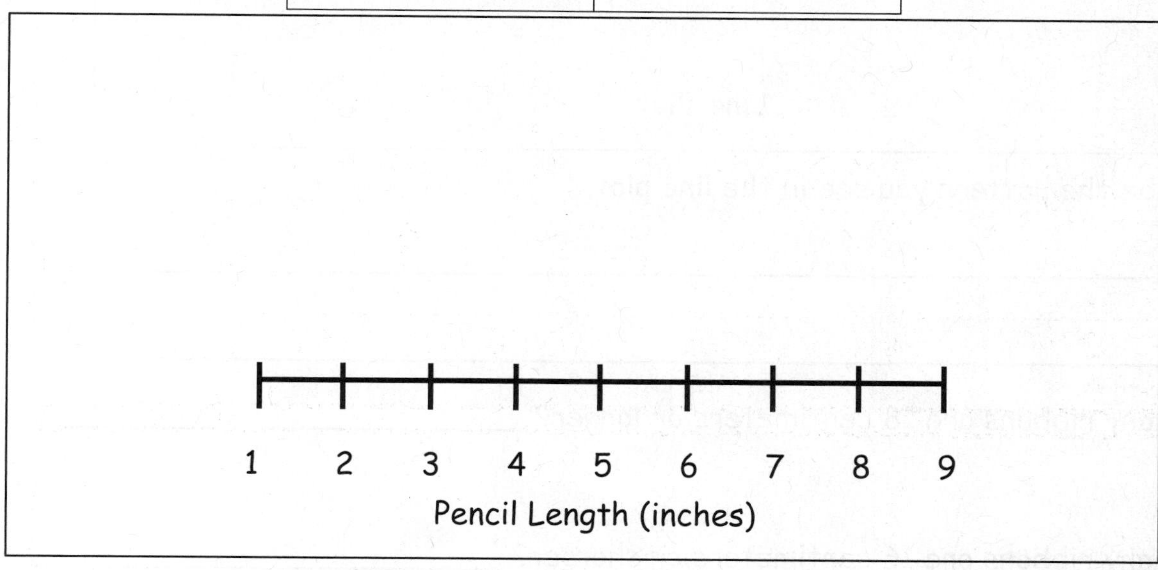

Describe the pattern you see in the line plot:

____

____

2. Scraps of Ribbon in the Arts and Crafts Bin

Length of Ribbon Scraps (centimeters)	Number of Ribbon Scraps
14	1
16	3
18	8
20	7
22	5

Line Plot

a. Describe the pattern you see in the line plot.

____

____

b. How many ribbons are 18 centimeters or longer? ____________________

c. How many ribbons are 16 centimeters or shorter? ____________________

d. Create your own comparison question related to the data.

____

____

Name ______________________________ Date ______________

Use the data in the tables to create a line plot and answer questions.

Length of Crayons in a Class Bin

Crayon Length (inches)	Number of Crayons
1	3
2	9
3	7
4	5

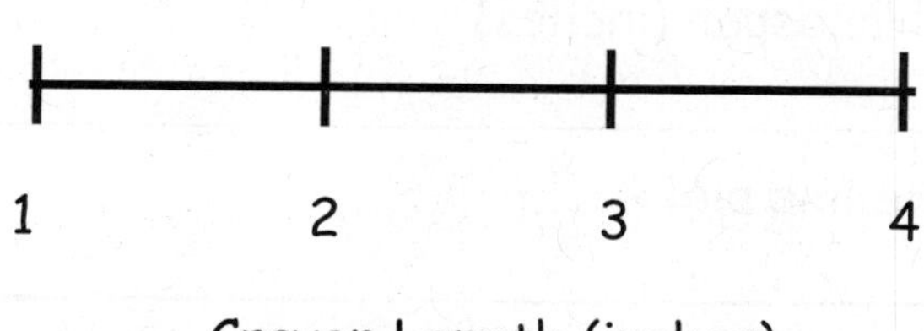

Crayon Length (inches)

Name _______________________________ Date ______________

1. Use the data in the tables to create a line plot and answer questions.

Handspans of Students in Ms. DeFransico's Class

Handspan (inches)	Number of Students
2	0
3	0
4	1
5	7
6	10
7	3
8	1

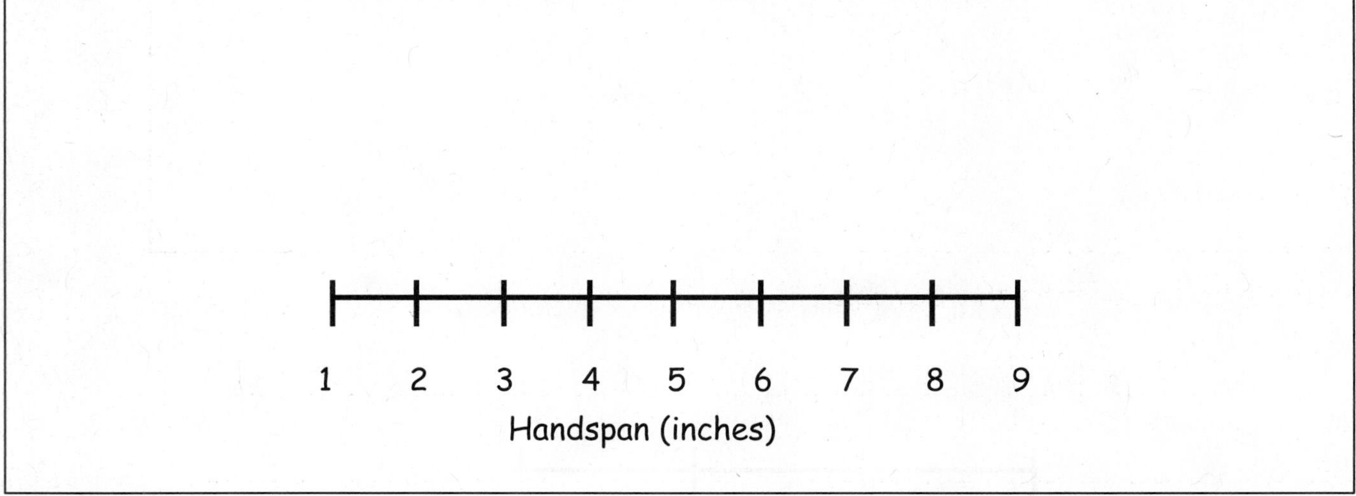

Describe the pattern you see in the line plot:

____

____

____

2. Use the data in the tables to create a line plot and answer questions.

Lengths of Right Foot of Students in Ms. DeFransico's Class

Length of Right Foot (centimeters)	Number of Students
17	1
18	2
19	4
20	6
21	6
22	2
23	1

Line Plot

a. Describe the pattern you see in the line plot.

____

____

b. How many feet are longer than 20 centimeters? ________________

c. How many feet are shorter than 20 centimeters? ________________

d. Create your own comparison question related to the data.

____

Lesson 25

Objective: Draw a line plot to represent a given data set; answer questions and draw conclusions based on measurement data.

Suggested Lesson Structure

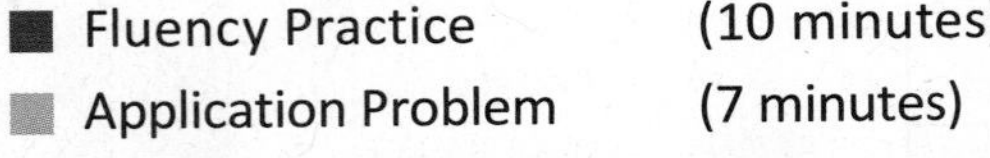

Fluency Practice	(10 minutes)
Application Problem	(7 minutes)
Concept Development	(33 minutes)
Student Debrief	(10 minutes)
Total Time	**(60 minutes)**

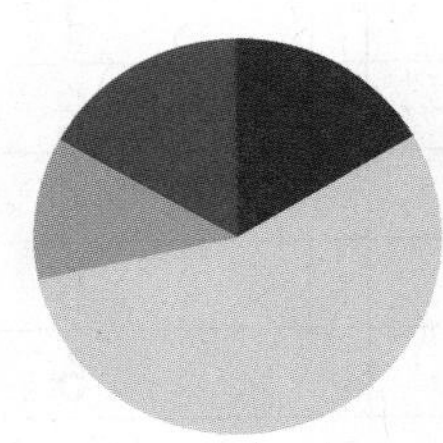

Fluency Practice (10 minutes)

- Decomposition Tree **2.OA.2** (5 minutes)
- Grade 2 Core Fluency Differentiated Practice Sets **2.OA.2** (5 minutes)

Decomposition Tree (5 minutes)

Materials: (S) Decomposition Tree Template (from G2–M7–Lesson 6)

Note: Students are given 90 seconds to decompose 36 inches.

T: (Distribute tree template.)

T: You are going to break apart 36 inches on your Deco Tree for 90 seconds. Do as many problems as you can. Go!

S: (Work for 90 seconds.)

T: Now exchange your tree with your partner and check each other's work. (Allow students 30–45 seconds to check.)

T: Return each other's papers. Did you see another way to make 36 inches on your partner's paper? (Allow students to share for another 30 seconds.)

T: Turn your paper over. Let's break apart 36 inches for another minute.

Grade 2 Core Fluency Differentiated Practice Sets (5 minutes)

Materials: (S) Core Fluency Practice Sets from G2–M7–Lesson 1

Note: During G2–M7–Topic F and for the remainder of the year, each day's fluency includes an opportunity for review and mastery of the sums and differences with totals through 20 by means of the Core Fluency

Practice Sets or Sprints. The process is detailed and Practice Sets are provided in G2–M7–Lesson 1.

Application Problem (7 minutes)

These are the types and numbers of stamps in Shannon's stamp collection.

Type of Stamp	Number of Stamps
Holiday	16
Animal	8
Birthday	9
Famous singers	21

Her friend Michael gives her some flag stamps. If he gives her 7 fewer flag stamps than birthday and animal stamps together, how many flag stamps does she have?

If the flag stamps are worth 12 cents each, what is the total value of Shannon's flag stamps?

Note: This two-step problem involves interpreting and comparing data using a table. Encourage students to use the RDW process and to draw a picture to visualize the *fewer than* situation.

NOTES ON MULTIPLE MEANS OF ACTION AND EXPRESSION:

The Application Problem can easily be extended for above grade level students. Here are some examples:

- How many stamps does Shannon have altogether?
- What is the value of the holiday and the famous singers stamps?
- What is the value of all of Shannon's stamps?

Concept Development (33 minutes)

Materials: (T) Document camera to project tables and line plots (S) Personal white boards, centimeter grid paper

Project or show the Bean Plant data table, as shown on right. Distribute one piece of grid paper per student.

Height of Bean Plant (cm)	Number of Students
9 cm	1
11 cm	4
12 cm	6
13 cm	7
14 cm	5
15 cm	3

Part 1: Plot measures of bean plant height.

The students in Mr. Shield's science class are growing bean plants. After five days, they measured the height of their bean plants in centimeters. The table shows their results.

T: (Read the scenario.) Let's create a line plot to display this data.

T: Turn and talk. What do you need to draw?

S: A number line. → X's above a number line to show the data from the table. → A number line that starts at 9 cm and ends at 15 cm.

S: Great! Get to work! Use the table to draw your line plot on the grid paper, just like you did

yesterday (as shown to the right). Don't forget to label it.

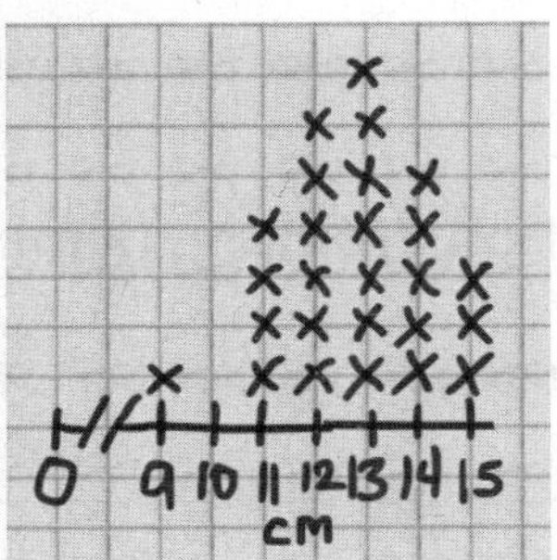

T: (Circulate and provide support while students work.)

T: Check your line plot with a partner. Did you have the same start point and endpoint? How did you label? How many X's did you draw for each height?

S: (Check and compare line plots for essential elements.)

T: Now, let's use our line plots to answer questions about the data. (The following is a list of suggestions.)

- Which bean plant height occurred most often?
- What is the difference between the tallest and shortest bean plant? How do you know?
- How many students are in this science class?
- Are there any measurements outside the main grouping? Why might this have happened?
- What do you think would happen in five more days if we watered and gave extra vitamins to the plants?

T: Yes! Now, let's look at data from students in a gym class. Here we go....

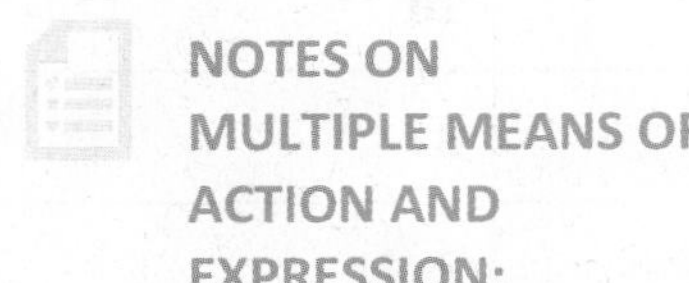

NOTES ON MULTIPLE MEANS OF ACTION AND EXPRESSION:

Support your English language learners by pointing to visuals of key terms such as *line plot, start point, end point,* and *intervals,* if these are already on your word wall. If not, find visuals for the terms and post them as continued reference for your English language learners during the lesson.

Part 2: Plot sit and reach distance.

In gym class, Mrs. Rincon measured the students' flexibility with the Sit and Reach test. The table shows how far the students were able to reach in centimeters.

T: (Read the scenario.) Go ahead and create a line plot to display the data.

S: (Draw their line plots, as shown on next page.)

T: Check your line plot with a partner. Did you have the same start point and endpoint? How did you label your plot? How many X's did you draw for each distance?

S: (Check and compare line plots for essential elements.)

T: Now, let's use our line plots to answer questions about the data. (The following is a list of suggestions.)

- How many students were the most flexible?
- What was the difference between the longest and shortest sit and reach distance? How do you know?
- How many distances were reached by only one student? Which distances?
- How many students can reach farther than 28 cm?
- Why aren't 24 cm and 32 cm listed in the table?

Sit and Reach (Distance in cm)	Number of Students
22 cm	1
23 cm	1
25 cm	1
26 cm	2
27 cm	3
28 cm	4
29 cm	3
30 cm	3
31 cm	1
34 cm	1

- What did you do on the line plot?
- How might this data be different for third-graders?
- What can we do to become more flexible? If we do those things, how might our data set change?

T: I hear some thoughtful responses today! You're ready for the Problem Set.

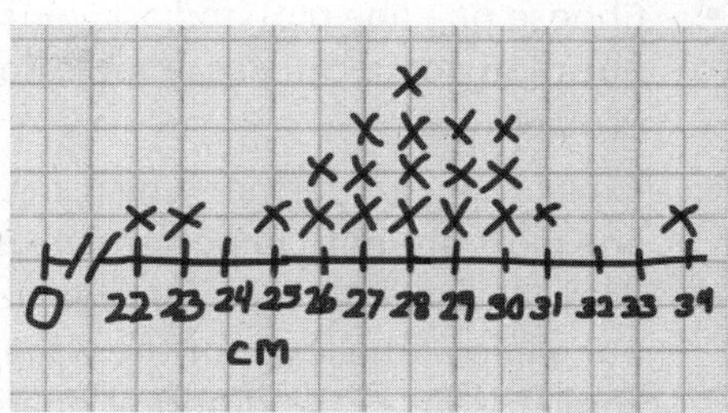

Problem Set (10 minutes)

Students should do their personal best to complete the Problem Set within the allotted 10 minutes. For some classes, it may be appropriate to modify the assignment by specifying which problems they work on first. Some problems do not specify a method for solving. Students solve these problems using the RDW approach used for Application Problems.

Student Debrief (10 minutes)

Lesson Objective: Draw a line plot to represent a given data set; answer questions and draw conclusions based on measurement data.

The Student Debrief is intended to invite reflection and active processing of the total lesson experience.

Invite students to review their solutions for the Problem Set. They should check work by comparing answers with a partner before going over answers as a class. Look for misconceptions or misunderstandings that can be addressed in the Debrief. Guide students in a conversation to debrief the Problem Set and process the lesson.

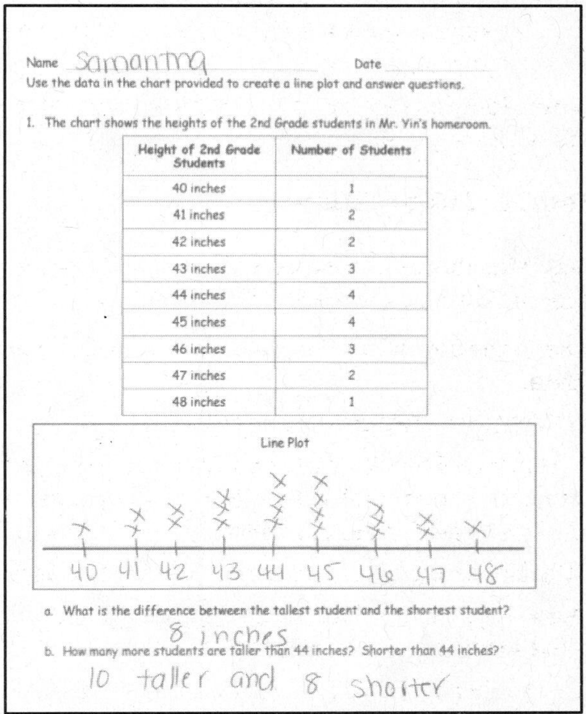

Name Samantha Date

Use the data in the chart provided to create a line plot and answer questions.

1. The chart shows the heights of the 2nd Grade students in Mr. Yin's homeroom.

Height of 2nd Grade Students	Number of Students
40 inches	1
41 inches	2
42 inches	2
43 inches	3
44 inches	4
45 inches	4
46 inches	3
47 inches	2
48 inches	1

a. What is the difference between the tallest student and the shortest student?

8 inches

b. How many more students are taller than 44 inches? Shorter than 44 inches?

10 taller and 8 shorter

You may choose to use any combination of the questions below to lead the discussion.

- Look at the line plots on your Problem Set. Did you label the units of the interval numbers? What are the units of the heights in Mr. Yin's class measured in? Is it important to label the line plot units? Why?
- What do you notice about the X's on the first line plot about heights and the X's on the statue line plot? (The first one is shaped like a curve, a small number of X's on each end, like a pattern. In the second line plot, the X's are in no particular order.) Why do you think this happened?

- Choose one line plot and ask your partner a question about the data that is not on the Problem Set.
- Explain to your partner why using tables and line plots are both important ways to look at data. (A table is useful for organizing data, but a line plot allows for the visual comparisons of the different quantities.)

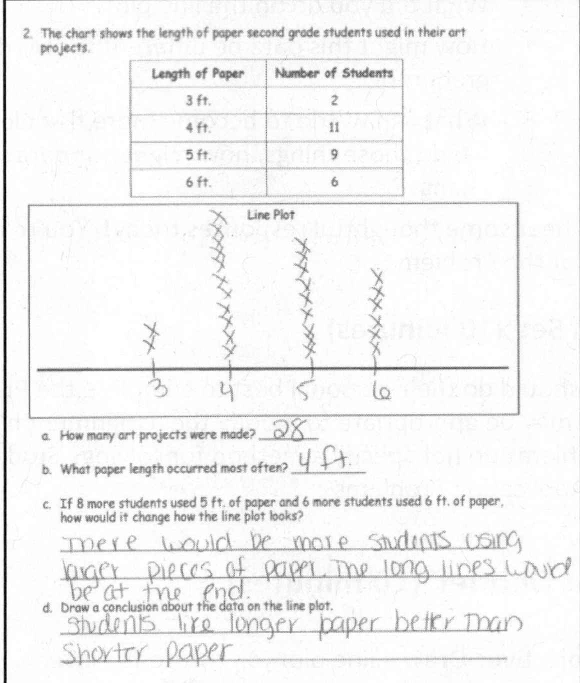
2. The chart shows the length of paper second grade students used in their art projects.

Length of Paper	Number of Students
3 ft.	2
4 ft.	11
5 ft.	9
6 ft.	6

a. How many art projects were made? 28

b. What paper length occurred most often? 4 ft

c. If 8 more students used 5 ft. of paper and 6 more students used 6 ft. of paper, how would it change how the line plot looks?

There would be more students using longer pieces of paper. The long lines would be at the end.

d. Draw a conclusion about the data on the line plot.

Students like longer paper better than shorter paper

Exit Ticket (3 minutes)

After the Student Debrief, instruct students to complete the Exit Ticket. A review of their work will help you assess the students' understanding of the concepts that were presented in the lesson today and plan more effectively for future lessons. You may read the questions aloud to the students.

Name ____________________ Date ____________

Use the data in the chart provided to create a line plot and answer questions.

1. The chart shows the heights of the second-grade students in Mr. Yin's homeroom.

Height of Second-Grade Students	Number of Students
40 inches	1
41 inches	2
42 inches	2
43 inches	3
44 inches	4
45 inches	4
46 inches	3
47 inches	2
48 inches	1

Line Plot

a. What is the difference between the tallest student and the shortest student?

b. How many students are taller than 44 inches? Shorter than 44 inches?

2. The chart shows the length of paper second-grade students used in their art projects.

Length of Paper	Number of Students
3 ft	2
4 ft	11
5 ft	9
6 ft	6

Line Plot

a. How many art projects were made? ________

b. What paper length occurred most often? __________

c. If 8 more students used 5 ft of paper and 6 more students used 6 ft of paper, how would it change how the line plot looks?

____

____

d. Draw a conclusion about the data in the line plot.

____

____

Name ____________________ Date ____________

1. Answer the questions using the line plot below.

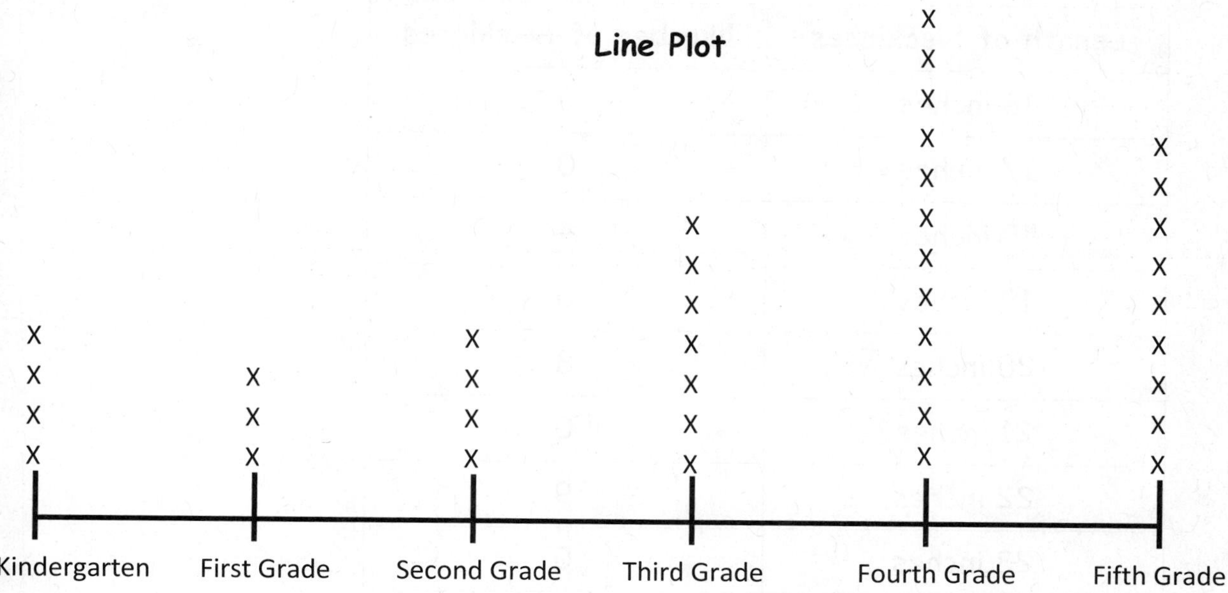

a. How many students went to the baseball game? ____________

b. What is the difference between how many first-grade students and how many fourth-grade students went to the baseball game? __________

c. Come up with a possible explanation for why most of the students are in the upper grades.

____

____

____

Name ______________________________ Date ______________

Use the data in the charts provided to create line plots and answer questions.

1. The chart shows the lengths of the necklaces made in arts and crafts class.

Length of Necklaces	Number of Necklaces
16 inches	3
17 inches	0
18 inches	4
19 inches	0
20 inches	8
21 inches	0
22 inches	9
23 inches	0
24 inches	16

Line Plot

a. How many necklaces were made? ___________

b. Draw a conclusion about the data in the line plot:

____

2. The chart shows the heights of towers students made with blocks.

Height of Towers	Number of Towers
15 inches	9
16 inches	6
17 inches	2
18 inches	1

Line Plot

a. How many towers were measured? ___________

b. What tower height occurred most often? ___________

c. If 4 more towers were measured at 17 inches and 5 more towers were measured at 18 inches, how would it change how the line plot looks?

____

____

d. Draw a conclusion about the data in the line plot:

____

____

Lesson 26

Objective: Draw a line plot to represent a given data set; answer questions and draw conclusions based on measurement data.

Suggested Lesson Structure

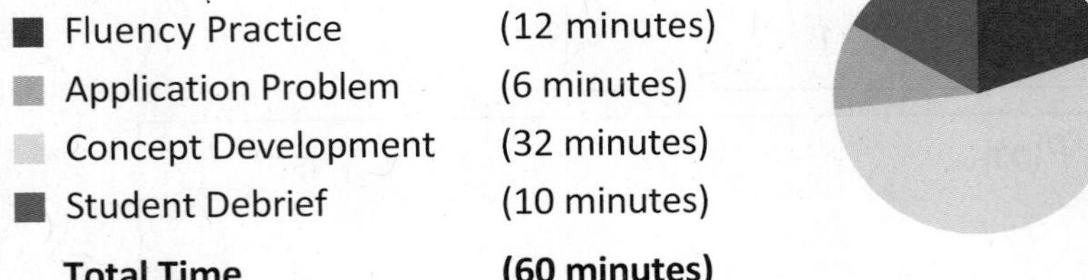

Fluency Practice	(12 minutes)
Application Problem	(6 minutes)
Concept Development	(32 minutes)
Student Debrief	(10 minutes)
Total Time	**(60 minutes)**

Fluency Practice (12 minutes)

- Making the Next Hundred **2.NBT.5, 2.NBT.7** (3 minutes)
- Making the Next Hundred to Add **2.NBT.5, 2.NBT.7** (4 minutes)
- Grade 2 Core Fluency Differentiated Practice Sets **2.OA.2** (5 minutes)

Making the Next Hundred (3 minutes)

Note: This fluency will review foundations that lead into today's lesson.

T: (Post 170 + ___ = 200 on the board.) Let's find missing parts to make the next hundred. If I say 170, you would say 30. Ready? 170.

S: 30.

T: Give the number sentence.

S: 170 + 30 = 200.

Continue with the following possible sequence: 190, 160, 260, 270, 370, 380, 580, 620, 720, 740, 940, 194, 196, 216, 214, and 224.

Making the Next Hundred to Add (4 minutes)

Note: This fluency will review foundations that lead into today's lesson.

T: When I say 9 tens + 4 tens, you say 10 tens + 3 tens. Ready? 9 tens + 4 tens.

S: 10 tens + 3 tens.

T: Answer.

S: 130.

Post on board:

90 + 40 = _____
/\
10 30

100 + 30 =

T: 90 + 40.

S: 130.

Continue with the following possible sequence: 19 tens + 4 tens, 29 tens + 4 tens, 29 tens + 14 tens, 9 tens + 6 tens, 19 tens + 6 tens, 19 tens + 16 tens, 29 tens + 16 tens, 8 tens + 3 tens, 18 tens + 3 tens, 18 tens + 13 tens, 28 tens + 13 tens, 8 tens + 5 tens, 18 tens + 15 tens, and 28 tens + 15 tens.

Grade 2 Core Fluency Differentiated Practice Sets (5 minutes)

Materials: (S) Core Fluency Practice Sets from G2–M7–Lesson 1

Note: During G2–M7–Topic F and for the remainder of the year, each day's fluency includes an opportunity for review and mastery of the sums and differences with totals through 20 by means of the Core Fluency Practice Sets or Sprints. The process is detailed and Practice Sets provided in G2–M7–Lesson 1.

Application Problem (6 minutes)

Judy bought an MP3 player and a set of earphones. The earphones cost $9, which is $48 less than the MP3 player. How much change should Judy get back if she gave the cashier a $100 bill?

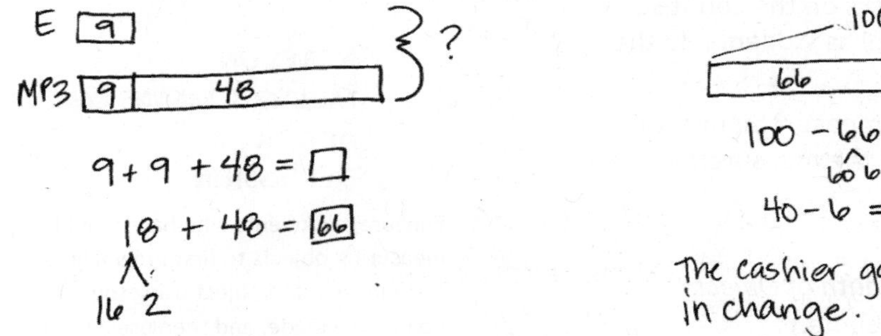

Note: This two-step problem encourages students once again to use the RDW process and make a tape diagram to visualize the relationships within the problem and correctly identify the question being asked.

Concept Development (32 minutes)

Materials: (T) Document camera to project tables and line plots (S) Rulers, grid paper, thermometer (real or Template C)

Project or draw Length of Items in Our Pencil Boxes data, as shown on the next page.

Part 1: Plot the length of items in our pencil boxes.

The students in Mrs. Washington's class each chose an item from their pencil box and measured its length. The table shows their results.

T: (Read the scenario, then pass out grid paper and rulers.) Let's create a line plot to display this data.

Length of Items in Our Pencil Boxes	Number of Items
6 cm	1
7 cm	2
8 cm	4
9 cm	3
10 cm	6
11 cm	4
13 cm	1
16 cm	3
17 cm	2

T: Talk with your partner: What do we need to draw?

S: A number line!

T: Turn your paper horizontally, and let's use rulers to draw a straight line. (Draw a line across the bottom of the paper as students do the same.)

T: Let's write 0 at the beginning of our scale and then put two diagonal hash marks between that and the next hash mark. (Model as students do the same.)

T: What's the smallest length measurement in our data set?

S: 6 centimeters.

T: Write 6 below the hash mark that follows 0. (Model as students do the same.)

MP.6

T: Remember, the double hash mark means that the numbers between 0 and 6 are not shown on the scale.

T: What is the greatest measurement in our data set?

S: 17 centimeters.

T: Yes. So, our number line needs to continue on to 17. Remember to draw the hash marks on the count scale where the gridlines meet. (Model as students do the same.)

T: We label our scale based on the measurement tool used. Look at the table. What is the measurement unit?

S: Centimeters!

T: Yes, so let's label that. (Write *Length of Objects (centimeters)* as students do the same.)

T: Talk with your partner: What do we do now?

S: We have to show the data. → We need to record the data by putting X's above the number line.

T: Go ahead and record the data. (Circulate and provide support as students work.)

T: Check your line plot with a partner. Do you have the same number of X's for each measurement? (Allow students time to compare.)

T: Now let's use our line plots to answer questions about the data. (The following is a list of suggestions.)

- What observations can you make about the data?

NOTES ON MULTIPLE MEANS OF ACTION AND EXPRESSION:

Encourage students who have trouble measuring objects to first draw a line the length of the object using the object as a guide, and then use a ruler to measure the line.

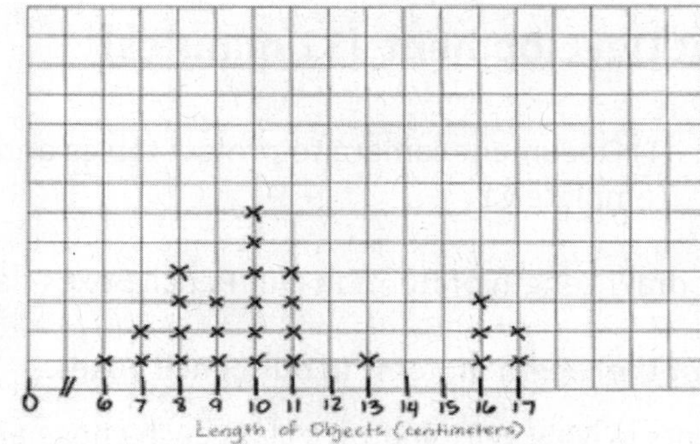

- What measurement occurred most often?
- What is the difference between the smallest measurement and the greatest measurement?
- Do you think the data would look different if the students each chose a different item in their pencil box to measure? Why?

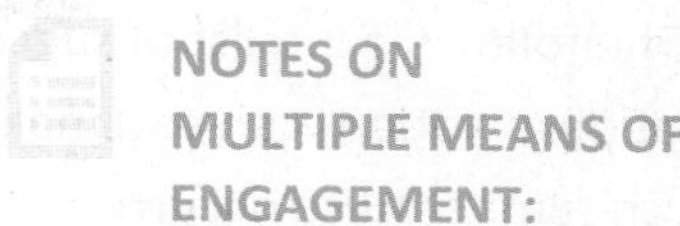

NOTES ON MULTIPLE MEANS OF ENGAGEMENT:

Scaffold the lesson for students with disabilities by placing the grid paper in their personal white boards. This allows students to practice marking the right number of X's onto the number line. Make sure they are transferring the data accurately by watching and asking questions as necessary: "How many items measured 10 cm? How many X's will you place above the 10 cm marker on the number line?"

Part 2: Plot temperatures in May.

Project or draw Temperatures in May table and data, as shown on right.

Mr. Enriquez's class measured the temperature each day during the month of May. The table shows the results.

Temperatures in May	Number of Days
59	1
60	3
63	3
64	4
65	7
67	5
68	4
69	3
72	1

T: (Read the scenario, and then show the thermometer from Template C.) Talk with your partner: Have you ever seen a **thermometer** before? What does this tool measure?

S: My mom and dad use a thermometer to take my **temperature** when I'm sick. → When you send me to the nurse, she takes my temperature. → The problem is talking about weather like when you watch the weather on TV. → You use a thermometer to know how hot or cold it is outside.

T: Yes, a thermometer is a tool that measures temperature.

T: We measure temperature in **degrees**, so today, for example, it's ___ (insert today's actual temperature) degrees outside.

T: Look at this thermometer and talk with your partner: What do you notice about the count scale?

S: The numbers are vertical, not horizontal!

T: Yes! Watch how I start the scale. (Model where to write the 0 and the double hash marks.)

T: Talk with your partner: Where will you mark the data points?

S: We have to put the X's next to the numbers. → This time the number line will be vertical and the X's will be horizontal.

T: Correct! Now, use the table to make a line plot of the temperatures during the month of May.

T: Remember to label it. (Circulate and provide support while students work.)

T: Now, check your line plot with a partner. Did you have the same start and end point? How did you label your plot? How many X's did you mark for each degree?

S: (Check and compare line plots for essential elements.)

T: Let's use our line plots to answer questions about the data. (The following is a list of suggestions.)

- What observations can you make about the data?
- Which temperature occurred most often?
- Which temperatures occurred least often?
- What is the difference between the highest temperature and the lowest temperature?
- How would a line plot recording data look next month? In a different season?

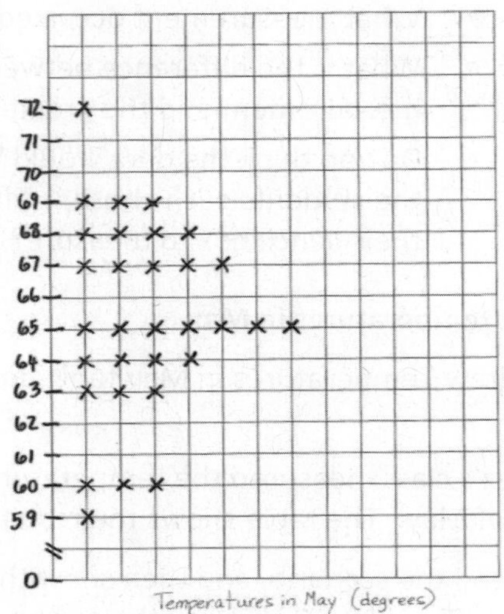

As students demonstrate proficiency creating and interpreting line plots, allow them to move on to the Problem Set.

Problem Set (10 minutes)

Students should do their personal best to complete the Problem Set within the allotted 10 minutes. For some classes, it may be appropriate to modify the assignment by specifying which problems they work on first. Some problems do not specify a method for solving. Students solve these problems using the RDW approach used for Application Problems.

Name Samantha Date

Use the data in the table provided to create a line plot and answer questions.

1. The table below describes the heights of basketball players and audience members who were polled at a basketball game.

Height (inches)	Number of Participants
25	3
50	4
60	1
68	12
74	18

a. How tall are most of the people at the basketball game? 74 inches

b. How many people are 60 inches or taller? 31

c. What do you notice about the people who attended the basketball game? Most of the people are tall

d. A line plot / table (circle one) is easier to read because: The lines would be too far apart

Student Debrief (10 minutes)

Lesson Objective: Draw a line plot to represent a given data set; answer questions and draw conclusions based on measurement data.

The Student Debrief is intended to invite reflection and active processing of the total lesson experience.

Invite students to review their solutions for the Problem Set. They should check work by comparing answers with a partner before going over answers as a class. Look for misconceptions or misunderstandings that can be addressed in the Debrief. Guide students in a conversation to debrief the Problem Set and process the lesson.

You may choose to use any combination of the questions below to lead the discussion.

- Look at the table made at a basketball game. If you had to guess how many basketball players and how many audience members there were, how would you make the groups, based on the data in the chart?
- Look at the pencil table on your Problem Set. Share with your partner why you thought so many pencils were 15 or 16 cm.

- Why did all of our line plots in today's lesson about the pencil box items look the same? (The whole class recorded the same data.)
- Can we make line plots horizontally and vertically? Does it change the data in any way? Talk to your partner about when you would use each. Why?
- Discuss with your partner a time in your life when you would need or want to organize information in a table or a line plot. How would it help you or make your life easier?

Exit Ticket (3 minutes)

After the Student Debrief, instruct students to complete the Exit Ticket. A review of their work will help you assess the students' understanding of the concepts that were presented in the lesson today and plan more effectively for future lessons. You may read the questions aloud to the students.

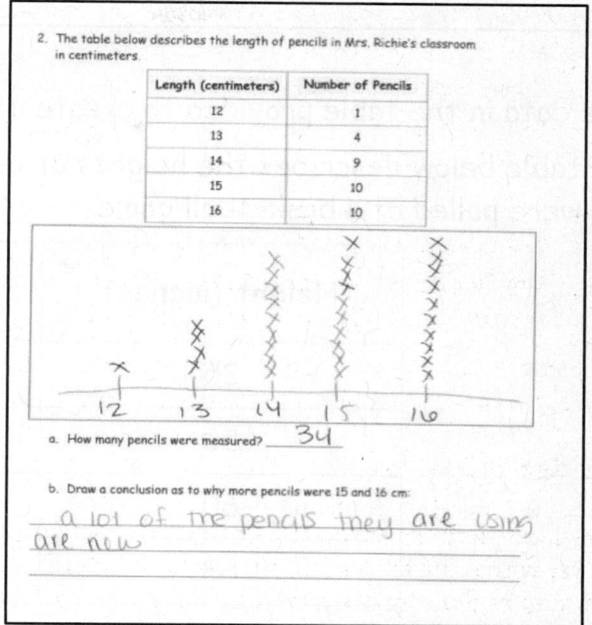

2. The table below describes the length of pencils in Mrs. Richie's classroom in centimeters.

Length (centimeters)	Number of Pencils
12	1
13	4
14	9
15	10
16	10

a. How many pencils were measured? 34

b. Draw a conclusion as to why more pencils were 15 and 16 cm: a lot of the pencils they are using are new

Name ______________________________ Date ____________

Use the data in the table provided to create a line plot and answer questions.

1. The table below describes the heights of basketball players and audience members who were polled at a basketball game.

Height (inches)	Number of Participants
25	3
50	4
60	1
68	12
74	18

a. How tall are most of the people at the basketball game? ____________

b. How many people are 60 inches or taller? ______________

c. What do you notice about the people who attended the basketball game?

____

d. A **line plot / table** (circle one) is easier to read because...

____

2. The table below describes the length of pencils in Mrs. Richie's classroom in centimeters.

Length (centimeters)	Number of Pencils
12	1
13	4
14	9
15	10
16	10

a. How many pencils were measured? ___________

b. Draw a conclusion as to why more pencils were 15 and 16 cm:

____

____

____

Name ______________________________ Date ______________

Use the data in the table provided to create a line plot.

1. The table below describes the heights of second-grade students on the soccer team.

Height (inches)	Number of Students
35	3
36	4
37	7
38	8
39	6
40	5

Line Plot

Name ______________________________ Date ______________

Use the data in the table provided to create a line plot and answer questions.

1. The table below describes the lengths of student shoelaces in Ms. Henry's class.

Length of Shoelaces (inches)	Number of Shoelaces
27	6
36	10
40	3
45	2

Line Plot

a. How many shoelaces were measured? ______________

b. How many more shoelaces are 27 or 36 inches than 40 or 45 inches?

____

c. Draw a conclusion as to why zero students had a 54-inch shoelace.

____

2. A **line plot / table** (circle one) is easier to read because...

____

3. The table below describes the lengths of crayons in centimeters in Miss Harrison's crayon box.

Length (centimeters)	Number of Crayons
4	4
5	7
6	9
7	3
8	1

a. How many crayons are in the box? ___________

b. Draw a conclusion as to why most of the crayons are 5 or 6 centimeters:

____

____

____

Length of Items in Our Pencil Boxes	Number of Items
6 cm	1
7 cm	2
8 cm	4
9 cm	3
10 cm	6
11 cm	4
13 cm	1
16 cm	3
17 cm	2

Temperatures in May	Number of Days
59	1
60	3
63	3
64	4
65	7
67	5
68	4
69	3
72	1

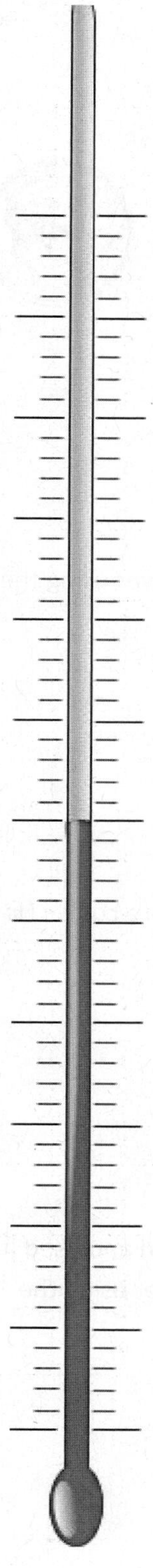

Name ______________________________ Date ____________________

1. Hank emptied his pockets and found these coins.

   a. How much money does Hank have? Write the answer using the $ or ¢ symbol. Explain your thinking using pictures, numbers, or words.

   b. Hank gave his brother Luke a quarter and some more coins. Now, Luke has 57 cents. Draw and label one possible picture of Luke's coins.

   c. Hank's sister Maria found a dollar bill under her bed and used it to buy an iced tea for 45 cents. How much change will Maria get back? Write the answer using the $ or ¢ symbol. Explain your thinking using pictures, numbers, or words.

2. Karen has 1 twenty dollar bill, 2 ten dollar bills, 4 five dollar bills, and 8 one dollar bills.
   a. How much money does Karen have? Write the answer using the $ or ¢ symbol. Explain your thinking using pictures, numbers, or words.

   b. Karen buys a book for 12 dollars and a fruit smoothie for 4 dollars. Karen gives the cashier the twenty dollar bill. How much change will she receive? Write the answer using the $ or ¢ symbol. Explain your thinking using pictures, numbers, or words.

3. Alex sorted the fruits in his shopping basket. The table below shows what he bought.

Oranges	Lemons	Bananas	Pears
2	5	3	4

   a. Draw and label a picture graph to represent the fruits in Alex's shopping basket.

b. Draw and label a bar graph to represent the fruits in Alex's shopping basket.

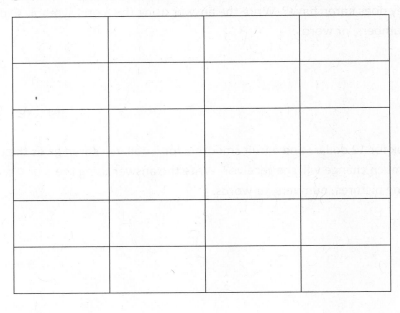

c. How many pieces of fruit did Alex buy in all?

d. How many more lemons and pears does Alex have than oranges and bananas? Explain your thinking using pictures, numbers, or words.

4. Denise found 4 nickels in the car, 32 cents in her room, and 21 pennies and 1 quarter in her desk drawer.
   a. How much money did Denise find in all? Write the answer using the $ or ¢ symbol.

   b. Denise spent 42 cents on one banana and lost 19 cents. How much money does Denise have left? Write the answer using the $ or ¢ symbol. Explain your thinking using pictures, numbers, or words.

Mid-Module Assessment Task Standards Addressed	Topics A–B
Use place value understanding and properties of operations to add and subtract.	
2.NBT.5	Fluently add and subtract within 100 using strategies based on place value, properties of operations, and/or the relationship between addition and subtraction.
Work with time and money.	
2.MD.8	Solve word problems involving dollar bills, quarters, dimes, nickels, and pennies, using $ and ¢ symbols appropriately. *Example: If you have 2 dimes and 3 pennies, how many cents do you have?*
Represent and interpret data.	
2.MD.10	Draw a picture graph and a bar graph (with single-unit scale) to represent a data set with up to four categories. Solve simple put-together, take-apart, and compare problems using information presented in a bar graph.

Evaluating Student Learning Outcomes

A Progression Toward Mastery is provided to describe steps that illuminate the gradually increasing understandings that students develop *on their way to proficiency.* In this chart, this progress is presented from left (Step 1) to right (Step 4). The learning goal for each student is to achieve Step 4 mastery. These steps are meant to help teachers and students identify and celebrate what the student CAN do now and what they need to work on next.

A Progression Toward Mastery				
Assessment Task Item and Standards Assessed	**STEP 1** **Little evidence of reasoning without a correct answer.** **(1 Point)**	**STEP 2** **Evidence of some reasoning without a correct answer.** **(2 Points)**	**STEP 3** **Evidence of some reasoning with a correct answer or evidence of solid reasoning with an incorrect answer.** **(3 Points)**	**STEP 4** **Evidence of solid reasoning with a correct answer.** **(4 Points)**
1 **2.NBT.5** **2.MD.8**	The student solves one out of five parts correctly.	The student solves two or three out of five parts correctly.	The student solves four out of five parts correctly.	The student correctly: a. Answers 78¢ and explains using pictures, numbers, or words. b. Draws and labels a coin combination that totals 57 cents, such as QDDDPP or QDDNNPP. c. Answers 55¢ and explains using pictures, numbers, or words.
2 **2.NBT.5** **2.MD.8**	The student solves one out of four parts correctly.	The student solves two out of four parts correctly.	The student solves three out of four parts correctly.	The student correctly: a. Answers $68 and explains using pictures, numbers, or words. b. Answers $4 change and explains using pictures, numbers, or words.
3 **2.MD.10**	The student solves fewer than three out of seven parts correctly.	The student solves three to four out of seven parts correctly.	The student solves five to six out of seven parts correctly.	The student correctly: a. Draws and labels the picture graph to show 2 oranges, 5 lemons, 3 bananas, and 4 pears. b. Draws and labels the bar graph to show 2 oranges, 5

A Progression Toward Mastery				
				lemons, 3 bananas, and 4 pears. c. Answers 14 pieces of fruit. d. Answers 4 more lemons and pears and explains using pictures, numbers, or words.
4 **2.NBT.5** **2.MD.8**	The student solves zero out of three parts correctly.	The student solves one out of three parts correctly.	The student solves two out of three parts correctly.	The student correctly: a. Answers 98¢. b. Answers 37¢ and explains using pictures, numbers, or words.

Name Teri Date ______________

1. Hank emptied his pockets and found these coins.

a. How much money does Hank have? Write the answer using the $ or ¢ symbol. Explain your thinking using pictures, numbers, or words.

25 + 40 + 10 + 3

25 + 50 + 3 = 75 + 3 = 78

Hank has 78¢.

b. Hank gave his brother Luke a quarter and some more coins. Now, Luke has 57 cents. Draw and label one possible picture of Luke's coins.

25 + □ = 57

(25) (25) (5) (1) (1)

c. Hank's sister Maria found a dollar bill under her bed and used it to buy an iced tea for 45 cents. How much change will Maria get back? Write the answer using the $ or ¢ symbol. Explain your thinking using pictures, numbers, or words.

45 + □ = 100

(5) (25) (25)

Maria will get back 55¢.

2. Karen has 1 twenty dollar bill, 2 ten dollar bills, 4 five dollar bills, and 8 one dollar bills.

   a. How much money does Karen have? Write the answer using the $ or ¢ symbol. Explain your thinking using pictures, numbers, or words.

   20 + 20 + 20 + 8 = $68

   Karen has $68.

   b. Karen buys a book for 12 dollars and a fruit smoothie for 4 dollars. Karen gives the cashier the twenty dollar bill. How much change will she receive? Write the answer using the $ or ¢ symbol. Explain your thinking using pictures, numbers, or words.

   12 + 4 = 16

   20 - 16 = 4 She will receive $4.

3. Alex sorted the fruits in his shopping basket. The table below shows what he bought.

Oranges	Lemons	Bananas	Pears
2	5	3	4

   a. Draw and label a picture graph to represent the fruits in Alex's shopping basket.

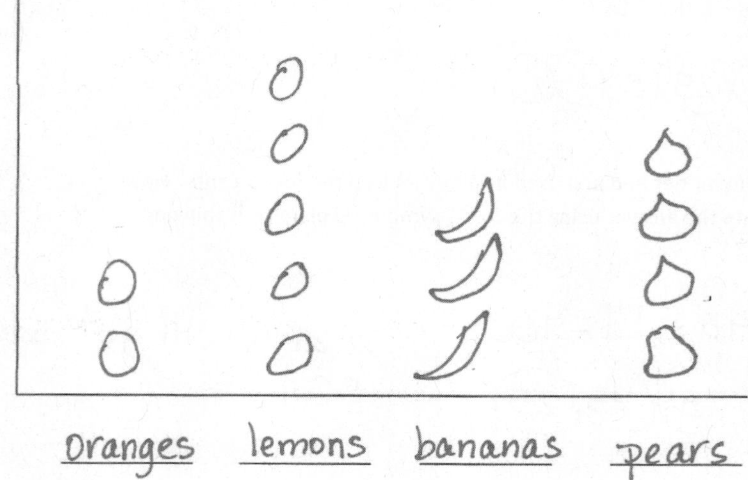

b. Draw and label a bar graph to represent the fruits in Alex's shopping basket.

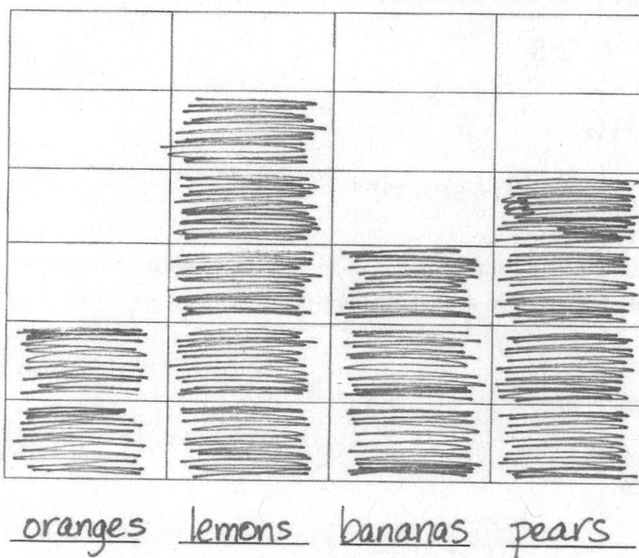

c. How many pieces of fruit did Alex buy in all?

2 + 3 + 5 + 4

5

10 + 4 = 14

Alex buys 14 pieces of fruit.

d. How many more lemons and pears does Alex have than oranges and bananas? Explain your thinking using pictures, numbers, or words.

5+4=9 2+3=5

9-5=4

Alex has 4 more lemons and pears.

4. Denise found 4 nickels in the car, 32 cents in her room, and 21 pennies and 1 quarter in her desk drawer.
   a. How much money did Denise find in all? Write the answer using the $ or ¢ symbol.

   20 + 32 + 21 + 25

   52 + 46 = 98

   Denise finds 98¢.

   b. Denise spent 42 cents on one banana and lost 19 cents. How much money does Denise have left? Write the answer using the $ or ¢ symbol. Explain your thinking using pictures, numbers, or words.

   98 − 42 = 56

   56 − 19 = 37

   Denise has 37¢ left.

Name ______________________________ Date ________________

Note: Do not pass out rulers until after students complete Problem 1(a).

1. a. Estimate the length of each item in inches.

The envelope is about ____ inches.

The pencil is about ____ inches.

The crayon is about ____ inches.

The scissors are about ____ inches.

b. Use a ruler to measure the length of the items above using inches and then centimeters. Round to the nearest unit, and then record the measurements in the table.

Envelope	Pencil	Crayon	Scissors
______ inches ______ centimeters	______ inches ______ centimeters	______ inches ______ centimeters	______ inches ______ centimeters

c. The envelope is ______ cm longer than the crayon.

d. For each measurement, which is greater, the number of inches or the number of centimeters?

____

e. Explain why.

2. Circle the appropriate tool for measuring each object.

a. The length of a book:	12-inch ruler	yardstick
b. The height of a flagpole:	12-inch ruler	yardstick
c. The length of a paper clip:	12-inch ruler	yardstick
d. The height of a doorway:	12-inch ruler	yardstick

3. a. What number is represented as Point A on the number line? ______

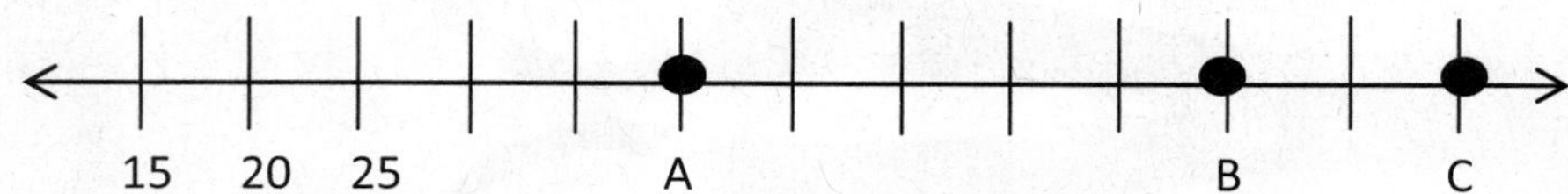

b. What is the distance between A and B? _______

c. What is 40 less than the number marked by Point C? Mark it as Point D on the number line.

4. Use the tables below to graph the data.

   a. Draw and label a line plot to show the length of pencils in the table.

Length	1 inch	2 inches	3 inches	4 inches	5 inches	6 inches	7 inches
Number of pencils	0	2	4	4	3	2	5

   b. Find the total number of pencils measured. __________

   c. Draw and label a bar graph to show the number of pencils in each student's desk.

Student Name	Jill	Sven	Rocco	Lyla
Number of Pencils	4	2	5	1

5. Draw a picture and write a number sentence to solve.

   a. The height of the dog's doorway is 19 inches. The height of the family's doorway is 78 inches. How much taller is the family's doorway than the dog's doorway?

   b. Albert saved 42 cents last week. This week he added a quarter, 2 dimes, and 13 pennies to his savings. How much money has Albert saved from the last two weeks? Write the answer using the $ or ¢ symbol.

End-of-Module Assessment Task Standards Addressed

Topics A–F

Use place value understanding and properties of operations to add and subtract.

2.NBT.5 Fluently add and subtract within 100 using strategies based on place value, properties of operations, and/or the relationship between addition and subtraction.

Measure and estimate lengths in standard units.

2.MD.1 Measure the length of an object by selecting and using appropriate tools such as rulers, yardsticks, meter sticks, and measuring tapes.

2.MD.2 Measure the length of an object twice, using length units of different lengths for the two measurements; describe how the two measurements relate to the size of the unit chosen.

2.MD.3 Estimate lengths using units of inches, feet, centimeters, and meters.

2.MD.4 Measure to determine how much longer one object is than another, expressing the length difference in terms of a standard length unit.

Relate addition and subtraction to length.

2.MD.5 Use addition and subtraction within 100 to solve word problems involving lengths that are given in the same units, e.g., by using drawings (such as drawings of rulers) and equations with a symbol for the unknown number to represent the problem.

2.MD.6 Represent whole numbers as lengths from 0 on a number line diagrams with equally spaced points corresponding to the numbers 0, 1, 2, ..., and represent whole-number sums and differences within 100 on a number line diagram.

Work with time and money.

2. MD.8 Solve word problems involving dollar bills, quarters, dimes, nickels, and pennies, using $ and ¢ symbols appropriately. *Example: If you have 2 dimes and 3 pennies, how many cents do you have?*

Represent and interpret data.

2.MD.9 Generate measurement data by measuring lengths of several objects to the nearest whole unit, or making repeated measurements of the same object. Show the measurements by making a line plot, where the horizontal scale is marked off in whole-number units.

2.MD.10 Draw a picture graph and a bar graph (with single-unit scale) to represent a data set with up to four categories. Solve simple put-together, take-apart, and compare problems using information presented in a bar graph.

Evaluating Student Learning Outcomes

A Progression Toward Mastery is provided to describe steps that illuminate the gradually increasing understandings that students develop *on their way to proficiency.* In this chart, this progress is presented from left (Step 1) to right (Step 4). The learning goal for each student is to achieve Step 4 mastery. These steps are meant to help teachers and students identify and celebrate what the student CAN do now and what they need to work on next.

A Progression Toward Mastery				
Assessment Task Item and Standards Assessed	**STEP 1 Little evidence of reasoning without a correct answer.** **(1 Point)**	**STEP 2 Evidence of some reasoning without a correct answer.** **(2 Points)**	**STEP 3 Evidence of some reasoning with a correct answer or evidence of solid reasoning with an incorrect answer.** **(3 Points)**	**STEP 4 Evidence of solid reasoning with a correct answer.** **(4 Points)**
1 **2.MD.2** **2.MD.3** **2.MD.4**	The student answers fewer than four out of eight parts correctly.	The student answers four or five out of eight parts correctly.	The student answers six or seven out of eight parts correctly.	The student correctly: a. Estimates the length of each item. b. Measures to the nearest whole unit to answer: ▪ Envelope is 4 in and 10 cm. ▪ Pencil is 6 in and 16 cm. ▪ Crayon is 3 in and 7 cm. ▪ Scissors are 5 in and 12 cm. c. Answers that the envelope is 3 cm longer than the crayon. d. Answers centimeters. e. Explains that centimeters have a smaller length unit than inches so there are more

A Progression Toward Mastery				
				centimeters than inches.
2 **2.MD.1**	The student answers one out of four parts correctly.	The student answers two out of four parts correctly.	The student answers three out of four parts correctly.	The student correctly answers: a. 12-inch ruler. b. Yardstick. c. 12-inch ruler. d. Yardstick.
3 **2.MD.6**	The student answers zero out of three parts correctly.	The student answers one out of three parts correctly.	The student answers two out of three parts correctly.	The student correctly: a. Answers 40. b. Answers 25. c. Labels D on the number line at 35.
4 **2.MD.9** **2.MD.10**	The student answers one out of five parts correctly.	The student answers two or three out of five parts correctly.	The student answers four out of five parts correctly.	The student correctly: a. Draws and labels a line plot to represent the given data. b. Answers 20 pencils. c. Draws and labels a bar graph to represent the given data.
5 **2.MD.5** **2.MD.8** **2.NBT.5**	The student answers one out of six parts correctly.	The student answers two or three out of six parts correctly.	The student answers four or five out of six parts correctly.	The student correctly: a. Draws a picture (e.g., tape diagram), writes a number sentence, and solves to get 59 inches. b. Draws a picture, writes a number sentence, and solves to get \$1 or 100¢.

Name Teri Date

Note: Do not pass out rulers until after students complete Problem 1(a).

1. a. Estimate the length of each item in inches.

The envelope is about 4 inches.

The pencil is about 5 inches.

The crayon is about 3 inches.

The scissors are about 4 inches.

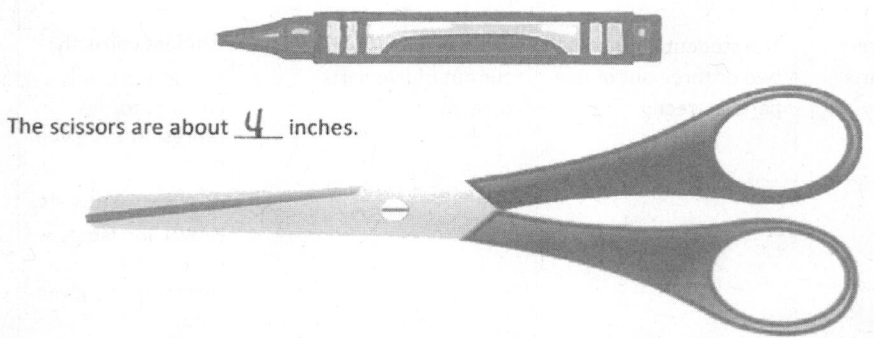

b. Use a ruler to measure the length of the items above using inches and then centimeters. Round to the nearest unit, and then record the measurements in the table.

Envelope	Pencil	Crayon	Scissors
4 inches 10 centimeters	6 inches 16 centimeters	3 inches 7 centimeters	5 inches 12 centimeters

c. The envelope is 3 cm longer than the crayon.

d. For each measurement, which is greater, the number of inches or the number of centimeters? centimeters

e. Explain why.

Centimeters are smaller than inches.

2. Circle the appropriate tool for measuring each object.

a. The length of a book: 12-inch ruler yardstick

b. The height of a flagpole: 12-inch ruler yardstick

c. The length of a paper clip: 12-inch ruler yardstick

d. The height of a doorway: 12-inch ruler yardstick

3. a. What number is represented as Point A on the number line? 40

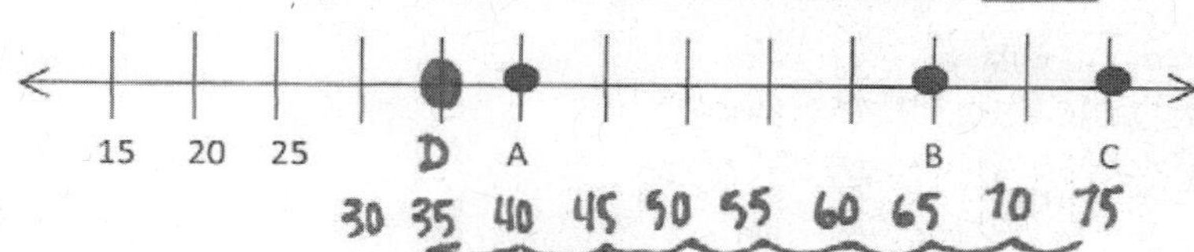

b. What is the distance between A and B? 25

c. What is 40 less than the number marked by Point C? Mark it as Point D on the number line.

75
- 40
35

4. Use the tables below to graph the data.
   a. Draw and label a line plot to show the length of pencils in the table.

Length	1 inch	2 inches	3 inches	4 inches	5 inches	6 inches	7 inches
Number of pencils	0	2	4	4	3	2	5

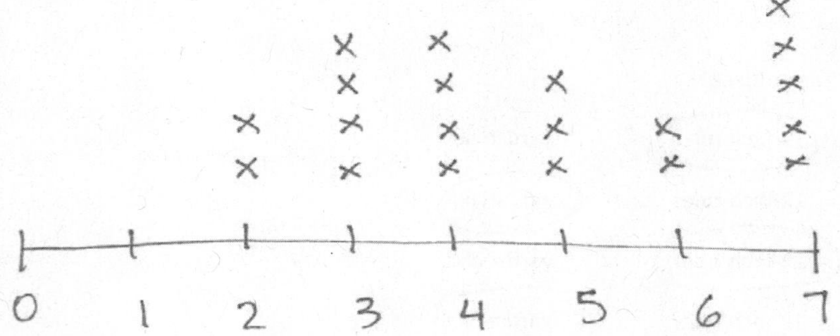

   b. Find the total number of pencils measured. 20

2+8+5+5
10 + 10 = 20

   c. Draw and label a bar graph to show the number of pencils in each student's desk.

Student Name	Jill	Sven	Rocco	Lyla
Number of Pencils	4	2	5	1

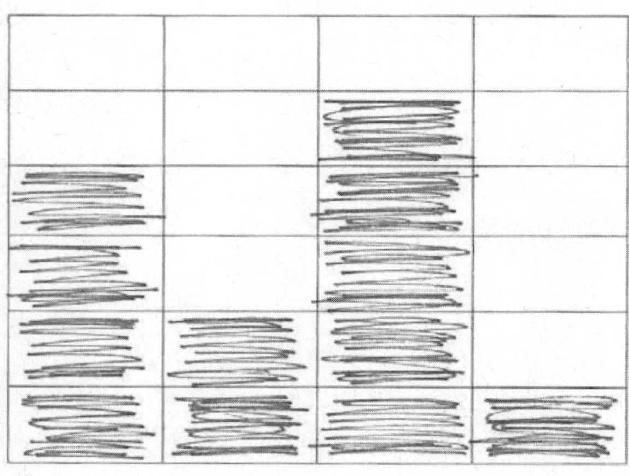

Jill Sven Rocco Lyla

5. Draw a picture and write a number sentence to solve.

   a. The height of the dog's doorway is 19 inches. The height of the family's doorway is 78 inches. How much taller is the family's doorway than the dog's doorway?

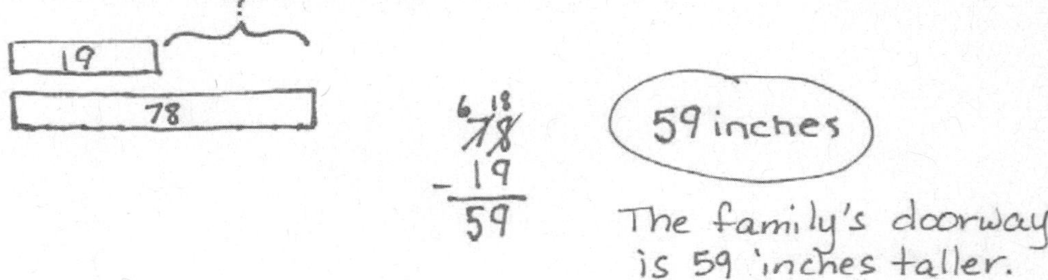

   b. Albert saved 42 cents last week. This week he added a quarter, 2 dimes, and 13 pennies to his savings. How much money has Albert saved from the last two weeks? Write the answer using the $ or ¢ symbol.

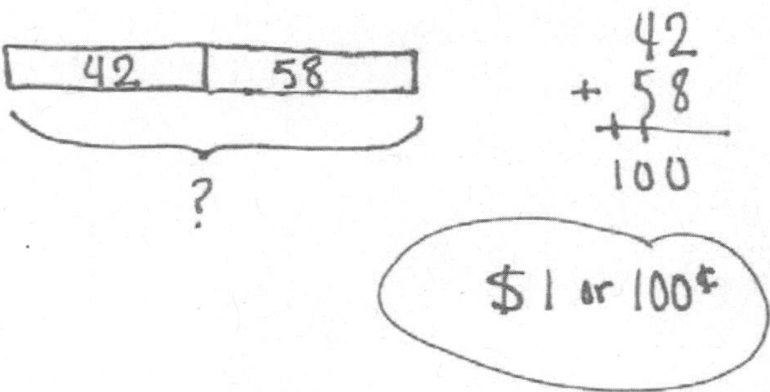

Albert saved $1.